The Citizens Advice Handbook

Practical, independent advice

Citizens Advice

PENGUIN BOOKS

PENGUIN BOOKS

Published by the Penguin Group
Penguin Books Ltd, 80 Strand, London WC2R ORL, England
Penguin Group (USA) Inc., 375 Hudson Street, New York, New York 10014, USA
Penguin Group (Canada), 90 Eglinton Avenue East, Suite 700, Toronto, Ontario, Canada M4P 2Y3
(a division of Pearson Penguin Canada Inc.)
Penguin Ireland, 25 St Stephen's Green, Dublin 2, Ireland
(a division of Penguin Books Ltd)
Penguin Group (Australia), 250 Camberwell Road, Camberwell, Victoria 3124, Australia
(a division of Pearson Australia Group Pty Ltd)
Penguin Books India Pvt Ltd, 11 Community Centre, Panchsheel Park, New Delhi – 110 017, India
Penguin Group (NZ), cnr Airborne and Rosedale Roads, Albany, Auckland 1310, New Zealand
(a division of Pearson New Zealand Ltd)
Penguin Books (South Africa) (Pty) Ltd, 24 Sturdee Avenue, Rosebank 2196, South Africa

Penguin Books Ltd, Registered Offices: 80 Strand, London WC2R ORL, England

www.penguin.com

First published 2005
1

Set in 9.5/12 pt PostScript Minion with TheSans display
Typeset by Rowland Phototypesetting Ltd, Bury St Edmunds, Suffolk
Printed in England by Clays Ltd, St Ives plc

Contents

Acknowledgements

This book would not have been possible without the enthusiasm and editing skills of Miranda Kemp and Liz Seward.

Introduction

We might like to think that there was a time when our lives weren't ruled by the millions of laws, regulations, codes of practice, guidelines and procedures that surround us today. The reality is that the freedoms we hold dear are all exercised within a delicately balanced framework of rights and responsibilities, enshrined in all of that legislation. We need those laws but, for most people, finding your way around the systems and structures that hold them, especially if it's urgent and you've got a crisis on your hands, can be a nightmare.

The *Citizens Advice Handbook* is designed to give you the basic information you need to get your head around a problem that needs solving, quickly and easily, whenever you need it. It gives advice about how to tackle the issue you face and where to look for further professional assistance and support.

In buying this book, you have bought into over sixty-five years of Citizens Advice Bureau expertise in giving information and advice to the public. Citizens Advice Bureaux know from experience that what people want is independent, reliable and jargon-free information about their rights and responsibilities. They want to know where they stand, what they can do about the problems they face and who can help them. This is what this book will tell you.

The advice and information in these pages is based on the CAB electronic information system, updated each month and used by all CAB advisers – mostly trained volunteers – to help people with nearly six million problems each year. No other information database can rival it for breadth and accuracy. Although you may be able to find all of this information elsewhere – in a thousand libraries and a million websites – the *Citizens Advice Handbook* is the only place you'll find it *all in one place* on your bookshelf.

Each chapter will give you:

- a practical understanding of a particular topic area;
- snapshot answers to some of the most common queries that Citizens Advice Bureaux get asked;
- *Who Can Help?* pointing you in the direction of further help and advice.

Some chapters also include a Jargon Buster to help you make sense of the relevant lingo.

Citizens Advice Bureaux give free, confidential, impartial and independent advice on a limitless range of subjects, including all of the ones in this book. If you can't find the answer you're looking for here, make an appointment at your local CAB. Just visit www.adviceguide.org.uk or look in your local telephone directory under 'C'.

About the Citizens Advice service

Citizens Advice Bureaux – all independent charities – have been a key part of local communities for over sixty-five years. Set up in 1939, to help people deal with problems at the outbreak of the Second World War, they now provide free information and advice from over 3,200 locations – in bureaux, from a variety of community venues, in people's homes, by e-mail, on the telephone and via a regularly updated website at www.adviceguide.org.uk.

Because the CAB service is so firmly rooted in the community, it also sees at first hand the immediate effects of the laws that govern our daily lives. This means it is able to campaign, locally and nationally, for improvements in policies and services that benefit us all. So CAB advice helps solve problems for individuals and the wider community.

- For online CAB advice and to contact a Citizens Advice Bureau go to www.adviceguide.org.uk
- to volunteer at your local Citizens Advice Bureau call 08451 264 264 or go to www.citizensadvice.org.uk/join-us
- to find out more about the campaigning work of the Citizens Advice service or to support its work go to www.citizensadvice.org.uk

The factual information in this book relates to England and Wales only and should be used as general guidance only, not legal advice. We have made every effort to provide information that is as accurate and up-to-date as possible but laws are constantly changing, and much depends on individual circumstances. Specific advice should be sought for specific situations, where necessary from a CAB adviser or a solicitor.

Important note: same-sex couples and civil partnerships

From December 2005, there will be far-reaching changes to the way that same-sex couples will be treated in law. From this date same-sex couples will be able to enter into a civil partnership by registering a formal commitment to one another. When they have registered a civil partnership they will have similar rights and responsibilities to married couples. These include:

- right to inherit from their partner if there is no will
- equal treatment with married couples in tax matters
- equal treatment with married couples in tenancy and housing matters
- equal treatment for the purposes of life insurance
- recognition for immigration and nationality purposes
- assessment of same-sex couple as a family unit when working out entitlement to welfare benefits and tax credits, including the right to bereavement benefits and retirement pensions
- duty to provide reasonable maintenance for a civil partner and any children of the family.

Where a same-sex couple have not entered into a civil partnership there are no changes to their legal position *except* for welfare benefit purposes. From December 2005, all co-habiting same-sex couples will be treated in the same way as opposite-sex co-habiting couples when their benefit is worked out. This means that many same-sex couples will lose out financially and receive less in benefits than they would have done previously, when they were treated as single people rather than as partners.

Family

1
Family

CONTENTS

INTRODUCTION

Families are central to our lives and are the social units in which most of us live. They are tiny microcosms of our wider societies and life within the family, for better or worse, teaches children how to live in the world.

These days, the 'traditional' family unit – if there ever really was such a thing – is changing. With separation and divorce on the increase, many children now live in single-parent families, or are not living with their birth parents at all but living in foster homes or permanently adopted. Step-families and families with same-sex parents are more common. At the same time, extended families, which provided a vital support network of aunts, uncles and cousins in the past, are now much more scattered.

Families, whatever their make-up, are where we live out every aspect of our lives and every family faces problems and challenges at one time or another. This section takes a 'cradle-to-grave' look at rights within the family, from how to get a birth certificate for a newborn and the vital difference between cohabitation and marriage to drawing up a will and how to have your ashes scattered where you want. It includes an A–Z of young people's rights and also looks at how the wider community can help families who are tackling problems like domestic violence.

BIRTH

Registering a birth

- All births must be registered within 42 days. A 'stillbirth' should normally be registered within 42 days and no later than three months after the birth.

A birth must be registered with the Registrar of Births and Deaths in the district in which the birth occurred. The address is in the telephone directory. There is no fee for registering a birth but there is a fee for an extra copy of the certificate.

What to do if a birth has not been registered

It is possible to apply to register a birth years after it occurred. You will need to give as many details as possible, such as the exact date and place of birth and including your or the child's full name and address. You should write to: GRO Corrections, PO Box 476, Southport, PR8 2WJ.

Birth certificates

There are two types of birth certificates:

- the full certificate. This is a copy of the entry in the birth register, giving all the recorded details.
- the short certificate. This only gives the child's full name, sex, date and place of birth. It does not give the name and particulars of the mother or father. A

short certificate is issued free of charge when a birth is first registered and is sufficient for most official purposes.

Obtaining copies of birth certificates

You can get a copy of a birth certificate in one of the following ways and a fee will be charged:

- by post or personal visit to the local register office where the birth was registered, or the local register office in the district where the birth took place
- by a personal visit to the Family Records Centre (0845 6037788). The address is: 1 Myddelton Street, London EC1R 1UW
- by post from the General Register Office. The address is: PO Box 2, Southport, Merseyside PR8 2JD
- by telephone/fax from the General Register Office (0845 6037788; fax 01704 550013), but this service is only available to credit card holders;
- online from the General Register Office at www.gro.gov.uk

You should provide as much information about the birth as possible. If you supply the index reference number of the entry, the fee will be lower than if you do not. The index reference number can be found by searching the indexes at the Family Records Centre or those larger libraries and public record offices that hold the indexes.

If you do not know your exact date of birth, a search will be made for one year either side of the year you give. If an entry cannot be traced, part of the fee paid will be kept and the balance returned, provided the balance is at least £2.

You can get a certificate, for social security purposes only, from the local registrar where the birth was registered. If you obtain the copy soon after the birth is registered, you will be charged a lower fee. Once the register has been passed to the Superintendent Registrar, the full fee is charged. The certificate will be kept by the Department for Work and Pensions (DWP).

Certificates after adoption

If you are aged 18 or over and have been adopted in England or Wales you can apply for a copy of your original birth certificate.

If all the birth details are known you should apply to the Superintendent Registrar in the district where your birth was registered. There is a fee for this. If you were adopted before 12 November 1975, you will have to see an experienced counsellor before you can get information from the original birth certificate.

If you were adopted on or after 12 November 1975, you can choose whether or not you would like to see a counsellor before getting information about your birth certificate.

You can also obtain a copy of the adoption certificate issued after the adoption order was granted.

Certificates from abroad

If you were born abroad, the birth may also have been registered in the UK. If so, a copy of the certificate can be obtained in the usual way – see above.

If the birth has not been registered in the UK, you may be able to get a copy of the birth certificate from the country where you were born. This can be done by contacting the relevant embassy in the UK. Alternatively, the Overseas Section at the General Register Office can help with enquiries. Their number is 0151 471 4001.

If you are unable to obtain a copy of your birth certificate from abroad, the Consular Division of the Foreign and Commonwealth Office (020 7270 3000) may be able to help. A fee is charged.

CHANGING A NAME

How to change your name

If you wish to be known by a different name you can change your name at any time, provided you do not intend to deceive or defraud another person. There is no legal procedure to follow in order to change a name. You simply start using the new name. You can change your forename or surname, add names or rearrange your existing names.

Although there is no legal way to change a name, you may want evidence that you have done so (see *Evidence of change of name*, p. 6). However, you cannot usually change details on your birth certificate, except in limited circumstances – for example, if you have changed gender since birth. Changing details on your birth certificate is complicated and, if you wish to do this, you should consult an experienced adviser.

Once you have decided to change your name, you can use the new name for all purposes: for example, publishing marriage banns, legal proceedings and obtaining or changing details on a driving licence or passport.

Changing a child's name

In the same way, a child's name can be changed at any time, provided it is not to deceive or defraud another person. There is no legal procedure that must be followed in order to change a child's name, providing all the people who need to give their consent have done so. The parent simply starts using the new name. A child's forename or surname can be changed, and names can be added or rearranged.

Again, the details on a child's birth certificate cannot be changed, except in limited circumstances, so if you wish to do so you should consult an experienced adviser.

If you are a child or young person under 16, your consent does not have to be given for your name to be changed. However, if you object to your name being changed you can apply for a court order to prevent the change, provided the court is satisfied that you have sufficient understanding of what is involved.

As a child or young person under 16 you cannot change your surname without your parent's consent.

Once a child's name has been changed it can be used for all purposes, such as starting school and registering with a GP. However, evidence may be required.

Who can change a child's name?

Where only one parent or person has parental responsibility for a child, that person can lawfully change the child's name. Where two or more people have parental responsibility for the child, one of them can lawfully change the child's name if all the others agree. Such agreements do not need to be in writing.

If there is a residence order in force, a child's name cannot be changed without the written agreement of anyone else who has parental responsibility or the permission of the court.

This means that where the parents are or have been married, neither can change the child's name without the consent of the other parent. If the parents have not been married, the mother can change the child's name without the father's consent unless he has acquired parental responsibility.

Evidence of change of name

You do not need legal proof that you have changed your name, provided that you can be identified by your new chosen name. However, there are some circumstances – for example, applying for a passport – when additional evidence of the change of name is required. The evidence required varies depending on the purpose for which it is needed and can include:

- a letter from a responsible person;
- a public announcement;
- a statutory declaration;
- a deed poll.

Letter

A letter from a responsible person, such as a GP, solicitor, minister, priest or MP, will often be enough evidence that you have changed your name. The letter should state that the person has known you in both names and that the change of name is to be used for all purposes.

Public announcement

You may want to record your name change by placing an advertisement in a local or national newspaper. This should state that you have stopped using your previous name and have assumed a new one. A copy of the advertisement can then be used as evidence that you have changed your name.

Statutory declaration

For most purposes, a statutory declaration is generally accepted as evidence of your change of name.

A statutory declaration is a statement recording your intention to abandon your old name and adopt a new one. Preparing a statutory declaration can be complicated. If you want to prove your change of name by making a statutory declaration you should consult an experienced adviser.

Deed poll

A deed poll is a formal statement to prove that your name has been changed. For most people it will not be necessary to prepare a deed poll as evidence that they have changed their name. However, there may be cases when a deed poll is required. For example, some professional bodies require members to produce a deed poll as proof of any name change.

As a child or young person under 18 you can only have your change of name recorded by deed poll by a person who has parental responsibility for you. However, if you are over 16, this can only be done with your consent.

Changing your name by deed poll can be complicated so, if you want to use a deed poll as evidence of change of name, you may want to seek the advice of an experienced adviser.

LIVING TOGETHER

This section is about the rights of unmarried couples who live together; this is known as cohabitation. In different areas of the law, you may not have the same rights as a married couple who live together. Unless it says otherwise, this information refers to same sex and heterosexual partners.

From December 2005, same-sex couples will be able to enter into a Civil Partnership that will give them similar rights and responsibilities to married couples – see p. xi.

If you want to set down your legal rights in certain areas of your relationship with your partner, you can make a series of agreements that will be recognized by the courts. These agreements can be about, for example, shared responsibility for your children, ownership of property that you live in, and ownership of jointly owned possessions. You will need the help of an experienced solicitor to do this.

Responsibility for children

A male partner is not necessarily assumed to be the father of his child. An unmarried mother will have sole responsibility for her child unless:

- the birth of the child is jointly registered with the child's father; *or*
- a formal agreement (this is called a parental responsibility agreement) is made with the father of the child; *or*
- a court order is made in favour of the father; *or*
- the father becomes the child's guardian (the father would only have responsibility if the mother died); *or*
- the father marries the mother.

However, both parents are responsible for supporting a child financially. If you are the father, you are financially responsible even if you are neither living with the mother nor named on the child's birth certificate. The Child Support Agency can contact you for maintenance if you no longer live with the child's mother.

If you separate, you and your partner may make an informal arrangement for contact with your child. If this is not possible, a court can be asked to intervene. The court order will usually allow contact between the child and the parent with whom the child is not living, unless there are exceptional circumstances.

Same-sex partners have no automatic parental responsibility for their partners' children. As a lesbian or gay partner you may be able to apply for a court order, which can give you certain limited rights.

Adoption

Unmarried couples who live together cannot adopt a child, although the law will change in 2005. Until then one partner must apply to adopt the child as a single person.

Death and inheritance

If your partner dies without leaving a will, you will not automatically inherit anything unless you and your partner owned property jointly. You both need to make wills if you want to make sure that the other partner inherits. However, unlike married partners, you will not be exempt from paying inheritance tax. Some same-sex couples get new rights in 2005 – see p. ix.

Debts

You and your partner are legally responsible for your own debts, for the whole of debts in joint names and for debts for which you have 'joint and several' legal responsibility. For example, if you are one of a heterosexual couple, you are responsible for paying all of a council tax bill, whether your partner contributes or not. If you have acted as guarantor for your partner, you will be legally responsible for the debt.

Money and possessions

The ownership of possessions can be complicated, but in general the rules are as follows:

- property you owned before you started living with your partner remains yours;
- if you bought an item, generally you will own it;

- property will be owned jointly if you bought it from a joint account;
- if you give property to your partner it will belong to your partner, though this can be difficult to prove;
- if you give your partner housekeeping money, any property bought with savings from it will probably belong to you.

Bank accounts

If you are living with your partner and you have separate bank accounts, neither of you will have access to money held in the other partner's account. If one partner dies, any balance in the account will be the property of the estate and cannot be used until the estate is settled.

If you have a joint account, both partners will have access to the money in the account. If the account is in joint names, on the death of one partner, the whole account immediately becomes the property of the other.

Financial support

Neither partner has a legal duty to support the other financially. If you are heterosexual partners living together and claiming Income Support or income-based Jobseeker's Allowance, tax credits, Housing Benefit or Council Tax Benefit, you will be treated as a couple and your income assessed jointly. This is not the case with same-sex couples until December 2005.

Voluntary agreements to pay maintenance to each other may be difficult to enforce.

Pensions

The rules of pension schemes vary. Whether or not you can benefit from a scheme to which your partner belongs will depend on the scheme. Most schemes offer benefits to dependent children and some will offer benefits to a dependent heterosexual partner. Benefits available to heterosexual partners, whether married or unmarried, should be available to partners in a same-sex relationship. If this is not the case there may have been unlawful discrimination. You can arrange a personal pension to give cover to whoever the scheme member wants, but you will probably have to pay large contributions to the pension fund.

Student grants

If you are a student living with your partner, your partner's income will be ignored when deciding if you are entitled to a student grant.

Housing

Tenants

If your partner is the sole tenant, you will usually have no rights to stay in the accommodation if your partner asks you to leave. This applies whether you live in private or public-sector accommodation. If you are in this situation, you should get help from an experienced solicitor.

It is advisable for partners who live together to be joint tenants as this gives them equal rights and responsibilities. It is possible to convert a sole tenancy to a joint tenancy if you and your partner and the landlord agree.

If you are a joint tenant and your partner leaves, you should get legal advice.

If your partner is the sole tenant and leaves, you will be in a very vulnerable position. If you are in this position, you should get legal advice. A court can transfer a tenancy, whether it is a sole or joint tenancy.

Owner-occupiers

A property may be owned in the sole name of one partner or may be owned jointly.

If your partner is the sole owner-occupier, you may have no rights to remain in the home if your partner asks you to leave, although you may be able to protect your position. You will need to get legal advice on this.

If your relationship ends, and there are children, courts can include property as part of an overall settlement to protect the children.

If you and your partner own your property jointly you can either be 'joint tenants' or 'tenants in common'. (This is different from being a tenant where you rent property from a landlord.)

If you are 'joint tenants', your property cannot be sold without the agreement of both of you. If one of you dies, their share of the property passes automatically to the other.

If you own your property as 'tenants in common', each of you will have a share of your home that you can dispose of as you like. It is up to you to decide how much each share will be. If one of you dies, you can leave your share to whoever you like.

Next of kin and medical consent

Some organizations – for example, hospitals and prisons – will usually accept the name of an unmarried partner who lives with you as the next of kin. If you want to name your partner as next of kin, you should insist on this. However, there is little you can do if the organization still refuses to accept it.

If your partner is to have an operation and the consent of the nearest relative is needed, you may be able to give this, although, strictly speaking, if there is a husband or wife, they will be the nearest relative. An NHS Trust will allow you formally to nominate your next of kin when you are admitted and this can be your partner.

Who can help?

Solicitors On-line (www.solicitors-online.com) is the website of the Law Society and can help you find a solicitor who is an expert in the area of law you need.

MARRIAGE

Who can get married?

According to UK law, a man and a woman may marry if they are both 16 years or over and free to marry – that is, single, widowed or divorced. The following people cannot marry:

- people aged 16 or 17 who do not have parental consent;
- people of the same sex;
- certain close relatives.

Young people

If you are 16 or 17 you cannot marry without parental consent. Each parent with parental responsibility is entitled to give parental consent. In some circumstances, other people may give parental consent.

Getting engaged

Engagements are mainly for cultural reasons and have limited status. However, they can be used, for example, in immigration law as evidence of intention to marry.

One of the parties can decide to end an engagement, as an agreement to marry cannot be legally enforced.

My fiancé and I have decided not to go through with the wedding. Can I keep the ring?

If an engagement is broken, a woman can keep the engagement ring unless, at the time she was given it, the man specifically said that it should be returned if the engagement were broken. Any other property belonging to the couple should be divided between them in the same way as property would be divided if the couple divorced. If the couple cannot agree about entitlement to property, either person can apply to a court to decide the issue, provided this is done within three years of the end of the engagement. Legal advice will be needed in these circumstances.

Where you can get married

Local authorities in England and Wales can approve premises other than Register Offices where marriages may take place. Certain churches are automatically approved premises. Applications for approval of premises can be made by the owner or trustee of a building but not by a couple who are marrying.

The premises must be regularly open to members of the public, so private homes are unlikely to be approved since they are not normally open to the public. Stately homes, hotels and civic buildings are likely to be thought suitable. Approval will not be given for open-air venues, such as beaches or golf courses. Generally, the premises will need to be permanent built structures, although it may be possible for approval to be given to a permanently moored, publicly open boat. Hot-air balloons or aeroplanes will not be approved.

If you want to get married in local authority approved premises you should obtain a list of premises from the local town hall.

How to marry

You can get married by a civil ceremony or a religious ceremony.

In both cases, the following legal requirements must be met:

- the marriage must be conducted by a person or in the presence of a person authorized to register marriages in the district; *and*
- the marriage must be entered in the marriage register and signed by both parties, two witnesses, the person who conducted the ceremony and, if that person is not authorized to register marriages, the person who is registering the marriage.

Civil marriage ceremonies

You and your partner must give notice of marriage in your local Register Office, whether or not you wish to marry in that district. The Superintendent Registrar then issues authority for the marriage and you may marry in any Register Office or local authority approved premises in any district.

In the period between the notice of intention to marry and the ceremony, anyone with strong grounds for objecting to the marriage can do so. Making a false statement is a criminal offence.

Both partners must be resident in England or Wales for seven days before notice is given (on the eighth day). A notice must state where the marriage is to take place. The marriage can then take place after fifteen days have elapsed from the date on which notice of the marriage is entered in the marriage notice book. There is a fee for giving notice of the marriage.

The marriage must usually take place within twelve months from the date of entry of the notice. If the marriage does not take place within that time, the process must be repeated.

Religious marriage ceremonies

The Church of England and the Church in Wales are allowed to register a marriage at the same time as performing the religious ceremony.

Ministers and priests of all other religions can be authorized to register marriages and must have a certificate or licence to do so from the local Superintendent Registrar. For Jewish and Quaker marriages, the authorization is automatic. For all other religions, if the official performing the ceremony is not authorized, either a Registrar must attend the religious ceremony or the partners will need to have separate religious and civil ceremonies.

Religious ceremonies and civil ceremonies

If a couple has been married in a Register Office, the partners can have a religious marriage ceremony afterwards. The partners are likely to be asked for their marriage certificate. A religious ceremony that does not comply with the conditions stated above, and which takes place before a civil wedding, is not a valid marriage under UK law and the couple's status will be that of cohabitees.

Do I have to fill in any forms to change my name when I get married?

No, you do not have to fill in any forms or get permission legally to change your name. You just start using your changed name instead of your old one. However, you may find that some organizations want to see written evidence of your name change. This could be a letter from a doctor, minister or solicitor, or an announcement in the press. You may prefer to make a statutory declaration or change your name by deed poll.

Anyone who is 16 or over can change their name at any time. You can change your forename, your surname or both. You can add new names or drop a name you do not want. You can use your new name for all purposes including getting married or applying for a passport. However, you cannot change your name for purposes of fraud.

Remarriage/second marriage

In the UK there are no legal restrictions to prevent a person who has been divorced or widowed from remarrying in a civil ceremony as long as the legal requirements described earlier are met.

Religions and denominations have different rules about whether someone can remarry in a religious ceremony. If you or your partner has been married before and you want a religious ceremony, you will need to check with an official of the relevant religion.

Blessing ceremonies

Even if you are not allowed to marry in a religious ceremony – for example, because you belong to a religion that does not permit marriage of people who are divorced, or if you are lesbian or gay – it may be possible to arrange for your relationship to be blessed in a religious ceremony. This is at the discretion of the religious official concerned.

Forced marriages

It is a criminal offence to force a person to marry. If you are afraid that you may be forced into a marriage in this country, the police should be contacted. This is also the case where there is concern that another person may be forced into a marriage.

If you are afraid that you may be forced into marriage overseas, you should, before travelling, contact the Community Liaison Unit at the Foreign and Commonwealth Office (020 7008 0230) for advice. If you are concerned about someone else who has travelled overseas, you should also contact the Community Liaison Unit.

ENDING A COHABITATION OR MARRIAGE

If you are living with your partner but are not married and your relationship ends, there is no need for you to take any legal action to formalize the separation. However, there may be issues concerning children, property and money to sort out. This can be done either by informal agreement or by a written separation agreement between you (see *Financial arrangements at the end of a relationship*, p. 24).

If you and your partner cannot agree, a court can order who should stay in the home in the short term and can also transfer a tenancy.

Once you are separating, or have separated, don't forget to inform:

- your landlord or local authority rent office;
- the local authority housing and Council Tax sections;
- your mortgage lender;
- the land registry;

- water, gas, electricity and telephone companies;
- your local social security office;
- the Inland Revenue if you are getting tax credits;
- schools;
- your bank or any other financial institution if you have a joint account – it may be advisable for one of the account holders to freeze the account to prevent the other withdrawing some or all of the money;
- hire purchase or credit companies;
- insurance companies, particularly if you have joint policies;
- the post office, if it is necessary to have mail redirected;
- your doctor, dentist, child health clinic.

Separating informally

If you and your partner are married you can separate by an informal arrangement. There is no need to notify anyone that you are no longer living together. However, it is advisable in practice to inform some or all of the people listed above.

If there is agreement between you and your partner, you can make arrangements about children, money, housing and other property without going to court. However, any informal arrangement made when separating may affect future decisions if you do ever go to court. A court may overturn an arrangement made by a couple that it considers to be unreasonable or, in the case of a child, not in the child's best interests.

Separation agreements

A separation agreement is a written agreement between a couple who intend to stop living together, setting out how they wish to resolve the issues of money, property and children. It is usually made by a married couple, but any couple can draw up an agreement as a way of resolving and confirming the arrangements they have come to.

Examples of what may be included are, an agreement:

- to live separately. This releases both partners from the duty to cohabit, which is part of the marriage contract. If one of you does not agree on separation, the agreement should not be included, as it will prevent any future right to sue for desertion in divorce proceedings.
- not to molest, annoy or disturb the other partner;
- to provide maintenance for the other partner, usually the woman. This would

normally say that maintenance will stop if the woman cohabits with another man. Any agreement not to apply to a court for maintenance is invalid.

- to provide maintenance for any children of the relationship. Any agreement not to apply to a court or to the CSA is invalid.
- on who the children should live and have contact with.

The advantage of a written agreement is that it is easier to ensure that you both understand what has been agreed. It also means that either partner can go to court to vary the order at a future date. It is advisable to consult a solicitor when drawing up a separation agreement, but you should work out in advance the general areas you want to cover. This will reduce the legal costs. Assistance may be available under the legal help scheme.

Judicial separation

A judicial separation is a court order which releases the partners of a marriage from the obligation to live together in the same way as a divorce. It is comparatively rare but can be used by couples who have a conscientious objection to divorce. The order does not dissolve the marriage so neither partner is free to remarry.

Divorce

You cannot apply for a divorce until you have been married for at least one year. There are no exceptions to this rule. To get divorced in England or Wales, the marriage must be recognized as valid by UK law and you must meet the residence rules.

If neither partner objects to the divorce it is called an *undefended* divorce. This is dealt with by a straightforward procedure, which does not necessarily require the use of a solicitor. If one of the partners does not agree to the divorce, it is called a *defended* divorce and will require the help of a solicitor.

Irretrievable breakdown

A divorce will be granted by the county court if you or your partner can show that the marriage no longer exists. Legally, this is known as the irretrievable breakdown of the marriage. For a marriage to have irretrievably broken down, one of the following must be proved:

- adultery;
- unreasonable behaviour;
- desertion;
- two years' separation with consent;
- five years' separation.

Adultery

A court may grant a divorce if one of you has committed adultery and the other partner finds it intolerable to continue living together. The decision that it is intolerable must be made within six months of the adultery taking place. A woman who is raped has not committed adultery but a man who commits rape has.

The court will need evidence of the adultery – for example, dates – and will only grant the divorce if it is satisfied that adultery has occurred and that the other partner could no longer live with the partner who has committed adultery.

If the divorce is undefended, the court will usually only need statements and details. If the divorce is defended, then proof will be necessary and this may be difficult and expensive.

Unreasonable behaviour

A court may grant a divorce if you or your partner has behaved so badly that the other can no longer tolerate living together. Unreasonable behaviour can include mental or physical cruelty, including violence or abuse, and less obvious things like dominating a partner and not letting the other leave the house or speak to neighbours and friends, or refusing to pay for house-keeping.

If the divorce is defended, a great deal of evidence and detail will be needed – for example, evidence from witnesses such as friends or medical evidence.

Desertion

A partner who has been deserted for two out of the last two and a half years can apply for a divorce without the agreement of the other partner. Living together for a total of up to six months during this period does not stop the desertion being continuous. A court will want proof of the desertion and, if the divorce is contested, there may be disputes over who deserted whom.

Separation for two years

If you have lived apart for two years continuously and you both agree to a divorce, a court will accept this as proof of irretrievable breakdown. The two years apart will still be continuous if you have actually lived together for up to six months in between.

Separation for five years

If you have lived apart for five years, either you or your partner can apply for a divorce without the other's agreement. The other partner can defend the divorce on the grounds that it would cause unreasonable hardship but a court will usually agree to a divorce where you have been separated for five years.

Applying for a divorce

The partner who is applying for the divorce is known as the petitioner. The other partner is the respondent.

If you want to start divorce proceedings you will need to obtain the necessary forms from the court. The court office will tell you which forms you need, but court staff are not allowed to give legal advice to either partner or help complete forms.

If you are applying for a divorce and want help in completing the forms you should consult an experienced adviser.

Undefended divorce

An undefended divorce is dealt with in the county court or the divorce registry in London. The partner who is applying for the divorce can go to any divorce county court. The address can be found in the local telephone directory. In an undefended divorce, the use of a solicitor is not usually necessary for the divorce procedure itself. However, it may be advisable to consult a solicitor for general advice prior to starting divorce proceedings. A solicitor can be useful for advice on whether there are sufficient grounds, which grounds are appropriate, and what evidence may be needed. If there are disputes over children, property or money which you and your partner cannot resolve, it is usually advisable to consult a solicitor.

Defended divorce

A defended divorce will normally be heard in the High Court, although proceedings can be transferred to the divorce county court.

In a defended divorce, both partners should always consult a solicitor.

When the case is heard, barristers will usually need to be employed as well. Solicitors' fees can become very high if there are lengthy disputes. It is advisable wherever possible for both partners to try to come to an agreement before going to court.

What the court will do

If the respondent does not intend to defend the divorce, the court will examine the petition and grant a decree nisi. No court hearing is needed. The marriage still exists at this stage

The court may, however, want to discuss arrangements about any children of the relationship and possibly meet the children if they are old enough (nine years and over). An undefended divorce can take up to six months if there are no children or money issues involved. It can take longer if children are involved and the court is not satisfied with arrangements being made for them.

If the respondent does not intend to defend the divorce, a date will be fixed for a court hearing and the court will decide whether to grant a decree nisi after the hearing.

Six weeks after the court grants the decree nisi, the partner who applied for the divorce can apply to the court for a decree absolute. The decree absolute is the final stage and will confirm the divorce. It will be granted provided that the court has approved the arrangements for any children.

Publicly funded legal services

Publicly funded legal representation is not available for an undefended divorce but it is available for matters concerning children, money and property connected with it. However, it is advisable to try to sort out matters of this kind as far as possible before going to court as this will reduce any legal costs that may have to be paid.

Publicly funded legal representation (usually called legal aid) may be available for a defended divorce. Anyone who does get legal aid in a matter involving property may have to pay part of the 'winnings' towards the costs and this can be expensive. A solicitor should explain this to you and should try to keep these costs as low as possible.

Financial arrangements at the end of a relationship

At the end of a relationship, both parents are responsible for supporting their children financially, regardless of whether a couple were married and regardless of where the children will live.

Neither partner has a duty to maintain the other at the end of a relationship if they were unmarried. However, if you were married, either partner can apply for maintenance from the other. You can do this regardless of whether you have children, and whether or not you are divorcing. There are three possible ways to arrange financial support:

- by voluntary agreement;
- through the Child Support Agency; *or*
- through the courts.

Voluntary agreement

A voluntary agreement between a couple whose relationship has ended can be formal or informal, verbal or written. You can agree, for example, that one of you will make weekly payments to the other for the support of children, or will meet rent or mortgage payments or household bills, or pay for the children's clothing and holidays.

Before you decide on the terms of a voluntary agreement, it may be useful to consult a solicitor for advice on what would be an appropriate arrangement. It may also be useful to have an agreement drawn up by a solicitor in case of future dispute or to obtain tax relief on payments. It may be possible to obtain help with the costs of advice on and the drawing up of an agreement under the legal help scheme.

An informal voluntary agreement avoids the need for, and the costs of, solicitors. However, there is no guarantee that a partner will keep to its terms.

Child Support Agency (CSA)

The Child Support Agency (CSA) assesses and collects maintenance payments in respect of children who are under 16 (under 19 if they are in full-time non-advanced education). If the children of a relationship are living with you and the relationship has ended, and you claim Income Support or income-based Jobseeker's Allowance, you will normally have to use the CSA to obtain maintenance for the children. If you claim Working Tax Credit or Child Tax Credit you do not have to use the CSA.

Through the courts

If you have been married and your relationship is ending, or has ended, you can apply to a court to order your partner or former partner to pay maintenance. The court will consider all the financial resources and assets of both partners, including pension arrangements.

In some circumstances, the court can also make an order for child maintenance to be paid.

A court can make an order for periodical maintenance payments to be made – that is, a specific sum at regular intervals – or for a specified lump sum. It can also make an order about pension arrangements.

If you want to apply to a court for maintenance for yourself or a child you should obtain the help of a solicitor. Publicly funded legal services may be available when making an application, but it may also be necessary to contribute to the costs from the proceeds of any financial arrangements made. Where pension arrangements are involved, you should also consider obtaining specialist financial advice.

Relationship breakdown and property

Courts can give one of the partners short-term rights to the home – for example, the right to stay, to have access to the home or to exclude the other person.

Courts can make long-term arrangements about property in certain cases where there are children or in judicial separation or divorce cases. In divorce, if there is a dispute about property, the court will deal with the dispute as part of the divorce.

Protecting a married partner's right to occupy the home

If you and your spouse are owner-occupiers, it is often the case that only one of you is the actual owner. If this is the case, and you are the partner who is not the owner, you will need to ensure that you keep your right to live in the property and to prevent the owner selling it without your knowledge. Even if you actually move out when the relationship ends, you may want to move back in again with the children. To retain your right, you must register your 'right of occupation' by completing a form and sending it to either the District Land Registry or the Land Charges Department in Plymouth, depending on where the title of the property is registered.

This procedure is not complicated and it is not necessary to consult a solicitor, but you may want to consult an experienced adviser.

Relationship breakdown and children

Once a marriage ends, decisions have to be made about who will care for any children of the relationship. Many parents are able to make arrangements amicably between themselves about where the children live and about visits by the other parent. However, if this is not possible, decisions can be made by the courts, including the transfer of property and tenancies.

Many couples split up but never get divorced. If you separate informally (or have never been married) you may not ever need to go to court. You can make arrangements for the children that may last indefinitely. But if you are unable to resolve a disagreement over the care of or contact with the children, you may need to ask the court to resolve the dispute.

If you are getting a divorce or judicial separation that involves court proceedings, the court will not grant the divorce or separation until it has looked at the arrangements for the children. If they are acceptable to both parents, the court will not make an order in relation to the child. It will only make a court order where it is necessary to do so to resolve a dispute.

Parental responsibility

The term *parental responsibility* covers all rights, duties, powers and responsibilities that a parent has for a child. This includes providing a home, feeding and clothing, providing protection and security, and ensuring that the child receives a satisfactory education.

If you were married at the time of your child's birth, or married each other since the birth, both partners will automatically have parental responsibility and continue to have it after divorce or separation. Each parent can exercise their parental responsibility independently of the other.

If you were not married, and do not subsequently marry each other, the mother has parental responsibility. However, the father will have parental responsibility if he registers (or re-registers) the birth of his child with the child's mother. If he has not registered and wants parental responsibility, he has to apply to a court for this to be granted.

What decisions can a court make?

A court will only make an order concerning a child if it feels it is in the best interests of the child to do so. The main orders that may be made by a court are for:

- a residence order to determine who the child should live with;
- a contact order to determine who the child should have contact with and what form of contact.

Residence order

The court can make a residence order in favour of:

- one parent. This means that the child must live with that parent.
- both parents. One residence order can be made in favour of both parents, even if they are not living together. The order will specify how much time the child will live with each parent.
- each parent. Each parent will have a separate order specifying how much time the child will live with them.

Contact order

The court will normally expect the parents to make their own arrangements to ensure that each of them maintains contact with the children. The court will only make a court order if they cannot agree.

The contact order may include conditions specifying where and how often contact should take place. It may also specify the type of contact – for example, visiting, telephoning or writing letters. Orders can also be made to allow contact between the child and, for example, other relatives or friends.

Family mediation

Family mediation is a way of assisting separating or divorcing couples to resolve disputes and reach agreed decisions on specific issues arising from the breakdown of a relationship. It involves both partners and aims to clarify the issues between them and to help them make decisions.

Two main types of family mediation are available:

- *out-of-court mediation*, where people can refer themselves or be referred by, for example, a solicitor or adviser; *and*
- *court-based dispute resolution*, where people are referred by the court when children are involved and seen at court.

Out-of-court family mediation

Out-of-court family mediation can be provided by a number of organizations. However, all family mediators should be members of the United Kingdom College of Family Mediators (see below). A couple can use family mediation services as soon as possible after they have decided their relationship is ending and they feel able to discuss any disputes.

Mediation can be helpful before divorce proceedings begin, to encourage co-operation between the couple and to prevent disputes intensifying and agreement becoming harder to reach in the future. Family mediation can also be used after a separation or divorce if new issues arise or there are outstanding issues to be resolved.

Couples referred to mediation by a solicitor may be eligible for the Family Mediation Scheme or other general publicly funded legal services for attending mediation.

There is a single professional body for family mediators, the **United Kingdom College of Family Mediators** (020 7904 7223; www.ukcfm.co.uk). You should check that any mediator is a member of this body to ensure that they are properly trained and supervised. The college has a directory that can be used to check whether a particular mediator is a member, or to find a mediator to use.

Court-based dispute resolution
Court-based dispute resolution schemes exist in divorce county courts and are provided by the children and family court advisory service. Some county courts do not have a dispute resolution scheme but may have a children and family reporter who can discuss some aspects of a case with a couple. Where a scheme exists, a couple who are divorcing or separating will be seen first by a children and family reporter with a district judge present. If there is a dispute over contact with children, or with whom the children will live, you will be referred to a children and family reporter for a meeting before being given a full court hearing.

Usually, both members of the couple will attend the meeting with the reporter, although you can ask to be seen separately as well. The reporter may also see the children separately. The children and family reporter will report the outcome of discussions to the district judge.

If agreement was reached at the meeting, the district judge can make an order to confirm what was agreed. If no agreement was reached, the district judge can order that a welfare report is produced before going any further with the case.

Court-based dispute resolution schemes are free.

Who can help?

www.ondivorce.co.uk is a website that provides a lot of information on the issues surrounding divorce and the ending of a relationship. It has links to information on child support, finding a solicitor, housing and mediation. It also has a bulletin board and a forum for discussion. The organization does not provide telephone advice.

DOMESTIC VIOLENCE

Domestic violence covers a range of situations where one person in some way harms another person with whom they have some pre-existing relationship. It can therefore be one person physically attacking another or it may be another form of abuse such as pestering with phone calls, installing a lover in the family home, or putting superglue in the locks of the victim's car doors. For the above actions to be counted as domestic violence, the victim and the perpetrator must have had some form of relationship, but they do not need to be heterosexual partners and they need not live in the same property.

If you are the victim of a violent relationship, get immediate practical advice on the options available, which may be to:

- attempt to stop the violence and stay with the perpetrator of the violence;
- leave home temporarily;
- leave home permanently;
- stay in the present home and get the perpetrator of the violence to leave;
- take legal action.

Finding somewhere safe to stay

If you are a victim of a violent relationship you may need somewhere safe to stay, either alone or with your children. The options are:

- stay at home if you think this is safe;
- stay with relatives or friends;
- stay in a women's refuge – this is only an option for women (with or without children);
- get emergency accommodation from the local authority under homeless persons law – this will usually mean a bed and breakfast hostel;
- get privately rented accommodation.

Women's Aid Refuges

Women's Aid Refuges are safe houses run by and for women suffering domestic violence. Refuges provide somewhere safe for women and their children to stay and allow some time and space for the women to think about what to do next.

Staff at refuges are specialists in dealing with domestic violence, and so can give a lot of emotional and practical support – for example, advice on benefit claims, which solicitors to use and, if necessary, how to contact the police.

To find out your nearest refuge with spaces available, you should contact the National Domestic Violence helpline (0808 200 0247). Helpline staff will do their best to find you somewhere safe to stay that night even if the local refuge is full. They are also happy to talk to women about any questions they have about refuges.

Going to the local authority

You will normally be considered to be legally homeless if it is not reasonable for you to occupy your home because of the risk or fear of domestic violence. Local authorities should deal sympathetically with applications from people who are in fear of violence. You can ask for a private interview, with someone of the same sex, and can take a friend with you for support.

The local authority may have a duty to provide interim accommodation for you while it decides whether you are legally homeless.

Going to privately rented accommodation

If you decide to go into privately rented accommodation you will be unlikely to be able to arrange it quickly. This is really only an option for people who have time to plan their departure and can afford this accommodation.

Longer-term solutions

Once you have found a safe place to stay for the short term, you will need to think about what to do in the longer term. You will need to consider:

● whether you wish to separate permanently from your partner – you should seek legal advice: see *Legal remedies and procedures* below;
● whether you want to take action to keep the violent partner away from you – you should seek legal advice: see *Legal remedies and procedures* below;
● housing. Your legal rights to the family home will depend upon the type of

housing you are leaving, the legal status of your relationship and whether or not you have children. You should get legal advice to ensure that you do everything possible to protect rights to the family home. Seek advice about the family home even if you are leaving permanently because, if your partner sells the home, you may lose money and possessions.

- children. If you have children you will need to decide if you are taking the children with you. You may need to use the courts to resolve who the children should live with and with whom they should have contact. You should seek legal advice: see *Legal remedies and procedures* below.
- money. You will need to sort out your benefit entitlement and tax arrangements and whether or not to apply to court for maintenance for yourself. You may also want to apply to the Child Support Agency for a maintenance assessment for your children. If you claim certain benefits, you will automatically be contacted by the Child Support Agency, and you should keep in mind that claiming maintenance from a violent partner could be distressing or threatening.

Legal remedies and procedures

If you want to discuss legal protection for yourself and your children, consult a solicitor who is experienced in family law work. Local Women's Aid groups, the police, rape crisis groups, or women's centres usually know of local solicitors who are both experienced and sympathetic. Your local CAB has the Law Society's Solicitors Regional Directory, which lists solicitors who specialize in family law work. Your local library may also have this directory.

You should make an appointment as soon as you feel ready, and you could take someone with you for support the first time you go to the solicitor. The initial interview will probably last quite a long time, during which the solicitor should discuss with you what courses of legal action are open to you and whether you are entitled to publicly funded legal services.

Who can help?

The **National Domestic Violence helpline** (0808 200 0247) is a 24-hour helpline providing access to advice and support to anyone experiencing domestic violence. The helpline is provided jointly by Women's Aid and Refuge.

Women's Aid (helpline: 0808 200 0247; www.womensaid.org.uk) can also give details of refuges and the availability of refuge places throughout the UK.

Welsh Women's Aid (helpline: 0808 801 0800) provides confidential information in English and Welsh.

Refuge (helpline: 0808 200 0247; www.refuge.org.uk) provides safe emergency accommodation through a network of refuges throughout the UK. It also offers a children's programme, individual and group counselling for women who have suffered abuse, help with resettlement and an outreach project for women from ethnic minority communities.

There are a number of police domestic violence units that have staff specially trained to help people experiencing domestic violence. They work closely with other organizations such as local solicitors and Women's Aid groups. Your local police station, in the phone book under Police, will be able to tell you if they have a domestic violence unit, or where the nearest one is.

Survivors UK Ltd (helpline 0845 122 1201; www.survivorsuk.org.uk) is a national helpline for men who have been victims of violence, sexual assault and rape. The helpline may be able to arrange counselling or a support group if you live in the London area. If you live outside London, Survivors UK may be able to provide details of an appropriate service outside the London area.

Everyman (helpline 020 7737 6747) is a national helpline for men who are violent, or concerned about their violence and the consequences of it. The helpline can provide telephone counselling and advice about local services. A face-to-face counselling service is also available but only in the London area.

M-Power (0808 808 4321; www.male-rape.org.uk) is a national helpline for men who have been raped, assaulted or abused in childhood or adult life. The helpline also supports partners (male and female) and family members of abused men.

Perpetrators of violence

There are several specialist organizations that can help violent people who want to stop being violent. Some are self-help groups run by others who have had experience of violent behaviour, others may be run by trained counsellors. It may also be possible for you to get help through your GP.

COMMUNITY CARE

Community care services are intended to ensure that you preserve as independent and satisfactory a style of life as possible. The services may be necessary because you are elderly, disabled or physically or mentally ill. The main aim in providing community care services is to enable you to remain living in your own home and to retain as much independence as possible. The local authority social services department will normally provide community care services or arrange for them to be provided.

Services that are available

There is a wide range of services that may be available under the heading of community care. The following list gives only the main examples:

- home care services;
- home helps;
- adaptations to the home;
- meals;
- recreational and occupational activities.

Home care services

Home care services generally mean help with personal tasks – for example, bathing and washing, getting up and going to bed, shopping, managing finances. Providing home care involves someone coming to your home at agreed times. This could be two or three times a day or even 24-hour care where necessary.

Home helps

Home helps can provide assistance with general domestic tasks including cleaning and cooking and may be particularly important in maintaining hygiene in the home.

Adaptations to the home

Adaptations to the home could be major or minor and can be particularly important in allowing you to remain at home. Major adaptations would include, for example, the installation of a stair lift or downstairs lavatory or the lowering of worktops in the kitchen. Minor adaptations would include, for example, hand rails in the bathroom.

Meals

The provision of meals as a community care service could mean a daily delivery of a meal or, in some areas, the delivery of a weekly or monthly supply of frozen food. It could also mean providing meals at a day centre or lunch club.

Recreational and occupational activities

A local authority can provide a range of recreational, occupational, educational and cultural activities, together with the necessary facilities – for example, at day centres. The activities could include lectures, games, outings, and help with living skills and budgeting. The local authority may also provide transport to enable you to make use of the facilities.

A local authority may also be able to provide radios, televisions and/or visiting library services.

Needs assessments

A community care service cannot normally be provided until you have had a *needs assessment* carried out by the local authority. The local authority must carry out an assessment for anyone who appears to need a community care service because they are, for example, elderly, disabled or suffering from a physical or mental illness.

It will usually be necessary to ask the local authority social services department to carry out an assessment. If you need an assessment you can ask for one or it can be requested by a carer – that is, someone who is looking after you.

If, after contacting the local social services department, there are problems with an assessment, it may be necessary to contact a specialist adviser, for example at a CAB.

An assessment is carried out by someone from or acting on behalf of the local authority's social services department. More than one person could be involved in carrying out the assessment, including a social worker, a physiotherapist and an occupational therapist. The assessment procedure may involve filling in a form but this will vary from area to area.

The assessment should take into account:

- your wishes as the person being assessed;
- whether you have any particular physical difficulties – for example, problems with walking or climbing stairs;

- whether you have any particular health or housing needs;
- what sources of help you have access to, such as carers, family or nearby friends, and their willingness to continue providing care;
- what needs these people who provide care may have.

Once an assessment has been carried out, the local authority has to decide whether or not to provide services to meet needs that have been identified. If the local authority is going to provide services these must be set out in a care plan. This should be given in writing if requested. The care plan will set out:

- the services which are to be provided, by whom, when and what will be achieved by providing them;
- a contact point to deal with problems over services;
- information on how to ask for a review of the services being provided if circumstances change.

Assessment for a carer

A carer is someone, often a relative or friend, who takes responsibility for looking after a disabled, ill or elderly person, and who does not provide the care as part of a job or as a volunteer with a voluntary organization. Some carers provide care for a few hours a week, others for twenty-four hours a day, every day. A carer does not have to be living with the person being cared for.

If you are a carer, you are entitled to ask for your needs to be assessed when an assessment is being carried out for the person you care for. You can ask to be assessed even if the person you care for is entitled to an assessment but does not want one. Some carers of disabled children can also have an assessment.

Local authorities can provide services direct to carers and offer you direct payments for your own needs. However, the results of the carer's assessment must be taken into account when the local authority decides what community care services the person being cared for will receive.

Paying for community care services

A local authority can charge for providing some community care services.

Some local authorities only charge for some services – for example, meals on wheels or home helps – while others charge for all services for which they are allowed to charge. Carers who are provided with services for their needs can be charged for those services.

A local authority must make information about charges generally available. If you are having your community care needs assessed by the local authority you must also be given full information on charges for any services provided.

Some local authorities make a flat-rate charge for a service – for example, meals on wheels. Other local authorities may want to know how much income – for example, social security benefits – and savings you have and then charge according to a sliding scale. Local authorities in England and Wales must comply with the following government guidance when assessing how much you can pay for services:

- they must not charge you if you get Income Support, income-based Jobseeker's Allowance or Pension Credit (guarantee credit only) and your overall income is less than a certain amount;
- the local authority should only take your savings and capital into account (but not the value of your home) if they are above a set limit;
- in England only, if the authority takes into account your disability-related social security benefit (for example, Attendance Allowance or Disability Living Allowance) it must assess any extra expenses you have as a result of your disability (for example, extra heating or laundry costs);
- the authority should offer you advice on social security benefits.

If you have been asked to pay for services and you think the charges are unreasonable or you cannot afford to pay them, you can ask for the charges to be reviewed.

Direct payments

In England, a local authority has a duty to provide direct payments to allow people with an assessed need for community care services to choose who provides these services. In Wales, a local authority may offer direct payments to:

- a disabled person of 16 or over;
- a disabled person with parental responsibility for a child;
- the carer of a disabled person or child for whom the carer has parental responsibility;
- a carer aged 16 or over;
- someone aged 65 or over.

Whether you can get direct payments, and how much you will get, will depend on your means. If you are accepted for direct payments, you will have to arrange your own services. Local support organizations may be able to help you with these arrangements and the **National Centre for Independent Living** (020 7587 1663; www.ncil.org.uk) can tell you which those organizations are.

MANAGING FINANCIAL AFFAIRS FOR SOMEONE ELSE

There may be times in life when you want to ask other people to manage your financial affairs for you. You might choose a close relative or friend. This might be because you think you may lose your mental capacity, or because you have had a physical illness or an accident resulting in physical injury. Ways of doing this are explored here.

Asking someone else to manage your financial affairs temporarily

Social security benefits

If you are temporarily unable to collect your benefit and it is normally paid into your bank or building society account, you should write to the bank or building society, asking them to give temporary power to someone else to operate your account (see below). If your benefit is normally paid by cheque, you can fill in the back of the cheque to allow someone else to cash it for you. If you want someone else to cash your benefit cheque for you on a regular basis, you should contact the office that deals with your benefit payments to let them know.

Bank accounts

If the only temporary power you want to give someone is the power to operate a bank account on your behalf, you should just write to your bank. Many banks have their own form, called a form for third-party mandate, which they will ask you to complete and return to them.

General financial affairs

If you want someone to handle your financial affairs for a temporary period, for example while you are on holiday or while you can supervise what they do, you need an ordinary power of attorney. A power of attorney is a legal document that authorizes one or more people to handle your financial affairs, including property, shares and money, either generally or in relation to specific items.

Power of Attorney

Ordinary power of attorney

If you want someone to look after your financial affairs for a longer period of time you can grant an *ordinary power of attorney*, which can relate to all your affairs or only to specific matters. You should not use an ordinary power of attorney if you have been diagnosed as having, or if you think that you may develop, any mental illness or degenerative disease that can lead to mental incapacity. This is because an ordinary power of attorney automatically comes to an end if you lose your mental capacity. If you have a physical illness or an accident resulting in physical injury, and you want someone else to look after your affairs, you should create an ordinary power of attorney.

Enduring power of attorney

If you have been diagnosed as having, or if you think that you may develop, a mental illness – for example, schizophrenia, or a degenerative brain disease leading to mental incapacity, like Alzheimer's disease – and you want someone else to manage your financial affairs either now or in the future, you should use an enduring power of attorney. Unlike an ordinary power of attorney, an enduring power of attorney can come into effect or continue in force after you lose your mental capacity. It will come into effect immediately if you do not specify in it that it should not take effect until you lose your mental capacity.

Who can grant a power of attorney?

Someone who grants a power of attorney is called a donor. In order to be a donor, you must have mental capacity and you can only grant the power of attorney to do things that you have the right and capacity to do yourself. Only the donor can make the decision to create a power of attorney and if you instruct a solicitor or advice worker to draft one for you, the solicitor or advice worker should only accept instructions or authorization from you, whether in person or in writing, and not, for example, from the person who is to become your attorney.

Children

A child under 18 can be a donor of an ordinary power of attorney, but a child can only give an attorney the power to do things that they can legally do as a child.

Who can be an attorney?

Anyone who has mental capacity can be an attorney. However, anyone who is, or who has been, bankrupt cannot act as an attorney under an enduring power of attorney. If an attorney becomes bankrupt, the enduring power of attorney is revoked.

Trust corporations such as banks can be an attorney and professional attorneys can charge for their services.

Responsibilities of an attorney

When you are appointed as an attorney you are placed in a position of trust and you must act in the best interests of the donor, using their money to meet the donor's best interests. As an attorney, you can only do the things the donor has authorized you to do, and you cannot delegate any duties unless the donor has authorized delegation.

Who can help?

The **Public Guardianship Office** (0845 330 2900; enduring power of attorney helpline 0845 330 2963; www.guardianship.gov.uk) offers information about enduring powers of attorney, and about the Court of Protection. They also supply some forms and can advise on current fees. Its staff cannot give legal advice or help people complete the forms.

DEATHS

Registering the death

The registration of the death is the formal record of the death.

When someone dies at home, the death should be registered at the register office for the district where they lived. If the death took place in hospital or in a nursing home it must be registered at the register office for the district in which the hospital or home is situated.

A death should be registered within five days but registration can be delayed for another nine days if the registrar is told that a medical certificate has been issued. If the death has been reported to the coroner you cannot register it until the coroner's investigations are finished.

It is a criminal offence not to register a death.

When you have registered the death, the registrar will give you a green certificate (for which there is no charge) to give to the funeral director. This allows either burial or cremation to go ahead. Occasionally a registrar may be able to issue a certificate for burial only (but never cremation) where no one has yet been able to register the death.

The registrar will also give you a form to send to the Department for Work and Pensions (DWP). This allows them to deal with the person's pension and other benefits.

Death certificate

The death certificate is a copy of the entry made by the registrar in the death register. This certificate is needed to deal with money or property left by the person who has died, including dealing with the will. You will need several copies of the certificate, for which there will be a charge.

Coroners

A coroner is a doctor or lawyer appointed by a local authority to investigate certain deaths. A coroner is completely independent of the authority and has a separate office and staff.

Anyone who is unhappy about the cause of a death can inform a coroner about it, but in most cases a death will be reported to a coroner by a doctor or the police.

A death cannot be registered until the coroner's investigations are complete and a certificate has been issued allowing registration to take place. This means that the funeral will usually also be delayed. Where a post-mortem has taken place the coroner must give permission for cremation.

Inquests

An inquest is a legal inquiry into a death. It is held in public (sometimes with a jury) by a coroner in cases where the death was violent or unnatural or took place in prison or police custody or where the cause of death is still uncertain after a post-mortem. The inquest should provide more information about how and why the death took place and whether anyone else was responsible. In some cases, a criminal prosecution may take place later.

Deaths abroad

If a death takes place abroad it must be registered according to the law of that country. The death should also be reported to the British Consulate, which may be able to arrange for the death to be registered in the UK as well.

Returning a body to the UK is expensive but the cost may be covered by any travel insurance taken out by the person. If the death was on a package holiday the tour operator should be able to help with arrangements.

When a body is returned to the UK, the Registrar of Births, Deaths and Marriages for the district where the funeral is to take place must be told and will need to issue a certificate before burial can take place. If cremation is to take place the Home Office also needs to give permission.

If the death was not due to natural causes the coroner for the district will also need to be told and an inquest may need to take place.

Donation of organs for transplant or the body for medical research

Donation of organs

The person who died may have wanted to donate organs for transplant. This will be easier if they were on the NHS Organ Donor Register (0845 60 60 400; www.uktransplant.org.uk), carried a donor card and had discussed the donation plans with their family. Relatives will still be asked to give their consent before donation. Most organ donations come from people who have died while on a ventilator in a hospital intensive care unit.

Donation of the body for medical education or research

Some people wish to leave their bodies for medical education or research and anyone wanting to do this will need to make arrangements before they die and tell their relatives. When the person dies, relatives should contact **HM Inspector of Anatomy** (020 7972 4551), who will advise on what should be done. If a body is accepted (and many bodies are not suitable) the medical school will arrange for eventual cremation or burial.

FUNERALS

A funeral can take place any time after death. Most funerals are arranged by the nearest relatives. However, if there are no relatives, anyone close to the person can arrange the funeral instead.

The person may have left instructions (in their will or somewhere else) about the type of funeral they wanted and whether they wanted to be buried or cremated. There is no legal obligation for relatives to follow these instructions. In some cases, relatives may want burial or cremation to take place abroad. The rules about this are very complex and the help of a specialist funeral director will be needed. Permission from a coroner is always needed before a body can be sent abroad.

If there are no relatives or friends to arrange a funeral, the local authority or health authority will arrange a simple funeral. The public authority that arranges the funeral will then try to recover the cost from any money left by the person who died.

Funeral arrangements

Funeral directors

Most funerals are arranged through a funeral director (who used to be known as an undertaker). It is important to find a funeral director who belongs to one of the professional associations, such as the National Association of Funeral Directors (NAFD) or the Society of Allied and Independent Funeral Directors (SAIF), since these associations have codes of practice and complaints procedures. Some local authorities also run their own funeral services by arrangement with a local firm of funeral directors. If a funeral director is not a member of a professional association and a complaint is not dealt with satisfactorily, you may need to take legal action against the funeral director.

Funeral costs

The person who arranges the funeral is responsible for paying the final bill and it is important to know where the money for the funeral will come from.

The person who died may have taken out a pre-paid funeral plan, paying for their funeral in advance. It is important to check their personal papers to see if they had a plan. If they did, this should cover the whole cost of the funeral.

If there is no funeral plan, the cost of the funeral will normally be met out of any money left by the person who has died and, where money has been left, the funeral bill should be paid before any other bills or debts. Even if the person's bank account has been frozen following the death it may be possible to have funds released from a building society or National Savings account on presentation of the death certificate. The person may also have had an insurance policy that will cover funeral costs. In other cases, relatives may need to borrow money until the person's money and property are sorted out. Some funeral directors will allow payment to be delayed until this has happened.

Some people do not leave enough money to pay for even a simple funeral. If this happens, the person arranging the funeral will have to pay for it, although other relatives or friends may be willing to contribute. There is no general death grant, but if you are in this situation and you receive a means-tested social security benefit (such as Income Support or Pension Credit) you may be able to get a payment from the Social Fund (known as a funeral payment) to cover the cost of a simple funeral. Even where a funeral payment is made, it may not cover the full cost of the funeral and you may still have to pay the difference.

The funeral director should always give a written estimate of the cost of the funeral, but the final bill may be higher. The bill will cover the costs of burial or cremation, the fees for the funeral service and the professional services of the funeral director. There will also be charges for extras, such as flowers, cars, service sheets and newspaper notices.

Other costs

Anyone who receives a means-tested benefit (such as Income Support) may be able to receive help from the DWP's Social Fund through a budgeting loan towards the cost of travelling to the funeral of a close relative.

If the person who is paying for the funeral is receiving a means-tested benefit it may be possible to receive help from the Social Fund through a funeral payment towards the cost of travelling to the funeral.

Burial or cremation

A burial can take place in a churchyard, a local authority cemetery or a private cemetery. Burials can also take place on private land, or in a woodland site. Anyone living within the parish has the right to be buried in the parish churchyard, if there is space, or in any adjoining burial ground. The person's religion is not relevant. Some churches may allow others to be buried there as well (for example, ex-parishioners or those with family graves). There is no right to be buried in any particular part of a churchyard or burial ground. Burials inside a church are not allowed in urban areas and are very rarely allowed elsewhere.

Most cemeteries are owned by local authorities or private companies and are non-denominational, although some have space dedicated to particular religious groups. In the case of a local authority cemetery, anyone living in the authority's area has the right to burial in the cemetery. Others may also be allowed burial, but for a higher burial fee.

In most cemeteries there are various categories of graves. Some graves do not give exclusive rights to burial while others give the right of exclusive burial for a set period of time. It is important to check the papers of the person who has died to find out if they have already purchased a grave space in a churchyard, cemetery or woodland burial ground. Although there is no law preventing burials on private land (including a garden), anyone wishing to do this should contact their local authority, who may issue a certificate confirming that the burial is lawful. The Natural Death Centre (020 7359 8391; www.naturaldeath.org.uk) can give advice on environmentally friendly burials, as well as on inexpensive funerals that do not need the services of a funeral director.

Most crematoria are run by local authorities. Five forms are needed before cremation can take place, including a certificate from the person's GP, countersigned by another GP, and an application form completed by a relative. These forms are available from the funeral director. The costs of cremation are usually considerably less than the costs of a burial.

Funeral service

The person arranging the service may choose any form of service. If you do not want any form of religious ceremony, the **British Humanist Association** (helpline 020 7079 3580; www.humanism.org.uk) can give advice on a non-religious (secular) service.

If you do not want a service of any kind, the funeral director can arrange for burial or cremation without any form of service.

If, for any reason, there is no body, a memorial service can be arranged instead of a funeral service.

Disposal of ashes

Ashes may be scattered or buried at the crematorium, either by crematorium staff or by relatives and friends. Ashes can also be buried in a churchyard or cemetery, often with a short service.

Ashes can generally be scattered anywhere, but if you wish to scatter ashes on private land you should get consent from the landowner.

Although UK law allows ashes to be taken abroad, many countries have strict rules on the importation of ashes and it is important to check before travelling.

Memorials

Churchyards and cemeteries have firm rules about the size and type of memorials that are allowed and it is important to check on these rules before ordering anything. Church of England churchyards usually have more rules than local authority cemeteries. Some woodland cemeteries permit wooden plaques, but most will only allow the planting of a tree. The design of the memorial may be subject to approval.

The funeral director will usually apply to the church or cemetery authority for permission to erect a memorial. The authority will normally charge for giving its permission. Names of local monumental masons can be obtained from the **National Association of Memorial Masons** (01788 542264).

The person erecting a memorial is responsible for maintaining it.

At a crematorium there will often be a Book of Remembrance and relatives may pay for an entry. It may also be possible to buy a memorial bush with a plaque.

If those attending a funeral have been asked to make donations to a charity, the funeral director will normally collect these and send them on to the charity. Relatives will be given a list of donations received.

Stillbirths

A stillbirth is a birth after the twenty-fourth week of pregnancy where the child is not born alive. In the case of a stillbirth, both the birth and death must be registered together at the register office within forty-two days.

A death certificate will not usually be issued. Many funeral directors make no charge for arranging the funeral of a stillborn baby and many cemeteries and crematoria also make no charge for burial or cremation.

Bereavement benefits

Bereavement benefits are payments made by the Department for Work and Pensions (DWP) to widows and widowers (see *If you are widowed*, p. 602).

Counselling and support

There are a number of organizations that can provide help and support if you have been bereaved.

For general counselling and support, contact **Cruse-Bereavement Care** (0870 167 1677; www.crusebereavementcare.org.uk).
For support following the death of a child, contact **Compassionate Friends** (0845 123 2304; www.tcf.org.uk).
For support following the sudden death of a baby (cot death), contact the **Foundation for the Study of Infant Deaths** (0870 787 0554; www.sids.org.uk).
For support following the death of a same-sex partner, contact the **Lesbian and Gay Bereavement Project** (020 7403 5969).
For support following a stillbirth, contact the **Stillbirth and Neonatal Death Society** (SANDS: 020 7436 5881; www.uk-sands.org).
For support following a miscarriage, contact the **Miscarriage Association** (01924 200 799; www.miscarriageassociation.org.uk).

WILLS

It is important for you to make a will, whether or not you consider you have many possessions or much money. It is important to make a will because:

- if you die without a will, there are certain rules that dictate how your money, property or possessions should be allocated (this may not be the way that you would have wished your money and possessions to be distributed);
- unmarried heterosexual couples cannot inherit from each other unless there is a will. This is also the case for all same-sex partners before 2005. Without a will, serious financial problems may arise for the remaining partner;

- married couples with children under 18 should consider what arrangements they want to make if either one or both of them die – you can appoint one or more individuals to act as guardian(s) for your children;
- unmarried couples with children under 18 should also consider what arrangements they want to make if either one or both of them die; it is even more important for unmarried couples to make provision for their children;
- it may be possible to reduce the amount of tax payable on the inheritance if advice is taken in advance and a will is made;
- if your circumstances have changed, it is important that you make a will to ensure that your money and possessions are distributed according to your wishes (for example, if you have separated and your ex-partner now lives with someone else you may want to change your will).

Solicitors and other help with writing a will

There is no need for a will to be drawn up or witnessed by a solicitor. If you wish to make a will yourself, you can do so. However, you should only consider doing this if the will is going to be straightforward.

It is generally advisable to use a solicitor or to have a solicitor check a will you have drawn up to make sure it will have the effect you want. This is because it is easy to make mistakes and, if there are errors in the will, this can cause problems after your death. Sorting out misunderstandings and disputes may result in considerable legal costs, which will reduce the amount of money in the estate.

Some common mistakes in making a will are:

- not being aware of the formal requirements needed to make a will legally valid;
- failing to take account of all the money and property available;
- failing to take account of the possibility that a beneficiary may die before the person making the will;
- changing the will (if alterations are not signed and witnessed, they are invalid);
- being unaware of the effect of marriage and/or divorce on a will;
- being unaware of the rules that exist to enable dependants to claim from the estate if they believe they are not adequately provided for. These rules mean that the provisions in the will could be overturned.

There are some circumstances when it is particularly advisable to use a solicitor. These are where:

- you share a property with someone who is not your husband or wife;
- you wish to make provision for a dependant who is unable to care for themselves;
- there are several family members who may make a claim on the will – for example, a second wife or children from a first marriage;
- your permanent home is not in the United Kingdom;
- you are not a British citizen;
- you are resident in the UK but there is overseas property involved;
- there is a business involved.

If you are a member of a trade union, you may find that the union offers a free will-writing service. A union will often use its own solicitors to undertake this work.

There are books that provide guidance on how to draw up a will. These can help you decide if you should draw up your own will and also help you decide if any of the pre-printed will forms available from stationers and charities are suitable. It is also possible to find help on the internet.

Will-writing services are available. However, will-writing firms are not regulated by the Law Society so there are few safeguards if things go wrong.

Costs

The charges for drawing up a will vary between solicitors and also depend on the complexity of the will. Before making a decision on who to use, it is always advisable to check with a few local solicitors to find out how much they charge. You may have access to legal advice through an addition to an insurance policy which might cover the costs of a solicitor preparing or checking a will. If you are a member of a trade union you may find that the union offers a free wills service to members.

It is also worth giving some thought to what you want to say in the will before seeing a solicitor. This should help reduce the costs involved.

The legal help scheme only covers the making of a will if you are eligible on financial grounds and are:

- 70 or over; *and/or*
- disabled; *and/or*
- a parent of a disabled person and wish to provide for that person in the will; *and/or*
- a single parent who wishes to appoint a guardian in your will.

What to put in your will

To save time and reduce costs when going to a solicitor, you should give some thought to the major points you want included in your will. You should consider such things as:

- how much money and what property and possessions you have – for example, property, savings, occupational and personal pensions, insurance policies, bank and building society accounts, shares;
- who you want to benefit from your will. You should make a list of all the people to whom you wish to leave money or possessions. These people are known as beneficiaries. You also need to consider whether you wish to leave any money to charity.
- who should look after any children under 18;
- who is going to sort out the estate and carry out your wishes as set out in the will. These people are known as the executors.

Executors

Executors are the people who will be responsible for carrying out your wishes and for sorting out the estate. They will have to collect together all the assets of the estate, deal with all the paperwork and pay all the debts, taxes, funeral and administration costs out of money in the estate. They will need to pay out the gifts and transfer any property to beneficiaries.

It is not necessary to appoint more than one executor, although it is advisable to do so – for example, in case one of them dies. It is common to appoint two, but up to four executors can take on responsibility for administering the will after a death. The people most commonly appointed as executors are:

- relatives or friends;
- solicitors or accountants;
- banks;
- the Public Trustee if there is no one willing and able to act.

It is important to choose executors with considerable care since their job involves a great deal of work and responsibility. You should always approach anyone you are thinking of appointing as an executor to see if they will agree to take on the responsibility. If someone is appointed who is not willing to be an executor, they have a right to refuse.

If an executor dies, any other surviving executor(s) can deal with the estate. If there are no surviving executors, legal advice should be sought.

Requirements for a valid will

In order for a will to be valid, it must be:

- made by a person who is 18 years old or over; *and*
- made voluntarily and without pressure from any other person; *and*
- made by a person who is of sound mind – this means the person must be fully aware of the nature of the document being written or signed and aware of the property and of the identity of the people who may inherit; *and*
- in writing; *and*
- signed by the person making the will in the presence of two witnesses; *and*
- signed by the two witnesses, in the presence of the person making the will, after it has been signed by that person. A witness or the married partner of a witness cannot benefit from a will. If a witness is a beneficiary (or the married partner of a beneficiary), the will is still valid but the beneficiary will not be able to inherit under the will.

Although it will be legally valid even if it is not dated, it is advisable to ensure that the will also includes the date on which it is signed.

As soon as the will is signed and witnessed, it is complete.

Once a will has been made, it should be kept in a safe place and other documents should not be attached to it. There are a number of places where you can keep a will:

- at home;
- with a solicitor;
- at a bank;
- at the Principal Registry of the Family Division of the High Court, a District Registry or Probate Sub-Registry for safe keeping. If you wish to deposit a will in this way you should visit the District Registry or Probate Sub-Registry or contact the Probate Department at the Principal Registry of the Family Division (020 7947 6000).

Searching for copies of a will

Postal application

When writing to request a copy of a will by post, the forename(s), surname, date of death and last known address of the person who has died must be provided to the **York Probate Sub-Registry** (01904 666777). They will pass requests to the probate registry keeping the will and grant of probate, which will in turn send the required copies direct to the individual. There is a fee for this service.

Personal application

You can make a personal search free of charge by going to the Principal Registry of the Family Division. If you want to inspect or take a copy of the will, there is a fee.

Local application

If you know which probate registry dealt with the will, it is possible to inspect the documents at that particular District (Controlling) Probate Registry. Copies can be obtained from the York Probate Sub-Registry or the Principal Registry of the Family Division. There is a fee.

How to change a will

When a will has been made, it is important to keep it up to date to take account of changes in circumstances. It is advisable for you to reconsider the contents of a will regularly to make sure that it still reflects your wishes. The most common changes of circumstances which affect a will are:

- getting married or remarried;
- getting divorced or separated;
- the birth or adoption of children, if you wish to add these as beneficiaries in a will.

You may want to change your will because there has been a change of circumstances. You must not do this by amending the original will after it has been signed and witnessed. Any obvious alterations on the face of the will are assumed to have been made at a later date and so do not form part of the original legally valid will.

The only ways you can change a will are by making:

- a codicil to the will; *or*
- a new will.

Codicils

A codicil is a supplement to a will that makes some alterations but leaves the rest of it intact. This might be done, for example, to increase a cash legacy, change an executor or guardian named in a will, or to add beneficiaries. A codicil must be signed by the person who made the will and be witnessed in the same way. However, the witnesses do not have to be the same as for the original will.

There is no limit on how many codicils can be added to a will, but they are only suitable for very straightforward changes. If a complicated change is involved, it is usually advisable to make a new will.

Making a new will

If you wish to make major changes to a will, it is advisable to make a new one. The new will should begin with a clause stating that it revokes all previous wills and codicils. The old will should be destroyed. Revoking a will means that the will is no longer legally valid.

Destroying a will

If you want to destroy a will, you must burn it, tear it up or otherwise destroy it with the clear intention that it is revoked. There is a risk that if a copy subsequently reappears (or bits of the will are reassembled) it might be thought that the destruction was accidental. You must destroy the will yourself or it must be destroyed in your presence. A simple instruction alone to an executor to destroy a will has no effect. If the will is destroyed accidentally, it is not revoked and can still be declared valid.

Although a will can be revoked by destruction, it is always advisable that a new will should contain a clause revoking all previous wills and codicils. Revoking a will means that the will is no longer legally valid.

Challenging a will

A person may want to challenge a will because:

- they believe that the will is invalid; or
- they believe that they have not been adequately provided for in the will.

There are strict time limits for challenging a will. If you want to challenge a will you should seek legal advice as soon as possible.

If a person who makes a will commits suicide, the will is still valid.

A-Z OF YOUNG PEOPLE'S RIGHTS

In this information, 'child' means someone aged under 14 and 'young person' means someone aged 14 or over but under 18. 'Parent' means someone with parental responsibility.

Abortion

Whatever age you are, you are entitled to a confidential consultation with a doctor, provided you make it clear that you do not want a parent to be told. However, a doctor who is unwilling to accept a request for confidentiality can refuse to discuss the matter. If you are a young woman under 16 who wants to discuss abortion with your doctor, check at the start of an interview whether the doctor is prepared to give you a confidential consultation.

If your doctor is unwilling to give a confidential consultation, or if you do not want to go to your family doctor for another reason, you should seek help from another agency, such as the Brook Advisory Clinic or a local family planning centre.

If you are under 16 and need treatment, a doctor will normally require parental consent. However, some doctors will perform an abortion without parental consent if they consider it is necessary for your welfare. But they will usually prefer you to discuss the matter with a parent and will try to persuade you to do so.

Adoption

If you are under the age of 18 you can be adopted. As a child, you will have little say over who adopts you, but you should be consulted by the adoption agency or social services department involved in the adoption.

If you are under 18, you have no legal right to know the identity of your birth parents. Once you reach 18, you have a right to apply to see your birth record and to use the **Adoption Contact Register**. The Register helps adopted people get contact details of birth relatives who have also registered.

To apply to the Adoption Contact Register, write to: Adoption Section, Room D09, The General Register Office, Trafalgar Road, Southport PR8 2HH.

Alcohol

It is an offence to give alcohol to a child under 5 (unless it is given by a doctor on health grounds). If you are 5 or over and under 16 there is no legal restriction on your drinking alcohol at home or on other private premises.

If you are under 14, you cannot normally go into a pub or other licensed premises where alcohol is sold and consumed during opening hours unless you are the landlord's child or live on the premises. However, a publican can apply for a children's certificate that will allow children under 14 to be taken into a pub by an adult. Children would normally have to leave by 9 p.m.

If you are aged 14 or 15 you can go into a pub but cannot buy or drink alcohol there. If you are aged 16 or 17 you can buy or drink wine, beer, cider or perry (but not spirits) with a meal in a hotel or restaurant or part of a pub set apart for eating meals.

It is normally an offence for a person under 18 to buy alcohol and drink alcohol in a pub – but see paragraph above. It is also an offence for a person to buy alcohol on behalf of a person under 18 that is to be drunk in the street. Anyone working in a pub will be committing an offence if they sell or allow a person under 18 to drink alcohol in a pub. However, they will have a defence if they can prove that they had no reason to suspect that the person was under 18.

If police suspect a young person of possessing alcohol (or something they believe to be alcohol) in a 'relevant place', they can confiscate it. A 'relevant place' is any public place (except licensed premises) or a place to which someone has gained access unlawfully. The police can also confiscate alcohol or what they think may be alcohol from a person of any age if they suspect some of it has been, or is intended to be, drunk by someone under 18 in a 'relevant place'. The police can arrest anyone who tries to prevent them confiscating what they believe to be alcohol.

Banking, credit and borrowing money

There is no legal age limit at which you can open a bank account but a bank manager can decide whether to allow a child or young person to open an account. There are restrictions on opening certain kinds of account – for example, as a young person you are not normally legally responsible for your debts so you are unlikely to be granted an overdraft.

If you are under 18 it is a criminal offence for anyone to send you material inviting you to borrow money or obtain goods or services on credit or hire purchase. However, if you are over 14 but under 18, you can enter into a credit or hire purchase agreement if an adult acts as your guarantor.

You can borrow money at any age, but access to loans may be limited because a contract between a lender and a young person will not usually be enforceable.

If you apply for a credit card when you are under 18 you will have your application turned down.

Betting and gambling

It is an offence for anybody to have a betting transaction with a person they know, or ought to know, is under 18.

Betting shops, gaming clubs and bingo

If you are under 18 you may not enter a public betting shop or gaming club. You can go into a licensed bingo club where bingo is played as long as you do not take part in the game. You can take part in a bingo game played in a social club or church club where the game has not been organized for private profit. You can also play bingo in a private club in which bingo is one of the club's activities, although the club may set its own age limit.

Fruit machines

If you are under 16 you can go into arcades but must not play on fruit machines giving a £10 or more cash payout.

If you are between 14 and 18 you can go into a pub, but you are not allowed to play on fruit machines with a cash payout of £10 or more. A sign stating that the machines are restricted to over-18s must be displayed.

There is no lower age limit for playing on fruit machines with a maximum cash or token prize of up to £8.

Lottery tickets and scratch cards

If you are under 16 you may not buy tickets (or scratch cards) in a registered public lottery. You may buy tickets in a private lottery.

Blood and organ donation

You are not allowed to donate blood unless you are considered to have sufficient understanding of what is involved.

If you are under 18 you can donate your body and organs on death but if you are under 16 you need to get your parents' consent to carry a donor card. Parental consent is also required before the organs can be used.

Body piercing

There are no legal restrictions on the age at which you can have your ears or other body parts pierced. However, some establishments may operate their own informal guidelines on obtaining parental consent.

Butane lighter fuels

It is illegal to sell a lighter fuel refill canister containing butane to children and young people if the seller knows that the contents are going to be abused.

Changing your name

You cannot change your name until you are 16 years old. Between 16 and 18 you can complete a change of name deed with parental consent.

Cigarettes

You can smoke cigarettes in private at any age. However, it is an offence punishable by a fine to sell tobacco, cigarettes or cigarette papers to anyone under 16. There are no legal restrictions on smoking for anyone aged 16 or above.

Contraception

There are no age restrictions on giving contraceptive advice and supplies. A doctor is allowed to prescribe contraception if you are under 16 without the consent or knowledge of a parent. However, they can inform your parent if they are concerned about your maturity.

Crime, police and the courts

If you are over the age of 10 you can be fingerprinted, photographed and searched while you are in police custody. If you are 16 or over and have been involved in anti-social behaviour you may be issued with a penalty notice. This is a notice for an on-the-spot fine.

Community support officers can also take action against young people if they are behaving in an anti-social way.

The procedures governing the treatment of children and young people by the police are set out in the codes of practice made as a result of the Police and Criminal Evidence Act (the PACE codes). If these procedures are not followed, the case may be dismissed. Disciplinary proceedings can be brought against police officers who break these codes of practice.

Criminal proceedings

A child under 10 is not considered to be capable of deciding whether an action is right or wrong. They cannot be taken to court and charged with a criminal offence. If you are aged 10 but under 14 years old you are considered to be responsible for a criminal offence and are treated in the same way as any young person under 18. This means that you can face criminal proceedings, although your case will normally be dealt with in a youth court.

Witnesses

If you are under 18 you will be expected to give evidence as a witness under oath in court unless the judge decides that you are incapable of giving reasonable testimony.

In child abuse cases, your evidence can be video-recorded as long as you are available for cross-examination. In sexual abuse cases the upper age limit for giving evidence by video link is 18 and in other cases of abuse the limit is 15.

Civil proceedings

If you are under 18, you cannot normally start court proceedings in your own name and a litigation friend – usually your parent – must act on your behalf.

As a child or young person you cannot normally be sued for breach of contract because, in most circumstances, you cannot enter into a contract that is enforceable in a court.

Anti-social behaviour

Anti-social behaviour is behaviour likely to cause alarm, distress, or harassment. Examples of anti-social behaviour include vandalism, graffiti, throwing fireworks in the street, throwing stones at trains, and causing a nuisance to others.

Negligence

As a child or young person you can be sued for negligence through your parent. Negligence is defined as failure to act with reasonable care so as not to cause damage to other people or property. An injured party has the right to sue for compensation. An example of negligence is riding a bicycle in a manner that results in personal injury or damage to property.

Legal assistance and advice

If you are aged 16 or over you can apply for assistance under the legal help scheme. You can apply in your own right in some circumstances and through a parent or guardian in others.

As a child or young person you can apply for other publicly funded legal services, generally through a parent or guardian.

A child or young person who has been arrested for a criminal offence has the same rights to legal advice (including criminal legal aid) as an adult.

Who can help?

The **Law Centres Federation** (020 7387 8570; www.lawcentres.org.uk) can provide addresses of local law centres.

Debt

As a child or young person you cannot normally be taken to court for debt. This is because you cannot usually make a legally enforceable contract. The exception is when debts are incurred for necessities – for example, food, clothing and shelter.

As a parent you are not usually under any obligation to pay the debts of your child. However, if you acted as a guarantor for a contract they entered into, you will be responsible for any debts under the agreement, even where the contract is not legally enforceable against the young person.

Discrimination

Race discrimination

It is illegal to discriminate against anyone, including a child or young person, on the grounds of race, colour, nationality or ethnic or national origins. If you have suffered race discrimination you may be able to take action against the organization or individual responsible.

If you have suffered racial harassment, which includes verbal abuse or threats, graffiti or physical attacks, you may be able to take action.

Sex discrimination

It is illegal to discriminate against anyone, including a child or young person, on the grounds of sex. If you have suffered sex discrimination you may be able to take action against the organization or individual responsible.

Disability discrimination

It is illegal to discriminate against anyone, including a child or young person, on grounds of disability. If you have suffered disability discrimination you may be able to take action against the organization or individual responsible.

Discrimination because of sexuality

It is against the law for an employer to discriminate against you at work because of your sexuality. However, there is no law covering discrimination because of sexuality in other situations. The **Lesbian and Gay Switchboard** (020 7837 7324: 24-hour helpline) can put people in touch with organizations that help young lesbian and gay people come out to their parents.

Religious or political discrimination

It is against the law for an employer to discriminate against you at work because of your religion or belief. However, there is no law covering discrimination on these grounds in other situations.

Driving

There are rules about the age at which you can drive a particular type of vehicle. For example, you can ride an electrically assisted pedal cycle from the age of 14, a moped or invalid carriage from the age of 16 and drive a motorbike, car or certain classes of van and lorry from the age of 17.

You are not allowed to supervise a learner driver until you are 21 and have had a licence yourself for three years.

If you drive a vehicle when you are 17 you must have third-party liability insurance, even though you cannot usually enter into a contract until you are 18.

Drugs

If you are in possession of illegal drugs you may face prosecution, depending on your age.

Films and videos

Film classification

There are restrictions on the films you can see in a cinema. The British Board of Film Classification (BBFC) issues certificates for all films as follows:

- U (universal) – suitable for all those aged four years or over;
- PG – unaccompanied children are admitted but parental guidance needed as some scenes are unsuitable for young children;
- 12A – no one under the age of 12 will be admitted, unless accompanied by an adult;
- 15 – no one under the age of 15 will be admitted;
- 18 – no one under the age of 18 will be admitted.

As well as these restrictions, a cinema manager has discretion over admission of any member of the public. In general, children under 5 outside London and under 7 in London are not allowed in a cinema unless accompanied by an adult.

Video classification

Most pre-recorded English language videos have to be classified and labelled according to their suitability for viewing by different age groups. The classification categories are:

- Uc (universal) – particularly suitable for pre-school children;
- U (universal) – suitable for all those aged four years or over;
- PG (parental guidance) – for general viewing but some scenes may be unsuitable for young children;

- 12 – only suitable for people aged 12 years or over; not to be supplied to anyone below that age;
- 15 – only suitable for people aged 15 years or over; not to be supplied to anyone below that age;
- 18 – only suitable for people aged 18 years or over; not to be supplied to anyone below that age;
- Restricted 18 – only to be supplied in licensed sex shops to people aged 18 or over.

It is an offence to supply a classified video to someone who is below the age specified in the classification.

It is an offence to supply an unclassified video unless it is exempt from classification.

PC and video games

Unless they depict activities considered unsuitable for viewing by children and young people, most PC and video games are exempt from the laws on classification because they do not realistically depict humans or animals. However, many video game distributors prefer to submit their games to the BBFC in borderline cases. The industry itself has introduced a self-regulatory system of classification for exempt videos which is run by the European Leisure Software Publishers' Association.

Flying

You are allowed to fly a glider from the age of 16. You can hold a private air pilot's licence from the age of 17 and a commercial air pilot's licence from the age of 18.

Glue sniffing

It is illegal to sell solvents to anyone under 18, but glue sniffing is not against the law. However, as a child or young person you can be arrested for glue sniffing in a public place and charged with breach of the peace.

Income tax

You are taxed independently on your income, in the same way as an adult. However, in general, if you are under 16 your parent enters details of your income on their own tax return.

If you are unmarried and under 18 and your parent gives you money that produces investment income – for example, money in a National Savings account – any resulting income over £5 will normally count as your parent's income and should be entered on their tax return.

If you are under 16 and want to make a claim to the Inland Revenue for repayment of overpaid tax, your parent, guardian or trustee must make the claim.

If you are under 16 and have a bank or building society account that pays interest, your parent can register to stop tax being automatically deducted from the interest, if you are a non-taxpayer.

Leaving home voluntarily

In most circumstances you can leave home without the consent of your parents or anyone with parental responsibility when you are 16. A parent or person with parental responsibility could take wardship proceedings in court, but it is unlikely that any court would order you to return home if you did not want to.

Local authority care

You can only be taken into care if you are under 18 and the local authority has obtained a court order. You have a right to know why you are in care, under what law, and how long you are likely to remain there.

You can be accommodated by a local authority without a court order if a parent requests it or gives permission. However, the local authority must take your wishes into account.

Marriage

If you are under 16 and marry, it will not be recognized by law unless your marriage took place in a country with a lower marriage age limit than 16.

If you are 16 or 17 and want to get married in a registry office, you need the written permission of a parent. If they refuse permission, you can apply to a magistrates' court, county court or the High Court for permission to marry. Anyone aged 18 or over can be married without parental permission.

Medical treatment

Registering with a GP

If you are under 16 you have no right to choose your own GP and must be registered by a parent. If you are aged 16 and over you can choose your own GP.

Confidentiality

If you are under 16 you are entitled to a confidential consultation with a doctor, provided you make it clear that you do not want your parent to be told. However, your doctor can refuse to discuss the matter if unwilling to accept your request for confidentiality. If you are aged 16 and above you are entitled to confidential advice and treatment.

Consent to medical treatment

If you are under 16 you can give your own consent to medical treatment provided you fully understand what is involved. If a doctor decides that you do not fully understand what is involved in giving consent, a person with parental responsibility for you can give consent on your behalf.

If you are under 18 and refuse treatment, a person with parental responsibility or medical staff may seek a court order to override you.

NHS charges

If you are under 16 or between 16 and 18 and in full-time education you are entitled to free prescriptions, dental treatment (including check-ups), eye tests, vouchers for glasses and free wigs and fabric supports. In Wales, any young person under 25 is entitled to free prescriptions.

If you are aged 16 and 17 and are not in full-time education you are entitled to free dental treatment (including check-ups). You may also qualify for help with other NHS treatment if you are on a low income.

If you are aged 16 or 17 and maintained financially by the local authority (either wholly or partly), you are entitled to free prescriptions, eye tests, vouchers for glasses, wigs and fabric supports.

Sexually transmitted diseases

If you think you have a sexually transmitted disease (STD) and want advice or treatment go to a family doctor, family planning clinic, pregnancy advisory service or STD clinic. If you are under 16 it is for the doctor to decide whether or not to act without consulting a parent. If you are concerned about confidentiality, you should check whether or not the doctor is prepared to treat you in confidence.

HIV/AIDS

If you want advice about HIV/AIDS you will need to seek specialist advice, for example, from the Terrence Higgins Trust (0845 1221 200; www.tht.org.uk).

Parents aged under 16

Mothers aged under 16

If you are under 16 and have a baby you have the same legal rights and responsibilities towards the child as any mother.

Benefits

If you live with your parents and they are claiming Income Support or income-based Jobseeker's Allowance, both you and your child can be included in the claim. If your parents are receiving either of these benefits, they can also claim a Social Fund maternity grant for you and your child. If they are claiming Housing Benefit, they can include you and your child in their claim. If your parents are getting Pension Credit, you cannot be included in their claim but they could claim Child Tax Credit for you and your child.

As a young mother, you can claim Child Benefit once the baby is born. If you are living at home and your parents are receiving Income Support or income-based Jobseeker's Allowance, any Child Benefit you receive will be treated as your parents' income and the benefit they receive will be reduced. If you are living with your parents and they are receiving Income Support, income-based Jobseeker's Allowance or Pension Credit (guarantee credit only), they will be able to claim free milk and vitamins on your behalf.

Education

Local education authorities have a duty to ensure that all children under 16 receive an education. If you become a mother, this duty remains.

Housing

As a young mother you will not normally be able to obtain privately rented or council accommodation because you are too young to be granted a tenancy. However, you can contact the local authority social services department and ask it to accommodate you, provided your parents agree.

Maintenance

As a young mother you can apply to the Child Support Agency for a maintenance assessment to be carried out in respect of your child.

Fathers aged under 16

As a father aged under 16 you may want to have a formal relationship with your child by applying for a parental responsibility agreement, residence order or contact order.

Maintenance

If you are aged under 16 and father a child, the Child Support Agency (CSA) can expect to pay maintenance for the child. Once the CSA is satisfied that you are the father, you will be expected to make maintenance payments when you begin earning or receiving a benefit.

Passports

Everyone who is travelling outside the UK must have their own passport. This includes babies and children.

You must have the consent of a parent to have a passport if you are under 18, unless you are married or a member of the armed forces. A parent can object to a passport being issued to a child or young person under 16.

Personal records

At any age, you have the right to see information kept about you, unless the person looking after the information considers you incapable of understanding the nature of the request you are making. If you are refused access to your records you can complain to the Information Commissioner.

As a parent you do not usually have the right to see information about your child kept on a computer record. This will only be allowed if the person looking after the information knows that the child has authorized the request, or – if the request is being made on behalf of a child or young person – is considered incapable of understanding the nature of the request.

Pets

There is no lower age limit for owning a pet. However if you are under 12 you cannot buy one without a parent being present.

Proof of age

There are many schemes that provide cards to help prove your age. Many local authorities and local colleges run card schemes. The Portman Group is an organization that works to prevent alcohol abuse by young people. The group can provide a Proof of Age card if you are over 18 and do not look your age. Applicants must pay a fee, complete a form and provide a photograph. A professionally qualified person must countersign both the form and the photograph. The form is available from some retailers or directly from the Portman Group (020 7907 3700; www.portmangroup.org.uk).

Punishment

Parents

Parents have a legal right to smack their child. However, if the violence they use is severe enough to leave a mark, for example a scratch or a bruise, they can be prosecuted for assault, or their child can be taken into local authority care.

School

No teacher in a school is allowed to inflict corporal punishment on a student of any age. A teacher is allowed to take restraining measures to prevent a child or young person committing an offence, causing or suffering personal injury or causing danger to property.

In care and other institutions

Corporal punishment must not be inflicted on any child or young person living in a children's home, secure unit, foster home provided by the local authority or voluntary organization, residential care home or young offender institution. If a child or young person lives in a private foster home, nursing or mental nursing home, or a youth treatment centre, mild smacking is allowed as long as it does not leave a mark.

Registered childminders

A registered childminder is not allowed to smack a child in their care.

Religion

A parent has the right to choose which religion their child will follow at home and at school or to choose that they shall follow no religion at all. However, a child or young person may choose their own religion if they have sufficient understanding. If a parent considers the child's chosen religion to be harmful, a court can be asked to intervene.

There is a general requirement on schools to provide religious education but it is possible for an individual child to be withdrawn from religious education.

Seat belts

Children travelling in the rear or front seats of a vehicle must normally wear a seat belt or, in the case of children below the age of 11, a child restraint. For children under the age of 14, the driver of the vehicle is responsible for making sure that they wear a seat belt or restraint where this is required by law.

Everyone over the age of 14 is responsible for wearing a seat belt when this is required by law. The driver or owner of the vehicle is not responsible for passengers over this age.

Sex and sexuality

It is legal for two people of the opposite sex or the same sex to have a sexual relationship if both of them are 16 or over and both of them consent to the sexual activity.

It is a criminal offence for someone of either sex to take part in sexual activity with someone under the age of 16, unless it is reasonable to believe that that person is 16 or older. Sexual activity includes sexual intercourse and intentional sexual touching. The penalties for an offence of this type are more severe if it is committed by someone who is 18 or over rather than someone who is under 18.

Where both people are under 16, each will be committing an offence if they have a sexual relationship. However, it is unlikely that there will be any prosecution if the sexual activity was mutual and non-exploitative. If someone under the age of 16 is sexually involved with someone else aged 16 or over, the younger person will not be committing an offence. However, the person over 16 could be charged.

Tattooing

It is an offence to tattoo anyone under 18 unless a qualified medical practitioner does it for medical reasons. Someone who tattoos anyone under 18 can be prosecuted unless they show they had good cause to believe the person was over 18.

Telephones

If you are under 18, you cannot open a telephone account because you cannot normally enter into a contract. You can buy a pay-as-you-go mobile phone as this does not require a contract.

Wills

If you are under 18, you cannot make a valid will unless you are in the armed forces or a seafarer. No one under the age of 18 can act as a trustee, executor or administrator of a will, but you can appoint a guardian to act on your behalf.

Who can help?

The **Children's Commissioner for Wales** (01792 765600; www.childcom.org.uk) can give children and young people living in Wales advice about their rights and welfare. The Commissioner can also help you make a complaint about your treatment if you are using the usual complaints procedure of an institution such as a school, care home or social services department. If your complaint is unsuccessful, the Commissioner may be able to carry out a separate investigation.

2

Health

CONTENTS

INTRODUCTION

It is hard to imagine what life must have been like, especially for
poor families, prior to the National Health Service (NHS). Before
then, some workers on low pay were entitled to see a doctor for
free, but this benefit often did not stretch to their wives or
children. Hospitals charged patients and, although sometimes
poorer families would be reimbursed, it still meant paying in the
first place, which many people simply could not do. People with
mental health problems were locked away, out of sight and out of
mind. Many older people who could no longer care for
themselves ended up in the workhouse, doing unpaid work in
return for food and a roof over their heads.

The new NHS – free to all at the point of delivery – was born on 5 July 1948, bringing access to healthcare services to the whole population, regardless of their ability to pay. It would be difficult to exaggerate the impact that the NHS has had on the health of the nation, cradle to grave – from establishing a vaccination programme for babies and children that protects the whole community to delivering appropriate care for older people approaching the last part of their lives. Huge medical and technological advances in recent years, like IVF treatments, gene science and successes in heart and liver transplant surgeries, have brought new challenges and an expansion in the demand for and provision of health services. The NHS is now the largest organization in Europe and is recognized as one of the best health services in the world by the World Health Organization.

This chapter covers the services provided by the NHS, how the system works and who to turn to if things go wrong.

JARGON BUSTER

- **GP** General Practitioner or doctor
- **NHS** National Health Service
- **PCT** Primary Care Trust. There are no PCTs in Wales – Local Health Boards in Wales have similar functions
- **A & E** Accident and Emergency
- **PALS** Patient Advisory Liaison Service
- **ICAS** Independent Complaints Advocacy Service

GENERAL PRACTITIONERS (GPs)

NHS numbers and medical cards

NHS numbers help staff across the NHS get up-to-date information on patients' health. However, if you do not have an NHS number, you can still get NHS treatment.

A hospital should give your baby an NHS number shortly after birth. If the baby was not born in hospital, a number will be given once the hospital has been told about the birth. If your baby was born abroad and does not have an NHS number, you can get one by registering with a GP.

To get a medical card for your baby, you may need to give their NHS number to a chosen GP. However, procedures for getting medical cards vary from area to area. If in doubt, you should ask your GP. If you do not have a medical card, or have lost it, you should contact your local PCT (Primary Care Trust), giving your name, address and date of birth, and the name and address of your previous GP. If possible, you should also give your NHS number.

You can register with a GP without a medical card by completing a form supplied by the GP. The PCT will then send you a new medical card.

Registering with a GP

If you are ordinarily resident in the UK, even if you are from abroad, you have the right to be registered with a General Practitioner, or GP for short. You can choose which GP you want to register with. However, the GP does not have to accept you and, if the GP decides not to do so, they do not have to give you a reason. You can obtain a list of local GPs from the PCT or the local community health council in Wales. You can also find details of GPs from NHS Direct and NHS Direct online (0845 4647; www.nhsdirect.nhs.uk in England or www.nhsdirect.wales.nhs.uk in Wales).

The list will describe the services offered by the GP and may also contain information on whether any alternative therapies are available within the practice. It may also give details of surgery hours, whether there is an appointment system and whether there are any special clinics run at the surgery.

You should take your medical card to the GP's surgery in order to register with the GP of your choice. You will need to fill in part A of the card and hand it to the GP or practice staff. A GP may wish to see you before agreeing to register you. The GP will forward the medical card to the PCT (or local health authority in Wales), which will send you a new medical card.

Children under 16 should be registered by their parent(s), but they do not have to register with the same GP as the rest of their family.

If you are staying somewhere in the UK for less than three months, you can ask to be registered with a GP on a temporary basis. You can also register temporarily if you move around the country and have no permanent address.

Unless the GP's register is full, or you live too far away for home visits, it is unlikely that the GP will refuse to register you. However, if you are refused the GP does not have to give a reason.

If you have been unable to register with a GP, you should contact the local PCT. You should send your medical card, with a letter giving the names of any GPs who have refused to register you, and of any GPs with whom you would prefer not to be registered.

The PCT will try to find a GP who is prepared to accept you. This will not necessarily be a GP of your choice. Once you have been allocated a GP, the GP must accept you and treat you, but can remove you from their list at any time without giving a reason. The PCT will then have to find you another doctor. The PCT cannot help you find another GP if you are already registered with one.

Treatment from a GP

You are entitled to treatment from a GP at the surgery where you are registered. You have no automatic right, however, to see your own GP.

A GP must provide any treatment which is immediately necessary in an emergency, even if you are not registered with them.

Outside surgery hours

All GPs must make sure that a service is provided for their patients when they are off duty. This service could be provided by, for example, other partners in a group practice, a rota between GPs, a commercial deputizing service (a locum), or a telephone number that patients can use out of hours.

Primary Care Trusts are responsible for ensuring that the standard of care provided by commercial deputizing services is satisfactory. If you are unhappy about the standards of treatment you have received, you should contact the PCT responsible for commissioning the deputizing service.

Home visits

You cannot insist that a GP visits you at home. A GP will only visit you at home if they think that your medical condition requires it. A GP can also decide how urgently a visit is needed.

If you were to become seriously ill after a GP had refused a home visit, the GP could be found to be in breach of their contract with the NHS, or could be found to have been negligent. You might therefore wish to make a complaint.

You can be visited at home by a community nurse if you are referred by your GP or by a hospital consultant. If you are not an urgent patient, you can make an appointment and should be visited on the day arranged.

You should also be visited at home by a health visitor if you have recently had a baby or if you are newly registered with a GP and have a child under five years.

Medication

If a GP decides you need medication, they will usually give you a prescription. In some cases – for example, if the surgery is in an isolated area – the GP may provide the medication themselves.

A GP must supply any drugs needed for immediate treatment in an emergency. There is no prescription charge for these.

Alternative therapies

Some GPs are qualified in alternative therapies and may offer these as part of their NHS treatment. In some areas GPs may be able to refer a client to alternative practitioners, but this option will not always be available.

Second opinions

You can ask your GP to arrange a second opinion from either a specialist or another GP. However, the GP does not have to do this if they do not think it necessary. You have no right to a second opinion.

You do have the right to see a GP competent to deal with your particular case. If a GP refers you for a second opinion, you cannot insist on seeing a particular practitioner. However, you should not be referred to someone you do not wish to see.

If the GP refuses to arrange a second opinion, you may wish to change your GP.

If a GP is unsure about a diagnosis, they could be found negligent if they failed to refer you to a specialist and you suffered as a result. If you have not been referred for a second opinion and have suffered as a consequence, you may wish to complain.

GP charges

There is no charge for basic GP treatment for NHS patients who live in the UK. There are charges for visitors from overseas, except in the case of an emergency. There may also be charges for certain services – for example, check-ups for employees and vaccinations for travelling abroad.

Changing your GP

You can change your GP at any time you wish without having to give a reason. If you tell the PCT that you want to change your GP, the PCT must give you details of how to do so and provide you with a list of alternative GPs.

You do not need the consent of your GP to change GPs. When you have found another GP willing to accept you, you should take your medical card to the new GP to be registered. You can then make an appointment to see the new GP immediately.

If you wish to change your GP, but cannot find a new one who will accept you, you should contact the Primary Care Trust, who should find you an alternative.

If your GP removes you from their register

A GP can remove you from their register without giving a reason, although it is considered good practice for reasons to be given. The GP will inform the health authority, which then notifies you. The removal from the register takes effect from the eighth day after the PCT receives the GP's notice, or from the date that you are included on another register if this is sooner. You are entitled to emergency treatment, or the continuation of treatment that is occurring more than once a week, until you are accepted by another GP. If you have been violent, or have threatened to be violent, towards your GP or practice staff, and the police have been informed, you can be removed immediately from the GP's list. You will only be accepted for emergency treatment by the GP who has removed you if the GP is satisfied that it is clinically necessary.

If you have been removed from a GP's list, you may wish to complain if you feel it was unreasonable to remove you.

If you move out of GP's area

If you are changing address, but are not moving too far, you may wish to stay with your current GP. You should ask the GP if they are willing to continue treating and visiting you at the new address. A GP can continue to treat you if you have moved out of their practice area, but they will have to assure the PCT that they are willing to continue visiting and treating you.

TREATMENT THAT MAY NOT BE AVAILABLE ON THE NHS

Access to some forms of treatment – for example, in-vitro fertilization – may be subject to the PCT's priorities. Some treatment may not be provided in your area. Access to some treatment may depend on your need. You can obtain details of those services not provided, and any prioritizing criteria, from the PCT.

If you are unhappy because a certain form of treatment is not available, you should complain.

CONSULTANTS

Your rights to see a particular consultant

You have no right to see a consultant or a particular doctor, although this can be requested. Your GP cannot insist that you see a particular consultant or doctor. You do have the right to see a doctor competent to deal with your case. If you have special reasons for seeing a particular consultant – for example, if your child is the consultant's patient – you could ask for an appointment, explaining your reasons for wanting to see them. If you still have difficulty in seeing the consultant, you could write to the hospital administrator or the consultant's secretary asking for their help.

You may wish to get a second opinion after seeing a consultant, either as an out-patient or as an in-patient. You will need to request this from the consultant, who may arrange for you to see someone else. If the consultant does not agree, you could ask your GP to help.

NHS DIRECT

NHS Direct is a confidential service offering advice and information about health problems and services. It provides 24-hour access to free health advice from experienced nurses. The line is intended to help people care for themselves by advising on the next course of action – for example, whether to stay at home and what self-treatment to take or whether to visit a GP or a hospital. NHS Direct can be contacted by telephone on 0845 46 47 (all calls are charged at local rate) or at www.nhsdirect.nhs.uk in England or www.nhsdirect.wales.nhs.uk in Wales.

Other information about NHS services

Other information about NHS services can be obtained through NHS Direct. NHS Direct cannot provide medical advice or counselling but can give information on:

- local charter standards;
- local medical services;
- waiting times;
- common diseases, conditions and ailments;
- how to complain about NHS services;
- maintaining and improving personal health.

MATERNITY SERVICES

If you are pregnant, you will be able to receive services from one or more of the following:

- midwives, based either in a hospital or in a local health centre or clinic. Midwives are responsible for the care of all normal pregnancies and labours. You do not need to be referred to a midwife by your GP.
- a GP. Not all GPs provide ante-natal care and arrange for delivery. If your GP does not provide this service, you may wish to register with another GP for your maternity care. The PCT can provide details of GPs who offer maternity care.
- an obstetrician based in a hospital. Generally, an obstetrician will only get involved if there are complications. However, you can request to see an obstetrician, even if the midwife or GP is providing all the care.

You may have a range of options to choose from on the type of ante-natal care you want and where you give birth. How much choice you have will depend on the area in which you live, but could include:

- full hospital care. This would only happen, in practice, if you require a high degree of medical intervention.
- shared care between a GP and hospital staff. Normally, you would return home shortly after the birth.
- a home birth, with the birth attended by, and ante-natal care provided by, a midwife and possibly a GP. You have the right to have your baby at home and may need to contact the supervisor of midwives to arrange for this. Alternatively, you could register with an alternative GP just for your maternity care.

Information on local maternity services can be obtained from your PCT, a community midwife, a health visitor or a GP. This information will include, for example, the type of care offered, where the birth can take place, what pain relief is offered and what tests are available and what they are for. In some areas, there are maternity charters that set out the rights of pregnant women and new mothers, and the standards of service you can expect.

If you are having difficulty obtaining the type of care you want, or you require more information on how maternity services are organized in your area, you should contact the supervisor of midwives at your local maternity hospital or at the PCT.

EMERGENCIES

If you need urgent medical attention, you can go directly to the accident and emergency (A & E) department of a hospital without needing a referral from your GP. Not all hospitals have accident and emergency departments.

If you need an ambulance to get to hospital in an emergency, this should arrive within a few minutes. The NHS plans give target maximum times for ambulance arrival, which differ between urban and rural areas.

It is the responsibility of the hospital providing the emergency treatment to meet the cost of treatment. If emergency admission as an in-patient is needed, the cost will be met by the PCT where you live.

Waiting times

If you go into an accident and emergency department (A & E), you should be assessed immediately.

You should be given a bed as soon as possible. Staff will try to ensure you do not wait more than four hours between attending the A & E department and admission, treatment or discharge, but this is not guaranteed. If you are using an out-patients' department you should be given a specific appointment time.

HOSPITAL CARE

Right to hospital treatment

You cannot receive NHS hospital treatment without being referred by your GP, unless you are attending a special clinic (for example, for the treatment of sexually transmitted diseases) or you need urgent medical attention in an emergency.

If you are violent and/or abusive to NHS staff, you may be refused NHS hospital treatment, or given a verbal or written warning before treatment is withheld or withdrawn. Violent or abusive behaviour could include verbal abuse, threats, violence, drug or alcohol abuse in hospital, and destruction of property. Each PCT can decide which types of behaviour could lead to treatment being withheld or withdrawn and how such policies are implemented. If you are violent or abusive to NHS staff and have severe mental health problems or are suffering life-threatening conditions, you will not be denied treatment.

Waiting lists

You may be unable to receive the hospital treatment you need immediately and may have to go on a waiting list. There are maximum waiting times for in-patient treatment. If necessary, treatment may be arranged in an alternative hospital to meet this guarantee.

There are also waiting time standards for a first appointment as an out-patient.

Waiting lists do not operate on a 'last come, last served' basis. Where you are on a waiting list depends on a range of circumstances and may change. If your condition deteriorates dramatically, your GP may recommend you be seen as a matter of greater urgency. How long you will have to wait for a date to see a specialist or have an operation will therefore depend on the severity of your condition, how busy the specialist is and other demands on the hospital facilities.

You can find out about waiting times at particular hospitals through the NHS Direct website. In Wales, information is available from the Health of Wales Information Service website (www.wales.nhs.uk).

If you are waiting to be admitted to hospital, you should contact the hospital appointments department or the consultant on a regular basis, reminding the hospital staff that you are still waiting. If you are prepared to go into hospital at short notice you should say so, in case a cancellation occurs. You should also keep your GP informed of your condition, particularly if it deteriorates.

Operation cancellations

If your operation is cancelled, you should be offered an alternative date. In most cases, this should be within twenty-eight days of the original date, and sooner for life-threatening conditions. If this does not happen you may want to complain.

An appointment for an operation should not be cancelled for non-medical reasons on the day that a patient goes into hospital. If it is cancelled on the day – for example, if the surgeon is unavailable or there is insufficient theatre time – an alternative date should be offered.

Visits

Most hospitals have visiting hours during which visits to patients can be made. A person has no automatic right to visit you, and your doctor may decide that visits would be detrimental to your health. There is usually also a limit to the number of people who can visit at any one time. The restrictions on visits from children are the same as those for other visitors.

If someone wishes to visit you outside visiting hours, they should discuss this with the ward sister. If they cannot get permission from the ward sister, they should contact the hospital administrator if they wish to pursue the matter.

Financial help with visits

If you are receiving Income Support or income-based Jobseeker's Allowance, you may be able to get help with travel costs to visit a sick relative from the Social Fund.

Children

There are things to consider if your child is going into hospital – for example, whether you can stay with your child, how much help you can give with feeding and looking after your child, and what will happen to your child's education. Action for Sick Children (020 7843 6444; www.

actionforsickchildren.org) may be able to advise on all these issues. It also produces a leaflet for parents whose child is going into hospital for the first time.

The Department of Health has strongly recommended to hospitals that they allow unrestricted visiting on children's wards. Hospitals should also allow parents to be with their children as much as possible. This could include allowing you to stay overnight at the hospital. You should make enquiries before your child goes into hospital about what arrangements can be made. If you are finding it difficult to visit a child in hospital – for example, if you have other children at home – you may wish to discuss this with the medical social worker at the hospital.

Single-sex wards

You do not have the right to be cared for in a single-sex ward. However, you do have the right to be informed before you go into hospital (unless it is an emergency or you are admitted to an intensive care unit) whether you will be in a mixed ward. If you wish to be cared for in a single-sex ward, you may have to delay your admission to hospital if this is not available immediately.

If a patient dies in hospital

If a patient dies in hospital, NHS staff should inform relatives and the patient's GP as soon as possible and advise the relatives of the arrangements that need to be made.

An NHS Trust may be responsible for the funeral arrangements if there are no relatives or the relatives are unable to afford the cost and do not qualify for a funeral payment from the Social Fund.

Hospital charges

There is no charge for most hospital treatment for NHS patients who live in the UK. There are charges for visitors from overseas, except in the case of an emergency. However, there are charges for the emergency examination and treatment of people involved in road accidents. There are also charges for certain services – for example, beds with more privacy, alternative menus, patients' telephones and televisions.

Financial help for hospital patients

If you are entitled to benefits or tax credits, your entitlement may be affected by being in hospital.

If you are concerned about the affect of hospitalization on benefits or tax credits you should consult an experienced adviser, for example at a CAB.

If you are on a low income, you may be able to get help with travel costs to hospital and with the cost of prescriptions, wigs and fabric supports.

Discharge from hospital

You should not be discharged from hospital until your care needs are assessed and arrangements made to ensure that you will receive any necessary services when you are discharged.

Any assessment should take into account your wishes, the wishes of your family and of any carer. You should be kept fully informed and involved, be given sufficient time to make decisions, and be told how to seek a review of any decisions made. You can ask for a reassessment of your needs if circumstances change in the future.

You may not be satisfied with arrangements for your discharge from hospital because, for example:

- you feel that you need to remain in hospital for further in-patient treatment;
- you are not satisfied with the community care services that have been arranged for you when you are to leave hospital;
- you do not want to be sent to a care home.

Before discharge takes place, you, or your family, carer or representative, have the right to ask for a review of the decision which has been made about your eligibility for continuing NHS care. In England, you can also ask for a review after discharge.

If you are not satisfied with arrangements that have been made for you after you have been discharged, you can complain. If you are not satisfied with any medical services you are receiving from the NHS, you should use the NHS complaints procedure. If you are not satisfied with community care services that have been arranged or provided by the local authority, you should complain to the local authority using its complaints procedure.

CONSENT TO MEDICAL TREATMENT

You should not be examined or given any treatment or operation without your consent, unless:

- you have a notifiable disease or are a carrier of a notifiable disease;
- you have been detained under the Mental Health Act, in certain circumstances;
- your life is in danger, you are unconscious and you cannot indicate your wishes;
- you are a child who is a ward of court and the court decides that a specific treatment is in your interests;
- a court or someone who has parental responsibility authorizes treatment. A person whose treatment is authorized by a court must be given an opportunity to defend their case against treatment in court.

In some cases, it is good practice to ask you, the patient, to sign a consent form, but in other cases consent can be obtained orally. For example, it is good practice to obtain written consent for any procedure or treatment carrying substantial risk or side effects. If you are capable, it is good practice to obtain your written consent for general anaesthesia, surgery and certain forms of drug therapy. Oral or written consent should be recorded in your notes with relevant details of health professionals' explanations.

Even if you sign a consent form, the signature may not be a valid form of consent if you have not been given appropriate information to be able to give informed consent. Similarly, consent for one procedure does not imply consent for a further procedure or form of treatment.

The doctor must inform you of the nature, consequences, and any substantial risks involved in the treatment or operation, before you give your consent. It is for the doctor to decide exactly how much to tell you, the patient.

Children

Young people aged 16 or 17 can give independent consent to their own treatment. It is not necessary to obtain the consent of a parent or guardian. A young person can be overruled by a court order.

However, if the young person is incapable of giving their own consent – for example, if they are severely disabled – the parent's or guardian's consent must be obtained.

Children under 16 can give their own consent to treatment provided they are judged capable by a doctor or PCT of understanding what is involved. There is no general test for assessing this capacity, and each case will be decided on its own merits.

If a child under 16 does not have sufficient understanding, parental consent (or a court order) will be required for any treatment, except in an emergency. If a child under 16 who does have sufficient understanding refuses treatment, treatment can still be given with their parent's or guardian's consent or by a court order.

Children or young people under 18 cannot give their own consent to experimental operations and blood donations, unless they have sufficient understanding of what is involved.

Experiments, medical research and teaching

In general, if a doctor wishes to carry out research on you, your consent has to be given. You should be given a full explanation of the procedures and risks involved. It should also be made clear to you that you can withdraw from the research at any time. Appropriate safeguards should always be in place to protect patient confidentiality.

No one can consent to research being carried out on another person. If your consent cannot be obtained, the research should not be done. However, if a child under 16 is not competent to decide, a parent or court can consent to the research on their behalf.

You have the right to refuse to participate in teaching without your treatment being affected. If you do not want to be involved in teaching, it is advisable to inform the hospital in advance.

Removal of organs after death

Unless you have said you do not want parts of your body used for research or donated to others after your death, whoever is legally responsible for the body can allow organs to be donated. This will usually be your personal representative. Before organs can be removed from the body, medical staff must be certain that brain death has taken place, and a death certificate must be issued.

Right to refuse treatment

You can refuse any treatment if you wish (but see *Consent to medical treatment*, p. 83, for exceptional circumstances). The doctor cannot act against specific instructions, so you should tell the doctor about any treatment you do not want.

If there are a number of alternative treatments that can be used to treat your condition, you should be given information on these. However, you cannot insist on a particular treatment if the doctor or consultant thinks this is not appropriate.

Forcing treatment on you against your will is assault. If you are assaulted, you should make a complaint. You may also wish to involve the police.

I have a terminal illness the symptoms of which mean that a time will come when I can no longer communicate. If I want to refuse further treatment at that stage, how can I make my wishes known?

You have a right to refuse or stop treatment at any time, even if this means you may die. It is illegal for a doctor actively to cause death, for example by massively increasing dosages of drugs which may bring about an earlier death. If you are concerned that you will be unable to make your wishes known at a later stage in an illness, it may be wise to tell the doctor at what stage you want to stop treatment. This is called making a living will.

You have the right to refuse medical treatment in most situations. However, consent to treatment isn't needed if you have a notifiable disease, have been detained in certain circumstances for psychiatric reasons (usually called being sectioned) or are unconscious and in need of lifesaving treatment and are unable to indicate consent. In fact, your consent is needed for most medical matters, but simply going to see a doctor can be regarded as implied consent for an examination or treatment. If you are concerned about a specific type of treatment, the doctor is obliged to describe other forms of treatment that are available. Forcing treatment on a patient who has refused can be considered assault.

Refusing treatment for a child

If a parent, guardian or child refuses to give consent for treatment which a doctor thinks is necessary, the doctor is still obliged to treat the child. The action the doctor takes will depend on how urgently the treatment is needed.

When a child's life is in danger, the doctor has the right to do whatever is needed to save the child's life, although the doctor may need to obtain a court order. If a parent or a guardian either fails to provide medical help for a child, or unreasonably refuses to allow treatment, they can be prosecuted for neglect.

RIGHT TO DIE

The law concerning whether a person has the right to die is unclear. You have a right to refuse or stop treatment at any time, even if this means that you may die. However, it is illegal for a doctor to omit or carry out treatment with the specific intention of inducing or hastening death. If you believe you may become so ill that you could no longer make the decision about treatment, you should tell the doctor beforehand at what stage you would want treatment to stop.

You may wish to draw up a written document setting out what you would want to happen if you became too ill to give consent to medical treatment. This is known as an advance directive or living will. Such a document may not be legally enforceable in the UK. However, an advance directive refusing treatment is legally binding on health care professionals. If you are concerned about being treated against your wishes, you should ensure you make this clear at the time the treatment is proposed.

ACCESS TO MEDICAL REPORTS AND HEALTH RECORDS

You have the right to see most health records held about you, subject to certain safeguards. You are entitled to be informed of the uses of the information, who has access to them and how you can arrange to see your records. You have a right, subject to certain safeguards, to see any medical report written for an employer, prospective employer or insurer by a medical practitioner who has responsibility for your ongoing care – for example, your GP or consultant and any medical practitioner who has treated you in the past. Information about your medical history should be kept confidential and should not be released without your consent to people who are not involved in your medical care. This includes your relatives, unless you are unable to give consent yourself.

HELP WITH HEALTH COSTS

Most NHS treatment is free, but there are a number of things for which there are usually charges. In some situations, for example if you are in receipt of certain state benefits or are a certain age, you may be able to get help with:

- prescription charges;
- NHS dental charges, including check-ups;
- sight tests;
- vouchers towards the cost of glasses and contact lenses;
- travel costs to and from hospital for NHS treatment;
- travel costs if travelling abroad for treatment;
- wigs and fabric supports – for example, abdominal and spinal supports, and support tights.

Help with prescription charges

Prepayment certificates

If you need frequent prescriptions but do not qualify to get them free of charge, you can buy a prepayment certificate which will save you money. You can get a certificate that lasts for either four or twelve months. You will usually benefit from buying a prepayment certificate if you have to pay for more than five prescription items in a four-month period, or more than fourteen items in a twelve-month period.

Before buying a prepayment certificate, check that you are not entitled to free prescriptions as it is very difficult to get a refund once you have paid for your certificate.

In England there are a number of ways to buy a prepayment certificate:

- over the phone from the **Prescription Pricing Authority** (PPA: 0845 850 0030);
- from the PPA website (www.ppa.org.uk);

- from the pharmacist;
- from your PCT.

In Wales, you can apply on form WP95, which you can get from your Local Health Board.

Help with health costs if you are on a low income

If you have difficulty in meeting your health costs and do not qualify for any other kind of help, you may be able to get help under the NHS low income scheme.

The amount of help you get will depend on the amount of income you have. You might not be entitled to any help at all if you have too much capital. There are two types of certificate: a full help certificate (HC2), and a limited help certificate (HC3), which tells you how much you have to pay.

To apply for either a full help certificate (HC2) or a limited help certificate (HC3), complete form HC1, which is available from local benefit offices, NHS hospitals, dentists, opticians and pharmacists. You do not have to wait until you need treatment before you apply for a certificate. Send the completed form HC1 to the Health Benefits Division (0845 850 1166).

NHS CHARGES AND PEOPLE FROM ABROAD

Your entitlement to free NHS treatment depends on the length and purpose of your residence in the UK, not your nationality. There may be charges for some NHS services, for example your dental treatment, and you may be entitled to help with these charges. Any free NHS treatment you receive, or any help with NHS costs, does not affect your immigration status.

If you are entitled to it, you can obtain free treatment immediately. There is no qualifying period.

Treatment that is always free of charge

Some hospital treatment is free of charge for everyone who needs it, regardless of how long they have been or intend to stay in the UK. This is:

- treatment for accidents and emergencies as an outpatient in a hospital's casualty department, or in a walk-in centre;
- compulsory psychiatric treatment;

- treatment for certain communicable diseases, such as tuberculosis, cholera, food poisoning, malaria and meningitis. Testing for the HIV virus and counselling following a test are both free of charge, but any necessary subsequent treatment and medicines may have to be paid for;
- family planning services.

Who can receive all NHS treatment free of charge

Some people from abroad can receive all NHS hospital treatment free of charge. If you are entitled to free NHS hospital treatment, your spouse and dependent child(ren) will also be able to receive free treatment, but only if they live with you permanently in the UK.

You can receive free NHS hospital treatment if you:

- have been living legally in the UK for at least twelve months when you seek treatment, and did not come to the UK for private medical treatment. Temporary absences from the UK of up to three months are ignored.
- have come to the UK to take up permanent residence – for example, if you are a former UK resident who has returned from abroad – or if you have been granted leave to enter or remain as a spouse;
- have come to the UK to work, either as an employee or self-employed person. This does not include people on short business trips.
- normally work in the UK, but are temporarily working abroad, have at least ten years continuous residence in the UK, and have been abroad for less than five years. However, if you are studying abroad you are not entitled to free NHS treatment.
- are receiving a UK war pension;
- are an asylum seeker or have been granted discretionary leave to remain or refugee status;
- are imprisoned in the UK or detained by UK immigration authorities;
- are a UK state pensioner who spends at least six months a year living in the UK and up to six months a year living in another EEA state (but are not a resident of that state);
- are working in another EEA country, or in Switzerland, but are paying compulsory UK national insurance contributions;
- are a student following a course of study that lasts at least six months or is substantially funded by the UK Government.

In addition, if you are living in the UK for a settled purpose for not less than six months you will not be liable for NHS charges. This includes, for example, if you have student or fiancé(e) status for immigration purposes.

It will be up to you to show the hospital or GP that you are in the UK for a settled purpose.

Who can receive some NHS treatment free of charge

You and your dependants are entitled to free NHS treatment if your need for it arose during your visit to the UK. A medical opinion may be needed in order to decide if treatment should be provided free of charge. This applies if:

- you are a national of an EEA country, living in an EEA state or Switzerland, or a refugee or stateless person living in an EEA state, or you are a non-EEA national who lives in an EU state and pays national insurance contributions there;
- you normally live abroad in a non-EEA state, and are receiving a UK state pension or other benefit, and have lived in the UK in the past for at least ten years;
- you have lived in the UK for at least ten years in the past, but now live in an EEA state or Switzerland, or in a non-EEA state with which the UK has a reciprocal agreement;
- you are a national or a resident of certain non-EEA countries with which the UK has a reciprocal agreement.

In addition, people from some countries can get free treatment if they have been referred to the UK for that treatment under the terms of the reciprocal agreement. There are also special arrangements with certain countries that enable people from outside the UK to get free treatment. The Department of Health can give details of countries with which the UK has a reciprocal agreement and for which there are special arrangements.

GPs and other non-hospital services

If you are entitled to free NHS hospital treatment you will not necessarily be able to receive treatment from a GP and other non-hospital services free of charge. Other non-hospital services available on the NHS include dental and optical treatment, district nursing, midwifery, health visiting, ambulance transport and family planning services.

A GP may, in practice, be flexible in deciding whether you are resident in the UK, in order to qualify for free treatment. You will usually have to show that your stay in the UK has some degree of permanence and stability.

If you are in the UK for less than three months, a GP may accept you as a temporary patient. Otherwise, a GP may offer to accept you as a private patient and you will have to pay for treatment.

You may have difficulty finding a GP or other practitioner who is prepared to register you. In this situation you should contact the Primary Care Trust.

Refusal of treatment

If you are not entitled to receive free NHS hospital treatment you will not be refused medical treatment that stabilizes a life-threatening condition – for example, for renal failure. Treatment will be given to deal with the emergency, but you will be expected to return home for it to be completed once the emergency is over.

I am coming to the UK from abroad. Can I get free NHS treatment?

Free treatment is available, but not automatically for every person who enters the UK from abroad. Emergency, compulsory psychiatric and contagious or infectious disease treatments are free. HIV diagnosis is free but treatment may not be.

As with UK residents, some NHS treatments have to be paid for (such as dentists and opticians), although help is available if you cannot afford to pay. People living or working in the UK are entitled to free treatment, but so are people who are taken ill whilst in the UK for a short stay. Some countries have an arrangement whereby UK residents can get free medical treatment there, and residents of that country can get the same in the UK – this is called a reciprocal agreement.

If you cannot pay for NHS treatment, urgent treatment will still be carried out on the NHS, but you will have to return home for continued treatment. If the need is not urgent, NHS treatment may be offered, but not for free.

Unless you have come to the UK specifically for medical reasons, this entitlement to free treatment extends to GP services, community nurses, midwifery and ambulances, although a GP may require proof of how long you intend to stay in the UK.

If there is not an emergency but treatment has to start immediately, you may be asked to give an undertaking to pay. In these circumstances, it is very important that you find out the likely cost.

If it is not urgent, you will be given the opportunity to refuse the treatment if you cannot afford it. Treatment can be delayed until you can raise the money. If you cannot do so, treatment will be refused.

Complaints about charges

If you are entitled to free hospital treatment, but have been told that you will be charged, you should contact the Primary Care Trust for a refund.

MAKING A COMPLAINT ABOUT THE NHS

You have the right to make a complaint about any aspect of NHS treatment using the NHS complaints procedure. To use the procedure you must usually be a patient or a former patient of the practitioner or institution concerned, although it is possible to complain on behalf of someone else. If you want to complain on behalf of another person, the hospital or practice must agree that you are a suitable representative.

There are NHS complaints procedures for all parts of the UK.

You should make your complaint as soon as possible after the problem incident. There are time limits for complaints.

It is not possible to get any financial compensation through the NHS complaints procedure. If you are seeking financial compensation you will need to take separate legal action.

Help with your complaint in England

The **Independent Complaints Advocacy Service (ICAS)** is a free, confidential and independent service that can help you make a formal complaint about your NHS experience. You can contact your local ICAS office direct, or through NHS managers at hospitals and GP practices, NHS Direct, and the Patient Advice and Liaison Service (PALS).

Contact numbers for local ICAS offices are:

London	0845 120 3784
South-East	0845 600 8616
Eastern (Bedfordshire and Hertfordshire)	0845 456 1082

Eastern (Cambridgeshire, Norfolk, Suffolk)	0845 456 1084
Eastern (Essex)	0845 456 1083
South-West	0845 120 3782
West Midlands	0845 120 3748
East Midlands	0845 650 0088
North-East	0845 120 3732
North-West	0845 120 3735
Yorkshire/Humberside	0845 120 3734

The **Patient Advice and Liaison Service (PALS)** gives general advice on how to complain and may be able to help you resolve a complaint. However, PALS is not able to take up formal complaints on your behalf.

You can contact your local PALS from:

• your local hospital, clinic, GP surgery or health centre;
• NHS Direct (0845 4647; www.nhsdirect.nhs.uk).

You can also get help from your local CAB to make a complaint about your NHS practitioner.

Taking legal action about your NHS complaint

If you are considering taking legal action about your NHS complaint, you will need to consult a solicitor.

You should be aware that these actions are costly and complex. All family practitioners are insured and legal action will usually be contested by an insurance company. Where the legal action is about the actions of an NHS employee of a trust or PCT, the NHS institution will be responsible for deciding whether to contest the action.

Complaints about professional misconduct

If you think that an NHS practitioner has been guilty of professional misconduct, it may be possible to complain to the practitioner's professional or regulatory body. Each body has a disciplinary committee that can investigate complaints. If a practitioner is found guilty of professional misconduct they can be prevented from practising in the future.

A-Z OF NHS AND LOCAL AUTHORITY SERVICES

Abortion

Certain women may be able to obtain an abortion through the NHS. General advice and help is available from GPs and family planning clinics. Help is also available from voluntary organizations, such as the **British Pregnancy Advisory Service** (08457 30 40 30), which runs its own clinics.

Aids and adaptations

Aids for disabled people are available from hospitals and local authorities' social services departments, as well as a number of voluntary organizations, including the British Red Cross. Council tenants should contact their local authority housing department for more information.

Alternative medicine

Some forms of alternative medicine (also known as complementary medicine) are available through the NHS from certain GPs and hospitals. The therapies most frequently available through the NHS are acupuncture, osteopathy, homoeopathy, chiropractic and aromatherapy.

Ambulances

Most ambulances are provided for patients by the NHS for both emergency and routine patient transport. Emergency ambulances can be contacted through the emergency telephone (999) service. Ambulances for routine journeys can be arranged through GPs or hospitals.

Breast cancer screening

Breast cancer screening is available through the NHS at three-yearly intervals for women aged between 50 and 64. Women aged over 64 can be screened on request.

Cervical screening

Cervical screening is available through the NHS every three to five years for women aged between 20 and 64. Women over 64 can be screened on request.

Chiropodists

State-registered chiropodists are available through the NHS to treat certain patients, including the elderly and disabled. Patients must normally be referred to a chiropodist by a GP or clinic. Anyone who does not come within a group entitled to NHS treatment will need to arrange private treatment.

Community nurses

Community nurses are employed by the NHS to provide home nursing care for patients. They are based at GP surgeries and health centres and can also be contacted through local community nursing offices.

Contraception

Contraceptive advice and supplies are available free on the NHS through GPs and family planning clinics. Free advice and supplies are also available from some voluntary organizations, for example the British Pregnancy Advisory Service.

Counselling services

Some GP practices provide free counselling services through the NHS.

Day centres

Local authority social services organize day care services for people with mental, physical and learning disabilities and for the elderly. There is usually a charge for these services.

Dentists

Lists of dentists who provide NHS treatment can be obtained from PCTs and, in Wales, community health councils. They can also be obtained from NHS Direct. Some groups of people are entitled to free treatment.

Disease and pest control

Local authority environmental health departments are responsible for investigating outbreaks of food poisoning and certain infectious diseases. They are also responsible for vermin control and the control of other health hazards – for example, excessive noise, dust or smoke.

General Practitioners (GPs)

Everyone is entitled to be registered with a GP. For help in finding a GP, contact your local health authority or NHS Direct. As well as providing health advice and treatment, GPs provide check-ups, take cervical smears, do immunizations and sign certificates for people unable to work because of illness. Many GPs also provide health promotion clinics, contraceptive services, minor surgery, counselling, maternity services and medical examinations for insurance and other purposes (for which they may make a charge).

Health visitors

Health visitors provide support through the NHS for families with children under five and for older patients. They are normally based at GP surgeries.

Home care

Local authority social services departments are responsible for providing home care (formerly called home help) services for older people and other people who need help at home with personal care – for example, washing and dressing. There is normally a charge for these services.

Hospitals

Most NHS hospital admissions and appointments take place through referrals by GPs but patients can attend an NHS hospital without a GP referral by visiting an Accident and Emergency department or by attending a special clinic for the treatment of sexually transmitted diseases.

Immunizations

The NHS provides immunizations for children and some adults. A charge may be made for immunizations needed for overseas travel.

Infertility treatment

Advice about infertility problems is available through the NHS from GPs. However, some forms of infertility treatment are not easily available on the NHS and patients may need to seek private treatment.

Maternity services

Antenatal and postnatal care is available through the NHS from GPs, midwives and hospitals. Expectant mothers are also entitled to free prescriptions and dental treatment from the time when the pregnancy is confirmed until one year after the birth. Women on low incomes are entitled to milk tokens and free vitamins during pregnancy.

Older people's services

A number of NHS services are available for older people. GPs should offer annual health checks to patients aged 75 and over. Help is also available from health visitors and district nurses. Local authority social services departments and some voluntary organizations – for example, Age Concern – provide various services, including meals on wheels and lunch clubs.

Optical services

General ophthalmic services are administered by health authorities. Some people are entitled to free eye tests and vouchers towards the cost of glasses or contact lenses, including all children under 16, some young people under 19, people aged 60 or over, people with certain eye conditions, people entitled to certain benefits and anyone else on a low income.

Pharmacists

Pharmacists (also known as chemists) are responsible for dispensing medicines. They can also provide information and advice about many common medical problems.

Physiotherapy

Physiotherapy is available through the NHS to patients referred for treatment by GPs or hospitals.

Practice nurses

Practice nurses are employed by GP practices to carry out a range of functions, including immunizations and basic health checks.

Prescriptions

Doctors, dentists and some nurses can prescribe a range of drugs and appliances on the NHS but can normally only prescribe a limited quantity of a drug at any time (usually one month's supply).

School health

Every school has a school doctor and nurse who carry out health checks on children attending the school, including tests on hearing, sight and growth. Parents have the right to be present at these checks. School nurses also provide health education and general advice on managing health problems in school.

Special clinics

The NHS provides special clinics to treat sexually transmitted diseases and genito-urinary infections. Most clinics are based in hospitals and patients need not be referred by their GP. For details of your nearest clinic, contact NHS Direct.

Terminal care

Care for the terminally ill is available through the NHS from GPs, hospitals, district nurses and others. There are also a number of NHS hospices providing palliative care for patients as well as hospices run by a number of voluntary organizations.

Walk-in centres

Walk-in centres are NHS centres staffed by nurses where patients can attend without an appointment for free advice and treatment for minor injuries. For the address of your nearest centre, contact NHS Direct.

Who can help?

Further information about NHS services can be obtained from **NHS Direct** (0845 4647) or at www.nhsdirect.nhs.uk (in England) www.nhsdirect.wales.nhs.uk (in Wales).

3
Housing

CONTENTS

INTRODUCTION

Shelter – a roof over your head – is one of our most basic human needs and the conditions in which we live profoundly affect the quality of our lives. It is reported that over a million children in Britain suffer from bad housing – living in damp and dilapidated conditions, or facing eviction over their family's rent arrears. It is clear that a lack of secure, long-term, adequate housing has a huge impact on the health of those families and their children's education and futures. Knowing how to tackle the housing problems you face is a good place to start. With many of us spending a large percentage of our monthly incomes on paying for our housing, through rent or mortgage repayments, making sure that we can live as comfortably as possible for what we can afford is important to everyone.

Whether you rent your place, either privately or from a social landlord or local authority, own it or want to get your foot on the property ladder, this chapter will help you to find – and keep – a home that you can call home. It looks at tenancy agreements, financial help you may get to pay for home improvements and how to get your landlord to do the repairs.

And, as the song says, everybody needs good neighbours, but unfortunately we don't all get them, so we take a look at common neighbour disputes and how to go about resolving them.

BUYING A HOME

The first thing to do is decide how much you can afford. You will need to look at how much money you have available yourself and how much you can borrow. There are a number of different financial institutions that offer loans to people buying a property, like building societies and banks, that will tell you whether they'll lend you money and if so, how much.

Some building societies now provide buyers with a certificate that states that a loan will be available provided the property is satisfactory. You may be able to get this certificate before you start looking for a property. Building societies state that this certificate may help you to have your offer accepted by the seller.

Before finally deciding how much to spend on a property, you need to be sure you will have enough money to pay for all the additional costs. These include:

- survey fees;
- valuation fees;
- stamp duty. This is payable on properties costing more than £60,000 and is at least 1 per cent of the purchase price;
- land registry fee;
- local authority search;
- fees, if any, charged by the mortgage lender or someone who arranges the mortgage, for example a mortgage broker;
- solicitors' costs;
- VAT;
- removal expenses;
- any final bills, for example gas and electricity, from your present home that will have to be paid when you move.

You should be aware that if you start the process of buying a property and the sale then falls through you may have already paid for a valuation or a survey. You won't get this back. If the solicitor has started any legal work you may also have to pay for the work done.

You will also have to pay a deposit on exchange of contracts, up to 10 per cent of the purchase price, a few weeks before the purchase is completed and the money is received from the mortgage lender.

Freehold, leasehold and commonhold

Freehold property
If the property is freehold, this means that the land on which the property is built is part of the sale and no ground rent or service charge is payable.

Leasehold property
A property may be leasehold, which means that the land on which the property is built is not part of the sale. You have to pay ground rent to the owner of the land, who is called the freeholder.

The length of a lease can vary and you should check that the length of the lease on the property you are interested in buying is acceptable to the mortgage lender.

In addition to ground rent on a leasehold property, you may have to pay an annual service charge. This usually happens with a flat. The service charge covers such items as maintenance and repairs to the building, cleaning of common parts and looking after the grounds.

A group of leaseholders living in the same building may have a right to buy the freehold of the building jointly. Even where you don't have the right to buy the freehold, you may have the right of first refusal to buy if the freeholder does decide to sell up. A group of leaseholders may be able to convert to commonhold ownership of their flats as long as all parties, including the freeholder, agree.

I am a leaseholder and I pay an annual service charge. The freeholder wants to increase his charge to cover repairs to the building. Do I have to pay?

A lease is a legal contract and you can only be charged for services if they are specified in the lease. You should check your lease carefully to see what has to be paid for and how much you can be charged.

The law gives you certain rights where your lease says that you have to pay for services, repairs, maintenance, insurance or management costs in addition to ground rent. These rights include the right to be given a summary of the costs on which any charge is based, the right to look at the accounts and receipts for the charge, the right to be consulted about major, non-urgent works and the right to challenge unreasonable charges.

If you are asked to pay for something that is not covered by your lease, or you think that a charge is too much, you should start by writing to the freeholder explaining why you think the charge is wrong. If you are not satisfied with the response you can challenge the amount by applying to a leasehold valuation tribunal. You can make a challenge either when the work is proposed or when you receive a bill, but not if you have already agreed to make the payment.

You and the other leaseholders in your block may wish to form a tenants' or residents' association and negotiate jointly with the freeholder through that association.

You can get further advice about leasehold from the **Leasehold Advisory Service** (0845 345 1993; www.lease-advice.org.uk).

Commonhold property

If the property is commonhold, this means that you can buy the freehold of a flat and own the common parts of the building jointly with the owners of other flats in the building (known as a commonhold association).

In commonhold, a ground rent or service charge is not payable. However, a share of the commonhold association's expenditure on maintenance, insurance and administration will be payable for the common parts of the building.

Making an offer

When you decide you would like to buy a particular property you do not necessarily have to pay the price being asked for it by the owners. You can offer less if, for example, you think there are repairs to be done that will cost money.

If the property is being sold through an estate agent, you should tell the estate agent what you are prepared to pay for the property. The estate agent will then put this offer to the owners.

If the owners do not accept the first offer put to them you can decide to make an increased offer. There is no limit on the number of times you can make offers on a property. If you make a written offer it will always be made subject to contract. This means that you will not be committed to the purchase before finding out more about the state of the property. If you make an oral offer this is never legally binding.

When your offer for the property has been accepted you will have to consider the following:

- whether a holding deposit is payable;
- arranging a mortgage;
- whether a survey is necessary;
- who will do the necessary legal work;
- whether you want to buy with someone else.

Once the owners have accepted your offer you may be asked to pay a small deposit to the estate agent. This is not usually more than £500. It is meant to show that you are serious about going ahead with the purchase. It is repayable if the sale does not go ahead.

Arranging a mortgage

If you have not already begun to arrange a mortgage, you should start to do this now. It should take about three weeks from the application for the mortgage to the formal offer being made by the lender. However, this timescale may vary.

Whoever agrees to lend the money will want to have the property valued. This is to make sure that the lender could get the loan back if for any reason you stopped paying your mortgage and the property had to be sold again. The valuation will be done by a surveyor on behalf of the lender but you will have to pay for this valuation. The fee will be payable in advance, usually when you send a completed mortgage application form to the lender.

If the amount of money to be borrowed is more than a certain percentage of the valuation of the property (usually 75–80 per cent), your lender makes it a condition of the loan that you take out extra insurance to cover the extra amount. You pay a single premium to your lender which is usually added to the loan. This is known as a higher lending charge.

Arranging a survey

The valuation that is done for whoever is lending the money is not a survey. You should consider whether or not to have an independent survey carried out in addition to the valuation. The survey would not only consider the value of the property but would also examine the structure of the property and should identify any existing or potential problems.

If the surveyor reports that there are some problems with the property you will have to consider whether you still want to go ahead with the purchase or want to negotiate further with the seller about the price. The surveyor will usually advise you as to how any problems they have identified should be dealt with and the likely costs of this. You can find more useful information about property surveys from the **Royal Institution of Chartered Surveyors** (www.rics.org/Property/ResidentialProperty).

Getting the legal work done (conveyancing)

The legal process of transferring the ownership of the property from the present owner to the buyer is known as conveyancing. You should decide who you want to do the conveyancing work. You can choose to do it yourself, although this can be complicated, or:

- use a solicitor; *or*
- use a licensed conveyancer.

Using a solicitor

Most firms of solicitors offer a conveyancing service. Although all solicitors can legally do conveyancing, it is advisable to choose a solicitor who has experience of this work.

Using a licensed conveyancer

You can use a licensed conveyancer to do your conveyancing. Licensed conveyancers are not solicitors but are licensed by the Council of Licensed Conveyancers (01245 349599), which you can contact to find out if a local conveyancer is licensed.

Before making a choice as to who will do the conveyancing, you should find out the probable costs. It is important to contact more than one solicitor or licensed conveyancer as there is no set scale of fees for conveyancing.

Buying with someone else

Legal ownership

If two or more people are buying the property jointly they will be joint 'legal owners'. The agreement of all legal owners is needed if the property is to be sold, although if there is a dispute an owner can apply for a court order to decide how the property sale should be handled.

Beneficial ownership

As well as the legal ownership of property, there is the 'beneficial ownership' to be considered. This means the shares in the property to which the owners are entitled.

There are two types of beneficial ownership: joint tenancy and tenancy in common. The most important difference is what happens when someone dies. Joint tenants all own all of the property, so if a joint tenant dies their share passes automatically to the remaining joint tenant(s). Tenants in common each have a share in the property that they can dispose of as they wish, either whilst they are living or through their will.

Steps in the legal work of buying a property

From having an offer accepted to exchange of contracts can take up to seven weeks and from exchange of contracts to completion can take up to four weeks. However, if there are any problems the time taken may be longer.

Once you have instructed the solicitor or a licensed conveyancer, the seller's solicitor or conveyancer draws up a contract that will eventually be signed by you and the seller. However, before the contract can be signed, your solicitor or licensed conveyancer must make sure that there are no problems with the ownership of the property, rights of way, access or future developments in the area that might affect the property.

While the solicitor or licensed conveyancer is making the enquiries, you should sort out how you will pay the deposit that has to be made when the contracts are exchanged. This deposit is usually 10 per cent of the price of the home.

Exchange of contracts

The final contract between you and the seller is prepared when:

- the solicitor (or licensed conveyancer) and you are satisfied with the final outcome of all the enquiries;
- any surveyor's report has been received and any necessary action taken;
- the formal mortgage offer has been received;
- arrangements about the payment of the 10 per cent deposit have been made;
- the date of completion has been agreed.

You and the seller each have a copy of the final contract which you must sign. These signed contracts are then exchanged. At exchange of contracts both you and the seller are legally bound by the contract and the sale of the house has to go ahead.

Completion

Completion of the purchase usually takes place about four weeks after exchange of contracts. On the day agreed for completion:

- the mortgage lender releases the money;
- the deeds to the property are handed over to your solicitor or licensed conveyancer;
- the seller must hand over the keys and leave the property by an agreed time.

The solicitor or licensed conveyancer will usually send their account to you on, or soon after, the completion date. You are in and the house is yours!

The right to buy your council-owned property

As a public sector tenant you will probably have the right to buy if you are a secure tenant of:

- a district council;
- a London borough council;
- a non-charitable housing association;
- a housing action trust.

You have the right to buy if you have been a public sector tenant for at least two years. This need not necessarily have been in your present accommodation. A tenancy with another public sector landlord can be included in this time.

As a tenant you will *not* have the right to buy if you are:

- a housing association tenant whose tenancy began on or after 15 January 1989;
- a tenant of sheltered housing or housing specifically designated for the elderly;
- bankrupt or about to go bankrupt. If you have rent arrears you will have to clear them before you have the right to buy.

If you are not sure whether you have the right to buy you should check with your landlord.

Discounts

As a tenant with a right to buy, you will get a discount on the price of the property. If you live in a house the discount will be between 32 and 60 per cent, depending on how long you have lived there. If you live in a flat the discount will be between 44 and 70 per cent, depending on how long you have lived there. The discount will not exceed the regional upper limits, which range from £16,000 to £38,000.

If you exercise the right to buy and sell the property within three years you will have to repay all or some of the discount.

How to pay

As a tenant who wants to exercise your right to buy, you should try to get a mortgage from a building society or high street bank. You could also contact a mortgage broker to see if they can arrange a mortgage.

However, if you cannot afford to buy the property outright you can still buy under the rent to mortgage scheme. Under this scheme you can buy a share of the property and make mortgage repayments on the amount you have borrowed for this. The landlord will retain ownership of the remaining share of the property.

How to apply

If you want to apply for the right to buy, you should ask your landlord for the Right to Buy Claim Form (Form RTB1), which the landlord must provide.

The right to acquire

As a secure or assured tenant of a registered social landlord – for example, a housing association or a local housing company – you may have the right to buy your home under a different scheme called the 'right to acquire'. The right to acquire only applies to a limited number of properties – for example, homes built with public funds on or after 1 April 1997.

For more information about the right to acquire in England, speak to your landlord or contact the **Housing Corporation** (0845 230 7000; www.housingcorp.gov.uk). In Wales, you should contact the **Welsh Assembly Government** (029 2082 5111; www.wales.gov.uk).

Shared ownership

Shared ownership schemes are intended to help people who cannot afford to buy a suitable home in any other way. A local authority or housing association will buy a property on your behalf. You pay rent to the local authority or housing association for part of the property and a mortgage on the rest. You will usually be able to buy further shares in the property at a later date.

To qualify for the scheme you must usually be a first-time buyer, and priority is given to local authority or housing association tenants. Other people in need of housing may also be considered for the scheme. You must be able to get your own mortgage to meet the purchase costs on a percentage of the property.

In Wales, the shared ownership scheme is no longer available to new purchasers.

More information about shared ownership is available from the **Housing Corporation** (0845 230 7000; www.housingcorp.gov.uk).

Homebuy

Homebuy is a scheme offered by housing associations to help you buy a home on the open market. The scheme is available to local authority and housing association tenants and to some other people in housing need. Help is limited to people who would not be able to buy a home without help from the scheme.

If you are accepted on to the Homebuy scheme you must be able to get a mortgage for a percentage of the purchase price of the property. This percentage varies depending on where you live. The housing association will lend you the remaining sum of the purchase price. You will need to repay the loan when the property is sold. The amount of money you will need to repay is usually a set percentage of the value of the property when it is sold. If the property has increased in value, this will mean that the amount that you repay will be larger than the amount that you initially borrowed.

If you are interested in Homebuy, you should contact your local housing association or, in England, the **Housing Corporation** (0845 230 7000; www.housingcorp.gov.uk) or, in Wales, the **Welsh Federation of Housing Associations** (029 2030 3150).

MORTGAGES

If you want to buy a home you may be able to borrow money to do this. The borrower offers the home as security against the loan. The lender has a legal charge against the property – that is, if you do not keep up the agreed repayments, the lender can take possession of the property. This is known as a mortgage. The loan will be for a fixed period and the borrower will be charged interest on the loan.

There are several types of mortgage available. The most common are:

- **repayment mortgage**. This is a mortgage in which the capital borrowed is repaid gradually over the period of the loan. The capital is paid in monthly instalments together with an amount of interest. The amount of capital that is repaid gradually increases over the years while the amount of interest goes down.

- **endowment mortgage**. This mortgage consists of two parts: the loan from the building society and an endowment policy taken out with an insurance company. You pay interest on the loan in monthly instalments to the building society but do not actually pay off any of the loan. The endowment policy is also paid monthly to the insurance company. At the end of the period of the mortgage the policy matures and produces a lump sum which pays off the loan to the building society.
- **pension mortgage**. This mortgage is primarily for self-employed people. The monthly payments consist of interest payments on the loan and contributions to a pension scheme. When the borrower retires there is a lump sum to pay off the loan and a pension.

A mortgage could be available from a number of different sources, such as banks, building societies, insurance companies (although they only provide endowment mortgages), finance houses and specialized mortgage com-

---

I have an endowment mortgage and have been told that there won't be enough money at the end of the mortgage term to pay for the house. What can I do?

There are over 10 million endowment policies linked to mortgages in the UK. An endowment mortgage combines an interest-only mortgage and an investment (the endowment policy). Throughout the term of the mortgage (usually twenty or twenty-five years) interest is paid on the amount borrowed to your mortgage lender and a monthly premium is paid on your endowment policy. The endowment premiums are invested with the intention that the endowment produces enough capital at the end of the term to pay off the mortgage. If your endowment policy doesn't reach this target you will have a shortfall and will need to pay part of the capital owed on your mortgage another way.

Many people were mis-sold endowment policies because the policy was not suitable for them. There are many reasons why an endowment policy may not have been right for you but, broadly, if you were not informed of the risks associated with using an investment product to repay your mortgage you have grounds for complaint. Find out more about problems with endowment mortgages from the Financial Services Authority (0845 606 1234; www.fsa.gov.uk).

panies. Some large building companies might arrange mortgages on their own new-build homes.

Using a broker to get a mortgage

Instead of going directly to a lender such as a building society for a mortgage, a broker could be used. A broker may be an estate agent, or a mortgage or insurance broker. They will act as an agent to introduce people to a source of mortgage loan to help them buy a home.

A broker may be used when it could be difficult obtaining a mortgage directly from a lender, for example when:

- the mortgage required is particularly large;
- the property is unusual in some way;
- more than two people wish to purchase the home jointly;
- you are self-employed and your income fluctuates.

There are rules about how much a broker can charge for their services.

SELLING A HOME

Finding a buyer yourself

If you wish to find a buyer for your home yourself, you must first decide what price you want to ask for the property. Many estate agents do free valuations so it is always possible to arrange for two or more local estate agents to provide this information. If you want a formal valuation, you could arrange for an estate agent to provide this but you would have to pay a fee.

In addition, you can find out about the cost of houses locally by looking at local papers, estate agents' windows and similar houses in the area.

You should also decide in advance if you are prepared to include any extras in the sale, for example curtains and carpets. These are known as fittings. A price for these can be included in the asking price or a separate price can be asked in addition.

There are some items that you must sell as part of the house unless you make it clear to the buyer that such items are not included in the sale. These are known as fixtures and include such items as fireplaces and a central heating system. However, in some cases it is not always clear whether something is a fixture or fitting so it would be useful for you to draw up a list of any items you intend to remove or are prepared to sell to avoid problems later.

Using an estate agent

If you wish to use an estate agent, you should enquire about local estate agents and find out the following information:

- what type of property the estate agent specializes in;
- whether the estate agent belongs to a professional association;
- how much the estate agent will charge;
- the reputation of the local estate agencies, if possible.

Estate agents' charges

Nearly all estate agents calculate their fees as a percentage of the final selling price of the property, usually between 1½ and 2½ per cent. This is known as the rate of commission and the estate agent must confirm the charges that will be made and the rate of commission when they agree to act for you.

Types of agreement you have with an estate agent

When you use one estate agent to handle the sale it is known as 'sole agency'. It is usual for the agreement to state that commission is only paid to the estate agent if they sell the property. If you find a buyer yourself, you don't have to pay the commission. If the agreement gives the estate agent 'sole selling rights' the agent is the only person who can sell. You would have to pay the agent under this type of agreement even if you find the buyer yourself.

If you appoint two or more estate agents to act together for you in selling the property, this is known as 'joint agency' or 'joint sole agency'. The estate agents involved share the commission when the property is sold regardless of which estate agent actually finds the buyer. The commission for the joint agency agreement is usually higher than for a sole agency.

If you appoint two or more estate agents independently, but the commission is only paid to the estate agent who finds the buyer, this is known as multiple agency.

What does the estate agent do?

The estate agent first of all visits the house in order to value it and decide on an asking price with you. You may wish to ask more than one estate agent to call and value the house. It is also advisable for you to check the price that the estate agent suggests by comparing it to similar houses in the local paper.

The estate agent will prepare details of the house to send out to people who are interested in buying it. These details will include the number and size of the rooms and all the fixtures and fittings that will be left in the house. The estate agent also arranges for the property to be advertised.

Deciding who to sell to

Whether you have arranged to sell the house yourself or used an estate agent you may find that you receive more than one offer for the house. You can sell the house to whoever you want and do not have to sell to the buyer who offers the most money. You may wish to take into account whether the buyer:

- is a first time buyer – this means they are unlikely to be in a chain of buying and selling and the sale may be more simple;
- has found a buyer for their own property. If so, is it part of a chain of buying and selling and how long is the chain?
- is paying cash or is likely to get a mortgage;
- wants to move at the same time as you.

If you are using an estate agent, it is often easier for the estate agent to find out this information from the buyer.

It is unlawful for a seller who uses an estate agent to discriminate against a prospective buyer on grounds of race, sex or disability, either by refusing to sell the property, or by offering it on less favourable terms.

If you are using an estate agent, the agent negotiates with the potential buyer(s) about the price. The estate agent should try and obtain the best possible price for you. If you are acting alone, you must negotiate yourself. You do not have to accept the first offer put to you and should not be rushed into making a decision quickly.

Accepting an offer

Even if you have accepted an offer, there is nothing in law to prevent you from changing your mind and accepting a higher offer from someone else. You should also bear in mind that when an offer is made and accepted, the potential buyer can also withdraw – for example, they may not get a mortgage, or the survey may show up some structural problem.

If you are handling the sale yourself it may be a good idea to keep the names and addresses of all potential buyers who make offers, in case the one you accept falls through.

COMMON PROBLEMS BUYING AND SELLING A HOME

Chains

A buyer or seller may find that they have problems because they are involved in a chain of buying and selling. This happens when a buyer or seller is selling and buying at the same time and the other people involved are also buying and selling. This creates a chain of buyers and sellers that may be very long and so delays may occur. It depends on the reasons for the delays as to what, if anything, you can do about them. If the problem is with a buyer further down the chain, the seller could look for another buyer or consider arranging a bridging loan until the property is sold.

Estate agents

If an estate agent is selling a property for you, there is a contractual agreement between yourself and the estate agent. If you have a problem with an estate agent it is usually necessary to check a copy of any written agreement between you both and establish what verbal agreements, if any, were made.

As the seller, you pay the estate agent for their services and the estate agent is therefore acting on your behalf. It is the seller's interest they will represent and the buyer should bear this in mind if they are interested in a house being sold through an estate agent.

The estate agent's bill is too high

You may think that the bill from the estate agent, after the sale is completed, is too high. It is important to check that the bill gives a clear breakdown of the costs – for example, the commission fee, advertising, VAT. Check the bill against the original agreement you made with the estate agent.

You decide not to sell

If you decide not to continue with the sale of your home, you may have to pay some estate agents' charges, for example to cover any costs the estate agent has already incurred. This will depend on the original contract between you and the estate agent.

You want to use an additional estate agent

If you have been using one estate agent this is known as 'sole agency'. When you agree a sole agency with an estate agent the contract will usually state how long this period of sole agency will last. At the end of this period you are free to use one or more additional estate agents.

If you use one or more additional estate agents before the period of sole agency has come to an end you are breaking the contract with the original estate agent. This means that if the new estate agent finds a buyer for the house you would have to pay commission not only to the new estate agent but also to the agent with whom you had the sole agency agreement. If the original agent found a buyer, the amount of commission that you would have to pay to the new estate agent would depend on the type of agreement you had with them.

However, you may be able to negotiate changing the sole agency agreement to a joint sole agency agreement with the original estate agency.

You want to change estate agents

You may want to change your estate agent. You should check the terms of the agreement you have with the estate agent to see if this is possible. If it is possible, you may still have to pay some charges to the estate agent to cover costs, such as advertising, that the estate agent has incurred.

You have found your own buyer

You may have found your own buyer for the property who has not come through the estate agent – for example, a friend may want to buy the property. You are entitled to sell to a buyer who has not been found by the estate agent but you may find that you will still have to pay the estate agent. What you have to pay will depend on your contract with the estate agent.

You are not satisfied with the service provided

You may not be satisfied with the service the estate agent is providing, for example:

- the estate agent may not be sending out details of your property to potential buyers;

- the advertising is not what you wanted;
- the details about the house are inaccurate or inadequate.

You may wish to consider complaining to the estate agent in writing or changing to a different estate agent.

Gazumping

The seller may accept an offer for their house and then inform you as the buyer that they have been offered a higher price by someone else. This is known as 'gazumping'. You may decide to offer a higher price in order to try and secure the house but there is no guarantee that you will not be gazumped again. There is nothing illegal about gazumping and the purchase price of a house is only legally settled when contracts are exchanged. You may, however, have entered into an agreement with the seller that the seller will not consider other offers during a set period before the exchange of contracts. If such an agreement exists, and you are gazumped during this period, you will be able to sue the seller for breach of contract.

Lenders

You are having difficulty in getting a mortgage

As the buyer, you may be having difficulty in getting a mortgage – for example, your salary is not enough or the property is unusual. Different lenders have different rules about giving mortgages and it may be worth your trying some other lenders.

The lender's valuation is less than the purchase price of the house

The lender may decide that the security value of the house is less than the amount that you have agreed to pay for it. This means that the lender will not lend as much money as you had requested. You may therefore try to negotiate a lower price with the seller. If the seller will not drop the price and you still want to go ahead with the purchase, you may have to borrow the difference from elsewhere if you do not have the extra money available.

If the seller will not lower the price, or you cannot pay the difference, you may consider if another lender would give the house a higher valuation.

There are delays in getting a mortgage offer

There may be a delay in the lender making a formal mortgage offer to you. Until the mortgage offer is made, contracts cannot be exchanged. You should contact the lender to find out if there is any reason for the delay – for example, if the lender is waiting for salary details from your employer. It may be possible for you to do something about the problem, such as contacting your employer yourself.

Offers

The offer to buy is withdrawn

The buyer may withdraw the offer they have made before contracts are exchanged. Until contracts are exchanged, the buyer is under no legal obligation to buy the home and does not have to pay for any of the costs that you, as the seller, may have incurred. However, you may wish to ask the buyer to contribute towards these costs.

The price offered is reduced

The buyer may decide to reduce the offer they have made for the house. If they do this before contracts are exchanged it is up to you as the seller to decide whether or not you want to accept this lower offer. However, once contracts have been exchanged the buyer is legally committed to paying the price stated in the contract. If they try to drop the price at this stage, you do not have to accept this lower price. If the sale is not then completed, the buyer will forfeit the 10 per cent deposit they paid when contracts were exchanged and you could also sue the buyer for any additional loss.

The seller withdraws their acceptance of the offer

The seller may withdraw their acceptance of the offer any time before contracts are exchanged – for example, if they have found another buyer or have decided not to sell. There is nothing you as the buyer can do about this but you could ask the seller for a contribution towards any costs you have incurred, for example survey fees.

The seller accepts more than one offer (contract race)

The seller may accept more than one offer and instruct their solicitor to send draft contracts to more than one potential buyer. The solicitor must inform all potential buyers that more than one contract has been sent out and that the first contract that is returned, signed and ready for exchange will get the house. This is known as a contract race and is quite legal. There is nothing you as the buyer can do except withdraw if you do not want to incur the necessary costs in getting the contract completed quickly.

Property

The buyer is dissatisfied with the state the property was left in

As the buyer, you may be dissatisfied with the state of the property when you move in – for example, it is dirty. There is nothing you can do about this because the seller is under no legal obligation to leave the house in a clean state. However, the seller is under an obligation to empty the house of all their furniture and belongings. If some belongings have been left in the house you should ask the seller to remove them. If the seller cannot or will not remove the items you will have to arrange to have them moved. Moving the items may cost you money and you could try to recover this from the seller. However, if the seller refuses to cover the costs you may have to take them to court to recover the money and this is unlikely to be worthwhile.

The seller's property is worth less than they paid for it (negative equity)

As the seller, you may find that the value of your house has dropped since you bought it. This may mean that if you sell it at its current value you will still owe money to your lender. This is called 'negative equity'.

There are a number of different schemes that have been designed to help someone with negative equity. For example, it may be possible to transfer the existing mortgage to a new property rather than pay it off and take out a new one. Different lenders will offer different schemes and you should discuss the situation with your lender.

Furniture and fittings have been removed

The seller must leave all the fixtures – for example, a fireplace – and any fittings that they agreed would either be included in the sale or paid for separately – for example, fitted carpets. If, as the buyer, you find that something has been removed you should check with your solicitor or licensed conveyancer whether or not the item should have been left. The solicitor or licensed conveyancer may be able to resolve the problem.

The property has been damaged between exchange and completion

A house may be damaged after contracts have been exchanged but before the sale is completed – for example, there might be a burst pipe or a broken window. It is the seller's responsibility to inform the buyer of any damage. It is, however, the buyer's responsibility to insure the property from the date of exchange of contracts and to have the repairs carried out. The buyer will then have to make a claim on their insurance policy.

Solicitors and conveyancing

There are delays in conveyancing

As the buyer or seller, you may think that there is an unreasonable delay in the conveyancing. You should find out from your solicitor or licensed conveyancer the reason for any delay. If the delay is unreasonable you should take this up with the **Consumer Complaints Service** (CSS) at the Law Society (01926 820082; www.lawsociety.org.uk) or the **Council of Licensed Conveyancers** (01245 349599).

The solicitor is not passing on the interest on the deposit

When a buyer pays a deposit on a property, this is held by the seller's solicitor or licensed conveyancer. Any interest earned on the deposit during the period is kept by the solicitor or licensed conveyancer and should be passed on to the seller at completion. The seller may need to ask for the interest as it is not always passed on. If the solicitor or licensed conveyancer refuses to pass on the interest, the seller should take this up with the **Consumer Complaints Service** (CSS) at the Law Society (01926 820082; www.lawsociety.org.uk) or the **Council of Licensed Conveyancers** (01245 349599).

The bill for the conveyancing is too high

If you, as the buyer or seller, think that the solicitor's or licensed conveyancer's bill is too high, you should not pay the bill but should first check that all the various costs are clearly itemized. You should ask the solicitor or licensed conveyancer to explain anything you do not understand. If you are still not satisfied with the amount of the bill, you may wish to consider taking further action against the solicitor or complaining to the **Consumer Complaints Service** (CSS) at the Law Society (01926 820082; www.lawsociety.org.uk) or the **Council of Licensed Conveyancers** (01245 349599).

You think your solicitor or licensed conveyancer has been negligent

As the buyer, you may think that the solicitor or licensed conveyancer has been negligent. For example, after the sale has been completed, you may discover there is a problem with the boundary wall or there is a road-widening scheme that will reduce the size of the garden, and this might mean that the value of your house is reduced. If this happens and you want compensation, you should seek legal advice about suing the conveyancer.

If you have a complaint regarding poor service or behaviour, you should follow any internal complaints procedures of the firm concerned. If you are not happy with the outcome you should complain about a solicitor to the **Consumer Complaints Service** (CSS) at the Law Society (01926 820082; www.lawsociety.org.uk). You will need to contact the CCS within six months of the end of the work your solicitor did for you, or within six months of your solicitor's final response to your complaint.

If you want to complain about a licensed conveyancer, you should contact the **Council of Licensed Conveyancers** (01245 349599).

Surveys and valuations

Carrying out the survey and/or valuation

If you are selling your property, a potential buyer will usually want a valuer and/or surveyor to inspect the property. You will have to allow the valuer/surveyor to look round the property if you want the sale to go ahead.

The circumstances in which a surveyor or valuer can be held legally responsible for any financial loss suffered by the buyer as a result of the survey or valuation are limited.

RENTING A HOME

Homelessness

Local authorities have a legal duty to provide help to certain people who are homeless or threatened with homelessness. You will qualify for help if you are 'eligible for assistance'. You also have to be legally homeless or threatened with homelessness, in priority need and not intentionally homeless. The local authority may also investigate whether you have a local connection with the area.

Local social services authorities also have responsibility for some homeless people. They have a duty to provide accommodation for children and young people over 16 who are leaving care, or who are in need for other reasons.

Local authority accommodation

If you are looking for local authority accommodation you should first check whether you qualify. Many people from abroad – for example, most asylum seekers and people who have spent significant time living away from the UK, even if they are UK citizens – do not qualify for housing. The rules on who can qualify for local authority housing are complicated, especially if you have just arrived in, or returned to, the UK from abroad.

Most local authorities have a housing register or waiting list of people who have applied to rent local authority accommodation. This is usually the only way you can apply for local authority accommodation.

Local authorities use different systems to give priority to applicants on their waiting lists. How priorities are allocated varies from one local authority to another, but factors normally taken into account will be:

- poor health made worse by housing conditions;
- lack of or shared use of some facility – for example, a bathroom or toilet;
- an inadequate number of bedrooms for the size of your family;
- length of time you have lived in the area;
- age (where access to sheltered or warden-supported accommodation is under consideration);
- length of time on the waiting list;
- separation from your family (including a family that is overseas) because of inadequate accommodation;
- homelessness – see *Homelessness*, p. 122.

Once accepted on a local authority waiting list, you may have to wait a long time before you are offered accommodation. Your local authority should be able to give you a rough idea of how long you will have to wait. You should make sure that you keep them informed of any changes likely to affect your application – for example, changes in the number or ages of your children. You may also have to renew your application regularly.

When you are made an offer, it may be accommodation owned by the local authority or by a housing association. In an area where the local authority's housing has all been transferred to a housing association, this may be the only option offered.

You will usually only be able to turn the offer down if it is unsuitable for your needs – for example, if you are disabled and there is no lift. However, there is usually a limit to the number of offers a local authority will make.

Housing associations

Housing associations are 'not-for-profit' organizations that provide housing for rent. There are many housing associations providing a range of accommodation. Some provide housing for certain types of people – for example, single parents or disabled people. Others provide general housing in the same way as a local authority.

Only some housing associations accept direct applications. Most require you to be nominated by the local authority, which means that you will need to apply to go on the local authority waiting list and ask to be nominated. Where a housing association does not insist on this, it may require that you are nominated by a local agency, for example an advice agency or the social services department. If a housing association does accept direct applications, the criteria each has for selecting tenants will vary.

In some areas the housing associations and local authority have joint waiting lists. This means you can register with the local authority and housing associations on the same form.

Home swap and home mobility schemes

HOMES (020 7963 0200; www.homes.org.uk) runs a number of national schemes that help people who want to move from one part of the UK to another.

The **HOMES mobility scheme** is a scheme that allows a local authority or housing association to nominate a tenant, or someone on its waiting list, to another local authority or housing association. If you are a local authority or housing association tenant, your landlord can decide to do this without asking you, but you can also ask to be nominated and can check the progress of your nomination regularly.

You can ask to be nominated if:

- you need to move into another area to take up a new job;
- you need to be nearer to friends or relatives so that you can give them support, or because you need support from them;

- you have other special reasons, for example if you have been a victim of domestic violence or racial harassment.

If you want to apply for the HOMES mobility scheme, you should contact your housing officer, explaining your reasons for wanting to move and saying where you want to move to.

The **Homeswap** scheme is designed to help local authority and housing association tenants exchange their home for another local authority or housing association home. You can register your details on a computer database, to be matched up with a tenant in the area to which you want to move. You can also view a copy of the Homeswap register at your housing office, and contact any tenant on it who is looking for an exchange. Contact HOMES (020 7963 0200; www.homes.org.uk) for more information.

Who can help find rented accommodation

Help the Aged (020 7253 0253; www.helptheaged.org.uk) produces a number of free publications giving advice about housing matters for older people, including one on care homes.

The **Shelternet** website (www.shelternet.org.uk) provides information about a range of housing options, including help for homeless people, private renting and home ownership.

Housing advice centres can offer advice and information about all aspects of housing. Some are run by local authorities while others are run by voluntary organizations. Details of independent housing advice centres are available in England from **Shelter** (020 7505 2000 or 0800 446441; www.shelter.org.uk) or in Wales from **Shelter Cymru** (01792 469400; www.sheltercymru.org.uk).

Shelter also operates a 24-hour freephone service (0808 800 4444) for anyone with a housing problem. The service is available via minicom and textphone, and a special translation service can be provided where necessary.

Accommodation agencies

An accommodation agency may be able to help you find accommodation owned by a private landlord. If you register with an agency you will be asked about the type of property you are looking for and how much rent you are willing to pay. You will normally be asked to give details of your job and income, and may also be asked to provide references from your employer, bank, and present or previous landlord.

When you register with an accommodation agency, it is only legally allowed to charge a fee when it finds you somewhere to live. Once you have signed a contract to accept the tenancy of a property, the fee the agency can charge is unlimited. As part of their fees, some agencies are allowed to include an administrative charge for preparing a tenancy agreement, making an inventory, and other costs of setting up a tenancy agreement.

It is against the law for an agency to ask for payment for:

- putting your name on its list or taking your details;
- providing a list of properties available for renting;
- a deposit that will be returned if no suitable accommodation is found.

If you are offered accommodation by an agency, you should inspect the property before accepting it and ensure you have full details about:

- the terms of the tenancy agreement;
- the amount of rent you will have to pay, and whether it includes any services, fuel and water charges;
- how much rent you will have to pay in advance;
- whether you will have to pay a premium and/or a security deposit and, if so, how much;
- whether the property has a mortgage. You can lose your accommodation if the property is repossessed due to the landlord's failure to keep up mortgage payments.
- the name and address of the landlord.

Where possible, you should use an agency that has signed up to the National Approved Letting Scheme (01242 581712; www.nalscheme.co.uk). Agencies belonging to this scheme have agreed to follow a set of standards that include a complaints procedure.

Organizations that belong to this scheme include the National Association of Estate Agents (01926 496800; www.naea.co.uk), the Royal Institution of Chartered Surveyors (0870 333 1600; www.rics.org), and the Association of Residential Letting Agents (0845 345 5752; www.arla.co.uk). These organizations will insist that member agencies keep deposits paid by tenants in a separate 'client account'.

An accommodation agency can refuse to register you. It may do this, for example, because:

- you are unemployed;
- you are on benefits;
- you are looking for accommodation for a family;
- of your sexual orientation.

If you experience discrimination for these reasons, you may be able to take action under human rights law. You should get specialist advice.

In most circumstances, it is illegal for an accommodation agency to discriminate on grounds of disability, race or gender, even where a landlord has said that they do not want a tenant of a particular race or gender, or with a disability. The only exception to this rule is where a landlord rents out a small property and lives on the premises, sharing some of the accommodation with their tenants.

Tenancy agreements

A tenancy agreement is a contract between you and your landlord. It may be written or oral. The tenancy agreement gives certain rights to both you and your landlord – for example, your right to occupy the accommodation and your landlord's right to receive rent for letting the accommodation.

You and your landlord may have made arrangements about the tenancy, and these will be part of the tenancy agreement as long as they do not conflict with law. Both you and your landlord have rights and responsibilities given by law. The tenancy agreement can give both you and your landlord more than your statutory rights, but cannot give you less than your statutory rights. If a term in the tenancy agreement gives either you or your landlord less than your statutory rights, that term cannot be enforced.

The tenancy agreement is a form of consumer contract and as such it must be in plain language that is clear and easy to understand. It must not contain any terms that could be 'unfair'. This means, for example, that the tenancy agreement must not put either you or your landlord in a disadvantageous position, enable one party to change terms unilaterally without a valid reason or irrevocably bind you to terms with which you have had no time to become familiar. An unfair term is not valid in law and cannot be enforced.

A tenancy agreement can be made up of:

- *'express'* terms. These include what is in the written tenancy agreement, if there is one, what is in the rent book, and/or what was agreed orally.

- *'implied'* terms. These are rights given by law or arrangements established by custom and practice.

'Express' terms of tenancy agreements

Most tenants do not have a right in law to a written tenancy agreement. However, social landlords like local authorities and housing associations give written tenancy agreements as a matter of good practice.

If you have a written agreement, it should indicate the type of tenancy you have. The tenancy agreement should be signed by both you and your landlord. Each tenant, if there are joint tenants, should receive a copy of the agreement.

Your landlord is obliged by law to give their address.

It is good practice for a written tenancy agreement to include the following details:

- your name and your landlord's name and the address of the property that is being let;
- the date the tenancy began;
- whether other people are allowed the use of the property, and if so, which rooms;
- the duration of the tenancy – that is, whether it runs out on a certain date;
- the amount of rent payable, how often and when it should be paid, and how often and when it can be increased. The agreement could also state what the payment includes, for example Council Tax or fuel.
- whether your landlord will provide any services – for example, laundry, maintenance of common parts or meals – and whether there are service charges for these;
- the length of notice you and your landlord need to give if the tenancy is to be ended. Note that there are statutory rules about how much notice should be given and these will depend on the type of tenancy and why it is due to end.

The agreement may also contain details of your landlord's obligations to repair the property, although it is rare for agreements to go into details. Your landlord's obligations to repair depend on the type of tenancy.

A tenancy agreement exists even if there is only an oral agreement between you and your landlord. For example, you and your landlord may have agreed at the start of the tenancy how much the rent would be and when it is payable, whether it includes fuel and bills such as water rates or whether your landlord can decide who else can live in the accommodation. Oral agreements can be difficult to enforce because there is often no proof of what has been agreed, or a particular problem may have arisen that the agreement did not cover.

'Implied' terms of tenancy agreements

There are obligations you and your landlord have that may not be set down in the agreement but which are given by law and are implied in all tenancy agreements. These terms form part of the contract, even though they have not been specifically agreed between your landlord and you.

Some of the most common implied terms are:

- that your landlord must carry out basic repairs;
- that your landlord must keep the installations for the supply of water, gas, electricity, sanitation, space heating and heating water in good working order;
- your right to live peacefully in the accommodation without nuisance from your landlord;
- your obligation to take proper care of the accommodation.

Rights given by law will vary according to the type of tenancy.

What documents and information the tenant must receive

By law, as a tenant, you must be given the following information:

- if you have a weekly tenancy (not a fixed-term or monthly tenancy), your landlord must provide a rent book or similar document. Your landlord commits a criminal offence if they fail to do so.
- your landlord's address;
- if you do not know the name of your landlord, you can make a written request to the person who receives the rent for the full name and address of your landlord. The agent must supply you with this information in writing within twenty-one days, after which they commit an offence.
- if the tenancy is an assured shorthold that started on or after 28 February 1997, your landlord must provide basic written terms of the agreement within twenty-eight days of your requesting this in writing.

PRIVATE SECTOR TENANCIES

Different types of tenancy agreements

Because of changes to housing law, the kind of tenancy agreement you have, and the rights that you and your landlord have under that agreement, depend on when the agreement was made. Understanding what those rights are can be complicated.

The tenancy began on or after 15 January 1989 but before 28 February 1997

If your tenancy is a private or housing association tenancy that began on or after 15 January 1989 but before 28 February 1997, you may be:

- an assured tenant;
- an assured shorthold tenant;
- an occupier with basic protection (see *Occupiers with basic protection*, p. 133).

Assured tenants

An assured tenant will not normally have a resident landlord and the landlord will not provide food or services. As an assured tenant, you will be paying rent for accommodation that you occupy as your only or principal home.

You are not an assured tenant if your accommodation is:

- a student let;
- a holiday let;
- a company let;
- business premises;
- a Crown tenancy;
- private accommodation arranged by the local authority because you are homeless.

As an assured tenant you have the right to stay in your accommodation unless your landlord can convince the court there are good reasons for eviction – for example, rent arrears or damage to the property – or that another of the terms of the agreement has been broken.

As an assured tenant you can enforce your rights – for instance, to get repairs done – without worrying about getting evicted.

As well as the right to stay in your home as long as you keep to the terms of the tenancy you will also have other rights by law including:

- the right to have the accommodation kept in a reasonable state of repair;
- the right of a partner of the opposite sex to take over the tenancy on your death (the right of 'succession').

Assured shorthold tenants (before 28 February 1997)

You will be an assured shorthold tenant if your tenancy is for a fixed period of not less than six months.

This is a less secure type of tenancy than an assured tenancy. After the fixed period ends, your landlord can apply to the court for possession as long as they have given two months' notice. If your landlord does not renew the agreement, you can stay on until your landlord serves notice that they want to repossess the property.

If you were not given a Notice of an Assured Shorthold Tenancy, or were given it after the tenancy started, you are an assured tenant.

You are not an assured shorthold tenant if the accommodation:

- is a holiday let;
- is a company let;
- is rented by you and you are a student from a university or college;
- is private temporary accommodation in which you are housed because you are homeless;
- has a resident landlord;
- is accommodation for which you pay no rent.

As an assured shorthold tenant you have the right to stay in the accommodation until the fixed term ends unless your landlord can convince the court there are reasons for eviction – for example, rent arrears or damage to property, or that one of the other terms of the agreement has been broken. You can stay on after the end of the fixed term, even if the agreement is not renewed, until your landlord gives you notice.

As an assured shorthold tenant you can enforce your rights – for instance, to get repairs done – but if you do, your landlord may decide not to renew the tenancy agreement at the end of the fixed term.

As well as the right to stay in your home for the fixed period as long as you keep to the terms of the tenancy, you will also have other legal rights including:

- the right to have the accommodation kept in a reasonable state of repair;
- the right to carry out minor repairs yourself and the right to deduct the cost from the rent;
- the right of a partner of the opposite sex to take over the tenancy on your death (the right of 'succession').

You may have a written tenancy agreement that may give you more rights than the minimum provided by law.

The tenancy began on or after 28 February 1997

Any new tenancy created on or after this date will automatically be an assured shorthold tenancy, unless:

- you are an occupier with basic protection (see below for more information);
- it was created following a contract made before 28 February 1997; *or*
- your landlord serves a notice on you stating that the tenancy is to be an assured tenancy; *or*
- there is a clause in the tenancy agreement stating that it is to be an assured tenancy; *or*
- the tenancy is one created by the death of a former protected tenant (see below for more information about protected tenancies); *or*
- the tenancy was previously a secure tenancy and became an assured tenancy.

This list of exceptions is not exhaustive. Only the most important exceptions are given.

If the tenancy is not an assured shorthold tenancy for one of the reasons given above, it will be an assured tenancy. Assured shorthold tenancies created on or after 28 February 1997 do not have to have a fixed-term period at the beginning of the tenancy, although your landlord may give a fixed term if they want. No written agreement or notice is needed to create an assured shorthold tenancy on or after 28 February 1997. An oral agreement is sufficient.

You will have the same rights as other assured tenants whose tenancy began before 28 February 1997 but after 15 January 1989.

However, there is one additional right to a statement from your landlord of the terms of the agreement. Your landlord must provide a written statement of the basic terms of the tenancy that are not already provided in writing. Failure to provide the statement is a criminal offence.

The tenancy began before 15 January 1989

If your tenancy began before 15 January 1989 you could be either:

- a protected tenant; *or*
- an occupier with basic protection.

Protected tenants

If you are a protected tenant you will:

- be paying rent for the accommodation; *and*
- not normally have a resident landlord; *and*
- not be provided with food or services by your landlord.

You will not be a protected tenant if your accommodation is:

- a bed and breakfast letting;
- a 'company' let.

Protected tenants have the strongest rights of any private tenants. As a protected tenant you have the following rights:

- security of tenure. Your landlord can only repossess the accommodation in certain specified circumstances.
- the right to have the rent fixed by the rent officer;
- the right to have rent increased only in certain circumstances;
- the right to have the accommodation kept in a reasonable state of repair;
- the right of a partner or another family member to take over the tenancy on your death.

Occupiers with basic protection
If you are not an assured tenant, assured shorthold tenant, or protected tenant, you may be what is called an occupier with basic protection. You may have basic protection if you have:

- a 'company' let (where a company holds the tenancy and provides accommodation for you as a member of staff);
- a student let granted by an educational institution;
- a resident landlord who does not share living accommodation with you, the accommodation is your landlord's only or main home and your landlord has been living there since the tenancy began and lives there when the tenancy ends. If your landlord shares living accommodation with you, you will not have basic protection – see *The right to stay in accommodation*, p. 137.
- accommodation provided by the Crown or a government department;
- accommodation provided by some housing co-ops and almshouses;
- accommodation provided by your employer in order for you to carry out your job. If you occupy accommodation because of your job (for example, a launderette assistant or a caretaker) you may not necessarily have to give up the accommodation if you leave the job.

The above list is not exhaustive.

Deposits and premiums

There are two types of deposit that you may be asked to pay by a landlord or an accommodation agency acting on their behalf. They are a holding deposit and a security deposit.

Holding deposits

A holding deposit is money a landlord or accommodation agency asks you to pay when you agree to rent a property but have not yet taken up the tenancy. This deposit will probably be deducted from the security deposit you pay when you move into the property.

Before making any payment, you should be sure you want to take up the tenancy as a holding deposit cannot be returned unless you are unable to move in for reasons beyond your control. Examples of this are if the landlord asks for more rent than was originally agreed, or the accommodation is not ready on the date the tenancy is due to begin.

Security deposits

A security deposit is money paid to a landlord (or an accommodation agency acting on their behalf) as security against, for example, rent arrears, damage to property or removal of furniture.

If you are asked to pay a security deposit you should check the condition of the property and its contents carefully. This is because, when the tenancy ends, you may be held responsible for anything that is missing or damaged, and may lose all or some of your deposit.

When a tenancy ends, the security deposit should be returned to you. It is reasonable for deductions to be made to cover, for example, damage to

---

I paid a deposit when I moved into my rented house. I have now moved out but the landlord will not return the deposit. What can I do?

A deposit is usually paid to a landlord or letting agency at the start of the tenancy. When the tenancy ends the landlord or agent should inspect the property and can make deductions from the deposit for any reasonable losses, such as rent arrears, damage to the property or furniture, or missing items.

Deductions should not be made for fair wear and tear.

If the landlord does not return the deposit or you disagree with the amount that has been deducted, you should try to negotiate. If that does not succeed, then consider taking court action against the landlord.

the property or furniture, missing items listed on the inventory, or outstanding rent you owe.

Premiums

A landlord can charge you a premium, or 'key money', for granting a tenancy. There is no limit on what can be asked by a landlord. If the amount appears unreasonable, you have no choice other than not to take the accommodation.

Rent deposit guarantee schemes

Some local authorities, housing associations and charities offer loans to pay a deposit of a month's rent on a private flat. Most schemes operate by lending the rent in advance, which you repay to the scheme. This may be through Housing Benefit. Most schemes guarantee to pay for any damage to the accommodation at the end of the tenancy.

You can get information about rent deposit guarantee schemes from the **National Rent Deposit Forum** (0121 616 5067; www.nrdf.org.uk). For details of local schemes, you should contact your local authority housing department.

Fixing and increasing the rent

Assured tenants

As an assured tenant you must pay whatever rent you agreed with your landlord when the tenancy began. Your landlord cannot normally increase the rent unless you agree or the tenancy agreement allows it. If the tenancy agreement allows your landlord to increase the rent, it should contain information about when and how the rent can be increased.

If a rent increase has not been agreed with your landlord, or if the tenancy agreement does not allow an increase, you may have the right to appeal to a local Rent Assessment Committee if you think the rent increase proposed by your landlord is too high. You can only do so if your tenancy is not fixed-term (that is, it does not run for a specific period only, for example six months or a year) and if your landlord uses a special procedure to increase the rent. If the tenancy agreement allows the rent increases, you cannot apply to a Rent Assessment Committee. Also, a Rent Assessment Committee can set a rent that is higher than that proposed by your landlord.

If you cannot afford to pay your rent, you may be able to apply for

Housing Benefit. You may also be entitled to other benefits if you are unemployed or on a low income.

Assured shorthold tenants

As an assured shorthold tenant you must pay whatever rent you agreed with your landlord when the tenancy began.

Your rent cannot normally be increased unless you agree or the tenancy agreement allows it.

In certain cases, your landlord can instead use a special procedure to increase the rent, which involves giving you a formal notice whose details are set down by legislation. It is in theory possible for certain types of assured shorthold tenant to appeal to a Rent Assessment Committee as assured tenants, but assured shorthold tenants have very little protection from eviction, and antagonizing your landlord can put you at risk of losing your home.

If you cannot afford to pay your rent, you may be able to apply for Housing Benefit. You may also be entitled to other benefits if you are unemployed or on a low income.

Protected tenants

As a protected tenant you must pay the rent you agreed with your landlord when the tenancy began. However, either you or your landlord can subsequently ask the Rent Officer to fix a 'fair rent'.

Your landlord cannot increase your rent if it has been registered as a fair rent by the Rent Officer. If no fair rent has been registered, your landlord cannot increase the rent unless you agree formally in writing, or either you or your landlord apply to the Rent Officer and the Rent Officer fixes a fair rent.

If you cannot afford to pay your rent, you may be able to apply for Housing Benefit. You may also be entitled to other benefits if you are unemployed or on a low income.

Occupiers with basic protection

As a tenant with basic protection you must pay the rent you agreed with your landlord when you moved into the accommodation. You cannot apply to the Rent Officer or to the Rent Assessment Committee to have the rent reduced. If your landlord wants to increase the rent you could try and negotiate. If you refuse to pay the increase this could lead to your landlord evicting you.

> ## I rent my flat privately and the landlord wants to increase the rent. Can he do this?
>
> It all depends on the type of tenancy agreement that you have. If your tenancy is for a fixed term (for example, six months) the rent cannot be increased during the fixed term unless the agreement states that it can, or you agree to the increase. When the fixed term ends, the landlord may ask you to sign a new tenancy agreement which charges a higher rent.
>
> If your tenancy is not for a fixed term, the landlord can charge a higher rent if you agree, or if the agreement allows for this, or by giving you the correct written notice. If the agreement allows for an increase, it should say when and how this should happen, for example annually.
>
> In some cases you can appeal against an increase if you think the amount of the increase is too much or if you think the notice of the increase was not issued correctly. If you start to pay the increased amount this means you have agreed to it and you cannot appeal against it.
>
> Some tenants have very little protection against eviction and could risk losing their homes if they disagree with the landlord about the amount of rent to be paid. If you cannot afford to pay your rent, remember you may be able to claim Housing Benefit.

The right to stay in accommodation

Your right to stay in the accommodation will depend on the type of tenancy you have.

Protected and assured tenants

Your landlord can only repossess the property if they can convince the court that there are reasons why you should be evicted – for example, you have rent arrears, you have damaged the property or you have broken one of the terms of the agreement.

Assured shorthold tenants

Tenancy began before 28 February 1997

As an assured shorthold tenant you have the right to stay in the accommodation for the duration of the initial fixed term unless you breach a term in the tenancy agreement or, for example, you are in rent arrears, or you have damaged the property.

If you stay in the home after the initial fixed term ends and your landlord does not intend to renew the agreement and wants possession, they will have to give you at least two months' notice to leave the property and will have to go to court for possession of the property if you do not leave. If your landlord takes no action you will become a statutory periodic assured shorthold tenant and your landlord will not be able to regain possession of the property without going through this procedure.

Tenancies created on or after 28 February 1997

Your landlord cannot evict you during the first six months of the tenancy, or during the initial fixed term, whichever is the longer, unless they have grounds for doing so, as for tenancies created before 28 February 1997.

At the end of this period your landlord can automatically get a court order to evict you, as for tenancies created before 28 February 1997.

Occupiers with basic protection

If you are a tenant with basic protection and you do not move out when your landlord has given you notice to quit and the notice period has expired, your landlord has to go to court for a possession order. This will normally be granted. If the tenancy is for a specified fixed term (for example, it is agreed that it lasts for six months or a year), your landlord does not have to give you notice to quit at the end of that term. However, your landlord still has to apply for a possession order to evict you. They can only apply once the fixed term has ended.

PUBLIC SECTOR TENANCIES

You are a public sector tenant if you are a tenant of:

- a local authority: these are district councils and London borough councils; *or*
- a Housing Action Trust (HAT); *or*
- a housing association (if the tenancy began before 15 January 1989); *or*
- a housing co-operative (if the tenancy began before 15 January 1989).

If you are a tenant of one of the above bodies you will be a secure tenant. However, HAT and local authority tenants may be introductory tenants for the first twelve months that they occupy their property.

If you are a housing association or housing co-operative tenant and your tenancy began on or after 15 January 1989, you will be an *assured* tenant.

Rights of secure tenants

As a secure tenant you have the right to stay in the accommodation unless your landlord can convince the court that there are special reasons to evict you – for example, if you have rent arrears, have damaged property or broken some other term of the agreement.

As a secure tenant you can enforce your rights – for example, to get repairs done – without worrying about being evicted. As well as the right to stay in your home as long as you keep to the terms of the tenancy, you will also have other rights by law, such as to sublet with your landlord's permission and for a resident member of your family to take over the tenancy on your death (the right of 'succession').

You will usually have a written tenancy agreement that may give you more rights than those set out above.

As a secure tenant you also have the right to complain to an ombudsman about certain problems. If you are a local authority tenant this will be the Local Government Ombudsman. If you are a housing association tenant it will be the Housing Ombudsman.

Rights of assured tenants

As an assured tenant you have the right to stay in your accommodation unless your landlord can convince the court there are good reasons for eviction – for example rent arrears or damage to the property, or that another of the terms of the agreement has been broken.

As an assured tenant you can enforce your rights – for instance, to get repairs done – without worrying about getting evicted.

As well as the right to stay in your home as long as you keep to the terms of the tenancy you will also have other rights by law including:

- the right to have the accommodation kept in a reasonable state of repair;
- the right of a partner of the opposite sex to take over the tenancy on your death ('the right of succession').

Fixing and increasing the rent

Secure tenants

Local authority tenancies
Rents for local authority tenants are fixed according to the local authority's housing policy and the amount of money it gets from central government. You cannot control the amount of rent payable, but may be able to claim Housing Benefit to help pay it.

Housing association and housing co-operative tenancies that began before 15 January 1989
The housing association or co-operative will usually have had the rent registered as a fair rent by the Rent Officer.

Once a rent has been registered, a new rent cannot usually be considered for the accommodation for two years. The rent can only be increased if:

- you ask for a new fair rent assessment after two years;
- your landlord asks for a new fair rent assessment after one year and nine months, although any new rent would not become effective until the end of two years.

An application for a rent increase can be made earlier, but only if the tenancy has changed drastically or if you and your landlord apply together.

If you need help paying the rent you may be able to claim Housing Benefit.

Assured tenants

Housing association or housing co-operative tenancies that began on or after 15 January 1989
As a housing association tenant whose tenancy started on or after 15 January 1989 your rent is the rent you agreed to pay your landlord at the beginning of the tenancy. It should be covered in your tenancy agreement. The tenancy agreement should also state when and how the rent can be increased. Registered social landlords must follow standards and procedures set down by the Housing Corporation. They should try to set rents that are affordable to people in low-paid employment. They should also provide each tenant with information on their policies, including those for setting rents. This information is often in the form of a handbook.

There is also a model tenancy agreement for registered social landlords' assured tenants, produced by the National Housing Federation, which says that assured tenants' rents should not be increased more than once a year.

If your tenancy agreement does not cover rent increases, you have the right to apply to a Rent Assessment Committee if you do not agree to the increase. However, the Rent Assessment Committee may agree to the rent increase, or may set an increase that is higher than that proposed by your landlord.

The right to stay in accommodation

Secure tenants

As a secure tenant you have the right to stay in the accommodation as long as you keep to the terms of the tenancy agreement with your landlord. However, if the tenancy agreement is broken – for example, because of rent arrears or nuisance to neighbours – your landlord can serve a notice on you and apply to the county court for eviction.

A public sector landlord can only evict you if they give you the proper notice and if one of the 'grounds for possession' applies.

What constitutes 'grounds for possession' is complicated. The landlord must apply to the county court to seek possession of the property and a secure tenant can only be evicted if the court grants a possession order to the landlord.

Assured tenants

If a housing association or housing co-operative tenancy began after 15 January 1989 it will be an assured tenancy. There will usually be a model housing association tenancy agreement, giving similar rights to those of secure tenants. In order to evict you, the housing association will have to give proper notice that it is going to seek possession. The housing association will then have to obtain a possession order from the county court by proving that one of the 'grounds for possession' applies.

Introductory tenants

Some local authorities and Housing Action Trusts (HATs) make all new tenants introductory tenants for the first twelve months of the tenancy. Introductory tenants have some but not all of the rights of secure tenants.

At the end of the twelve months, provided there have been no possession proceedings against you, the introductory tenancy will be converted by your landlord to a secure tenancy.

It is very easy for a landlord to evict an introductory tenant.

COMMON PROBLEMS WITH TENANCIES

Sounds silly, but I don't know who my landlord is!

If you do not know the identity of the landlord, you can write to the person who last collected your rent asking for your landlord's full name and address. You should send this letter by recorded delivery and keep a copy. If the person to whom you have written does not reply within twenty-one days, this is a criminal offence. You can inform the Tenancy Relations Officer of the local authority, who can prosecute the person who has failed to provide the information.

Before contacting the Tenancy Relations Officer, you should consider whether this might provoke your landlord into retaliating with threats or attempted eviction.

If you need to find out your landlord's identity because of an emergency, such as a burst pipe, it may be quicker to inform the local authority of the emergency. The local authority has special powers to enter and carry out any necessary work, and can take steps to find out who your landlord is in order to recover its costs.

My landlord thinks he can come and go as he chooses. Can he do that?

Your landlord has a right to reasonable access to carry out repairs. What 'reasonable access' means depends on why your landlord needs to get access. For example, in an emergency, your landlord is entitled to immediate access to carry out any necessary work.

Your landlord also has a right to enter the property to inspect the state of repair, but they should always ask for your permission and should give you at least twenty-four hours' notice.

If you are staying in lodgings where it is agreed that your landlord provides a room-cleaning service or where you share a room with other lodgers, your landlord can enter without permission.

Your landlord does not have a right to enter in any other circumstances unless they have a court order.

We feel harassed by our landlord

It is an offence for your landlord to do anything that they know is likely to make you leave the home or prevent you from exercising your legal rights. This would include, for example, repeatedly disturbing you late at night or obstructing access to the home, creating noise, disconnecting supplies of water, gas or electricity where your landlord knows that this is likely to drive you out or discourage you from insisting on your legal rights.

If you are subjected to harassment, the matter should be reported to the Tenancy Relations Officer of the local authority or to the police.

We rent a house and want to take in a lodger or sub-tenant. Can we do that?

A lodger is someone who lives with the person who occupies the accommodation, is provided with meals and services (such as cleaning and provision of linen), and who may not have any separate accommodation of their own. A sub-tenant has their own separate accommodation (at least one room) and will not normally be provided with meals and services.

Secure tenants can take in lodgers without the landlord's permission. Some private tenants can take in lodgers without the landlord's permission, but you should seek the help of an experienced adviser before doing this.

As a local authority or housing association tenant you have to get your landlord's permission to sub-let part of your accommodation to sub-tenants, but your landlord cannot refuse unreasonably. Sub-letting all of the accommodation can be a ground for possession. This means your landlord can evict you.

In other cases, the right to sub-let depends on the tenancy agreement. If you are a private tenant you should seek your landlord's permission before sub-letting unless the tenancy agreement specifically allows this. There is no appeal against a private landlord's refusal to allow sub-letting.

Our landlord wants to bring in another tenant – the house is already overcrowded. What can we do?

A home is considered overcrowded if:

- there are more than the 'permitted number' of people living there (the 'permitted number' will depend on the size of the accommodation); *or*
- two or more people of the opposite sex aged 10 or over, who are not living together as husband and wife, have to sleep in the same room.

The local authority can, in certain circumstances, prosecute both the landlord and the occupier of an overcrowded dwelling.

If you are in privately rented accommodation and you are on the local authority housing register/waiting list, you should inform the housing department that you are living in overcrowded accommodation. If you are not on the housing register/waiting list you should apply to go on it. If you are living in local authority accommodation, you should inform the housing department of your situation and ask for a transfer.

We have just rented a flat as 'furnished' but it has very little furniture in it. How furnished does a furnished flat have to be?

If a property is let furnished, as a tenant you could expect a level of furnishing that would be reasonable to allow you to live in the accommodation. This would include:

- table and chairs in the kitchen/living room;
- sofa and/or armchairs in the living room;
- a bed and storage for clothes in each bedroom;
- heating appliances;
- curtains and floor coverings;
- a cooker, fridge, kitchen utensils and crockery.

If you think that the provision is not adequate, you can provide your own furniture, unless the tenancy agreement does not allow this.

If you are not happy with the condition of the furniture when you move in, you could consider discussing this with your landlord. Your landlord might agree to replace it. You could check what was listed in the inventory, if one exists, or tenancy agreement about the condition of the furniture.

Any furniture provided by your landlord must be fire resistant, unless the landlord is letting a room in their own home, or letting the whole home on a temporary basis.

All new and second-hand upholstered furniture sold should meet the fire safety regulations, and carry a label to say so. The labels should be permanently attached to a hidden part of the item. If a piece of furniture does not carry a label saying that it meets the regulations, it is likely that the item does not meet the regulations and must be replaced. The landlord is committing a criminal offence if the furniture does not meet the fire safety regulations.

The landlord is not providing the services we think she should be. Can we make her?

If the tenancy agreement specifies that your landlord should provide certain services – for example, gardening or lighting common parts – you must make them do so.

If your landlord is not providing the agreed services, or is providing an inadequate level of service, you may wish to negotiate with the landlord to enforce the agreement.

Who is responsible for repairing any damage to the property?

Your landlord is usually responsible for external and major structural repairs. You are usually responsible for internal decoration and for making sure that furniture and other contents, and fixtures and fittings, are not damaged because of your negligence.

You will not usually be responsible for making good any deterioration caused by 'fair wear and tear'. Your exact responsibilities will normally be described in the tenancy agreement.

You must take care of the property by doing the little jobs that can reasonably be expected of you – for example, unblocking drains and mending fuses.

You should also inform the landlord about any situation that could cause damage to the property, for example a leak in the roof.

If your landlord claims that you have damaged the property, they will normally keep all or part of any deposit you may have paid to cover the cost of damage.

Who is responsible for 'wear and tear'?

Over a period of time, most household furniture and contents deteriorate as a result of normal use – for example, floor coverings will become worn. This is known as 'wear and tear', and you would not be responsible for replacing these items.

If the extent of the wear and tear means that it causes a hazard – for example, springs in an armchair begin to stick through the upholstery – your landlord should repair or replace such items.

If your landlord has supplied an appliance such as a cooker or a washing machine that was working at the beginning of the tenancy, they have a responsibility to repair or replace it if it breaks down, unless this is the result of your negligence.

If there is damage or loss of furniture or contents, the cost may be covered by your landlord's or your own insurance.

The tenancy agreement may state who is liable for any damage or loss to contents. The liable person should consider arranging an insurance policy to cover this liability.

You are responsible for arranging insurance cover for any contents or possessions that you own.

Our landlord wants us to move out while he does repairs. Do we have to?

If your landlord wants to carry out improvements, they must either get your permission to enter the home and do the work, or get a court order authorizing them to take possession of the home. This also applies if the repairs are so extensive that they cannot be done unless you move out. Your landlord may have to provide alternative accommodation for you. If you do not want to move, your landlord has the power, in some circumstances, to apply to the county court to repossess the property.

If your landlord wants you to leave so that improvements or repairs can be done, you should not agree to this until you have obtained independent advice on your rights.

We think we are going to have trouble getting our deposit back at the end of the tenancy. What are the rules?

If you paid a deposit to your landlord at the start of a tenancy as security for any rent arrears or damage to property, this should be returned at the end of the tenancy if the accommodation has been left in good condition and there are no arrears.

If your landlord refuses to return the deposit or makes deductions, you should check the terms of the tenancy agreement or the agreed inventory (if there was one) to see what the deposit was supposed to cover. In cases of damage to property, it will often be cheaper for you to make good the damage before your landlord comes to inspect the property than for your landlord to charge for the cost of getting repairs done.

If your landlord persists in refusing to return a deposit, you could use the small claims procedure in the county court to try and get it back.

Can I keep a pet in my rented flat?

You can keep pets as long as it is not specifically forbidden in the tenancy agreement and it does not cause a nuisance to neighbours. However, you should normally seek your landlord's permission because, even if you have a legal right to keep pets, if your landlord does not approve they may seek to evict you for some other reason.

Can I pass my tenancy on to someone else?

Passing on a tenancy to someone else is called assignment. The rules about who can and who cannot assign tenancies are very complex.

When a tenant dies, there are rules that may allow the tenancy to be passed on to the tenant's partner or, sometimes, another member of the family who has been living with the tenant. These rules apply regardless of anything stated in a tenancy agreement. A tenancy agreement can increase the basic rights of a tenant, but it cannot take these rights away. The rules are different for different kinds of tenancy.

I left some property in my rented flat after I left and the landlord is being difficult about me getting it back.

Property you left behind still belongs to you and normally should be returned to you when you ask for it.

If you leave things behind when you give up a tenancy, your landlord may charge for the cost of clearing them out of the home.

ENDING A TENANCY

Tenancy ended by landlord

There are many rules that govern the notice needed to end a tenancy agreement. The rules cover the length of notice needed, the form in which it must be given and the dates on which it must take effect.

In most cases, your landlord has to serve a special notice on you before he can apply to the court for an order to evict you from your home (this is called a possession order). The rules vary depending on what kind of tenancy it is and, in some cases, more than one notice is needed.

If a private landlord wants to end a tenancy on the date the agreement expires, they must usually serve a notice conforming to special rules.

Tenancy ended by tenant

You generally have to give the same amount of notice as your landlord to end the tenancy agreement.

If you want to end a fixed-term agreement before it is due to expire, you can only do so with the permission of your landlord or if there is a term in the agreement that allows for this. Otherwise you may end up liable for the rent for the remainder of the time covered by the fixed-term agreement.

If you have given notice to your landlord and then change your mind and want to stay on, there are different rules on this for different kinds of tenancy.

If you leave without giving proper notice, your landlord may be entitled to charge rent up to the date when notice should have expired, or up to the end of the tenancy agreement if it is a fixed-term agreement and you did not give any notice at all.

However, your landlord is expected to re-let as soon as possible after they become aware that you have left, even if no notice was given. Your landlord can only charge you for any unavoidable loss of rent due to your early departure.

Facing eviction

How your landlord can evict you and get possession of the accommodation will depend on the type of tenancy you have.

Once your landlord or you have given notice, this does not necessarily mean you can be evicted. In nearly all cases a court order is needed, and further notice of court proceedings is often required. Whether the court will allow the eviction will depend on the kind of tenancy and the reasons for seeking eviction. However, in some cases a court order may not be necessary. For example, a court order for eviction is not needed to evict you from your home if you have a resident landlord and the tenancy started after 15 January 1989.

If your landlord has an order from the court giving them possession of the property, you do not have to leave until the date on the order.

If you are threatened with eviction you should always get advice.

REPAIRS

If you are living in rented property that is in an unsatisfactory condition, there are several ways of getting repairs or improvements done.

This is a very complex area of the law and trying to get a repair done may put a tenant at risk, so what action you take will depend on your housing security. It will also depend on which repair responsibilities are yours and which are your landlord's.

You should not stop paying your rent because of bad housing conditions. If you are in rent arrears, your landlord may take action to get you evicted.

The landlord's general responsibilities

By law, your landlord has a number of repairing responsibilities, including repairing and keeping in working order:

- the structure and exterior of the premises, including drains, gutters and external pipes;

- the water and gas pipes and electric wiring (including, for example, taps and sockets);
- the basins, sinks, baths and toilets;
- fixed heaters (for example, gas fires) and water heaters (but not gas or electric cookers).

Your landlord has these duties by law, no matter what is written in the tenancy agreement. However, if you ask your landlord to do these repairs they may attempt to regain possession of the property or not renew the agreement when it expires. Before attempting to use this general right to repairs you should consult an experienced adviser.

The tenancy agreement may specify additional repairing obligations.

Common parts
Your landlord is normally also responsible for repairs to common parts of the building – for example, stairways, lifts, hallways or garden paths shared with other tenants or your landlord.

Electrical and gas appliances
Your landlord is responsible for ensuring that any electrical appliances supplied with the accommodation are safe. This includes heaters, cookers, kettles, and any other electrical goods.

If you are concerned that an electrical appliance is not safe, you could contact the trading standards department of the local council.

Your landlord must also arrange and pay for safety checks on gas appliances and any necessary work to be carried out on appliances at least once every twelve months. The checks must be carried out by a person who is registered with the **Confederation of Registered Gas Installers** (0870 401 2300; www.corgi-gas-safety.com).

Your landlord must keep a record of inspection dates, any defects identified and any remedial action taken. You must be given a copy of this record.

If your landlord does not carry out regular inspections of gas appliances, or if they refuse to give you a copy of the inspection record, you could contact the local office of the Health and Safety Executive (HSE), which has a duty to enforce the safety requirements. The HSE also operates a special **Gas Safety Advice Line** (0800 300363 – 24-hour freephone).

Disabled tenants

As a disabled private tenant you may be able to have alterations carried out to your home. You will first have to get the need for the alterations assessed by the local authority social services department. Alterations could include the installation of a stair lift or hoist, or adaptation to a bathroom or toilet.

You may also be able to get a disabled facilities grant to make the home more suitable.

Local authorities' duties and unfit property

Local authorities have a duty to take action against private landlords, housing association landlords, or registered social landlords if:

- the condition of the property affects the health of the occupier – for example, if it is damp, infested with insects or has dangerous wiring; or
- the property causes a 'nuisance' to people living nearby – for example, if damp is coming into a person's property from next door, or if rotten windows may fall into the street and injure others.

This duty covers disrepair in common parts of blocks of flats, such as unhygienic rubbish chutes and noisy central heating.

If you think that the condition of the property is either affecting health or causing a nuisance, you should complain to the Environmental Health Department of the local authority. They must investigate and, if appropriate, give your landlord a notice instructing them to carry out the necessary repairs. If your landlord does not comply with the notice they could be prosecuted and the local authority can carry out the repair work itself.

These authorities also have a duty to take action against a private landlord, housing association landlord or a registered social landlord if the property does not meet certain housing standards and is 'unfit for human habitation'. A property must:

- be structurally stable; and
- be free from serious disrepair; and
- be free from dampness prejudicial to the health of the occupier; and
- have adequate heating, lighting and ventilation; and
- have an adequate supply of piped, wholesome water; and

- have satisfactory facilities for preparing and cooking food, including a sink with a satisfactory supply of hot and cold water; *and*
- have a suitably located toilet, for the exclusive use of the occupier; *and*
- have a suitable sewer and drainage system; *and*

The house I rent is very damp. I told the landlord but she has not done anything about it. What else can I do?

As a tenant, you have the right to have the structure of your home kept in good repair by the landlord. This includes some of the installations in the home such as heating and hot water systems. You will often be responsible yourself for repairs to internal decoration and for minor repairs such as a blocked sink. Details about repairs are usually set out in a written tenancy agreement that describes the landlord's and tenant's responsibilities. If you do not have a tenancy agreement the law may still give you some basic rights. However, you should always check what sort of tenancy agreement you have before you complain about housing conditions, as some landlords try to evict tenants who wish to enforce their legal rights to repair.

When you have decided that your repair should be done by the landlord, you must tell them about the repair that is needed. You should write out a description of the problem and collect evidence such as photographs, a report from environmental health officers, and medical reports if the disrepair is affecting your health or the health of someone in your household.

If the landlord still fails to carry out the work you could consider contacting the Environmental Health Department at your local authority, or you could take the landlord to court. If your landlord is a registered social landlord such as a housing association or is a private landlord, then the local authority may be able to force them to take action. If you are a tenant of the local authority itself, then you should make a complaint using the authority's complaints procedure.

You should carry on paying your rent while you try to get the repair work done, as your landlord may try to evict you if you have rent arrears.

- have a suitably located fixed bath or shower and hand basin, each of which has a satisfactory supply of hot and cold water for the exclusive use of the occupier.

If your property does not meet these standards, it will be declared unfit and your landlord will be ordered to do the necessary repairs. If your property cannot be repaired, the local authority may order that it is not to be occupied or that it is demolished. In this case, it will rehouse you.

'Right to repair' schemes

Tenants of local authorities and registered social landlords (including housing associations) can use 'right to repair' schemes to claim compensation for repairs that the landlord does not carry out within a set timescale.

If you are a tenant of a registered social landlord you are entitled to compensation if you report a repair or maintenance problem that affects your health, safety or security and your landlord fails twice to make the repair within the set timescale. There is a flat rate award, plus a daily rate up to a maximum amount, for each day the repair remains outstanding. A maximum cost for an eligible repair may be set by the individual landlord. You should contact your landlord for more details about the scheme.

Local authority tenants have a right to repair scheme similar to that of registered social landlord tenants. Under this right to repair scheme, if repairs are not carried out within a fixed timescale, you can notify the landlord that you want a different contractor to do the job. The local authority must appoint a new contractor and set another time limit. You can then claim compensation if the repair is not carried out within the new time limit.

As a local authority tenant you can currently use this 'right to repair' scheme for repairs that your landlord estimates would cost up to £250. You can also claim up to £50 compensation. There are twenty types of repairs that qualify for the scheme, including insecure doors, broken entry-phone systems, blocked sinks and leaking roofs.

A repair will not qualify for the scheme if the local authority has fewer than a hundred properties, is not responsible for the repair or decides it would cost more than £250.

Taking action about repairs

If you are a tenant thinking of taking action about disrepair in your home you should seek the advice of an experienced adviser, who will be able to advise you on the possible courses of action, including one or more of the following:

- negotiating with your landlord;
- using the law;
- using the Ombudsmen;
- campaigning with others.

Negotiating with the landlord

If you think your landlord has an obligation to carry out a repair you should first consult an experienced housing adviser to check whether you can try to have the repair done without risking losing your accommodation. An adviser will also be able to check whether your landlord is obliged by law to carry out the repair.

It may be worth trying to negotiate amicably with your landlord, even if they do not have a legal duty to carry out a repair.

It is also advisable to put a repair request down in writing. You should keep copies of letters written to your landlord.

If you are a tenant of a local authority, housing association or registered social landlord you should find out how long your landlord usually takes to carry out repairs. This may depend on the urgency of the repair. If your landlord refuses to do repairs or delays in carrying out agreed repairs, you should try to negotiate. You may need specialized help to do this. If negotiations fail, you may need to take legal action to enforce your rights to repair.

Using the law

There are a number of laws that cover your right to have your property repaired. These laws are very complex. In all cases, before starting legal action you will, in most cases, need an expert's report on the disrepair.

Private prosecutions

If you are affected by the poor condition of a property, you can take out a private prosecution against your landlord. If the prosecution is successful, your landlord will be ordered to do the repairs and will be guilty of a criminal offence if they do not carry them out. This is useful for local authority tenants, who may not be able to use other types of action against the local authority. However, criminal legal aid is not available to pay for your legal costs.

Civil court action

If a property is in poor condition, your landlord may have broken the tenancy agreement by failing to carry out repairs. Your tenancy agreement may include specific details of what repairs your landlord has agreed, either in writing or orally. In addition, even if there are no specific terms in the tenancy agreement, certain repairing responsibilities will be implied by legislation. If your landlord has broken the tenancy agreement, you can sue your landlord and, if successful, get a court order requiring your landlord to carry out the repairs. You may also be able to get compensation. Publicly funded legal services may be available.

If you intend to take action, you must give your landlord written notice of the repairs that need doing. You will not be able to start court action until a reasonable time for your landlord to carry out the repairs has elapsed.

Using the Ombudsmen

Local Government Ombudsman

The Local Government Ombudsman investigates cases of management inefficiency and unreasonable delay by local authorities. As a local authority tenant you can complain to the Local Government Ombudsman if you are dissatisfied with any aspect of how a problem over a repair has been dealt with. Tenants of other landlords can only complain about dissatisfaction they have with the authority's exercise of, or failure to exercise, its duties.

You cannot complain to the Local Government Ombudsman until you have gone through the local authority's own complaints procedure. A complaint to the Ombudsman may take quite a long time to be investigated, but usually no more than three months. The Ombudsman can also make a recommendation for a local authority to pay compensation. The Ombudsman's recommendations cannot be enforced but local authorities do usually comply.

If you are dissatisfied with the way in which the local authority exercised, or did not exercise, its legal obligations or powers, you can also complain to the Local Government Ombudsman. Contact details of the Local Government Ombudsmen for your area are listed in the chapter on Civil Rights.

Independent Housing Ombudsman

In England, all registered social landlords are members of the Independent Housing Ombudsman scheme, including housing associations and local housing companies. Some private landlords may also be members. You can complain to the Independent Housing Ombudsman about any aspect of the way in which a landlord has handled a request for a repair. You cannot complain to the Independent Housing Ombudsman until you have gone through your landlord's own complaints procedure. Contact details of the Independent Housing Ombudsmen are listed in the chapter on Civil Rights. Complaints about maladministration by registered social landlords in Wales should be made to the Housing Performance and Finance Division of the National Assembly for Wales (029 20 826938).

Campaigning with others

If you know that there are a number of tenants affected by the disrepair, it may be effective to start a campaign against your landlord. This is likely to be more effective if your landlord is a local authority or a registered social landlord (including a housing association), which could be sensitive to bad publicity. A successful campaign should involve as many people as possible and publicity in the local or national media can be effective. It may also be useful to lobby local councillors, MPs and the chair of the housing committee (if your landlord is a local authority).

HOME IMPROVEMENTS

A local authority can offer different types of help with home improvements. It will have its own rules about the types of help it will offer, and about the conditions you must meet in order to qualify for help. To find out if you can get help with home improvements, and the help available in your area, contact your local authority. Your local authority can give you help to:

- adapt, improve, or repair your home. This could be in the form of a grant or loan. It could be by providing labour, tools, or cheap materials to help you carry out the work. It could be by providing details of builders who can carry out the work, or by providing free or low-cost surveys, or advice on carrying out repairs. *Or*

- buy a new home if it decides that this would be a better way of improving your living conditions than carrying out work on your current home. The help could be in the form of a grant or loan. *Or*

- buy a new home if it has decided to buy your current home. The help could be in the form of a grant or loan. *Or*
- demolish your home, or build a new home if your previous home has been demolished. The help could be in the form of a grant or loan.

If you or someone you live with are disabled, you may be able to get a disabled facilities grant to help you adapt, improve or repair your home.

Your local authority can help improve a building, part of a building, a caravan, or a boat, as long as the property is your home, or it is available for you to live in as your home.

Your local authority will have its own rules about the conditions you must meet in order to get help. For example, it might say you cannot get a grant if your savings are over a certain limit. Although the local authority can have its own rules, it cannot have rules which are completely rigid or unreasonable. For example, it cannot say it will never give any grants, and it must take your individual circumstances into account if you apply for help.

If you rent your home and apply to your local authority for help with home improvements, you will need to get your landlord's permission before the local authority will agree to help you. If your home is in need of repair, your landlord may have to do the repairs you need. If your home is in need of serious repair and you apply for help, your local authority may decide it is unfit for human habitation.

Disabled facilities grants

There are special rules for getting a disabled facilities grant and these are different from the rules that apply for getting help with home improvements. A disabled facilities grant is a grant that you can get from your local authority for work that is essential to help a disabled person live an independent life. You can, for example, get a disabled facilities grant for the following things:

- making it easier to get in and out of your home, for example by widening doors or providing ramps;
- making it easier to get to a living room, bedroom, toilet, bathroom or kitchen, for example by putting in a stair lift, or providing a downstairs bathroom;
- providing suitable bathroom or kitchen facilities;
- providing or improving a heating system;
- ensuring your safety, for example by providing a specially adapted room in which it would be safe to leave you unattended, or by providing improved lighting for better visibility;

- helping you get around at home so you can care for someone who lives with you and needs care.

A local authority must give you a disabled facilities grant if you meet the conditions for getting one.

Owner-occupiers, landlords, tenants, licensees, and occupiers of some houseboats and park homes can apply for a disabled facilities grant, provided the work is for the benefit of a disabled person who lives or will live in the property.

To apply for a disabled facilities grant, you need to fill in a form that you can get from your local authority. They may ask for information or for tests to be carried out before you make a formal application. You may also need to get approval for building regulations, planning, listed building or conservation area purposes.

Your local authority may have a list of local architects, surveyors and builders who specialize in renovation work that you could ask to see when choosing a contractor for the work to your home. If you intend to carry out the work yourself, you will not be able to claim for the cost of your labour.

Once you have applied for a grant, your local authority must tell you about its decision in writing as soon as it can, and no later than six months after you applied.

You can only get a disabled facilities grant if the work you need done on your home is:

- necessary and appropriate to meet your needs. Your local authority will normally ask an occupational therapist for their opinion on whether or not you need the work done. *And*
- reasonable and practicable, given the age of your home and the condition it is in. For example, if your home is in a serious state of disrepair, it might not be practical to do the work you need.

A disabled facilities grant will be no more than £25,000 in England and £30,000 in Wales, although your local authority can top this up as it can give you other help with home improvements. The amount of grant you get depends on your income and savings.

If you live in rented accommodation and are applying for a disabled facilities grant for work to a communal area of the property in which you live, you should make sure that you are responsible for doing the work. If your landlord is responsible for doing the work, you will not be able to get a grant and your landlord may be able to apply for a grant instead.

If you rent your home and apply to your local authority for a disabled facilities grant, you will need to get your landlord's permission before your local authority will agree to help you. If your home is in need of repair, your landlord may have to do the repairs you need. If your home is in need of serious repair and you apply for a disabled facilities grant, your local authority may decide it is unfit for human habitation.

If you wish to challenge a decision by your local authority on a disabled facilities grant, the **Royal Association for Disability and Rehabilitation** (020 7250 3222) may be able to help you do this.

The rapid response adaptations programme in Wales

If you live in Wales, and are physically disabled or aged 60 or over, you may be able to get help under the rapid response adaptations programme. You can get help with small-scale alterations to your home so that you can be discharged from hospital and return to live safely at home. You may also be able to get help if you are not in hospital. You can get various adaptations to your home under the programme.

You must be referred to the programme by a health professional. You cannot apply directly yourself. To get help, you have to be a homeowner or a tenant. You must usually be aged 60 or over, and/or have a physical disability, and:

- be in hospital; *or*
- have recently been discharged from hospital; *or*
- want to carry on living independently at home.

The work to your home should be finished within fifteen days of the day you were referred to the programme.

The rapid response adaptation programme is run by **Care and Repair Cymru** (029 2057 6286).

Home improvement agencies

Home improvement agencies (HIAs) are not-for-profit organizations run by housing associations, local authorities and charities. They can help people who own their own homes, or who live in privately rented accommodation, and who are elderly, disabled, or on a low income to repair, maintain or adapt their home.

For example, an HIA can:

- arrange for repairs to be carried out to your home;
- help you to get funding for repairs to be carried out to your home;
- give you advice about a range of issues that affect your living conditions;
- organize the fitting of small aids and adaptations to help you live independently in your home;
- install security measures to your home such as door and window locks, door chains and viewers.

Foundations (in England: 01457 891909; www.foundations.uk.com) and Care and Repair Cymru (in Wales: 029 2057 6286) can put you in touch with your local organization, if one exists.

Home energy efficiency scheme

The home energy efficiency scheme (HEES) provides grants that help to cover the costs of home insulation and of improving energy efficiency. It is available to owner-occupiers and people renting accommodation. You may also be able to get other help with insulating your home.

PLANNING AND PLANNING PERMISSION

Planning laws are there to protect the environment in towns and the countryside. It is a very complex area and the rules differ from area to area, so it is important to check with the planning department of your local authority whether planning permission is required before you start making any changes to your house or land.

If you carry out work without the proper permission, there can be serious consequences and the local authority has powers to enforce planning laws. For example, it could order you to knock down a building erected without permission.

The local authority has the responsibility to ensure that 'development' of land is carried out in the public interest and that the character of an area is not adversely affected by new buildings or changes in the use of existing buildings or land. 'Development' is building or engineering work, or changes in the use of land. For the purpose of planning permission 'buildings' include any structure or erection, which would cover, for example, fences, flag-poles, and a steel structure covering a swimming pool. Local authorities have a development plan for their area that sets out the local planning authority's policies and proposals for development in the use of land in their area.

If planning permission is required, and the local authority refuses to grant it, you can appeal. In most circumstances, other people can object to the granting of planning permission and the local authority has to take these objections into account.

When is planning permission always required?

A planning application is always needed:

- for additions or extensions to a flat or maisonette;
- if you want to change the use of the property – for example, if you want to:
  divide off part of the house to rent out as a separate home for someone else to live in;
  use a caravan in your garden as a home for someone else;
  start up a business at home, so that the main use of the property is no longer residential;
- for planned works near a highway. Developments that might affect the user of a highway are generally not permitted without planning permission, and if you want to carry out work near a highway or which affects a highway you should seek specialist advice. The definition of a 'highway' is very broad and includes footpaths, bridleways and alleyways.
- if you live in a conservation area. A conservation area is an area of 'special architectural or historic interest whose appearance or character it is desirable to preserve or enhance'. The rules about planning permission for houses in conservation areas may be different to other areas. *Or*
- if you live in a national park; *or*
- if you live on the Norfolk or Suffolk Broads; *or*
- if you live in an area of outstanding natural beauty; *or*
- if you live in a listed building. A listed building is a building designated by the Government as a building of special architectural or historic interest. If you live in a listed building, there are two separate systems of controlling work to or near the building. The two systems are *planning permission* and *listed building consent*.
- if more than half of the area of the land around the original house will be covered by additions or other buildings;
- if the extension or addition is bigger than certain prescribed limits. In all cases, 115 cubic metres is the maximum that can be added to the volume of the original house without making a planning application.

- if the extension or addition is higher than certain prescribed limits;
- to build any kind of addition or extension to the roof of a house in a conservation area, national park, AONB, or the Broads;
- to build an addition or extension:

  to any roof slope which fronts a highway; *or*

  that would add more than 50 cubic metres to the volume of the house, or more than 40 cubic metres to the volume of a terraced house; *or*

  if you wish to change significantly the shape of the house; *or*

  if the roof extension would rise above the highest part of the existing roof or raise the roof.

When is a planning application not usually required?

The right to carry out work in some circumstances without making a planning application is called a *permitted development right*. However, the local authority can decide to withdraw some or all of these permitted development rights in its area.

A planning application is not usually required for:

- a normal domestic television or radio aerial. However, a planning application is necessary to install a satellite dish or antenna if it is going on a chimney and it would be more than 45 centimetres in any dimension (diameter, depth, width), excluding mounting brackets.
- repairs or maintenance;
- minor improvements, for example painting the house;
- internal alterations;
- the insertion of windows, skylights or rooflights, provided that they do not alter the shape of the house or alter the shape of any roof facing a highway. However, if the client wants to put in a new bay window, this will be treated as an extension of the house.
- the installation of solar panels that do not project significantly beyond the roof slope;
- re-roofing the house. However, any additions to the roof are treated as extensions to the house.

Applying for planning permission

There are several things that you can do to try to ensure that your application is successful. Your local planning department may be able to give you an informal opinion and some local authorities will make an informal site visit if you request. It might be helpful to discuss your proposals with neighbours before applying, so you can take their comments into account. Your neighbours may even agree to write in support of your application.

If the proposal is controversial, you could consider applying for planning permission that would be limited to you. This would mean that only you could carry out the works or use the building in a different way. (Usually, a planning decision applies to the land and not to the individual applicant so that if a new owner buys the land, they are subject to the decision and may make use of it.)

To make a planning application, you will need to approach the planning department of the local authority, which should usually determine a planning application (make a decision) within eight weeks. However, it may ask to extend this period, for example if the issues involved are complex or a lot of people will be affected by the decision.

You can appeal if the local authority refuses an application for planning permission.

Other types of approval

Whether or not you need planning permission to carry out work, you may need another sort of approval. For example:

- listed building consent. It is a criminal offence to carry out work that needs listed building consent without first obtaining it.
- conservation area consent;
- consent to prune or chop down a tree;
- building regulations approval. Building regulations approval is completely separate from planning permission and a different department of the local authority will deal with it. This will normally be the building control department and a client should contact this department before carrying out work if there is any doubt about whether building regulations approval is required.
- to consider a relevant right of way.

Planning and wildlife

If bats or other protected species of animals live in the roof of your property, you must notify English Nature or the Countryside Council of Wales if you wish to carry out any work that might disturb the animals, and obtain a licence before carrying out the work.

Planning and phone masts

Each mobile phone company operates a network of phone masts, which carry mobile phone messages across and beyond England and Wales.

A mobile phone company can erect a mast of up to 15 metres. However, it must make a planning application, and the local authority will then give members of the public fifty-six days in which to make representations about the application.

When deciding whether to allow the application, the local authority must take into account health and environmental concerns. It must also consult with any nearby school or college. Local authorities must also encourage the sharing of masts by multiple companies.

If you are concerned about a planning application for a mast, you can object to the local authority. You may also want to contact the mobile phone company direct.

Who can help?

If you are concerned about the possibility of health risks resulting from a mobile phone mast, you can seek advice from the **National Radiological Protection Board** (01235 831600; www.nrpb.org.uk).

In England, the **Office of the Deputy Prime Minister** (020 7944 4400; www.odpm.gov.uk) publishes guidance on the erection of masts, entitled 'Planning Policy Guidance Note 8: Telecommunications', and a 'Code of Best Practice on Mobile Phone Network Development'.

In Wales, the **Welsh Assembly Government** (029 2082 5111; www.countryside.wales.gov.uk) has published guidance entitled 'Planning Guidance (Wales), Technical Advice Note (Wales) 19'.

In England, the **Campaign to Protect Rural England** (020 7981 2800; www.cpre.org.uk) can also provide information and advice about challenging planning applications for telecommunications masts.

Objecting to proposals

Your local planning authority must have a development plan for its area and all large-scale development that takes place – for example, the construction of a housing development or a hypermarket – must comply with the local development plan. If the development plan shows, for example, that a particular area of land is designated for residential use, it should not be used for a large commercial enterprise. In most circumstances, any large- or small-scale development or building activity must be compatible with both planning law and building regulations.

If you are concerned about the environmental impact of any form of development or building work, you should contact the planning department at the local authority.

If you wish to object to the proposals of a neighbour or commercial developer, you should first of all try to discuss the matter and suggest alterations to the scheme that would be mutually acceptable.

If this is not successful, there are several possible options to consider. Before deciding which option to pursue, you should find out as much detail as possible about the proposal by inspecting the application. You could also ask the planning department to send you a copy of the application and drawings. The local authority has to send copies to people who are unable to visit the office, for example because of mobility difficulties, and is likely to charge a fee. Ask in advance how much the fee is. It is, however, best to visit the office if possible, since you could then find out about other proposals affecting the same site and look at any previous decisions that might be relevant.

Any objections to the proposal should be sent in writing to the planning officer dealing with the application. You could also make contact with the local residents' or tenants' association or other local organizations that might support the objection.

We have just bought a house on a private estate and have been told by our new neighbour that we are not allowed to put up a fence around our front garden without planning permission. Can this be right?

When the local authority originally gave planning permission for the building of your estate, they may have done so on the condition that no fences were put up. These conditions may restrict your right to carry out work which you would normally be allowed to do without planning permission. The planning department of the local authority will have a record of all existing planning permissions and you should contact them to see whether you need to make a new application for planning permission to carry out the work.

Who can help?

Planning Aid (020 7929 9494) is a free service providing independent professional advice on town planning for community groups, residents' associations and individuals who cannot afford professional fees.

COMMON DISPUTES WITH NEIGHBOURS

It is not possible to provide a standard set of guidelines for how to deal with every neighbour problem, because the problems are so varied and the solution to any particular dispute will depend on the individual circumstances.

So this section is in two parts:

- common neighbour disputes, which describes some common disputes and indicates which of the alternative courses of action would be most suitable in each case; *and*
- how to deal with a neighbour dispute. This outlines the range of actions that may need to be taken to resolve a neighbour dispute.

Access to a neighbour's land for repairs

If you want to carry out repairs to property or land you may need to have access to neighbouring property or land in order to carry out these repairs.

There may be a right of entry specifically for the purposes of inspection or repair in the property's legal documents. If there is no such right, or no agreement can be reached, the law allows you as the person wishing to carry out repairs to apply to the county court for an access order allowing you to enter your neighbour's land to carry out the repairs. There is a fee for the application.

Amenities that are shared

There may be amenities shared between two or more properties – for example, drains and pipes, shared drives or the roof of a block of flats. Responsibility for maintaining them and rights to use them – for example, putting up an aerial on a shared chimney – are usually outlined in the property's legal documents.

The legal documents may give you as a property owner rights over your neighbour's property. Sometimes these rights are not included in the legal documents but have arisen out of long, continuous and unchallenged use (usually twenty years). A right to use, for example, a pipe through a neighbour's property implies a right to go on that neighbour's property to undertake repairs, although any damage incurred to that property must be made good. If access is refused, an application can be made to a county court for an access order – see above.

Where there is a shared amenity that is in need of repair the first step is to find out who is responsible for repairs. However, the legal documents may not always provide clear evidence and, in this case, it is probably best to settle in advance that the costs will be shared between owners.

The next stage will probably be to get a surveyor or architect to inspect and report on the part of the property requiring repairs. Estimates will have to be sought and finally a contract made with builders. It is essential that at each stage when a cost is incurred the household initiating the repairs has the consent of the other parties responsible.

If some or all of the property involved is rented, the landlord may be liable for repairs.

Boundaries, fences and walls

If a dispute arises between neighbours about the boundary between their properties, it will be necessary to establish who owns the disputed land. The primary evidence will be contained in the legal documents. Clear evidence of this kind is normally conclusive.

However, the boundaries between properties can differ from those described in the title documents or lease in certain circumstances. The most common are where they have been changed by agreement or by encroachment (occupation without permission). For more useful information about boundary disputes, see the Royal Institution of Chartered Surveyors' website (www.rics.org).

Duty to erect a barrier
Generally, as a property owner you do not have to erect and maintain any type of barrier, for example a fence, wall, trellis or railing, around your property. Some of the exceptions include where:

- there is a clause in the title documents or lease;
- the property is next to a street and may cause danger;
- the land is used for dangerous purposes – for example, storing chemicals;
- a barrier is necessary to prevent animals, other than domestic pets, from straying.

Who can use or repair a barrier

In order to decide who can use and repair a barrier, it is first necessary to establish who owns it. The rules for working out ownership are the same as for other boundaries. In other words, the legal documents may specify who owns the fence, or you may have evidence that it belongs to you.

If the barrier belongs to you alone, you can use it as you wish, without your neighbour's consent, providing it is safe. The neighbour has no rights over the barrier. For example, they could not use it to support trailing plants without your permission. If a fence is jointly owned, each neighbour can use it for support, provided neither makes it unsafe. Any repairs should be financed jointly.

As a property owner you do not have to repair your barrier unless the title documents or lease contain such obligations. However, if the barrier causes damage or injury, your neighbour could take you to court for compensation.

If, as a property owner, you have a barrier next to the street, this should be kept in good repair to prevent it becoming a nuisance or danger to people using the street. If a passer-by is injured by the barrier – for example, if it has barbed wire, or falls down on someone in the street – that person can take you to court for compensation.

Party walls

There are special rules covering structural work to walls that stand across the boundary of land belonging to different owners, or which are used by two or more owners to separate buildings. The owner must notify neighbours about any work they intend to carry out. These rules allow for the agreement or objection to any work within certain time limits, and compensation and temporary protection for buildings and property. If there is no agreement an independent surveyor can be appointed to decide what work can be done, and how and when (for more useful information about party walls, see www.rics.org).

Planning restrictions on barriers

Planning permission is not generally needed before erecting a fence or wall, provided it is no more than one metre in height if next to a highway, or two metres elsewhere. If you wish to exceed these limits, you will need to get planning permission from the local authority.

Children

Noisy children

Noisy children in themselves are not a 'nuisance'. If someone is disturbed by a neighbour's children – for example, a shift worker who wants to sleep during the day – the only real solution is a conciliatory approach to the neighbour.

Damage done by children

If a neighbour's child causes damage to a property, a conciliatory approach to settle the matter is probably the best solution. Legally, the child can be sued for damages if they are old enough to know what they were doing. In practice, this is unrealistic since few courts would look favourably on such an action, and a child is unlikely to have much money to pay any damages. However, the parents of the child may be liable for negligence and damages if they have trusted the child with something dangerous that was beyond their capability to use responsibly, for example an airgun. The parents may also be liable if they have failed to exercise the control that would be expected of a parent given the child's age.

Balls and ball games

If a child throws a ball into a neighbour's property, the neighbour should either hand it back or allow it to be collected. However, as it is a trespass for the ball to cross the neighbour's boundary, even if it was unintentional, the neighbour would be entitled to financial compensation if any damage had been caused.

Noise

Dealing with noisy neighbours

As a first step, you should talk to your neighbour making the noise and ask them to reduce the noise. If the noise is not reduced and your neighbour is a tenant, it may be worth contacting your neighbour's landlord. If the problem persists it is useful to keep a record/diary of the disturbances that can be used as evidence in any future action.

Local authorities have extensive powers to deal with noise nuisances. You can ask the Environmental Health Officer (EHO) to investigate the noise. They are able to measure the level of noise and to give an expert opinion on how it rates as a noise nuisance. Local authorities have powers to seize noise-making equipment.

If the EHO considers there is a noise nuisance and has been unable to resolve the matter by discussion, the authority can then serve a notice on the person causing the noise, or on the owner or occupier of the property. If the person causing the noise does not comply with the notice, the local authority can prosecute them. The local authority can also apply for an injunction. (An injunction is a court order that forbids a particular someone taking a particular action.)

Local authority tenants who suffer noise nuisance can contact the Local Government Ombudsman, who may be able to recommend compensation if the local authority has failed in one of its duties. Tenants of housing associations and other registered social landlords (and of some private landlords) can contact the Independent Housing Ombudsman. See *Civil Rights*, p. 453, for details of how to complain to the Ombudsman.

Noise in the neighbourhood

Loudspeakers (except for the police, ambulance and fire brigade) must not be used in the streets between 9 p.m. and 8 a.m. It is illegal to use loudspeakers in the street at any hour for advertising, entertainment, trade or business. There is an exemption from this rule for vehicles that sell food (such as ice cream), but loudspeakers or chimes on these vehicles may only be used between the hours of noon and 7 p.m. in such a way as not to annoy people nearby. Any complaints about noise from loudspeakers or chimes should be made to the police or to the environmental health department of the local authority.

All local authorities have the power to deal with noise nuisance from vehicle alarms and other street noise, for example music. This includes the power to break into the vehicle and silence the alarm if it is creating a nuisance.

Burglar alarms

There is no national law that controls noisy burglar alarms. In London, a local authority may have the power to enter a building and silence an alarm, where the alarm has been operating for an hour and is causing a noise nuisance. A local authority officer can enter a building by force only with a warrant and accompanied by a police officer. The local authority can recover the cost of silencing the alarm from the occupier of the premises.

The National Society for Clean Air and Environmental Protection (01273 326313) can provide general advice on noise. It also produces an excellent series of leaflets on noise pollution.

Parking space

Unless there are local parking restrictions giving a right to a particular space, residents do not have automatic rights to a parking space on a public road. However, they do have a right of access to their drive. If there is a shared drive, then each person has a right of access and neither should block the drive. The local authority and the police have wide powers to remove vehicles that are illegally parked, causing an obstruction on the highway or been abandoned.

Trees

Overhanging branches

If your neighbour's tree hangs over your property, the neighbour should be asked to trim back the tree. If this is not done, you have the right to trim the tree back to the boundary line (but see *Tree preservation orders*, below). Any branches and/or fruit removed belong to the tree's owner and should be returned.

An overhanging tree may also be a danger. For example, most parts of a yew tree are poisonous. If you suffer any damage or injury, the tree owner will be liable to pay compensation if you take court action.

Dangerous trees

Local authorities have powers to deal with trees on private property that are in a dangerous condition. A local authority can:

- make any tree safe, if asked to do so by the owner of the land on which the tree stands – the local authority will recover the costs of doing this from the owner; *and/or*
- make a tree safe on someone else's land, if asked to do so by a neighbour whose property is threatened by the tree and the owner of the land on which the tree stands is not known; *and/or*

• serve a notice on someone who has a tree in a dangerous condition that is threatening to damage the property of a neighbour if that neighbour asks the local authority to take action. The owner of the tree must comply with the notice. If they do not, the local authority will do the necessary work and recover the costs from the owner. The owner can appeal to the county court against the notice.

If you want the local authority to take action, you should contact the planning or technical services department, who will check the condition of the tree. It is up to the local authority to decide if the tree is in a dangerous condition. If it considers it to be safe, it does not have to take any action.

Roots

If the roots of your neighbour's tree spread into your property they can be removed using the least damaging method available, unless there is a tree preservation order on the tree – see below. If you have to enter the tree owner's property to do this, you must give reasonable notice.

You may also wish to consult your insurers, if there is a possibility that your property may be damaged by the roots. If the roots have already caused damage, the tree owner is liable to pay compensation but it must be shown that the tree owner knew, or ought to have known, of the danger.

Tree preservation orders

If you wish to prevent a tree being lopped by your neighbour, you could contact the local authority to see if they will place a tree preservation order on it. All trees in an area designated as a Conservation Area are automatically protected.

Hedges

If a neighbour's hedge is tall and blocks out light, the person affected by the nuisance can prune the roots or branches. However, no one should attempt to reduce the height of a hedge without obtaining advice from a solicitor. In addition, some hedgerows are protected by law.

If you have a problem with a neighbour's high hedge and you haven't been able to solve the problem with the neighbour themselves, you can get the local authority involved. For a fee, the authority will look into the problem and may order the neighbour to cut the hedge back down to two metres.

Hedgeline (024 7638 8822; www.hedgeline.org) is an organization that can give advice to victims of hedge nuisance who are members of the organization.

How to deal with a neighbour dispute

Approach the neighbour
You should first make a complaint to the neighbour. If it seems that either of you will be unable to keep their temper during such a meeting, it may be advisable to write.

Sometimes a neighbour may be made to see that their behaviour is anti-social if representations come from a group of neighbours.

If an initial approach to the neighbour has failed, there may be local mediators who are able to help. **Mediation UK** (0117 904 6661) will be able to give information about mediators in the area.

Contact the landlord
If the offending neighbour is a tenant and refuses to co-operate when approached directly, it may be appropriate to contact the landlord.

If the property is owned by the local authority, the authority's housing department should be approached. It may be prepared to contact the offending neighbour to help resolve the problem.

If the property is owned or run by a housing association, it may have a housing welfare officer who deals with disagreements between tenants.

A private landlord can also apply for possession on the grounds that a tenant has been a nuisance to neighbours. If it is possible to find out who the landlord is, they might be prepared to talk to the tenant about the problem.

Call the police
You can call the police if it is possible that a criminal offence is being committed. The most likely offences in the case of neighbour disputes are breach of the peace or assault.

Contact the environmental health department
In cases where neighbours may be breaching public health or pollution laws, you can approach the local authority environmental health department.

An environmental health officer will usually contact the neighbour and attempt to resolve the matter informally. If this fails, a notice may be served on the neighbour, requiring the abatement of the nuisance. This means they are required to stop, or deal with, the nuisance.

Contact the planning department

The local planning department has the power to investigate if there has been a breach of planning control. The authority can issue an enforcement notice if the neighbour has carried out building work without permission or is using the land for an unauthorized purpose.

Consult a solicitor/take court action

Solicitor's letter
A letter from a solicitor may be helpful in making a neighbour realize that you are serious about your complaint. It may be particularly effective in making tenants realize that the next stage might be eviction by their landlord. It may also be necessary when, for example, there is genuine disagreement as to who is responsible.

Taking court action
Although a particular dispute may be resolved successfully through the courts, the relationship between neighbours may be damaged irretrievably. It can also be very expensive unless you are eligible for publicly funded legal services.

ANTI-SOCIAL BEHAVIOUR

Anti-social behaviour is acting in a way that causes or is likely to cause harassment, alarm or distress. To be anti-social behaviour, the behaviour must be persistent. There can be a fine line between anti-social behaviour and disputes between neighbours over relatively minor inconveniences. Anti-social behaviour can include:

- intimidation of neighbours and others through threats or actual violence;
- harassment, including racial harassment;
- verbal abuse;
- homophobic behaviour;
- noise;
- dumping rubbish;

- animal nuisance;
- vandalism, property damage and graffiti.

If you want to take action about anti-social behaviour you should first try and establish who is responsible for the behaviour. It is also important to establish whether the behaviour is deliberate or unintentional.

To deal with anti-social behaviour you can do one or more of the following:

- take action yourself, including going to court if you want compensation or an order to stop the behaviour from recurring;
- get the landlord to take action;
- get the local authority to take action;
- get the police or a community support officer to take action.

Taking action yourself

If you want to take action about anti-social behaviour you can:

- contact the tenants' association where you live (if there is one), particularly over behaviour that may also be affecting other people;
- seek mediation;
- start a criminal prosecution in court, which could lead to the perpetrator being fined or imprisoned;
- take civil proceedings in court to claim compensation or apply for an order to stop the perpetrator continuing with their behaviour.

If you are thinking of taking any legal action you should get advice first.

Asking the landlord to take action

You can ask your landlord to take action. You should find out whether the landlord has a policy and procedures for dealing with anti-social behaviour. Any landlord can take action against anti-social behaviour, although it is more likely that local authorities and registered social landlords (including housing associations) will be willing to take action. Remember that landlords have discretion to take action, not a duty to do so.

If you are a local authority or registered social landlord tenant you will normally have a housing officer to whom you can refer a complaint about anti-social behaviour of a neighbour. If you have a private landlord you will have to contact the landlord or their agent.

What the local authority can do

If you are suffering anti-social behaviour, you can ask the local authority to deal with it, regardless of whether you are a local authority tenant or not. The local authority can:

- apply to the county court for an order to stop or prevent certain anti-social behaviour;
- apply to a court for an order to stop public nuisance, which includes drug-dealing;
- take action to stop noise, nuisance and threats to health;
- take action to evict the person responsible for the behaviour, if they are a local authority tenant;
- prosecute where the behaviour is a criminal offence;
- apply for an anti-social behaviour order.

What the police can do

The police can take action about any anti-social behaviour that is a criminal offence and can charge someone who has:

- attacked another person, causing physical or psychological damage;
- wilfully damaged someone else's property;
- behaved in a threatening or intentionally abusive way;
- incited racial hatred or violence by, for example, distributing racist leaflets.

The police can also get a court order to close down properties that have been taken over by drug dealers. Entering the property will then become an offence and the property will be sealed.

You should bear in mind that although the police may charge someone, there is discretion whether or not a prosecution will follow the charge.

The police can issue on-the-spot fines (penalty notices) for some types of anti-social behaviour and can also apply to court for an anti-social behaviour order.

What community support officers can do

Community support officers can take action about anti-social behaviour in certain circumstances. For example, they can order people to stop cycling on the pavement, disperse groups of young people who are gathering in a public place and escort young children home if they are out unattended late at night.

4
Education

CONTENTS

INTRODUCTION

Parents voicing concern over increased testing, while others are
jailed for allowing their children to skip school, MPs arguing over
student fees and the pilot of a new baccalaureate-style system in
Wales. The educational landscape is very different from 1870
when free primary schooling was first introduced. The 1944
Education Act delivered free secondary education and
comprehensive education became government policy in the 1960s.
Today, the numbers of young people going on to further

education are at an all-time high and the range of part and full-time courses available to adult learners is vast. But, with increased opportunity and the extension of choice, comes an ever more complicated education system. In this chapter, we look at what kinds of education are available, who has a right to free education and the funding available for those who don't, the responsibilities of parents and what happens if they fail in their duties, and how to deal with problems at school. We look at further and higher education choices and how to secure financial help to carry on studying, as well as bullying, home education and what happens if you take a gap year.

Note: the term 'parent' is used throughout this chapter to describe either or both parents, or the child's guardian, or another person who has custody of the child.

JARGON BUSTER

National Curriculum:

Foundation stage	The first stage of the National Curriculum for children aged three to the end of the reception year at school
Key Stage 1	The second stage of the National Curriculum for children between the ages of 5 and 7
Key Stage 2	The third stage of the National Curriculum for children between the ages of 7 and 11
Key Stage 3	The fourth stage of the National Curriculum for children between the ages of 11 and 14
Key Stage 4	The fifth stage of the National Curriculum for students between the ages of 14 and 16
DfES	Department for Education and Skills
LEA	Local Education Authority
ELB	Education and Library Board – Northern Ireland
OFSTED	Office for Standards in Education
SEN	special educational needs
EWO	education welfare officer

EMA	external marking agency
CTC	City Technology College
LSC	Learning and Skills Council
CETW	National Council for Education and Training in Wales
UCAS	Universities and Colleges Admissions Service

THE BASICS

Types of school

There are two main types of school to choose from – local education authority (LEA) maintained schools and independent schools.

The bulk of LEA-maintained schools are *community schools*, owned and funded by the LEA but run by the school's own governing body. Admissions policies are set and administered by the LEA.

Other types of LEA-maintained schools are:

voluntary controlled schools, owned by a voluntary organization, usually a church, run by the governing body and funded by the LEA. The admissions policy is usually set and administered by the LEA.

voluntary aided schools, owned by a voluntary organization, usually a church, and run by the governing body. The school is funded partly by the LEA, partly by the governing body and partly by the voluntary organization. The admissions policy is set and administered by the governors in consultation with the LEA and other schools in the area.

foundation schools, owned and run by a governing body, but funded by the LEA. The admissions policy is set and administered by the governors, in consultation with the LEA and other schools in the area.

An **independent school** is funded by fees, sometimes quite substantial, paid by parents and, sometimes, by charitable trust funds. The governing body runs the school and, along with the head teacher, sets the admissions policy.

There are other types of schools not maintained by the LEA, such as:

city technology colleges (CTCs), which are independent non-fee-paying schools in urban areas, funded by commercial sponsors and the Department for Education and Skills (DfES).

specialist schools, which have a special focus on their chosen subject area, but must meet the full National Curriculum requirements and deliver a broad and balanced education to all pupils.

academies, which are publicly funded independent schools that provide a free education for local pupils.

special schools for pupils with special educational needs (SEN). The LEA might pay your child's fees at a special school if they feel it best meets your child's needs.

early learning organizations. They could be independent playgroups, private day nurseries or independent schools for 3- and 4-year-olds. A part-time place might be free if your child is 3 or 4, but you'll usually have to pay fees if you want your child to go on a full-time basis.

Compulsory school age

Everyone between the ages of 5 and 16 must receive full-time education, either at school or out of school, and your LEA has to find a school place for your child. Plus, the LEA must provide full-time education to anyone who wants it between the ages of 16 and 19, at a school or sixth form college. That includes children who are living in the area temporarily, like a child whose parent is in the armed forces, or who has come from abroad.

By the same token, it is up to you to make sure that your child receives education during the compulsory school age years. If you fail in that duty, legal action could be taken against you.

When does my child have to start school?

A child does not have to attend school until the beginning of the term following their fifth birthday, although most LEAs accept children into school at the beginning of the term during which the child becomes five. All young people can leave school on the last Friday in June of the school year that they reach 16. In addition, some schools allow some 14- to 16-year-olds to drop compulsory subjects and, instead, attend up to a day a week in a workplace, or at college.

Pre-school education

You may want (or need) to find your child a place in a nursery, or other early education setting, prior to their reaching compulsory school age. You can find out what is on offer in your area via the LEA. A range of places provide early education, such as nursery schools, nursery classes in primary schools or reception classes in primary schools, playgroups, private day nurseries and independent schools.

In England and Wales, every 4-year-old, and, in England, every 3-year-old, is entitled to a free early education place. It should be for at least two and a half hours each day, for five days a week, during normal term times. Even if the place would normally charge fees, you will not have to pay for at least two and a half hours each day, but if your child attends for longer than that, you may have to pay for extra hours. Schools and groups in the scheme will provide information about how to apply for a place and about the education they offer.

STARTING SCHOOL

Choosing a school

You have the right to express a preference for your child's school (but don't have to). Expressing a preference does not mean that your child will be offered a place at that school but the LEA usually has a duty to try to comply with your choice, subject to the school's admission policy.

When you have decided which school you'd like your child to go to, you will need to tell either the school or the LEA, depending on what type of school you have chosen. The school or LEA will be able to supply you with the relevant application form.

Admissions policies

The policy will vary from one school to another but criteria often include:

- if your child has a brother/sister already attending the school;
- how far your child lives from the school;
- whether your child lives within the 'catchment area' of the school;
- whether the school is a religious school, and whether your child follows that particular religion;
- whether the school gives priority to parents who express a preference for a single-sex or co-educational school;
- whether your child has been excluded from two or more schools. The LEA or governing body can refuse to admit pupils who have been excluded from two or more schools.

- whether the school selects its pupils on the basis of academic ability. Grammar schools select pupils wholly on academic ability. Some other schools select some pupils on their academic ability.

What you can do if your choice of school is refused

If your child does not get offered a place at the school of your choice, the school or LEA must tell you why. It may be because a particular school is popular and therefore over-subscribed.

You can talk informally to the LEA or governing body about changing the decision, which may avoid using the formal appeals procedure and might resolve the matter more quickly. There is usually a time limit on appeals, so be careful if you have informal discussions that there is still time to appeal after that.

If, after discussion and negotiation, the LEA or school still refuses to accept your choice of school, and they are offering your child a place at a school that you find unacceptable, you can appeal to a local appeal committee. The school or LEA should give you information about how to appeal against a decision, and what the time limits are.

Children with special educational needs (SEN)

A pupil is defined as having SEN if he or she has a learning difficulty that requires special educational provision to be made. Pupils with SEN, between the ages of 2 and 19, are entitled to receive full-time education appropriate to their needs and that may be in a special school or a mainstream school, or somewhere else. You can educate your child at home if you choose, as long as the education is satisfactory and has been approved by the LEA. If your child has SEN, or you feel they may have, contact your LEA to discuss those needs as soon as possible prior to their starting school. There are also a number of organizations who can offer advice and support, such as the **Centre for Studies on Inclusive Education** (0117 328 4007), which gives SEN information and advice for pre-school children and school pupils up to the age of 19. **Parents for Inclusion** (Helpline: 020 7582 5008) is a self-help organization giving information, advice and support on education matters to parents of children with learning difficulties. **Contact a Family** (020 7608 8700) links up parents of children with learning difficulties to other individual families and to local support groups.

> *My daughter has just been diagnosed as autistic. Can she continue to go to our local primary school?*
>
> Your daughter should be assessed by the LEA and may be given a statement of special educational needs (SEN). All children with SEN should be provided with education that suits their needs. This education may be in your local primary school, a special school or somewhere else, depending on her needs. If you do not feel that the education being offered to your child is best suited to her, you have a right of appeal over any decision made. You can get more advice and support from the **Centre for Studies on Inclusive Education** on 0117 328 4007.

Children with a disability

Schools must not treat children with a disability less favourably than other children, and this applies to both pupils and prospective pupils. You can find out more about discrimination and education in the chapter on Civil Rights. More information is also available from the **Disability Rights Commission** (DRC: www.drc-gb.org). Other organizations who offer advice and support are the **Council for Disabled Children** (020 7843 1900), an information service to parents and professionals on the needs of disabled pre-school children, pupils and students; **Disability Wales** (029 2088 7325) and the **Royal National Institute for Deaf People** (www.rnid.org.uk) – 0808 808 0123 (freephone); textphone: 0808 808 9000 (freephone). The RNID Information and Casework Service provides information to deaf and hard-of-hearing people who may have been discriminated against in education.

EDUCATION OUTSIDE SCHOOL

Home education

Some people decide, for a variety of reasons, that the education on offer within a school environment is not what they want for their child and decide to educate at home. This is perfectly legal and the LEA has a duty to ensure that the out-of-school education arranged for your child is satisfactory. Organizations who can support you, if you are considering home education, are the **Home Education Advisory Service** (01707 371 854; www.heas.org.uk) and **Education Otherwise** (0870 730 0074; www.education-otherwise.org.uk).

Can I educate my child at home?

Yes, you can. An LEA must provide a full-time education for a child of 'compulsory school age' by law and a parent must make sure that their child of 'compulsory school age' receives an education. But the law does not say a child must go to school. A parent can arrange for a child to be taught at home. However, the LEA must make sure that this education is of good quality. If you want to teach your child at home you should talk to the LEA about it.

Pupils who have been permanently excluded (expelled) from school

If your child is permanently excluded (expelled) from any school, the LEA has a duty to provide other suitable education. This may be a place in another school or at a special educational unit (sometimes called pupil referral units, PRUs), or provision of home or individual tuition. If you want your child to go back to the same school, you have a right to appeal against your child's exclusion. If you find yourself in this position, seek advice from the **Advisory Centre for Education** (ACE) exclusion line (020 774 9822) or your local CAB.

Illness

If your child cannot attend school because of sickness or injury, the LEA must arrange suitable education for them. It might be in a hospital school, a hospital teaching unit, or at home.

If your child is admitted to hospital for more than five working days, they are entitled to properly planned education and should have their educational needs assessed as soon as is reasonable after admission. If they are in hospital for five working days or less, their school can set them work to do.

Education during and after pregnancy

If your daughter cannot attend school because she is pregnant, your LEA still has a duty to provide suitable alternative education, for example home tuition. It would be reasonable to expect a minimum of ten hours a week. In practice, you may find that the provision is more limited. Many LEAs provide only one session each week and others none at all. However, lack of resources is not a sufficient reason for failure to provide suitable alternative education. If you feel she is not receiving suitable education in these circumstances, you can get advice and support from the **Advisory Centre for Education** (ACE: 0808 800 5793).

LEARNING

From learning by rote to letting pupils decide whether to attend lessons at all, what our children learn and how they learn it has been the subject of hot debate since education became compulsory.

National curriculum

What we do know is that all pupils in LEA-maintained schools must follow the national curriculum, whereas those in independent schools need not. Most LEA-maintained schools will teach other subjects alongside the national curriculum, and a pupil will usually be able to choose which of these they study. If the school does not offer a subject or combination of subjects your child wants to study, you can try and persuade the school to offer them. The school may be able to re-timetable subjects if a particular combination of subjects is asked for, or you could suggest that your child studies a subject at another school. If a restriction on the choice of subjects offered is affecting other pupils, you may wish to consider involving the parents' association.

Key stages

The **Foundation stage** is the first stage of the National Curriculum and is for children aged three until the end of the reception year of primary school.

Key Stage 1 lasts two years and covers the education for children between the ages of 5 and 7.

Key Stage 2 covers National Curriculum learning over four years, when your child is aged 7–11.

Moving to secondary school is a big step and marks the beginning of **Key Stage 3**, which covers the ages 11–14.

Key Stage 4 covers the last two years of compulsory education(14–16 years).

Students whose first language is not English

If English is not your child's first language, you might feel he or she needs extra tuition to improve the standard of their written and spoken English, or you may wish them to have teaching in their first language at school. However, there is no requirement for LEAs or governing bodies to teach English as a second language, or, in England, to provide teaching in a first language other than English. All students in mainstream schools in Wales can study Welsh.

Sex education

My child's class is to be show a sex education video, but I feel my child is too young for 'the birds and the bees'. Is there anything I can do?

In most primary schools, governing bodies must consider whether to offer sex education and at what age to do this. They should have a written sex education policy for parents to see. In LEA-maintained secondary schools, sex education (including education about HIV and AIDS and other sexually transmitted diseases) must be provided for all registered pupils. You can withdraw your child from all or part of the sex education provided, if you wish, but not from those aspects of the national curriculum which cover the reproductive process, usually in science lessons.

There is no requirement to provide sex education at an independent school.

Religious education and collective worship (assembly)

Religious education must be taught in all schools, except independent schools, and information should be given to you about the religious education your child will receive at a particular school.

Most schools must teach an agreed syllabus for religious education, which reflects the fact that religious traditions in England and Wales are mainly Christian, although it must take account of the other principal religions in Britain. Teaching should be non-denominational, although individual lessons about particular denominations are allowed.

An act of collective worship, what used to be called assembly, must take place each school day in community schools, voluntary and foundation schools. The form the 'collective worship' takes will depend on the type of school, but it must be mainly of a broadly Christian character and non-denominational. City technology colleges (CTCs) are expected to make broadly similar provision for collective worship as other state schools. Independent schools are not obliged to hold a daily act of collective worship.

Homework

Your child may be pleased to hear that pupils do not legally have to do homework. However, schools are encouraged to draw up reasonable homework policies that detail sanctions for not doing homework. If the pupil does not do homework, as set out in these policies, the school could argue that the pupil is in breach of school policy and rules and could take steps to discipline them.

Home–school agreements (HSAs)

A home–school agreement (HSA) is a document drawn up by a school's governing body in consultation with the parents of all registered pupils. Parents and perhaps pupils will be invited to sign the HSA, but if parents refuse or fail to sign they or their children should not be penalized in any way and the terms of the HSA are not legally binding.

SCHOOL LIFE

Charges

All schools, except of course independent schools, must provide free education. Also they must not charge for any activity (or materials, books, exam entry fees or equipment connected with an activity) that is an essential part of the national curriculum or the religious education syllabus or is part of the syllabus for a prescribed examination. They cannot charge for something that takes place wholly, or mainly, during school hours.

What activities can the school charge for?

It is common practice for schools to request a voluntary contribution from parents towards the cost of school equipment, for example. They should make the voluntary nature of the contribution quite clear and state that the children of parents who do not contribute will not be discriminated against in any way. Sometimes a school may ask for voluntary contributions for an activity or trip and will specify that the trip will not go ahead unless the majority of parents agree to contribute. You may feel that this is unfair pressure, but it does not amount to discrimination.

The LEA and governing body must make it clear which activities they will charge for and where circumstances mean they will not – for example, if a parent is on a low income. If you have a problem about being asked to pay for activities, you might want to seek advice from the Advisory Centre for Education (ACE) or your local CAB.

School records

LEAs and schools are required to keep information on each pupil's educational progress. They may also keep a record of other information about the pupil's medical history, family background, personality and predictions of future potential. Some will store all the information on computer, while others will keep manual records. You and your child are entitled to see school records. The record must be disclosed within fifteen days of receiving the written request for it and you should not be charged more for it than the cost of photocopying or postage. In Wales, the head teacher can arrange for the record to be translated into Welsh, English or any other language that they feel to be appropriate. If a fee is charged for the translated record it should be no greater than for the original record.

If you think that any part of the school record is inaccurate, write to the LEA or school holding the record. If it is inaccurate it must be amended.

School records will not be disclosed if the record would give information about another pupil, if disclosure would cause serious harm to the pupil in question or to someone else or if the record holder believes the record is relevant to whether the pupil is at risk of child abuse, or has been a victim of child abuse.

Holidays during term time

You are allowed to take your child out of school for two weeks' annual holiday (in any one year) during term time, but only with the agreement of the school.

If you want to take more time off for a holiday during term, you'll have to get the permission of the head teacher. If your request is refused, you can ask the governing body to consider your request. However, most governing bodies will only agree to allow more than two weeks' holiday in what they consider to be exceptional circumstances. Even if they do agree, you should bear in mind that your child may not be allowed to return to the school after the holiday.

Can I take my children out of school to celebrate Islamic festivals like Eid, at the end of Ramadan?

Yes, you can. Pupils are allowed time off school to celebrate major religious occasions, even if they also attend the school's own acts of collective worship. It is good practice to let the school know in advance, if your child will be absent for these reasons.

School uniform

Whether or not your child has to wear a school uniform depends on the school they attend. Many schools do have a school uniform policy stating that certain items must be worn, while others cannot. The policy may also specify a certain make of clothing, but if you can buy a similar but not necessarily identical garment to the specified item at a much lower price, this should be allowed.

A school's uniform policy must be reasonable and must not discriminate on grounds of sex or race. Religious and cultural requirements must also be considered when drawing up a school-uniform policy.

Some LEAs give help with the cost of school clothing in the form of one-off grants when the pupil starts school, while others pay regular grants as the pupil grows and needs new clothing. Some are cash grants while others give vouchers to be used at local shops.

Some schools keep a stock of second-hand clothing that it gives to pupils who fall within its criteria for help, or run a second-hand uniform shop where the clothing can be bought cheaply by any parent.

If your child is disabled and you are on Income Support or income-based Jobseeker's Allowance, you may be eligible for a community care grant from the Social Fund to help with the cost of school clothing. Contact your local CAB for advice.

Meals at school

All schools must make provision for meals in the middle of the day. They must provide free supervised facilities for pupils to eat a packed lunch and may provide school meals for all pupils. A school that decides to provide school meals for all pupils can decide how much to charge.

Your child may be eligible for free school meals if you get income-based Jobseeker's Allowance or Income Support, or if you are receiving support as an asylum seeker, or if you receive Child Tax Credit and your income is below a certain level.

At City Technology Colleges (CTCs), the governing body decides whether or not to provide free school meals and, if so, to whom. So if your child is a student at a CTC, you should check what provision that particular school makes.

And, these days, all school meals provided by LEA schools have to meet certain nutritional standards.

Safety at school and on school trips

You might be surprised to know that schools do not have to provide insurance cover for accidents to pupils. You may wish to arrange individual accident insurance for your child. Speak to your LEA as some negotiate special terms with insurance companies.

However, teachers have a duty of care towards pupils while they are on the school premises or taking part in a school activity, such as a school trip. This duty of care will apply even if you have given permission for your child to take part in the activity. You should inform the school if your child has a medical condition or disability which means that they are more likely to be injured or that extra care should be taken – for example, if your child is a haemophiliac. All accidents should be recorded by the school.

Examinations

If you child is unhappy with the results of their external examinations, such as GCSEs or A levels, you can ask the head teacher to submit an 'enquiry on results' or appeal to the examinations board on their behalf, no later than 20 September following the summer GCSE/A level examinations.

Your child is entitled to re-sit an exam if they missed it the first time, or if they want to try to improve their grade, but you may be required to pay the examination fee.

PROBLEMS AT SCHOOL

Most problems at school can be resolved by talking to your child's teacher or their year tutor, who will usually be able to clarify the problem and provide more information and may be willing to support and work with you, if this is in the best interest of your child. The vast majority of problems or areas of concern can be resolved in this way.

If you feel you need to take it further, you can go to the head teacher or the governing body, via the clerk of the governing body or a parent governor. All LEA-maintained schools in England must have a formal complaints procedure and you can ask the school for a copy of their procedure.

If the matter remains unresolved, or you are still not happy, you may be able to appeal to the LEA or to the organization that set up the school. For example, if your child is at a church school, you may be able to appeal to a local diocesan board. If the right of appeal is to the LEA, you could talk to your local councillors before the appeal as they may be on the appeal committee or may be willing to give advice and support. If you are considering appealing, you may want to speak to a CAB advisor.

Harassment and discrimination at school

Incidents of sexual harassment by pupils or teachers should be reported to the head teacher. Sexual harassment by a teacher is considered to be gross misconduct and could lead to the teacher's dismissal.

Some schools have clear anti-racist policies and will take positive steps to discourage racism and stop racist attacks, either at school or on the way to and from school. It is important that parents bring all incidents to the head teacher's attention.

It is unlawful for a school, or any other provider of education, to discriminate against disabled pupils (both current and prospective pupils), and LEAs must now develop plans to make schools accessible to disabled pupils. You can find more information about discrimination at school in the chapter on civil rights (p. 447).

Punishment

Corporal punishment is unlawful in all schools (including independent schools) and for children receiving nursery education, although staff can use reasonable physical force to break up a fight between pupils, or to stop pupils endangering themselves, other pupils or school property, or to prevent a pupil from committing a criminal offence.

Teachers can, however, use 'reasonable non-physical' means to punish a pupil for unacceptable conduct or behaviour. That might mean extra work during school hours or being told off. Detention after school hours is allowed, whether or not a parent consents to the detention, as long as it is known by both pupils and parents that detention is a disciplinary measure, that the detention is carried out by an authorized teacher, the detention is reasonable, the school takes the pupil's safety into account and the pupil's parent has been given twenty-four hours' written notice of the detention.

Some schools have special units attached to the school that specialize in helping pupils with disruptive behaviour.

Bullying

My child is being bullied at school; what can I do?

First of all, talk to your child to hear what they have to say. Then arrange to speak to the child's teacher. You should find out how they usually deal with a problem about suspected bullying and how they are going to take the matter forward. You can also find out whether the school has a written anti-bullying policy. If so, ask to see it.

If you are not satisfied with the teacher's response, ask to see the head teacher. If you are still not happy, you could contact the governing body of the school and/or the LEA. If the bullying is really severe, it is possible that it could be considered a criminal activity.

There are several organizations that may be able to help you and provide support if you think your child is being bullied. Advice is available from www.dfes.gov.uk and www.parentcentre.gov.uk; you can also contact the **Anti-bullying Campaign** on 020 7378 1446 or **Bullying Online** (www.bullying.co.uk).

Exclusion from school (being expelled)

What can I do if my daughter is expelled from school?

Children can be excluded from school for a short time if they have broken a rule that the school considers important. They can be permanently excluded (expelled) if the school decides that their behaviour has been very unacceptable. The ways in which this happens will depend on what sort of school your daughter goes to and the ways to appeal will also vary according to the type of school. If she is permanently excluded from any school, your LEA still has a duty to provide her with other suitable education. The Advisory Centre for Education runs a dedicated exclusion helpline on 020 7704 9822.

Truancy

If you find out that your child is truanting, try to resolve the problem by talking to the school. The LEA education welfare officer (EWO) may be asked by the school to visit your child at home to find out why they are truanting and offer advice. A school can exclude a pupil from school for persistent truancy.

HELP WITH THE COSTS OF EDUCATION

You and your family may be entitled to financial help, depending on your financial circumstances, from the LEA, the governing bodies or parents' associations. Some charities give out grants to parents, but often have a limited amount of money to give and usually have very specific criteria that must be met in order to get a grant.

Your child may be entitled to free school meals, school milk, school clothing, or school transport. You might get the costs of visiting your child at special school.

You can apply for help whenever you think you may be eligible, but you might find the amount of money available for the year is limited, so the sooner you apply in the school year, the better. Speak to the LEA or the school about what help is available.

School milk

Schools may provide milk to pupils, but you'll have to pay for it unless you are on Income Support or income-based Jobseeker's Allowance, when it will be free. Some schools take part in schemes that offer free school milk to children under 5; in Wales, Key Stage 1 pupils are entitled to free school milk.

School transport

Your child's transport costs will be paid, until he or she is 16, if the LEA considers that transport is needed to get to the nearest suitable school. This is the case even if the nearest suitable school is in a different LEA area, or it is an independent school.

A car allowance may be paid to you if you take your child to school or to a pick-up point agreed by the LEA.

Visiting a pupil at a maintained special school

Your LEA may pay all or some of your travel costs to visit your child, if they board at an LEA-maintained special school that is some way from your home. You may need to get a letter of support from your doctor, social worker or child's teacher.

Grants for other needs

LEAs have a very wide discretion to make grants to enable pupils in maintained schools to take advantage of the educational facilities available to them without causing hardship to their families. However, the money available for these grants is likely to be limited and usually will be given only for activities or items that are not part of the school curriculum – for example, a grant may be given for travelling costs to attend an interview or towards the costs of a musical instrument. Contact your LEA for more details.

EDUCATION CHOICES AT 16

More and more young people are choosing to continue their studies after the age of 16, to increase their chances of better paid and more satisfying employment during their working lives.

Where to study

The LEA only has a duty to provide full-time education for students up to the age of 16, so not all schools in your area will have provision for 16–19-year-olds. The extent to which you can choose where to study will therefore depend on what is available in the local area. Schools and colleges offer a range of different types of courses. Sixth form colleges and colleges of further education usually provide a wider variety of courses than those normally available in schools. Further education and tertiary colleges are more likely to offer vocational courses than are schools and sixth form colleges.

What to study

Courses that may be available include GCSE courses, A levels, AS levels and vocational courses.

Vocational courses, which often prepare you for a particular job, include:

- Business and Technology Education Council courses (BTEC);
- City and Guilds of London Institute courses;
- Royal Society of Arts (RSA) courses;
- General National Vocational Qualification (GNVQ) and National Vocational Qualification (NVQ) courses;
- specialized foundation courses – for example, in art and design or accountancy.

For more information about your choices at 16, speak to your school or the careers/Connexions service (www.connexions.gov.uk).

Students with learning difficulties or disabilities

> ### I am a wheelchair user and want to go to college after my A levels. What do I need to consider?
>
> You should contact the colleges that interest you and get hold of their prospectuses. Read each prospectus carefully to find out how accessible the college is for wheelchair users and how it caters for the needs of wheelchair users. If the prospectus does not tell you all you want to know, contact the college concerned for further information. You may wish to ask for an interview to discuss accessibility. If your course requires you to go on a work placement, then make sure the college can arrange one that is suitable for your needs. Also you can call the **National Bureau for Students with Disabilities** (SKILL) on 0800 328 5050 for more advice.

If you have a statement of special educational needs and stay on at school, the LEA must provide the special education specified in your statement. However, if you continue your education at a college outside the control of the LEA, like a sixth form or tertiary college or other further education college, that college does not have to comply with your statement.

It is unlawful for any school or provider of further education or higher education to discriminate against disabled pupils. Providers of post-16 education must also supply assistance to disabled students if needed – for example, equipment or a sign language interpreter. If you have particular support needs, you should discuss these at an early stage with the school or college you are interested in attending, so that any necessary arrangements can be made.

You may find it useful to speak to SKILL (0800 328 5050; www.skill.org.uk), which gives advice and information for students with disabilities and special educational needs. Some careers/Connexions offices have a careers officer to advise students with special educational needs.

I've been refused a place at my local tertiary college. Can I appeal?

You have no right of appeal but colleges will normally have appeal procedures which you could use. Incidentally, if you had applied to another school (rather than a college) and been refused a place, you could have appealed.

Further information and advice

If you are a student aged between 16 and 19 you can get further information and advice from:

- your school, which can usually offer advice on courses that are available and career options. The school may have a careers teacher and may keep careers information in the school library.
- the local careers/Connexions office, which provides careers guidance for 13–18-year-olds. Information is available about courses, entry requirements and grants.
- libraries. Some branch libraries and all central reference libraries will have up-to-date prospectuses for all local colleges as well as general careers guides.
- local colleges, which produce a prospectus with details of courses available and will also give advice on entry requirements and the purpose of courses.

EDUCATION CHOICES AT 18

This section looks at what your choices are if you are 17 or over and are currently in education and have just taken or will be taking A level or AS exams, a BTEC National Certificate or Diploma or a General National Vocational Qualification (GNVQ) course. This information also applies if you have been out of education for a while but have qualifications or work experience equivalent to the normal higher education entry requirements.

Higher education qualifications

There are three categories of qualification for which you may study at this level:

Diplomas and certificates

Courses that lead to a higher education diploma or certificate are usually vocational courses in business or technology subjects. The diploma or certificate may be awarded by the college or may be a national qualification. The most common are the BTEC Higher National Certificate and Higher National Diploma, which are awarded by the Business, Technology and Education Council, part of Edexecel, and the Diploma of Higher Education, which is awarded by universities and colleges of higher education under their own validating powers.

Degrees

Degree courses usually concentrate on one or two subjects and may be vocational (for example, medicine or engineering) or academic (for example, English or history). It is becoming increasingly possible to study a combination of subjects that may or may not be related.

If you attend a university, the degree will be awarded by the university. If you attend a college of higher education the degree will be awarded by a body that has degree-awarding powers, such as a local university or the Open University.

Access courses

Some local colleges may run access courses for people who did not get qualifications at school. An access course lasts for one year and will count instead of GCSE and A levels for entry to a degree course.

Foundation degrees

Foundation degrees are designed to provide technical knowledge and skills. They are available on a full-time or part-time basis and also by distance learning or on the internet. There are no national entry requirements and individual institutions can set their own.

Professional qualifications

Professional qualifications are needed to work in a wide range of professions – for example, teaching, architecture, medicine, accountancy and surveying. Qualifications for some professions are laid down by law – for example, medicine and teaching. Other professions have set up their own standards and qualifications (for example, accountancy and surveying).

Applications to do a professional qualification course leading to a full-time Diploma of Higher Education, a Higher National Diploma or a degree should be made through UCAS.

Help to choose the right course

Further information and advice on choosing an appropriate course can be obtained from a variety of sources, including:

- the school or college where you are currently studying, as it is likely to have a careers adviser and/or reference materials in the library;
- the local careers/Connexions service;
- libraries. Some branch libraries and all central reference libraries keep up-to-date prospectuses for the local colleges and usually for most other universities and colleges. They often also have independent guides to careers and courses.
- the universities or colleges you are interested in. Write or telephone for a free prospectus. You may be able to speak to one of the course tutors. Open days are often held where you can meet the course tutors and other students on the course and find out what the campus is like.
- the UCAS handbook, which will be available from your school or college careers service or UCAS or for reference in a local library or careers office;
- students' unions. Many students' unions produce alternative prospectuses and guides to their university or college. These can be obtained from the students' union and will usually have to be paid for.
- the professional body for the career you are interested in pursuing;
- educational organizations that give general advice and information.

Universities and Colleges Admissions Service (UCAS)

You can apply to up to eight universities or colleges through the Universities and Colleges Admissions Service (UCAS), the clearing house for admissions to universities throughout the United Kingdom (0870 1122211; www.ucas.ac.uk).

If you are applying to several universities or colleges on a UCAS application form, you should be aware that each of your choices will see the form. This means that you should try to choose subjects or courses that are linked, even if they are not exactly the same in content, for at least some of your choices. For example, if you apply to study maths at one university, English at another, and art at another, each university might wonder whether you are really committed to doing the course if it offered you a place.

If you do not get the place chosen

There is no right of appeal against the refusal of a place by a university or college unless you think you were discriminated against on grounds of sex, race or disability. However, once you have received a conditional offer of a place (for example, on condition you get two B grades and one C at A level),

---

Help! My A level results are lower than expected. What can I do?

If your A level or other exam results are lower than you expected, you may not have good enough grades to get the place you have been offered by a university or college. However, the institution may still offer you a place. This may happen if the other applicants have also got lower results than they expected, or other applicants have taken up other offers, which leaves the course undersubscribed. It is important to act quickly. Telephone the university or college that offered you a place to check whether they will still accept you. You could try to get a place on another course at a different college. Many national newspapers will have lists of which colleges have places available and there is a computerized database, called ECCTIS, available at many schools, colleges or careers offices, as well as some libraries.

if you meet the precise terms of the offer, the college or university is committed to take you.

Taking a gap year

You can apply for deferred entry, which means that you apply in the normal way but do not start the course for a year or more. You may want to defer entry to gain work experience or to travel abroad. Most universities and colleges will accept deferred entry and many positively encourage it, particularly if what you propose to do during this period is linked to the course you are applying for. Before applying for deferred entry, check with the individual course admissions tutor. If you are considering applying for deferred entry, you can tell the university or college when you make your initial application, or at any time before you start the course.

FEES AND FINANCIAL SUPPORT FOR STUDENTS

Fees

Full-time students aged 16–18 who are studying at an LEA-maintained school or college will not be charged tuition fees. Part-time students and students over 19 may be charged fees and the amount will vary between individual colleges.

Financial support

If you choose to go on to further or higher education, you may be able to get financial help. Help includes:

- an Educational Maintenance Allowance;
- Income Support, income-based Jobseeker's Allowance, Housing Benefit and Council Tax Benefit;
- help towards your tuition fees if your income is less than a set amount;
- loans to cover your living costs;
- help if you are disabled;
- travel expenses;
- help if you are an asylum seeker or refugee;
- sponsorship.

Full and up-to-date information about financial help for students is available at the DfES website (www.dfes.gov.uk).

Can my son get financial help to go to college after his GCSEs?

An LEA does not have to give financial help to any student over the age of 16. However, it does have the power to help if it chooses to. Each LEA has its own rules for helping students in further education. They may give a certain amount of money in the form of either an Education Maintenance Allowance (EMA) or an LEA grant. If your home is in Wales you may be able to get an Assembly Learning Grant to help with the costs of your studies, even if the college is not itself in Wales.

It is also possible that your son may get Income Support, income-based Jobseeker's Allowance, Housing Benefit or Council Tax Benefit. However, the rules for claiming these benefits if you are a student are restricted to certain kinds of student and many will not be able to get help in this way.

Colleges also have their own funds that can be used to help individual students. Each college has its own rules for giving out these funds. Your son can find out more about these from the college itself.

State benefits and tax credits

The rules about students and benefits are complicated. If you are a student and want more information about benefits, contact the National Union of Students (England 020 7272 8900, Wales 029 2037 5980) or a Citizens Advice Bureau.

Higher education – grants and loans

The main forms of financial support available to students are help towards tuition fees (which does not have to be repaid) and loans towards living costs. Other help for students in financial hardship, for disabled students and for carers is also available.

There are a number of ways that you can secure financial support if you choose to go on to higher education. The Department for Education and Skills (DfES) produce a very good leaflet called *Financial Support for Higher Education Students – A Guide*, which is available at www.dfes.gov.uk/studentsupport or from the DfES Students Support Orderline on 0800 731 9133.

Sponsorship

Some companies offer sponsorship to a student, usually for a sandwich course, on condition that the student works for the company for a specified period during or after the course.

WHO CAN HELP?

You will find contact details for other relevant organizations in the appropriate sections above. The help given by these organizations, and those listed below, is free unless otherwise stated. However, most will make a charge for publications. The address and telephone number of your LEA will be in the local telephone directory.

Organizations giving general advice

The **Advisory Centre for Education** (ACE: 0808 800 5793 advice line; www.ace-ed.org.uk) is an independent information and advice service for parents, governors, teachers and others in England and Wales.
The **British Council** (020 7389 4004; www.britishcouncil.org) is the national office for information and advice on all forms of educational visits, exchanges and working holidays.
Childline (0800 1111; www.childline.org.uk) provides a free confidential phone counselling service for any child with any problem twenty-four hours a day, every day.
Children in Wales (029 2034 2434; www.childreninWales.org.uk) has been responsible for guiding policy decisions that affect young people in Wales.
The **Gifted Children's Information Centre** (GCIC: 0121 705 4547) offers a free telephone advice and information service and will deal with written enquiries on receipt of an SAE. GCIC have a particular interest in

dyslexia and left-handedness, Attention deficit/Hyperactivity disorder (ADHD) and Asperger syndrome.

The **Independent Schools Information Service** (ISIS: England: 020 7798 1560; Wales: 01843 855 341; www.isis.org.uk) gives advice and information to parents considering private education for children up to the age of eighteen.

The **National Association of Gifted Children** (NAGC: 0845 450 0221; www.nagcbritain.org.uk) offers support to parents and others on how to deal with a gifted child from the age of about 18 months to 14 years.

The **National Association of School Governors** (NASG: 0121 643 5787) gives information and advice to parents and governors on all aspects of being a governor and the work of governing bodies.

Parentline Plus (0808 800 2222; www.parentlineplus.org.uk) runs courses for parents, produces books and leaflets and has a free, confidential helpline for anyone looking after a child.

Parentsnet (www.learning.wales.gov.uk/parents) is a Welsh Assembly Government website that provides information about education in Wales.

Service Children Education UK (SCE: 01962 880880) gives advice and information to members of the Navy, Army and Air Force on their children's education, up to the age of 18.

Young Minds (020 7336 8445; Parents Information Line: 0800 0182138; www.youngminds.org.uk) provides a service for parents or carers of children and young people experiencing difficulties at school owing to mental health problems.

Organizations for students

The **Association of Commonwealth Universities** (ACU: 020 7380 6700) provides an information service about universities in Commonwealth countries.

The **British Council** (020 7930 8466; www.britishcouncil.org) offers youth exchange grants to help organized groups of young people, usually between the ages of 14 and 30, to establish continuing links with a group of similar background and interests from another country.

The **British Universities Transatlantic Exchange** (BUTEX: 020 7133 2364; www.butex.ac.uk) programme covers some eighty higher education institutions in the UK, most of which have exchange arrangements with universities and colleges in North America.

Connexions service (www.connexions.gov.uk) gives information and advice for 13–19-year-olds about learning and personal life.

The **Fulbright Commission** (020 7404 6880) gives information and advice to British students who want to study at an American university.

The **National Union of Students** (NUS: England: 020 7272 8900; Wales: 029 2037 5980; www.nusonline.co.uk) gives information and advice on most educational and welfare issues affecting students, including help to a student who is having a problem getting a grant.

The **National Academic Recognition Information Centre for the United Kingdom** (0870 990 4088; www.naric.org.uk) provides an advisory service for people who need to relate overseas academic qualifications to qualifications awarded in the UK. There is a fee charged for this service.

UKCOSA (020 7288 4330 administration only; www.ukcosa.org.uk) provides support for people who work with international students and acts as a facilitator for the exchange of ideas on international education.

Universitas 21 (www.universitas21.com) is a multinational consortium of higher education institutions. It offers students the opportunity to spend time studying abroad.

Adult education: organizations that give help and advice

Information about local adult education is available from colleges, libraries and the LEA.

The **Basic Skills Agency** (020 7405 4017) will answer enquiries about basic education (reading, writing, numeracy) where the LEA or library is unable to provide it.

Learndirect (0800 101 901; www.learndirect.co.uk) is a government scheme to encourage people to learn new skills and improve existing skills. It offers courses in basic computer skills as well as numeracy and literacy courses. Courses are available full or part time, both to those working and to those studying full time.

The **Open University** (01908 653231; www.open.ac.uk) is a university for part-time students who wish to take a course leading to a qualification such as a diploma or degree. Students study at home and are provided by the university with study materials.

Distance learning and home study courses

The **Open and Distance Learning Quality Council** (020 7612 7090; www.odlqc.org.uk) sets standards for distance learning and home study courses.

The **Association of British Correspondence Colleges** (020 8544 9559; www.homestudy.org.uk) is a voluntary association of correspondence colleges that comply with a code of ethics guaranteeing certain standards of service in their dealings with students.

Organizations for employees and trade union members

The **Workers' Educational Association** (WEA: England: 020 7375 3092; South Wales: 029 205 52277; North Wales: 01766 781900; www.wea.org.uk) has local branches which run day, evening and residential courses and summer schools.

The **TUC Education Service** (020 7636 4030; www.tuc.org.uk) runs courses for shop stewards, union officers and health and safety representatives.

Supervisory and standards setting bodies

OFSTED (England: 020 7421 6744; www.ofsted.gov.uk); ESTYN (Wales: 029 2044 6446; www.estyn.gov.uk).

Daily Life

1
Employment

CONTENTS

INTRODUCTION

Work: it's a four-letter word but most of us do it at some stage,
paid or unpaid. The majority of men, women and children have
always worked to survive, on land and sea, and then in the
sprawling cities that grew up from the industrial revolution. Low
wages and appalling conditions drove workers, like the Tolpuddle
Martyrs, to form trade unions, which have done so much to
secure decent wages and safer conditions for working people.
Successive governments of all political persuasions have legislated
and regulated working terms and conditions. Huge social
changes, like the rise of paid female employment and part-time
employment, have been the motivation for new rights designed to
deliver a work–life balance, and the deregulation of many
industries has spurred the introduction of the National Minimum
Wage. In recent years, Europe has been the source of many
individual employment rights, such as the Working Time
Directive (with its right to paid holidays), health and safety law,
and rights to consultation. This chapter includes what your basic
rights at work are, finding work, a self-employment checklist and
what to do if you think you have been unfairly treated at work.

JARGON BUSTER

Statutory rights	by law; already on the statute book
Contractual rights	for example, written into your contract of employment given to you by your employer
Occupational	something specific to your trade or profession
NMW	National Minimum Wage: the minimum hourly rate that a UK worker can be paid

SSP	Statutory Sick Pay: a minimum fixed amount payable to workers who are off sick
SMP	Statutory Maternity Pay: a minimum fixed amount payable to women on maternity leave
Whistle-blowing	when an employee makes public a concern about malpractice
Employment tribunals	used to be called 'industrial tribunals' – legal bodies that deal with complaints about employment rights

RIGHTS AT WORK

Your rights at work will depend on:

- your statutory rights – the rights you have by law; *and*
- your contract of employment.

Your contract of employment cannot take away rights you have by law (statutory rights). So if, for example, you have a contract that states you are only entitled to two weeks' paid holiday each year, when by law employees are entitled to four weeks' paid holiday each year, that part of your contract is invalid and does not apply and your right under law (to four weeks' holiday in this case) applies instead.

If your contract gives you greater rights than you have under law – for example, five weeks' paid holiday each year – then your contract applies.

Statutory rights

Statutory rights are legal rights based on laws passed by Parliament and nearly all workers, regardless of the number of hours they work each week, have certain legal rights.

Statutory rights that most workers have are:

- the right to a *written statement of the main terms of employment*. All employees, regardless of the number of hours they work each week, are entitled to receive a written statement from their employer, within two months of starting work, that describes the main terms of their contract of employment. The statement must give details about job title, wages, hours of work, holiday entitlement, sick pay, pension schemes, notice and the company or organization's grievance and disciplinary procedure.
- the right to an *itemized pay slip*. All employees are entitled to an individual written payslip, at or before the time they are paid. The payslip must show

gross pay (that is, pay before any tax or National Insurance has been taken off) and take-home pay, after deductions such as tax, National Insurance, pension and union dues. Deductions that change from week to week – for example, tax and National Insurance – must be listed each time, with the amount of the deduction and what the deduction is for. Deductions that do not change, for example union dues, only have to be shown once a year. This applies from the day you start work.

- the right to be *paid at least the national minimum wage*. This applies from the day you start work.
- the right *not to have illegal deductions made* from pay. This applies from the day you start work.
- the right to at least *four weeks' paid holiday* each year. There are some workers who are not entitled to paid holiday.
- the right to *time off for trade union duties and activities*. This applies from the day you start work. The time off does not necessarily have to be paid. Employees also have the right to be accompanied by a trade union representative to a disciplinary or grievance hearing.
- the right to *paid time off to look for work if being made redundant*. This applies once you have worked for two years for the employer.
- the right to *time off for study or training for 16–17-year-olds*. This applies from the day you start work.
- the right to *paid time off for antenatal care*. This applies from the day you start work.
- the right to *paid maternity leave of twenty-six weeks* and the *right to return to work after this maternity leave*. This applies from the day you start work. If you have worked for ten months or more for your employer, you will be entitled to additional maternity leave.
- the right to *paid paternity leave*;
- the right to *paid adoption leave*;
- the right *to ask for flexible working*;
- the right to take *unpaid parental leave* for both men and women (if you have worked for the employer for one year) and the right to reasonable time off to look after dependants in an emergency (applies from the day you start work);
- the right under Health and Safety law to work a *maximum 48-hour working week*. This applies from the day you start work.
- the right under Health and Safety law to *weekly and daily rest breaks*. This applies from the day you start work. There are special rules for night workers.
- the right *not to be discriminated against* on grounds of sex, race, disability, religion or sexual orientation. This applies from the day you start work.
- the right to *notice of dismissal,* provided you have worked for your employer for at least one calendar month.

- the right to *written reasons for dismissal* from your employer, provided you have worked for your employer for one year. Women who are pregnant or on maternity leave are entitled to written reasons without having to have worked for any particular length of time.
- the right to claim *compensation if unfairly dismissed*. In most cases you will have to have worked for one year to be able to claim unfair dismissal.
- the right to claim *redundancy pay* if made redundant. In most cases you will have to have worked for two years to be able to claim redundancy pay.
- the right *not to suffer detriment or dismissal for 'blowing the whistle'* on a matter of public concern (malpractice) at the workplace. This applies from the day you start work.
- the right of a *part-time worker* to the *same contractual rights* (pro-rata) as a comparable full-time worker;
- the right of a *fixed term employee* to the *same contractual rights* as a comparable permanent employee.

Many employees will be entitled to Statutory Sick Pay if they are off work due to sickness. In addition, some employees may receive occupational sick pay from their employer but this will depend on their contract of employment. You may also have additional rights that may be set out in your contract of employment.

Workers not entitled to statutory rights

Not everyone is entitled to these statutory rights. These people include:

- anyone who is not an employee – for example, an agent or freelance worker. However, some workers are entitled to certain rights such as the National Minimum Wage, limits on working time and other health and safety rights.
- employees who normally work outside the UK;
- members of the police service. However, members of the police service are covered by discrimination law.
- members of the armed forces. However, members of the armed forces are covered by discrimination law.
- merchant seamen or share fishermen;
- workers in inland waterways or lake transport are not entitled to paid holidays or limits on their working hours by law and have to rely on their contract;
- trainee doctors are not entitled to paid holidays although they do now have limits on their working hours by law. They have to rely on their contract for rights to holidays.

When is a worker not a worker?

If you are a subcontractor, freelancer or a casual or agency worker, you are probably not an employee, but a worker. Sometimes it is not obvious whether someone is an employee – you may be, even if the person you work for calls you something else. If you have any doubt about your status, you should seek advice.

Rights under the contract of employment

The contract of employment is the agreement made between you and your employer. This could be in the form of a written or verbal agreement. In addition, the contract of employment will also include 'custom and practice' agreements. These are how things are usually done in the workplace – for example, if the employer always gives the employees a day's holiday in August. Even though this is not mentioned in the written contract, this will form part of the contract of employment as it is the usual practice.

If the written contract says one thing, but in practice all the employees have been doing something else with the employer's knowledge, the 'custom and practice' would form the contract rather than the written statement.

A trade union may have negotiated an agreement with an employer about conditions at work. The negotiated agreement will often form part of a contract of employment, particularly if the conditions negotiated are more favourable than the previous ones.

Illegal contracts of employment

Some contracts of employment will be illegal if:

- the employee gets all or part of their wages as 'cash in hand'; *and*
- tax and National Insurance contributions are not paid; *and*
- the employee knows they are getting paid in this way to avoid paying National Insurance and tax.

WAGES

There are a number of statutory rights associated with wages.

Rights to pay

All workers are entitled to be paid for the work they have done. They are also entitled to be paid if they are ready and willing to work but their employer has not provided them with any work to do.

Workers are also entitled to be paid if they cannot work because they are off sick or on holiday, or away from work on maternity leave, paternity leave or adoption leave, or parental leave. In most of these situations, the worker will be entitled to their usual wage while off work. There are some exceptions to this rule, such as:

- a parent on maternity leave, paternity or adoption leave, or parental leave, is entitled to a certain amount of paid leave but the law sets out the rate at which this must be paid and it may not be as much as their usual wage;
- an employee on sick pay. By law, most employees are entitled to the legal minimum Statutory Sick Pay. Their contract may give them more pay than this. In either case their sick pay may be less than their usual pay.
- workers may be entitled to unpaid time off work in other circumstances – for example, in a family emergency, or on jury service.

There is no legal right to have wages paid in any particular way – for example, for an employee to have their wages paid direct into their bank account.

National Minimum Wage

In the UK, most workers aged 16 or over are entitled to a national minimum wage (NMW). The minimum wage covers you whether you are in a permanent job, working for an agency or on a short-term contract.

Some workers are not covered by the NMW, including:

- workers under the age of 16;
- some apprentices;
- au-pairs and nannies if they are living with a family and not paying for accommodation or meals;
- self-employed people;

- members of the armed forces;
- voluntary workers;
- some trainees on government schemes.

How much is the National Minimum Wage?

There are four different rates of pay under the NMW. From October 2005:

- for workers aged 22 and over the rate of pay is £5.05 an hour;
- for workers aged between 18 and 21 the rate of pay is £4.25 an hour;
- for workers aged 16 and 17, the rate of pay is £3.00 an hour;
- for workers aged 22 and over on the trainee rate of NMW the rate of pay is £4.25 an hour.

The NMW is an average hourly rate that must be paid for each hour worked over a certain period of time. If you are paid weekly, this period of time is a week, and if you are paid monthly the period is a month. As long as your average pay an hour is not below the NMW during this period, you may earn less than the NMW for some hours.

If you think you are not getting the NMW

If you think you should be getting the NMW but aren't, you can ask your employer to tell you why not.

If you are a member of a trade union, you could ask for advice from your representative. If your employer will not talk about the NMW, or you don't feel able to approach them, you can contact the **National Minimum Wage Helpline**, staffed by the Inland Revenue, on 0845 600 0678 (local rates apply); minicom 0845 915 3296.

If you think your employer is aware of the NMW and is not paying it, you can contact the NMW Helpline, who will tell the NMW enforcement agency. This agency is run by the Inland Revenue and can investigate employers who do not pay NMW to their workers. If you do not want your employer to know that you have contacted the NMW enforcement agency, you must tell them that you want to remain anonymous. In some cases, reporting an employer can lead to bullying or unfair treatment at work.

You cannot be forced to agree to a wage that is lower than the NMW. If your employer has tried to force or persuade you to sign an agreement that gives you less than the NMW, this agreement will not be legally binding.

Go to www.tiger.gov.uk for guidance for both workers and employers on how the NMW works. It will help you to calculate whether or not you are receiving the NMW.

Wages for agricultural workers

Agricultural workers are entitled to a set minimum hourly pay depending on how old they are and the kind of work they do. They have a set rate for standard pay and a set rate for overtime pay.

If you think you are an agricultural worker and are entitled to a particular level of pay, in England and Wales you should contact the **Agricultural Wages Helpline** for more information on 0845 000 0134 (calls charged at local rate).

Deductions from wages

By law, your employer is only entitled to make certain deductions from your pay. If an employer does not pay their employee at all, this counts as a 100 per cent deduction. There are rules about what counts as pay for the purposes of when the employer can make deductions.

In most cases, an employer can only lawfully make a deduction from an employee's pay if the deduction is:

- required to be made by law. For example, employers are required to deduct tax and National Insurance from their employee's pay by law. *Or*
- allowed for by the employee's contract. This means that there must be a specific clause in the contract which allows for that particular deduction to be made. The deduction can then only be made lawfully if the employee is given a written copy of that term in the contract before any deduction is made under it. This would cover deductions such as union dues or payments to a pension scheme. *Or*
- the deduction has been agreed to in writing by the employee before it is deducted.

There are particular additional rules for shop workers that make it unlawful for an employer to deduct more than 10 per cent from the gross wages of a shop worker, if the deduction is for stock shortages or cash shortages.

There are particular deductions an employer can make that do not have to fit into the categories listed above. These deductions are:

- a deduction because the employee has been genuinely overpaid;
- a deduction made because the employee took part in industrial action;
- a deduction made by an employer under a court order or an order from an employment tribunal, such as an attachment of earnings order.

What counts as pay?

When considering whether your employer can make a deduction from your wages, the following all count as wages:

- normal pay including fees, bonuses and commission;
- holiday pay;
- payments ordered by an employment tribunal, such as payment of wages between an employee being dismissed and being given their job back;
- payments that have to be made by law instead of wages, such as guarantee payments when the employee takes time off to do union work or look for a job if they are to be made redundant;
- Statutory Sick Pay;
- Statutory Maternity Pay, Statutory Paternity Pay and Statutory Adoption Pay.

Tips and service charges

Tips in cash that are voluntarily given by a customer to a worker, such as a waiter, count as a gift from the customer to the worker and therefore do not form part of the worker's pay. Even if the cash tips are pooled by all the workers and shared out amongst them, they still remain gifts to the workers and are not part of their pay.

If a service charge is compulsory – that is, it is added to all bills automatically – it is the property of the employer. The employer can share it out between the workers as the employer wishes, and if a worker is paid part of this compulsory service charge, it will form part of the worker's wages.

If a tip is paid by a customer voluntarily by adding an extra amount to a credit card or cheque payment, the tip is the property of the employer. The employer can share it out between the workers as the employer wishes and if a worker is paid part of this voluntary additional payment, it will form part of the worker's wages.

Bank holidays

Unless your contract of employment gives you bank holidays *in addition* to your four weeks' statutory paid holiday, bank holidays are included when calculating the four weeks' holiday. So if, for example, you have five days off in a year for bank holidays, and you do not get these bank holidays in addition to statutory holiday, you will be entitled to these five days plus another three weeks of holiday.

> ## I am confused about whether I am entitled to have bank holidays off work.
>
> Most workers are entitled to four weeks' paid holiday. However, there is no automatic right to have any bank or public holidays off or to be paid for them. Any rights that you have to time off for bank or public holidays will depend on what it says in your contract of employment.
>
> If you are given bank or public holidays off, they can count as part of your four weeks' holiday, unless your contract of employment specifically says that you get these holidays in addition to your four weeks' holiday.

There is useful information about paid holiday on the ACAS website (www.acas.org.uk).

Lay-offs and short-time working

If your employer has no work for you to do, they may put you on short-time working or lay you off. Short-time working means you will receive only part of your normal wage. If you are laid off, you will not usually get paid. A person who is laid off or put on short-time working may be entitled to a payment from their employer, called a 'guarantee payment'.

Sickness

Being paid for time off sick

If you are off for four days in a row or more and you earn more than a certain amount each week, you will be entitled to Statutory Sick Pay (SSP) – money paid by employers to employees who are away from work because they are sick. It is the minimum amount you can be paid when you are off work because you are sick. Your contract of employment may give you extra rights to more sick pay than this, called contractual sick pay. You should check your contract to see what you are entitled to.

To qualify for SSP you must be a worker aged between 16 and 65. This includes agency workers, workers on fixed-term contracts and part-time workers. SSP can last for up to twenty-eight weeks. Contractual sick pay may last for longer. You will need to check your employment contract to see if this applies to you.

If you cannot get SSP, or if you have been off sick for more than twenty-eight weeks, your employer will give you form SSP1 and tell you why. You can use form SSP1 to claim Incapacity Benefit from your local benefit office if you are not entitled to either SSP or contractual sick pay.

How much sick pay will you get?
You will be paid either SSP or, if your contract of employment gives you more pay when you are off sick, you will be paid what it says in your contract. This might not be your normal rate of pay, but it should not be less than SSP. You cannot get SSP for the first three days you are off sick. For these three days you will only be entitled to sick pay if your contract of employment allows for it. After this, you should get the daily rate of SSP for each day you are off sick when you would normally be working. SSP is paid at a fixed weekly rate. If SSP is your only income while you are off sick you may be able to claim other benefits, such as Housing Benefit.

If you can, you should tell your employer straight away that you are ill and unable to go to work. If you do not, you could lose some or all of either SSP or contractual sick pay, unless you have a good reason for not telling them. Your employer can refuse to pay you contractual sick pay for the days you are off and do not call in sick.

Your employer may have rules about what to do if you cannot come to work because of illness. They can, for example, insist that you tell them you are ill on the first day that you cannot go into work. Your employer must let you know what these rules are in advance. You will have to keep to the rules if you want to get all the sick pay you are entitled to.

If you are only getting SSP and no contractual sick pay, there are some things your employer is not allowed to do. Your employer cannot, for example:

- ask you for a medical certificate until your eighth day of illness;
- say you must phone in by a certain time of day to tell them you are sick;
- say you must phone in more than once a week when you are off sick;
- say you must phone in yourself, and not allow someone else to do it on your behalf.

However, your employer can make rules like these about the payment of any contractual sick pay you are entitled to.

If you are off sick because of a disability

If you are disabled and your employer refuses to give you sick pay when you are off sick for a reason connected with your disability, your employer could be breaking the law and you may be able to make a complaint to an employment tribunal for unfair treatment because of your disability. For help, contact ACAS (08457 474747; www.acas.org.uk) or the **Disability Rights Commission** (0845 7622 633).

If you are off for several short periods of time

If you are off sick for more than four short periods (four to seven days) in a year, your employer can contact Medical Services to look into the reasons you have given for missing work. Medical Services are contacted by your employer through the Inland Revenue. They may contact your doctor to ask for information about your illnesses. Medical Services cannot contact your doctor unless you give them permission to do so. If the Medical Services report says you have been off work without good reason, your employer may refuse to pay you SSP. You can appeal against this decision if you think it is wrong.

If you are off for long periods of time

If you have long periods of time off work, your employer can contact Medical Services to decide if you are fit enough to do your job. If the Medical Services report says you have been off work without good reason, your employer may refuse to pay you SSP. You can appeal against this decision if you think it is wrong.

What you can do if your employer won't pay you SSP

If you think your employer did not pay SSP when they should have done, or paid you too little, you can ask them for a written statement that tells you:

- the days you got SSP, if any;
- how much SSP you got for each of those days;
- why they did not pay you for days when you were sick.

If you still think your employer's decision is wrong, you can send a copy of the statement to your nearest Inland Revenue office and ask for a formal decision from the Board of Inland Revenue. You must do this within six months of the first day when you think SSP should have been paid. You should think carefully about doing this, as it may have a negative effect on your relationship with your employer, or even put your job at risk. You should get specialist advice first.

> ## I spent the whole of my holiday from work in bed sick!
>
> If you become ill while you are on holiday leave you may be able to get time off at a later date to make up for losing your holiday, if your contract of employment allows for this. If this applies to you, you should get SSP while you are sick. If you become ill while on holiday and your employment contract does not allow you to take time off at a later date, you should get a mixture of SSP and holiday pay to make up your wages to your normal amount of pay.

If you are dismissed for taking time off sick

If you are dismissed while you are receiving SSP, your employer must go through a proper dismissal process and must give you form SSP1. This explains why SSP is no longer being paid. You should complete the form and take it to your local benefit office to claim either Incapacity Benefit or Income Support. If you believe you have been dismissed because you are ill, or because you have asked for SSP, you may be able to complain to an employment tribunal. You should get advice immediately as there are strict time limits to make a tribunal claim.

If you are dismissed because of your disability

If you are disabled and your employer dismisses you for taking time off sick for a reason connected with your disability, your employer could be breaking the law. You may be able to make a complaint to an employment tribunal for unfair treatment because of your disability. You should get advice immediately as there are strict time limits for making a claim to an employment tribunal.

Unpaid time off work

Almost all employees have rights to take time off work, not necessarily with pay, for the following:

- to participate in trade union activities;

- to perform 'public duties', for example being a JP, local authority councillor or school governor;
- to care for their children. People who have worked for their employer for one year have the right to thirteen weeks' unpaid parental leave. Generally, leave must be taken before a child is five years old. You are entitled to paid maternity leave, paternity leave and adoption leave.
- to attend to unexpected problems with dependants, for example where child-minding arrangements break down. A dependant includes anyone who reasonably relies on the employee.

PARENTAL RIGHTS AT WORK

'Work-life balance', 'family-friendly': call it what you will. Working parents have the right to:

- paid and unpaid maternity leave;
- paid paternity leave;
- paid and unpaid adoption leave;
- request flexible working hours.

These rights are in addition to their rights to:

- unpaid parental leave for parents of children under five;
- unpaid time off to care for dependants.

MATERNITY RIGHTS

Statutory maternity rights

There are a number of rights for pregnant women given by the law. These are known as statutory rights:

- the right of all pregnant women to take time off work for antenatal care;
- the right of all pregnant women to work in a safe environment;
- the right of all pregnant women to claim unfair dismissal and/or sex discrimination if dismissed because of pregnancy;
- the right of all pregnant women to take twenty-six weeks' maternity leave;
- the right of some pregnant women to be away from work for up to fifty-two weeks;
- the right of some pregnant women to Statutory Maternity Pay;
- the right to return to work after you have had the baby.

The statutory rights outlined above are minimum rights and many women will have better rights in their contract of employment.

Workers who do not have statutory maternity rights

Some workers do not have any statutory maternity rights. These include:

- women who are normally employed abroad (unless they have a work connection with the UK);
- self-employed women;
- policewomen and women serving in the armed forces are entitled to Statutory Maternity Pay and can claim sex discrimination but are not entitled to the other rights for pregnant women workers.

Time off for antenatal care

Any woman (except those listed above) who is working and pregnant will qualify, regardless of how long they have worked for their present employer, and regardless of how many hours they work each week.

You can have time off for appointments for antenatal care if your doctor, midwife or health visitor advises that it is needed. Your employer should pay your usual wage for the time off, as long as you only have a reasonable amount of time off. However, if you take a lot of time off you may be treated as if you are off sick and will only get paid if your contract of employment allows for you to be paid sick pay. If you are off sick, you may qualify for Statutory Sick Pay or Incapacity Benefit.

After the first antenatal appointment, you will have to show your employer, if requested, a medical certificate stating that you are pregnant and an appointment card for the antenatal care.

If your employer refuses to allow time off for an antenatal care appointment or refuses to pay, you can complain to an employment tribunal within three months of the appointment. You should get advice immediately as there are strict time limits for making a tribunal claim.

Right to work in a safe environment

An employer is under a legal duty to make the working environment safe for all employees, and particularly for women of childbearing age, to work in. This means that the employer must assess what health and safety risks there are in the workplace and, specifically, what risks may be posed to pregnant women, women who are breastfeeding and women who have given birth in the past six months.

Where there is a health and safety risk in the workplace, the employer must take action to eliminate the risk by:

- taking any legal action required – for example, ensuring that pregnant women do not come into contact with hazardous chemicals;
- altering your working conditions or hours of work so you are not put at risk – for example, a shop assistant could be given a chair so she does not have to stand for long periods;
- if altering your working conditions or hours is not possible, the employer must consider offering you different work, at the same pay;
- if offering you different work is not possible, your employer must suspend you on medical grounds and pay you full pay while you are suspended.

Dismissal or unfair treatment because of pregnancy

If you are dismissed because of pregnancy and you are an employee, you can claim unfair dismissal. It does not matter how long you have worked for your employer or whether you work full or part time. This is because the law says that it is automatically unfair to dismiss a woman because she is pregnant. A woman who is unfairly treated (suffers detriment) in connection with her pregnancy or maternity can make a claim to an employment tribunal. An example of unfair treatment would be that she is passed over for promotion because she is pregnant.

Dismissal because of pregnancy does not affect your entitlement to any of the other maternity rights: for example, you will retain the right to return to work. If you qualify for Statutory Maternity Pay but are dismissed because of pregnancy before the beginning of the fourteenth week before your baby is due, you will still remain entitled to Statutory Maternity Pay.

For help, contact **Maternity Alliance** (020 7490 7638; www.maternityalliance.org.uk) or the **Equal Opportunities Commission** (0845 6015901; www.EOC.org.uk). ACAS can also help.

Ordinary maternity leave

All women employees (apart from those listed under 'Workers who do not have statutory maternity rights' above) are entitled to twenty-six weeks' maternity leave. It does not matter how long you have worked for your employer, nor how many hours you work, you will still have this entitlement. Some women who have worked for their employer for twenty-six weeks by the beginning of the fifteenth week before the baby is due may be entitled to a longer period of maternity leave.

Before taking maternity leave

You must tell the employer, preferably in writing, by the end of the fifteenth week before the baby is due:

- that you are pregnant;
- the date your baby is due;
- the date you want your maternity leave to start.

You must produce a medical certificate (MATB1), if your employer asks for one, showing when your baby is due. You can get your MATB1 from your midwife or GP.

Once your employer has received your notice that you want to take maternity leave, they must write to you within twenty-eight days and tell you the date on which you are expected to return from leave.

When does your maternity leave start?

You can start your twenty-six weeks' maternity leave at any time in, or after, the eleventh week before your baby is due. However, the maternity leave will start automatically if you are off work for any reason to do with your pregnancy from the sixth week before your baby is due.

When does your maternity leave end?

Your maternity leave will finish at the end of the twenty-sixth week after you went on maternity leave. If this means that you would have to go back to work within two weeks of the birth (four weeks if you work in a factory), your maternity leave will be extended so that you have two (or four) weeks off after the birth.

You do not have to give the employer any notification of your return to work unless you are returning early. You just return to work at the end of the twenty-sixth week of maternity leave.

If your employer refuses to take you back after maternity leave, this will count as a dismissal and you can claim unfair dismissal and sex discrimination. For help, contact **Maternity Alliance** (020 7490 7638; www.maternityalliance.org.uk) or the **Equal Opportunities Commission** (0845 6015901; www.EOC.org.uk). ACAS can also help.

Your contractual rights during 26 weeks' maternity leave

During the twenty-six weeks' maternity leave, all your rights (except your rate of pay) under your contract of employment will continue as if you were still at work – for example, the right to holiday pay or the right to receive a pay increase.

You do not retain your contractual rights to your usual pay while you are on maternity leave. However, you may have a clause in your contract that gives you paid contractual maternity leave (either at your usual rate of pay or at a different rate). Otherwise, you may be entitled to SMP or Maternity Allowance.

Additional maternity leave

The workers listed under 'Workers who do not have statutory maternity rights' (see p. 227) have no right to *any* maternity leave.

If you have worked for the same employer for at least twenty-six weeks at the beginning of the fifteenth week before your baby is due (roughly, you will have been employed for ten months on the date the baby is due), you are entitled to twenty-six weeks' additional leave. This additional leave is on top of the twenty-six weeks' ordinary maternity leave to which all pregnant workers are entitled. This means you can get fifty-two weeks' statutory maternity leave altogether.

You can be absent from work from the beginning of the eleventh week before your baby is due, until the twenty-sixth week after the end of the ordinary maternity leave (a total of fifty-two weeks). It is up to you to decide how much time you actually take off during this period. There is a helpful calculator on the TIGER (Tailored Interactive Guidance on Employment Rights) website that can help you calculate any additional maternity leave and when it might begin (www.tiger.gov.uk).

If you are entitled to additional maternity leave because you have worked for long enough for your employer, you only have to give the same notice as required for a woman who takes only twenty-six weeks' maternity leave. You do not have to give separate notice of your wish to take the extra leave.

Maternity leave and continuous employment

Some employment rights, such as the right to claim statutory redundancy pay, depend on how long you have worked for your employer. The length of time you have worked for your employer is the length of your 'continuous employment'. It is important, therefore, to note that time spent on maternity leave counts when calculating how long you have been with your employer.

Statutory maternity pay

Who can claim it?

Some women cannot claim Statutory Maternity Pay (SMP) from their employer because they have no entitlement to maternity leave. They are those listed under 'Workers who do not have statutory maternity rights' above.

You can claim SMP if:

- you have worked for the same employer for twenty-six weeks continuously into the fifteenth week before your baby is due. It does not matter how many hours each week you work. For example, if your baby is due the week beginning 5 May 2006 (expected week of childbirth), fifteen weeks before that is the week beginning 20 January 2006 (the qualifying week), and twenty-six weeks before the qualifying week is the week beginning 22 July 2005. So you would have to have started work on or before 22 July 2005 in order to qualify for SMP if your baby is due in the week of 5 May 2006. *And*
- you are pregnant at, or have had the baby by, the eleventh week before the week the baby is due; *and*
- you have average weekly earnings of at least the national insurance lower earnings limit. This is worked out on your average earnings in the eight weeks up to the fourteenth week before your baby is due. There is a helpful calculator on the TIGER website that can help you calculate if you are entitled to SMP (www.tiger.gov.uk).

If you are not entitled to Statutory Maternity Pay you may be entitled to Maternity Allowance paid by the Department for Work and Pensions (DWP).

When is SMP paid?

SMP is paid for up to twenty-six weeks and this period is known as the maternity pay period (MPP). The earliest the MPP can begin is the eleventh week before the baby is due. The latest the MPP can begin is the week after the week when the baby is born. You can choose when you want the twenty-six weeks to start within this period, unless you are sick.

If you are sick with a pregnancy-related illness in the six weeks before your baby is due, the MPP will start the week following the week you become sick. If you are sick with a non-pregnancy-related illness you can claim Statutory Sick Pay until the week the baby is due.

How much is SMP?

For the first six weeks of maternity leave, SMP is paid at 90 per cent of your average gross weekly earnings (that is, before tax and National Insurance contributions are deducted). For the remaining weeks, it is paid at 90 per cent of your gross weekly earnings or £100 a week, whichever is lower.

To claim SMP you must tell your employer at least twenty-eight days before you decide to start maternity leave that you will be off work because of the birth. Your employer will want to see a medical certificate (a MATB1) and you must get one and show it to your employer. SMP is paid by your employer in the same way and at the same time as your wages are normally paid, for example weekly or monthly. Your employer then claims the money back from the Government.

If your employer refuses to pay SMP, you can complain to the Inland Revenue, which will decide whether or not you should be getting SMP.

Statutory maternity pay and returning to work

The right to Statutory Maternity Pay does not depend on going back to work. You will still receive it, even if you do not go back. You will not have to pay back any SMP if you do not return to work.

Contractual maternity pay

You may have both contractual rights and statutory rights to maternity leave. Contractual rights will usually be better than statutory rights. If they are not, you can ignore them and rely on your statutory rights.

You will need to look at your contract of employment to find out what your contractual rights are to maternity leave and maternity pay.

If you are in one of the groups which do not qualify for statutory maternity rights, you may still be entitled to contractual maternity rights. If you think you have contractual maternity rights but you are not sure how to enforce them, or if you are not sure what your contractual maternity rights are, you should seek advice.

Returning to work

All women have the right to return to their old job after twenty-six weeks' ordinary maternity leave. After your twenty-six weeks' ordinary maternity leave you do not have to give your employer notice that you are returning to work, you can just turn up for work on the day you are due back.

If you are not allowed to return to work you will have been dismissed and you can claim that your dismissal is automatically unfair for a reason to do with your pregnancy or maternity leave. You could also claim sex discrimination. Both of these claims can be made regardless of how long you have worked for the employer or how many hours a week you work. You should get advice immediately as there are strict time limits for making a claim to an employment tribunal.

If you are sick at the end of your 26 weeks' ordinary maternity leave

If you are sick when you are due back to work at the end of your twenty-six weeks' maternity leave you must get a medical certificate to send to your employer. Your maternity leave will end at the end of the twenty-sixth week and you will then go on to sick leave. You will be protected from unfair dismissal for an additional four weeks after the twenty-six weeks' maternity leave if you are sick for this period.

If an employer tries to dismiss a woman who is sick at the end of her maternity leave, and so cannot return to work, this is likely to be sex discrimination and if you are in this position you should seek advice.

Right to return to work after additional maternity leave

If you have been working for your employer for a certain period of time and therefore qualify to take maternity leave of longer than twenty-six weeks, you do not have to inform your employer of the date you intend to return as it will be expected that you will return at the end of your additional maternity leave. If you want to return to work before your additional maternity leave runs out, you will need to inform your employer of this, in writing, at least twenty-eight days before you want to return.

If you wish to return to work after additional maternity leave, you should be offered your old job back, unless this is not reasonably practicable. If this is the case, you must be offered a job that is suitable for you and appropriate

in the circumstances, on the same terms and conditions as your old job –
for example, your pay must be at least the same as your old job.

If you are returning from additional maternity leave and your employer
does not offer your old job back or a suitable alternative, you can claim
unfair dismissal and sex discrimination.

Right to return part time

You have no automatic right to return to work part time after maternity
leave. However, you may have the right to ask for flexible working and any
refusal by your employer to allow flexible hours or part-time working may
be sex discrimination. If this is the case you should get advice.

Small firms

If the firm you work for had only five workers or fewer before you went on
additional maternity leave, the employer does not have to take you back if
it is not 'reasonably practicable'. This only applies to women on additional
maternity leave, not to women on the ordinary twenty-six-week maternity
leave.

Benefits and tax credits

Working Tax Credit and Child Tax Credit

You can claim Working Tax Credit or Child Tax Credit if you are receiving
Statutory Maternity Pay or Maternity Allowance. You can claim Child Tax
Credit if you already have a child, or once the new baby is born if it is your
first child.

Maternity Allowance

If you do not qualify for Statutory Maternity Pay, you may be entitled to
Maternity Allowance paid by the Department of Work and Pensions.

Income Support

If you are on maternity leave you may be able to claim Income Support if
your income is below a certain level. This may apply even if you are getting
Statutory Maternity Pay or Maternity Allowance.

If you are entitled to Income Support you may also be entitled to a
lump-sum payment for maternity needs from the Social Fund.

Who can help?

Further advice on pregnancy and maternity rights is available on the **Equal Opportunities Commission** website (www.eoc.org.uk), from the DTI (www.tiger.gov.uk) and from **Maternity Alliance** (www.maternityalliance.org.uk).

PATERNITY LEAVE

Statutory paternity rights

If you are a working father you are entitled to one or two weeks' paternity leave when you and your partner have a child. You can also qualify for paternity leave when you adopt a child. Most fathers will be entitled to Statutory Paternity Pay for their paternity leave. Statutory Paternity Pay is paid at the same rate as Statutory Maternity Pay.

To qualify for paternity leave for a birth you must:

- be employed by your employer for at least forty-one weeks by the time your baby is due;
- be the biological father of the child, or be married to or be the partner of the baby's mother (this includes same-sex partners);
- have some responsibility for the child's upbringing;
- have given your employer the correct notice to take paternity leave.

To qualify for paternity leave for an adoption you must:

- be employed by your employer for at least twenty-six weeks by the time you are matched with your child for adoption. (You will not be entitled to paternity leave or pay if you already know the child – for example, if it's your stepchild).
- not be taking adoption leave. (Where you and a partner are adopting a child one of you can take adoption leave and the other can take paternity leave.)
- have some responsibility for the child's upbringing;
- have given your employer the correct notice to take paternity leave.

When can you take paternity leave?

If you are taking paternity leave for a birth, the leave can start either on the day the baby is born or on a date that has been agreed in advance with your employer. Your paternity leave cannot start before the baby is born and, if you are agreeing a date later than the birth of your baby, it must be completed within fifty-six days of the birth.

If you are taking paternity leave for an adoption, the leave can start either on the day that the child is placed with you, or on a date that has been agreed in advance with your employer. If you are agreeing a leave date later than the date the child was placed with you, the leave must be completed within fifty-six days of the adoption date.

Telling your employer about your paternity leave

You need to be able to show your employer that you are entitled to paternity leave. To do this you must give the employer the following information:

- your name;
- the date the baby is due or the date of the birth. If you are adopting a child you should give the date that you were matched with your child or the date on which the child is placed with you.
- the date when you would like your paternity leave (and pay) to start;
- whether you are taking one or two week's paternity leave;
- a declaration that you are entitled to paternity leave;
- a declaration that you are taking leave to support the mother or care for the child.

(There are self-certificates available on the DTI website (www.dti.gov.uk) that you can use to provide this information to your employer.)

You must also give your employer notice that you want to take paternity leave. The notice must be in writing if your employer asks for written notice. You must give notice fifteen weeks before the baby is due or, if this is not practical, as soon as possible once you know you want to take leave. If you are adopting a child, you must give notice no later than seven days after the date you are matched with your child for adoption. If this is not practical you must give notice as soon as possible once you know you want to take paternity leave.

If you change your mind about when you want to take paternity leave you can, but you should give your employer twenty-eight days' notice of the changed date.

The **Department of Trade and Industry** (DTI) website (www.dti.gov.uk) has more information about paternity leave and the DTI TIGER website (www.tiger.gov.uk) can help you calculate paternity leave and pay.

ADOPTION LEAVE

If you are a working parent matched with a child for adoption, or who has a child placed with you for adoption, you may be entitled to adoption leave. You must have worked for your employer for at least twenty-six weeks ending with the week in which you were notified that you had been matched with your child.

If you adopt a child from overseas you must also have worked for your employer for at least twenty-six weeks: either twenty-six weeks ending with the notification of a match or twenty-six weeks from the start of your employment if you've changed jobs since you were notified of the match.

Adoptive parents are entitled to up to twenty-six weeks' ordinary adoption leave, followed immediately by twenty-six weeks' additional adoption leave. Most parents will be entitled to Statutory Adoption Pay during the twenty-six weeks' ordinary adoption leave and it is paid at the same rate as Statutory Maternity Pay. Additional adoption leave is usually unpaid, although you may be entitled to some contractual adoption pay during this leave.

You must notify your employer that you want to take adoption leave no more than seven days after you have been notified that you have been matched with a child for adoption, or as soon as is practical after this. You must tell your employer the date on which you expect the child to be placed with you and the date on which you want your statutory adoption leave to start. The partner of a person who adopts, or in a couple the person who is not taking adoption leave, may be entitled to paternity leave and pay.

Again, the Department of Trade and Industry (DTI) website (www.dti.gov.uk) has more information about adoption leave, and the DTI TIGER website at www.tiger.gov.uk can help you calculate adoption leave and pay.

FLEXIBLE WORKING

If you are the parent of a child under 6 (or under 18 if your child is disabled), you have the right to ask to work flexibly and your employer should consider your request seriously. It is important to understand that, although you have the right to ask for flexible working hours, you do not have the right to flexible working. (This will depend on your employer, who must consider your request seriously but is not compelled to grant it.) You must also have worked for your employer for at least twenty-six weeks and must be responsible for your child on a day-to-day basis. You can make one request to work flexibly each year. Flexible working can include working part time, working school hours, working flexitime, home working, job sharing, shift working, staggering hours and compressing hours (where you work your total number of agreed hours over a shorter period).

There is a standard procedure that employees and employers must follow when making a request to work flexibly and considering the request. Visit www.tiger.gov.uk and www.acas.gov.uk for more information about flexible working rights.

HEALTH AND SAFETY

All employers have a statutory duty to take care of the health and safety of all their employees: for example, they should provide first-aid equipment, protective clothing and adequate means of escape in case of fire, and ensure all machinery is safe.

In addition, there are specific rules covering the following:

- cleanliness;
- noise;
- machinery;
- lifting and carrying heavy weights;
- hazardous substances;
- toilets;
- washing facilities;
- drinking water;
- seating;
- first-aid facilities;
- temperatures;
- computers.

Hours and rests

Nearly all workers have the right not to have to work for more than forty-eight hours on average a week. Night workers cannot work an average of more than eight hours in each twenty-four-hour period. Workers aged 18 and over (adult workers) are entitled to one day off each week. Workers aged 16–18 (adolescent workers) are entitled to two days off each week.

Adult workers are entitled to eleven hours consecutive rest each day, and a minimum twenty-minute rest break if their working day is longer than six hours. Adolescent workers are entitled to twelve hours consecutive rest each day, and a minimum thirty-minute rest break if they work for longer than four and a half hours.

The **Health and Safety Executive** website for workers (www.hse.gov.uk/workers) provides information on workers' rights and responsibilities. The HSE also has an information line (08701 545500). If you believe your workplace is unsafe or unhealthy you should contact the local Health and Safety Executive or the local authority's environmental health department.

HARASSMENT AND DISCRIMINATION

It is unlawful to discriminate against a person at work because of their:

- sex;
- race;
- disability;
- colour;
- nationality;
- ethnic or national origin;
- religion;
- sexual orientation.

Discrimination can be either direct or indirect. Direct discrimination occurs when a person is treated less favourably at work because of their sex, race, religion, sexual orientation or disability. For example, if an Asian employee is not selected for promotion because of their race, this is direct discrimination.

Indirect discrimination occurs where a particular employee cannot meet a requirement that is not justifiable in terms of the work and they are at a disadvantage as a result. For example, if the employer only gives training to full-time workers, this would indirectly discriminate against women, as most part-time workers are women.

Harassment is also a form of discrimination. Harassment can include verbal abuse, suggestive remarks and unwanted physical contact. You may also be discriminated against if you are victimized because you have tried to take action about discrimination, either on your own behalf or on behalf of someone else.

Discrimination on grounds of sex

Employment and training

It is unlawful for an employer to discriminate on the grounds of sex. Employment is defined as employment under a contract, which includes employees and self-employed people contracted to do a job personally. Discrimination in employment also includes discrimination in recruitment and in vocational training.

Equal pay

A form of unlawful discrimination occurs where a female or male employee is paid less than an employee of the opposite sex for doing the same or similar work.

The Equal Pay Act 1970 gives a person the right to be treated equally in terms of pay in comparison to a member of the opposite sex. The people who are being compared must be working in the same place or working at different establishments for the same employer. A woman who believes she is being discriminated against would have to show that she is employed:

- in 'like work' – that is, work that is the same or broadly similar to a man's; *or*
- in work that has been rated as equivalent to a man's job under a job evaluation study; *or*
- in work which is of equal value to that of a man in terms of, for example, effort, skill and decision making.

Transsexual people

It is unlawful to discriminate in employment and vocational training against someone who intends to undergo, is undergoing, or has already undergone gender reassignment.

Married people

In the case of employment, it is sex discrimination to discriminate against a person of either sex for being married. There is no provision covering discrimination against a person for being single.

Positive action

The law against sex discrimination does allow positive action in favour of one sex, particularly in training and advertising. Positive action is intended to redress the effects of previous unequal opportunities by providing special encouragement to the minority sex without actively discriminating against the majority sex. Examples of positive action are:

- a training agency may use positive action if it appears that very few or no people of one sex have been engaged in a particular kind of work over the past twelve months;
- an employer who has very few or no employees of one sex engaged in a particular job, or in management positions, may use positive action to provide training for that work to employees of the minority sex only;
- a trade union or political party is allowed to use positive action to ensure that members of both sexes are represented at all levels of the organization. A trade union can, for example, reserve seats on a committee for one sex where it is under-represented.

Discrimination on grounds of race

It is unlawful for an employer to discriminate against someone on the grounds of race. This includes all employers, no matter how small. Most workers, including employees, trainees and those who are self-employed, have legal protection from race discrimination in all aspects of employment including recruitment, selection, promotion, training, pay and benefits, redundancy, dismissal and terms and conditions of work.

Trade unions have a duty not to discriminate against their members or those wishing to become members.

When race discrimination is not illegal

There are some situations where race discrimination is permitted.

If certain conditions or requirements in employment can be shown to be a 'genuine occupational qualification' they may not be discriminatory. For example, it may be justified for the owner of a Chinese or a Greek restaurant to ask for a Chinese or a Greek waiter because the restaurant setting requires this. It is justifiable for a hostel for Asian women who have suffered violence to specify that it wants only Asian women workers on the grounds that the women would find it easier to relate to and communicate with people of the same racial group.

Race discrimination is not unlawful if the job involves working for a private household, working abroad for most of the time or when, with regard to certain jobs, the Crown is the employer.

Discrimination on grounds of disability

It is against the law for an employer to:

- discriminate directly against a disabled person;
- treat a disabled person less favourably because of their disability, unless the treatment can be 'justified' (see below);
- fail to make 'reasonable adjustments' to the workplace to enable a disabled person to work or to continue in work (see below);
- harass a disabled person, for example by making jokes about their disability;
- victimize a disabled person for taking action under the Disability Discrimination Act, or for helping someone else take action.

An employer can only treat a disabled person less favourably if they have a justifiable reason for doing so that cannot be overcome by making 'reasonable adjustments'. For example, an employer would be justified in rejecting someone with severe back pain for a job as a carpet fitter, as they cannot carry out the essential requirements of the job.

The Disability Discrimination Act gives examples of the types of adjustments that an employer might have to make. These include:

- making physical adjustments to the premises;
- supplying special equipment to help a disabled person do their job;
- transferring a disabled person to a different post or workplace;
- altering a disabled person's hours of work or giving them extra time off.

When an employer is deciding whether an adjustment is reasonable they can take into account several considerations, including the cost of making an adjustment and the size of their business. In the case of an existing employee, an employer can also take into account the disabled person's skills and experience and the length of time they have worked for the employer.

Discrimination on grounds of sexual orientation

It is unlawful for an employer to discriminate against you on the grounds of your sexual orientation. This means that you cannot be discriminated against or harassed in the workplace because you are gay, lesbian, bisexual or heterosexual. You are protected whatever your sexual orientation.

If you think you have been discriminated against because of your sexual orientation, you may want to seek advice as soon as possible because there is a strict three-month time limit for taking legal action on these grounds.

You can find more information on the website of the **Advisory, Conciliation and Arbitration Service** (ACAS: www.acas.org.uk).

Discrimination on grounds of religion and belief

It is unlawful for an employer to discriminate against you on the grounds of your religion or belief. Religion or belief generally means any religion, religious belief or similar philosophical belief. It does not include purely political beliefs. You are also protected from discrimination whatever your employer's religion or belief, and whether you are already working for them or are applying for a job.

If you think you have been discriminated against because of your religion or belief, you may want to seek advice as soon as possible because there is a strict three-month time limit for taking legal action on these grounds. You can find more information on the website of the Advisory, Conciliation and Arbitration Service (www.acas.org.uk).

I think I'm being treated unfairly because of my religion. Is this legal?

I'm Jewish and need to take Friday afternoons off work in winter to get home before dark and prepare for the Sabbath. At the moment, my boss is happy to let me do this and make up the time during the rest of the week. However, he is thinking of introducing a new shift pattern which means I will not be able to do this any more. Can he do this?

It is unlawful to discriminate against any worker because of their religion or belief. For example, if your employer is introducing a new shift pattern which will be difficult for you because of your religion, it may be that you are the victim of indirect discrimination on religious grounds. Your employer would have to show exactly why it is essential for you to work on Friday afternoons. If he is unable to show that there is no other reasonable way to reorganize your work, his behaviour towards you may count as discrimination on religious grounds.

Discrimination on grounds of age

At the moment there is no specific law to protect someone who is being discriminated against/harassed on the grounds of their age, although a voluntary code on age diversity was introduced in 1999. It sets out a standard of non-ageist practice that employers should aim for regarding recruitment, selection, training, promotion and redundancy. Age discrimination law is due to be introduced into the UK in 2006.

Bullying at work

Your employer should protect you from being bullied at work. The **Advisory, Conciliation and Arbitration Service** (www.acas.org.uk) has useful guidance about workplace bullying and harassment and, if you are a member of a union, they will also be able to provide information and help. If you are being harassed or victimized at work because of your sex, race, disability, sexual orientation or religion, seek advice as soon as possible. The organizations **Bully Online** (www.successunlimited.co.uk) and the **Andrea Adams Trust** (aat@btinternet.com) also provide information on bullying.

TRADE UNIONS

You have the right to join a trade union, and should not be refused a job, dismissed, harassed or selected for redundancy because you are a member of, or wish to join, a trade union.

You also have the right not to join a trade union if you wish, and should not be refused a job, dismissed, harassed or selected for redundancy because you refused to join.

A member of a trade union has the right to take part in trade union activities, for example recruiting members, collecting subscriptions and attending meetings. Any form of industrial action – for example, going on strike – is not considered a form of trade union activity.

Trade union activities must take place either outside the employee's normal working hours or at a time agreed with the employer. An employee has no right to be paid for this time off work unless their contract allows for this.

You can get further information and advice about trade unions from the **Trades Union Congress** (020 7636 4030).

WHISTLE-BLOWING AT WORK

There is some protection for workers who are concerned about malpractice at work and who publicly disclose information about their employer's activities. This is called 'whistle-blowing'. The information disclosed must relate to one or more of the following:

- a criminal offence;
- a failure to comply with a legal obligation;
- a miscarriage of justice;
- a health and safety issue;
- damage to the environment;
- an attempt to cover up any of the above.

For further information and help, contact **Public Concern at Work** (020 7404 6609; www.pcaw.co.uk).

SURVEILLANCE AT WORK

Employers have the right to monitor the following activities of their employees:

- postal communications;
- telephone calls;
- faxes;
- e-mails;
- internet use;
- workplace behaviour (by CCTV).

Surveillance is only permitted by law if:

- the monitoring is relevant to the employer's business;
- the telecommunications system is provided for use partly or wholly in connection with the employer's operation;
- the employer has made all reasonable efforts to inform users that their communications will be intercepted.

Ideally, an employer should have a code of conduct or policy about surveillance. If it has been agreed with the employees, it will form part of the contract of employment and can be the basis for disciplinary action.

Some employers monitor their workers without informing them that this is happening – for example, by use of hidden cameras or audio devices. This is very rarely legal and guidance under data protection law says that secret monitoring should not be allowed in private areas at work, such as staff toilets, unless there is serious crime involved, such as drug dealing. If you think that your employer has been monitoring you in a way that is not allowed, you can contact the **Information Commissioner** (01625 545 745 or visit www.informationcommissioner.gov.uk) to assess whether your employer is meeting their obligations under data protection law. There is no charge for this. If the Commissioner decides that your employer is not complying with the law, recommendations can be made to them or an enforcement notice can be issued. The Information Commissioner cannot award you compensation.

SUNDAY WORKING

Shop workers (including betting-shop workers) have certain rights if they are asked to work on Sundays.

Employees of a catering business do not count as shop workers and are not protected from having to work on Sundays. This includes employees of pubs, restaurants and cafés.

Shop workers have the same rights to limits on hours of work and entitlements to rest breaks, under Health and Safety law, as other workers.

MAKING A COMPLAINT TO YOUR EMPLOYER

Grievance procedures enable you to raise concerns with your employer about your job, your terms and conditions, or the way your employer or people at work treat you.

Your employer must by law have a grievance procedure to allow you to raise concerns, and must tell you what it is. Within two months of starting work, a new employer must give you written details about the job, including information about terms such as pay and hours. This statement must also set out the employer's disciplinary and grievance procedures and tell you who to go to if you have a grievance.

If you have a problem with your employer you should usually try to sort it out informally first. Raise the matter with the person named in the grievance procedure or, if this isn't possible, go to the next most senior person after the named person. If you cannot sort the problem out informally and want to pursue the grievance, you must follow the statutory minimum grievance procedure. Usually, you will also have to use this procedure to raise a grievance if you have already left a job but want to follow up a complaint with your ex-employer.

The standard three-step grievance procedure is:

1. The written statement
2. The meeting
3. The appeal meeting

1. The written statement

You must send your employer a written statement, setting out your grievance. It should include as much detail as possible, including dates and times. You must keep a copy of this written statement. As a general rule, you will not be able to take your grievance to an employment tribunal later on unless you have provided the information about the grievance to your employer and have given them at least twenty-eight days to respond.

You may find it helpful to state in the written grievance how you would like the matter to be resolved. Be positive – suggest options if you think there are different ways of solving the problem that you would be happy with.

You can find a sample grievance letter for you to adapt and use on the **Department of Trade and Industry** website (www.dti.gov.uk).

2. The meeting

Once you've sent your employer the written statement of your grievance, they must arrange a meeting with you to discuss the issue. Your employer should be allowed enough time to think about what you have said but should not delay the meeting for an unreasonable time.

You have a right to be accompanied at the meeting by someone who works with you or by a trade union official. You have a duty to attend the meeting, which must be held at a time and place that is reasonable for you and anyone accompanying you. If either of you is disabled, your employer must ensure that you have no problems getting to or joining in the meeting.

If you do not attend, a tribunal may later find you at fault for not completing the procedures and reduce your compensation.

If, for an unforeseeable reason, you or the person accompanying you cannot attend, the employer must arrange another meeting and you must attend. If this meeting also has to be cancelled for an unforeseeable reason, then no further meetings need to be held and the necessary procedures would have been complied with.

Prepare carefully for the meeting and discuss the matter fully with anyone accompanying you. If there is anyone there you don't know, ask your employer to introduce them.

Set your case out calmly and clearly and explain what you have done to try and resolve the problem informally. You could also make some further suggestions as to how the problem might be resolved. Try to keep the discussion to the point of the grievance.

After the meeting, your employer must tell you their decision and what action they are going to take.

Your employer should tell you about your right to appeal against the decision. You must use your right of appeal before you take a claim to an employment tribunal. If you do not, any compensation award will be reduced.

3. The appeal meeting

If you decide to appeal, you must tell your employer. It is advisable to do this in writing. Keep a copy of the letter, as you may need it if your case goes to an employment tribunal. Your employer must arrange a further meeting to discuss your appeal. Again, it must be at a reasonable time and place and you have a right to be accompanied.

Where possible, a more senior manager should deal with your appeal.

You have a duty to attend the meeting. If you do not attend, a tribunal may later find you at fault for not completing the procedures and reduce your compensation.

After the meeting, your employer must decide what they are going to do and tell you what it is. This is their final decision and if you are not happy with it and you think your rights have been infringed you may be able to take your case to an employment tribunal.

If an employer does not follow proper procedures a tribunal may decide they have acted unreasonably. This would mean you would have been unfairly dismissed.

There are some situations where you will not need to follow the formal grievance procedure. You will not need to follow it if:

- more than one employee is affected by the same grievance and the matter is being dealt with by the recognized trade union;
- you have suffered harassment and it's reasonable to believe that you will suffer further harassment if you use the formal grievance procedure;

- it is reasonable to assume that there is a serious threat of violence or damage to property by one of the parties to the grievance;
- it is impracticable to begin or to complete the procedure within a reasonable time, or – where you have already left your job – to deliver a written grievance to your ex-employer.

DISCIPLINARY ACTION AND DISMISSAL

The statutory minimum disciplinary and dismissal procedure

Your employer must by law have a disciplinary and dismissal procedure and must tell you what it is. Within two months of starting work, a new employer must give you written details about the job, including information about terms such as pay and hours. This statement must also set out the employer's disciplinary and dismissal procedure or refer you to a document which sets out the procedure.

By law, if your employer is considering taking disciplinary action or dismissing you, they must comply with the statutory minimum three-step disciplinary procedure detailed below. Your employer's disciplinary and dismissal procedure may have more steps than the statutory minimum procedure. If so, your employer should follow this fuller procedure.

The standard three-step dismissal and disciplinary procedure is:

1. The written statement
2. The meeting
3. The appeal meeting

1. The written statement

If your employer is considering disciplinary action or dismissal, their first step should be to send you a written statement, setting out exactly the complaint made against you. If you think information is missing – for example, the date of the misconduct – then ask your employer to provide it in good time for the hearing.

It would usually be reasonable for your employer to provide you with evidence from any investigation that has been held so you have an opportunity to consider the information.

Read the statement and any other documents carefully.

2. The meeting

Once your employer has sent you the statement, they must arrange a meeting with you to discuss the issue. You should be allowed enough time to think about what your employer has said but should not delay the meeting for an unreasonable time. The employer must not take any disciplinary action before the meeting.

You have a right to be accompanied at the meeting by someone who works with you or by a trade union official. You have a duty to attend the meeting, which must be held at a time and place that is reasonable for you and anyone accompanying you. If either of you is disabled, your employer must ensure that you have no problems getting to or joining in the meeting.

If you do not attend, a tribunal may later find you at fault for not completing the procedures and reduce your compensation.

If, for an unforeseeable reason, you or the person accompanying you cannot attend, the employer must arrange another meeting and you must attend. If this meeting also has to be cancelled for an unforeseeable reason, then no further meetings need to be held and the necessary procedures would have been complied with.

Prepare carefully for the meeting and discuss the matter fully with anyone accompanying you. If there is anyone there you don't know, ask your employer to introduce them. Your employer should explain how the meeting will be held, who will speak and when. They should then set out the allegations made against you and the evidence that supports them. Listen to what your employer has to say and give your side of the case calmly and clearly when asked to do so. The employer must give you the opportunity to set out your case at the meeting.

Preparing a written note before the hearing may help – your companion or a CAB can help you with this.

Take notes of what is being said and done – your employer will not always take notes and they may be needed later.

After the meeting, your employer will tell you their decision and what action they are going to take.

Your employer should tell you about your right to appeal against the decision. You must use your right of appeal before you take a claim to an employment tribunal. If you do not, any compensation award will be reduced.

3. The appeal meeting

If you decide to appeal, you must tell your employer. It is advisable to do this in writing. Keep a copy of the letter, as you may need it if your case goes to an employment tribunal. Your employer must arrange a further meeting to discuss your appeal. Again, it must be at a reasonable time and place and you have a right to be accompanied.

Again, if you do not attend, a tribunal may later find you at fault for not completing the procedures and reduce your compensation.

You have a duty to attend the meeting. If, for an unforeseeable reason, you or the person you have chosen to come with you cannot attend, the employer must arrange another meeting and you must attend it. If this meeting also has to be cancelled for an unforeseeable reason, then no further meetings need be held and the necessary procedures would have been complied with. Prepare carefully for the meeting and discuss the matter fully with the person accompanying you. Take notes at the meeting.

After the meeting, your employer must decide what they are going to do and tell you what it is. This is their final decision and if you are not happy with it and you think your rights have been infringed you may be able to take your case to an employment tribunal.

If an employer does not follow proper procedures a tribunal may decide they have acted unreasonably. This would mean you would have been unfairly dismissed.

Warnings

Employers often use a system of verbal and written warnings in disciplinary action, which will increase in seriousness leading to final written warnings or dismissal. Your employer is not required to follow the three-step procedure above if they simply want to issue a warning to you – even a final written warning. However, if they are thinking of taking any other action, such as deducting wages or demotion, they do have to follow the procedures.

Suspensions

Your employer can suspend you on full pay without having to go through the procedures. However, if your pay is reduced the procedures will have to be followed.

If you are unsure about how to proceed, seek advice from your local CAB, ACAS or your union rep.

Unfair dismissal

A dismissal may be fair or unfair depending on the circumstances of the dismissal.

Have you been unfairly dismissed?

You need to work through the following steps to identify whether you can make a claim for unfair dismissal:

- **Step 1** – do you have the right to make a claim for unfair dismissal?
- **Step 2** – have you actually been dismissed?
- **Step 3** – have you been discriminated against?
- **Step 4** – was the reason for the dismissal one which means the dismissal was automatically unfair?
- **Step 5** – if the dismissal was not for one of the reasons in step four, was the dismissal fair or unfair, and did your employer act reasonably in dismissing you? You may be able to claim that you have been unfairly dismissed to an employment tribunal, provided you have worked for your employer for one year. Only an employment tribunal can decide if a dismissal was fair or unfair, taking into account all the circumstances of the case. You can also make a claim for unfair dismissal if your employer did not follow proper procedures, which include consulting you before dismissing you.

In all cases, if you make a claim of unfair dismissal to an employment tribunal and you win your claim, the employment tribunal can award you compensation for the unfair dismissal from your employer and/or tell your employer to give you your job back. It is very rare, however, for tribunals to tell employers to give an employee their job back. It is much more usual for the tribunal to award compensation to the employee.

In all cases, when making a claim to an employment tribunal the claim for unfair dismissal must be made within a very strict time limit.

Step 1: Who cannot claim unfair dismissal?

There are some employees who can never claim unfair dismissal. They are:

- people who are not employees, such as independent contractors or freelance agents. Employers often claim that people who are actually employees are self-employed. It is important to check the relationship between the employee and their 'employer', because this will determine the employee's actual employment status.

- police officers;
- members of the armed forces;
- share fishermen;
- people who work outside Great Britain;
- registered dock workers;
- employees above the normal retirement age for their occupation.

You can only make a complaint of unfair dismissal if you are below the normal retirement age for your job, unless you are making a claim for unfair dismissal for a reason that is an automatically unfair one.

The retirement age must be the same for men and women and might not be the same as the state retirement age. For example, fire-fighters are expected to retire at 55 and cannot make a claim for unfair dismissal after that age. If there is no normal retirement age for the job, or if there is one but it is never enforced, then you can make a claim up to the age of 65.

Step 2: Have you actually been dismissed?

All the following count as dismissal:

- your employer ends your employment with or without notice;
- your employer does not renew a fixed-term contract that has run out;
- you are made redundant, including if you take voluntary redundancy;
- your employer refuses to take you back after a strike or lockout;
- constructive dismissal. This is when your employer makes it impossible for you to carry out your work so you resign.
- you resign under pressure from the employer;
- you are a woman on maternity leave, and your employer refuses to allow you to return to work after maternity leave;
- self dismissal. An employer may argue that you have dismissed yourself by behaving in a way that brings the contract to an end. However, unless it is obvious that you have actually resigned, you will have been dismissed by your employer.
- you have been laid off or put on short-time working when your contract does not allow for this.

The following will not count as dismissal:

- you resign without any pressure from your employer or leave by mutual agreement;

- you are suspended on full pay;
- your employer withdraws a job offer before you start work;
- circumstances change and you can no longer continue to work for your employer (known as frustration of contract);
- you are laid off or put on short-time working and your contract allows for this, and then you claim redundancy. You are then actually resigning.
- you receive an ambiguous dismissal from your employer and it is not clear if the employer is dismissing you or not.

Step 3: Have you been discriminated against?

You may believe that you have been dismissed because of your sex, race, disability, religion or sexual orientation. You can make a claim for discrimination to an employment tribunal instead of, or in addition to, a claim for unfair dismissal. You do not have to have worked for any particular length of time to be able to claim discrimination.

If you have been dismissed for a discriminatory reason you will almost always have been unfairly dismissed. However, in order to claim unfair dismissal, you will need to have worked for your employer for one year.

Step 4: What is the reason for the dismissal and is it one that means the dismissal is automatically unfair?

The reason for the dismissal dictates what action you can take. The reason your employer has given you may not be the real reason for the dismissal. Generally, an employer can dismiss an employee when they want. Unless your work colleagues or trade union are prepared to take industrial action to make your employer change their mind, the only way you may be able to get your job back is to claim unfair dismissal.

You may be able to negotiate with your employer so that you do not lose your job. All employers must follow a dismissal or disciplinary procedure before the employee can be dismissed (see section above). If you are facing dismissal you should always get advice.

Automatically unfair dismissal (where it does not matter how long you have worked for the employer)

If the reason for the dismissal was any of those listed below, an employment tribunal will automatically decide that the dismissal was unfair. If you were dismissed for one of the following reasons you can still claim unfair dismissal regardless of how long you have worked for the employer and regardless of how old you are:

- because you are pregnant or on maternity leave or a related reason;
- for trying to enforce a right you have under law;
- for taking action over a health and safety issue;
- if you are a shop or betting worker refusing to work on a Sunday;
- for carrying out your duties as a trustee of an occupational pension fund;
- because you are a trade union member or have taken part in trade union activities including official industrial action, or have acted as an employees' representative;
- because you have 'blown the whistle' on a matter of public concern at work.

Automatically unfair dismissal (where you must have worked for your employer for one year)

If you have not been dismissed for one of the reasons listed above, but have been dismissed in any of the following circumstances, an employment tribunal will find that you have automatically been unfairly dismissed. However, in order to bring a claim, you must have been employed by your employer for at least one year:

- if your employer has not followed proper dismissal or disciplinary procedures before dismissing you (see section above);
- if the dismissal is as a result of the business you work for having been taken over by a new owner, the dismissal will be automatically unfair and you can make a claim provided you have worked there for one year.
- if the dismissal is as a result of your not declaring a spent conviction.

Remember: a claim to an employment tribunal must be made within three months of the date of the dismissal.

Step 5: Is the reason for the dismissal one that is not automatically unfair?

If you have not been dismissed for one of the reasons in Step 4, then the dismissal may have been fair or unfair depending on the reason for it and the procedures followed by your employer in dismissing you. If the reason for the dismissal was not one of those in step four, you will have to have worked for one year for your employer in order to make a claim to an employment tribunal.

Reasons for claiming unfair dismissal where you will have to have worked for one year are:

- your employer says you are not capable of doing the job;
- your employer says you do not have the necessary qualifications to do the job;
- your employer says your conduct has been poor;
- your employer says you have done something illegal;
- your employer says you are redundant;
- your employer has given some other reason for dismissing you.

It is important to remember that there is a three-month time limit, starting from the date the employee is dismissed, during which any claim must be made to an employment tribunal.

Constructive dismissal

Constructive dismissal occurs if you resign because your employer breaches the employment contract, by taking action such as cutting your pay, changing your working conditions, and so on, and so makes it impossible for you to continue working. Constructive dismissal is a type of unfair dismissal and you will therefore have to have worked for your employer for one year to be able to make a claim to an employment tribunal.

Notice periods

Most employees have a legal right to a period of notice if dismissed. Many employees will have extra rights to notice under their contract of employment. There will always be a contract of employment, even if there is nothing written down. Even if the law or your contract of employment does not give you the right to a minimum amount of notice, you are still entitled to 'reasonable' notice. In most circumstances, if your employer wants to dismiss you, they must follow the proper dismissal and disciplinary procedures set out above which are laid down by law.

Who has no legal right to minimum notice?

Some employees have no legal right to a minimum period of notice (but see also under 'Reasonable notice' section, below). These include:

- those employed for less than one calendar month by their employer. Employees on fixed-term contracts who have worked for their employer for one month have the right to notice.
- Crown servants;

- seamen employed on a ship registered in the United Kingdom under a crew agreement;
- employees who have been dismissed for gross misconduct. If you have been accused of gross misconduct, you may wish to make a claim to an employment tribunal. There is a strict time limit for doing so.

If you have no legal right to notice, you will still be entitled to 'reasonable' notice or the notice your contract gives you, except when you have been dismissed for gross misconduct, when you will not be entitled to any notice under your contract or any 'reasonable' notice. For this reason, it is important to check the real reason for the dismissal.

How much notice should you get?

The law gives all employees the right to a minimum amount of notice, except those listed above. This period of notice is:

- one week for employees who have worked for their employer for one month but less than two years; *or*
- two weeks if the employee has worked for their employer for two whole years; *and*
- one extra week for each further whole year's employment at the date the notice period expires, up to a maximum of twelve weeks' notice in total.

Contractual notice

Your contract of employment may give you more notice than the minimum the law gives you. However, you can never get less than the minimum, no matter what your contract says.

If your contract does not specify a period of notice, you may still have the right to a minimum period of notice because of custom and practice. For example, if everyone who works for your firm has always been given at least three weeks' notice, you would have the right to this much notice.

'Reasonable' notice

If the law does not give you the right to notice, and there is no notice period in your contract (whether written, spoken or through custom and practice), you will still be entitled to 'reasonable' notice. What is reasonable will often depend on your pay period. For example, if you are paid weekly, you could argue that a week is reasonable, and if you are paid monthly, you could argue that a month is reasonable. You won't be entitled to reasonable notice if you have been dismissed for gross misconduct.

How much notice is an employer entitled to?

The notice you should give your employer before resigning should be in your contract. If your contract does not say how much notice you must give your employer then, if you have worked for one month or more, the minimum notice you should give is one week. If you have worked for less than one month, the notice period should be reasonable. If your contract says you must give your employer more notice than this, you must give the amount of notice in your contract. Your contract may set out how much notice you must give, whether it must be written, and when you should give it.

If you leave your job without giving proper notice, your employer may try to withhold part or all of the money owed to you. In general, employers are not legally entitled to withhold money owed but it will depend on what it says in your contract.

Pay

Pay during your notice period

If you work your normal working hours in your notice period, you are entitled to be paid your normal pay.

You may not be able to work during the notice period because you are:

- willing to work but are given no work to do;
- on holiday;
- off work through sickness or injury.

If you do not work during the notice period for one of the reasons above, the law says you should usually still get your normal wage. However, there is an exception to this rule. If your contract gives you at least one week's notice more than the law gives you, you lose your legal right to be paid during the whole of the notice period. In this case you would just be entitled to the pay specified in your contract.

Pay in lieu of notice

If your employer has dismissed you without giving you notice that the law or your contract says they should have, your employer should pay you in lieu of notice. 'In lieu' means 'instead of'. This is also called severance pay. The only exception to this is when you have been dismissed because of gross misconduct.

The amount of pay in lieu of notice you should get will depend on how much notice you are entitled to. You should get pay in lieu at the rate of your normal wages. For example, if you are entitled to four weeks' notice, but are only given one, you will be entitled to three weeks' pay in lieu of notice. You may be entitled to more than this, depending on what your contract says.

ENFORCING RIGHTS AT WORK

Employment tribunals

Employment tribunals are legal bodies that deal with complaints about employment rights. A tribunal is made up of a legally qualified chairperson and two other people representing the employer's and the employee's sides of industry.

If you wish to enforce your rights at work you can complain to a tribunal. A tribunal can deal with problems on the following:

- written statement of terms and conditions;
- maternity rights;
- holiday rights;
- itemized pay statements;
- unpaid wages;
- sex discrimination/equal pay;
- race discrimination;
- disability discrimination;
- discrimination on grounds of sexual orientation;
- discrimination on grounds of religion or belief;
- some health and safety issues;
- unfair dismissal and redundancy.

If you complain to an employment tribunal, you may risk losing your job. There are time limits within which you must take a case to a tribunal. These vary but generally a claim for unfair dismissal/illegal deduction from wages/ discrimination must be made within three months of the last day worked, or of the date of the last deduction or of the date of the discriminatory act. A claim for redundancy pay must normally be made within six months of leaving the job. It is very important therefore that, if you are considering making a claim to an employment tribunal, you should get help from an experienced adviser as soon as possible, for example at a Citizens Advice Bureau.

What is wrongful dismissal?

If your employer does not give you the rights you are entitled to under your contract of employment – for example, your employer does not give you the correct notice of dismissal that you are entitled to under your contract – this is known as a breach of contract.

Your employer may pay you an amount of money as compensation instead of giving you notice of dismissal or allowing you to work out your notice. This is called pay in lieu of notice. If there is a term in your contract that allows your employer to pay you 'pay in lieu of notice' instead of giving you notice, then provided you are paid the correct amount of pay in lieu, there will be no breach of contract.

If your employer does not give you the correct notice and does not pay in lieu instead, or does not pay the right amount of pay in lieu of notice, you may be able to claim compensation for the breach of contract by making a claim for wrongful dismissal. You can make a claim for breach of contract to the employment tribunal at the same time as making a claim for unfair dismissal. Compensation for breach of contract will be in addition to any compensation you can also claim for unfair dismissal.

You can claim compensation for breach of contract for other things, such as if your employer takes back your company car when it is a term of the contract that you have a company car for all the time that you are an employee (including your notice period).

REDUNDANCY

Redundancy is a form of dismissal. Therefore, in order to claim redundancy, you must normally have been dismissed from your job. You must have been dismissed because you are genuinely redundant, otherwise you will have been unfairly dismissed.

If you resigned, you will not be redundant. You may, however, be able to argue that, although you have resigned, you have actually been dismissed. This is called constructive dismissal and occurs when you have been put in a position where you have no choice but to resign – for example, you have been made to resign under pressure or you have been made to take another job that is not suitable.

If you volunteered for redundancy, this will usually count as a dismissal. There are special rules that apply if you have been dismissed because the business has been transferred to a new owner. There are also special rules that apply if you think you may have been dismissed or chosen for redundancy for a discriminatory reason – for example, if all the people chosen for redundancy are part-time, this would usually be sex discrimination.

If you are facing redundancy and are a member of a trade union, the trade union is the first place you should go for help. You should get advice as soon as possible.

Redundancy procedure

Where a job disappears, or is moved, causing a redundancy, the employer must follow a recognized procedure when selecting who is to be made redundant. The employer must also follow a proper procedure when dismissing an employee.

The employer must use a procedure that is fair, objective and non-discriminatory, using objective criteria. There is no legal definition of what is a fair and objective procedure, but cases that have gone to employment tribunals have established principles of good employment practice that employers should follow. These are:

- the employer will try to give as much warning of the redundancies as possible;
- the employer will use objective criteria when deciding who will be made redundant;
- the employer will try to ensure that the selection for redundancy is fair and in accordance with the criteria set;
- the employer will try to find alternative employment for the employee.

Unfair selection for redundancy is a type of unfair dismissal. Someone who has been unfairly selected for redundancy may therefore be able to claim compensation for unfair dismissal as well as redundancy pay.

Notice of redundancy

The required statutory notice is one week if you have been employed for at least one month but less than two years, two weeks if you have been employed for two years, three weeks for three years, and so on, up to twelve weeks. After twelve years' service, the statutory notice period is twelve weeks.

Discrimination

It is unlawful to have redundancy selection criteria or a redundancy procedure that involves discriminating on the basis of disability, sex, race, religion or sexual orientation. It is also unlawful to have criteria based on whether employees chosen to be made redundant are part-time or pregnant, as this would be sex discrimination. This is the case even if the criteria or procedure have been agreed with the work force.

You do not have to have worked for your employer for any qualifying period to be able to claim compensation for discrimination from an employment tribunal.

Suitable alternative job offers

If your employer intends to make you redundant, they must consider whether there are other jobs available that you would be capable of doing. If such suitable employment is available, it should be offered to you. If it isn't, normally this would mean that you were unfairly dismissed. Whether an alternative job offered is suitable will depend on the terms of the job offered and your skills, abilities and circumstances. Factors such as pay, status, hours and location are relevant when deciding if a job is a suitable alternative. Your employer does not have to offer a similar position or a position in the same workplace.

The offer of alternative employment must be made before your current job ends. It can be made in writing or can be verbal. It must give you enough details about the new job so you know what the difference is between your existing job and the new job. You must also be offered a trial period in the new job.

Your employer may offer you a number of alternative jobs. Each offer must give sufficient detail and you are entitled to a trial period in each, if you wish.

If you are considering the offer of another job with your employer you have a right to try out the job before you decide whether or not to take it, without losing the right to statutory redundancy pay. You can work in the new job for a trial period of four weeks. The trial period will start immediately the previous job ends. At any time during the period you can decide that the job is unsuitable. If you unreasonably refuse the alternative job after the trial period, you will not have a right to a statutory redundancy payment.

Leaving or getting another job during the redundancy notice period

If you are under notice of redundancy and have found another job, you may leave to take the new job during the notice period and still be entitled to a statutory redundancy payment provided certain conditions are met.

Redundancy pay

A redundancy payment is compensation because an employee's job has disappeared. If you are entitled to redundancy pay, you will get a statutory redundancy payment from your employer. You may be entitled to a larger amount of compensation because your employer has a contractual redundancy scheme.

If your contract gives you less redundancy pay than you are entitled to under law, the statutory amount will apply.

If you have contractual rights to redundancy pay, the way it is calculated and when it should be given will be in the contract.

Who is entitled to a statutory redundancy payment?

Only some employees are entitled to a statutory redundancy payment. To be entitled, you must:

- be an employee. Self-employed people or members of a partnership do not qualify.
- be under 65, or below the normal retirement age for your occupation if this is less than 65;
- have worked for the employer for at least two calendar years continuously since the age of 18;
- not be in an excluded occupation (see below).

If you do not meet these conditions, you won't get a statutory redundancy payment, even if you are genuinely redundant. If you are excluded from statutory redundancy pay you may be entitled to contractual redundancy pay. Check your contract of employment.

Excluded occupations

Most public employees – for example, civil servants and police officers – cannot claim a statutory redundancy payment as they have contractual arrangements that give them similar or better payments. Share fishermen can never claim a statutory redundancy payment.

Losing the right to a statutory redundancy payment

Even if you are entitled to redundancy pay, there are reasons you might not get it, for example:

- if your employer claims to have offered you a suitable alternative job, you may lose the redundancy pay (see above);
- if you want to leave before the date your employment is due to end – because, for example, you have found another job (see above).

How much is a statutory redundancy payment?

The amount of a statutory redundancy payment depends on:

- how long you have worked for your employer; *and*
- your age; *and*
- your weekly pay.

Statutory redundancy pay is worked out as follows:

- 1½ weeks' pay for each complete year of employment when you were aged between 41 and 64 inclusive;
- 1 week's pay for each complete year of employment when you were aged between 22 and 40 inclusive;
- ½ week's pay for each complete year of employment when you were aged between 18 and 21 inclusive. Employment before the age of 18 is ignored when working out statutory redundancy pay.

If you are made redundant when you are within a year of the age of 65, your redundancy payment is reduced by 1/12 for each complete month after your 64th birthday. This tapering gradually reduces entitlement to redundancy pay to nothing by the time you reach 65.

You cannot get a statutory redundancy payment once you reach the age of 65.

The maximum number of years of employment that can count is twenty. Employment is counted up to the relevant date, which is the date your notice expires. If you have not been given any notice, it is the date on which the notice would have expired had you been given it.

Weekly pay

The weekly pay that will be used to work out the redundancy payment will usually be your normal weekly gross pay at the time you were made redundant up to the maximum limit. This means that if you changed from full-time work to part-time work and are then made redundant, your weekly pay will be calculated at the part-time rate. Gross pay is pay before deductions such as tax and National Insurance are made.

A week's pay does not include overtime pay unless the overtime was regular and compulsory. Where earnings vary each week, an average of the twelve-week period leading up to the redundancy will be used. If commission is paid regularly, this should be included in a week's pay. An average should be calculated – for example, an amount that could be expected in a year, divided by the number of weeks worked in a year.

There is a maximum limit on the amount that can count as a week's pay. This applies even if you earned more than the maximum amount. There is a ready reckoner for calculating the number of weeks' pay due at www.adviceguide.org.uk that will give you a rough guide to how much statutory redundancy pay you will get.

When making a payment, your employer must give you a written statement saying how it is calculated.

Claiming a statutory redundancy payment

Your employer is responsible for paying a statutory redundancy payment to you on, or soon after, the date of your dismissal. You do not need to make a claim unless your employer fails to pay or claims that you are not entitled to the payment.

What to do if your employer refuses to make a statutory redundancy payment

If you have a right to a statutory redundancy payment, but your employer refuses to make it, you should make a written request for the payment. If your employer still refuses payment, you will have to make a claim to an employment tribunal within six months of the date of dismissal to get the money. However, remember that if you want to claim unfair dismissal or sex or race discrimination, the time limit to apply to an employment tribunal is three months.

A statutory redundancy payment may affect your entitlement to benefits and your tax position.

Claiming redundancy pay if the employer has ceased trading

If your employer is insolvent and a receiver or liquidator has been appointed to deal with the company's affairs, you should claim your redundancy payment from the National Insurance Fund. You can contact the fund on 0845 145 0004.

If your employer has ceased trading but is not insolvent, write to your employer claiming the redundancy payment. If the employer does not pay the statutory redundancy pay, you must apply to an employment tribunal within six months of your dismissal. If an employment tribunal decides that you are entitled to statutory redundancy pay but your employer still does not pay it, you can make an application to the National Insurance Fund for your redundancy payment.

Other redundancy rights

Right to notice of redundancy

Because redundancy is a form of dismissal, you will still be entitled to your statutory or contractual period of notice of dismissal, if your employer plans to make you redundant.

Time off to look for work

If you have been given notice of redundancy, you are entitled to paid time off to look for a new job providing that by the time your notice period ends you have worked for your employer for two years. The following employees are not entitled to paid time off to look for work:

- employees who have worked for their employer for less than two years;
- overseas employees;
- merchant seamen;
- share fishermen;
- members of the armed forces;
- police service employees.

There is no definition of how much time the employer has to give, but it must be reasonable. What is reasonable will vary according to the circumstances – for example, the difficulty of finding work in certain areas, the time and travel involved and the range of jobs you are looking at. In addition to these legal rights, you may have rights that have been negotiated by the trade union, if any, or from your contract.

SELF-EMPLOYMENT

If you are considering self-employment, you will need to give some thought to the different ways of trading and which would be most appropriate for your business. The business could take one of three legal forms:

- a sole trader. This is the simplest way of starting a business.

- a partnership. This is similar to a sole trader except that two or more people run the business.
- a limited company. This gives the business a completely separate identity from the people who run the business. It is more complicated to set up.

In addition to one of the above legal forms, self-employment can also involve one of the following trading practices:

- a co-operative. This is a business that is collectively owned and controlled by the people who work in it. At least two people must be involved.
- a franchise. A franchise is an agreement that allows the person buying the franchise the right to run a branch of a business that someone else has set up.

It is extremely important that accurate and detailed records of the business are kept. You may be able to keep your own books or employ a bookkeeper or accountant, but if you are trading as a limited company you will need the help of an accountant.

Tax

As a self employed person, you will be taxed differently to an employee. You will be responsible for paying income tax on your earnings and will usually need the help of an accountant. There are special tax reliefs and allowances that self-employed people can claim. If you are newly self-employed, you should register with the Inland Revenue by calling the helpline for the Newly Self-Employed. The helpline number is 08459 154515.

VAT

Value Added Tax (VAT) is a tax on goods and services that is paid to Customs and Excise. Whether or not a self-employed person has to pay, and in some cases has the right to choose to pay, VAT depends on the type of business and how much the business sells. Your accountant should be able to tell you whether you should be paying VAT or not.

Premises

Working from home has the advantage of low costs but you will need to make sure that the tenancy agreement, mortgage agreement or title deeds of the property do not place any restrictions on business use. You may also need to get local authority planning permission. If you are buying or renting property from which to trade, you need to make sure the property has been approved for business use. Planning permission may also be necessary.

As a self-employed person, you have a duty to make sure that your business premises and working environment meet health and safety requirements. Further information is available from the local health and safety executive or environmental health department of the local authority.

Insurance

Depending on the business and how you trade, you will be required by law to take out certain types of insurance. Other types of insurance are not compulsory but it is important to consider which ones are appropriate. The types of insurance you may need are:

- employer's liability insurance. If you employ other people you must have this insurance. It provides cover for claims made by employees who are injured or become ill as a result of their employment.
- vehicles insurance. Vehicles used for business must be insured for business purposes even if already insured for private use.
- public liability insurance. This provides cover against claims by members of the public who have been injured or had property damaged as a result of carelessness at work by you or your employees.
- premises insurance. Insurance will be necessary for the premises you work from, even if you work from home and there is already a policy. This is because the insurance will usually only cover residential use.
- contents, stock and materials insurance. This insurance will be necessary to cover the replacement costs of stock, materials and the contents of the premises even if work is being done from home and there is already a home contents insurance policy.
- health and accident insurance. These will pay a regular income or lump sum if you are unable to work because of an accident or sickness.

Immigration status

Setting up in business may affect your immigration status and you should therefore get good advice before doing so.

Employing other people

If you employ other people you will be responsible for paying wages, tax, National Insurance contributions and Working Tax Credit where relevant. You will have to meet the requirements of employment law and health and safety regulations.

National Insurance contributions

As a self-employed person you may have to pay National Insurance contributions for yourself and any employees. Whether you have to pay contributions for yourself, and if so what type, depends on how much you earn. Whether contributions have to be paid for any employees depends on what they earn. The payment of contributions will affect the benefits a person can claim in the future. You can contact a telephone helpline for information about National Insurance contributions, Statutory Sick Pay and Statutory Maternity Pay on 0845 714 3143.

Benefits and tax credits

As a self-employed person you may be able to claim benefits or tax credits, depending on your income and other circumstances.

Trading names and licences

You need to consider whether you wish to use a trading name for the business. If so, there are restrictions on the names businesses can use. You may also need to get a licence depending on the type of business.

Further help in setting up a business or co-operative

Banks can be useful sources of information and advice if you are thinking of setting up in business.
Chambers of Commerce are local organizations that give information, advice and training to businesses in their town or area. Most give free advice to members, but charge for services to non-members. Some Chambers of Commerce serve particular ethnic minorities.

The **Small Business Service** (0845 600 9006 helpline) is a government agency providing general information on starting up a small business. It operates the Business Link National Contact Centre (www.businesslink.gov.uk), designed to deliver information and advice to small businesses in the UK. It also operates a network of local providers throughout the UK, which can provide independent and impartial advice. The **Countryside Agency** (in England only: 01242 521381; www.countryside.gov.uk) can help small businesses in rural areas. Normally the agency only helps manufacturing or service industries and businesses employing less than twenty skilled employees, and will not help agricultural and horticultural businesses.

Local enterprise agencies give free general advice and support to small businesses. Training courses are also available, and are often free. Details of local enterprise agencies are available from the National Federation of Enterprise Agencies (01234 831 623; www.nfea.com or for business advice www.smallbusinessadvice.org.uk).

The **National Federation of Small Businesses** (01253 336 000; www.fsb.org.uk) is a pressure group that promotes the interests of all self-employed people.

The **British Franchise Association** (01491 578049) is the trade association for franchising companies. It was set up to promote franchising and establish standards.

The Prince's Trust (0800 842 842) helps young unemployed people aged 18–30 to set up their own businesses. In Scotland the age limit is 18–25. The Trust can give loans, ongoing business advice and help with marketing. The Trust is particularly interested in helping people from ethnic minorities, disabled people and ex-offenders.

Livewire (0191 261 5584; www.shell-livewire.org.uk) is a national scheme sponsored by Shell, to help young people aged 16–30 to set up in business. Young people with projects can discuss their ideas with local advisers and financial awards may be given. There is usually a closing date for the scheme each year. Each entrant to the scheme will be paired with an adviser who will help them on an individual basis to plan and develop their business idea.

Instant Muscle (020 8319 5660) is a charity that helps unemployed people to set up their own businesses or find a job. It provides training, practical advice, help with preparing a business plan, and individual business counselling. Instant Muscle also offers help and support during the first two years of trading.

Co-operatives UK (0161 246 2959) is the national federation for worker co-operatives. It produces model rules and model employment contracts that are used by most co-ops in the UK. It gives advice on setting up and running a co-operative, community business or community enterprise, particularly on the legal requirements necessary.

Brecon Business Centre (01874 610 054) is responsible for the economic and social development of mid-Wales. It provides advice and support to small businesses, including advice about setting up in business, preparing a business plan and whether the business idea is viable, and can help investigate sources of money, find suitable premises and set up financial control systems, for example bookkeeping.

Equality Direct (0845 600 3444; www.equalitydirect.org.uk) runs a free, confidential advice line for employers. It provides advice and information on equality issues and general people management.

Disabled Entrepreneurs Network (www.disabled-entrepreneurs.net) is a regional networking service for disabled people. It provides advice and support for disabled people who run their own business or who want to set up in business.

Jobcentres sometimes advertise details of self-employment possibilities for unemployed people, including contract work and commission only vacancies. They may also be able to provide information on starting a small business or arranging a franchise. If you want information you should speak to your Employment Services Adviser.

HELP FINDING WORK

The main government employment schemes are provided through Jobcentres, where you can get more details. Some employment schemes are compulsory for people claiming Jobseeker's Allowance (JSA) while others are voluntary. You can also find information at Jobcentres about employment schemes for the self-employed, training schemes, the New Deal and other types of help on offer.

Help for disabled people

Every Jobcentre has a Disability Employment Adviser (DEA) attached as part of a Disability Service Team (DST), providing specialist advice to disabled people and actual or potential employers. The DEA can advise on practical help through the Access to Work scheme, the Job Introduction Scheme and supported employment.

> *When I was younger I got into trouble with the police. I'm applying for jobs now and I'm worried my conviction will stop me getting work. Do I have to tell employers about my criminal record?*

The information that you have to give will depend on the length and type of sentence that you received and the job that you are applying for. You will always have to declare a prison sentence of more than two and a half years (or an equivalent period of youth detention or custody) if you are asked about any criminal record by an employer. This applies to a suspended or partially suspended sentence too. When you are calculating the time it is the length of the original sentence that counts, not how long you actually spent in custody. So, if the sentence was for five years but you were given parole after two years, you will still have to declare the offence.

You will also always have to declare any conviction if you are applying for a job where you will be working with children or vulnerable adults. For example, you will have to declare all convictions if you are applying to teach, work in the healthcare sector, work as a childminder, or as a social worker.

However, if you are not working with children or vulnerable people, there are some offences that do not have to be declared after a certain period of time has passed. If your conviction falls into this category the conviction is considered to be 'spent' and does not have to be declared, even if an employer asks you directly about your criminal record. This fixed period is known as a 'rehabilitation period' and runs from the date of conviction. The length of the rehabilitation period depends on the sentence that you received rather than the type of offence that you committed. Some will be spent more quickly then others.

You can find full details of the rehabilitation periods and more information about criminal records at www.disclosure.gov.uk/docs/pdf/simple guide to ROA.pdf

2

Communications

CONTENTS

INTRODUCTION

From 1875 when Alexander Graham Bell was granted a patent for his 'multiple telegraph' device, through to the world's first television broadcasts in 1935 and on to the development of the internet by Tim Berners-Lee in the late 1980s, advances in communication are at the heart of modern economic, financial and social life. Few in the developed world are without access to telephones and TV and the internet is central to many people's working lives. But hard on the heels of the benefits come the legislation and the pitfalls, along with concerns about privacy and data protection. In this chapter, we cover what to look out for when you are choosing phone service providers and the standards you can expect from them, television licences, and where to get help to protect your private information from misuse.

JARGON BUSTER

ISP	Internet Service Provider
CPS	carrier pre-selection – a phone service that allows a BT customer to make calls using another phone company
Network operator	the company that allows airtime so that you can make and receive calls
Service provider	the company that buys airtime from the network operator and sells it to shops, outlets or the public
Pay-as-you-go	where calls are paid for in advance

PHONE SERVICES – LAND LINES

You can choose between a range of phone service providers for phone lines and equipment providers for telephone handsets, faxes and switchboards. As well as BT, other phone service providers now include NTL (incorporating Cable and Wireless plc) and Energis Communications (for business customers only). There are also various cable phone service companies. Before choosing a phone service provider find out what phone services are available and how much they will cost. Take into account the cost of equipment rental, line and call charges, and call facilities such as call waiting. Also, check whether cheaper rates are offered for particular payment methods, like direct debit, the standards the phone service providers offer, any extra help for older or disabled customers and what the company's policies are on debt and disconnection.

Each phone service provider issues a code of practice that covers issues like repairs, maintenance, disconnection and their complaints procedure. Check the code of practice before choosing a service provider. For the addresses of where to obtain copies of the Codes of Practice of the individual phone service providers, see *Complaints about a phone service*, p. 281.

Phone directories and directory enquiries

BT produces a phone directory. You can choose not to be included in this if you do not want to give general access to your phone number.

No charge is made for a listing in the telephone directory.

If you are listed in the directory, your telephone number will also be available from companies that provide directory enquiries. Calls to directory enquiries are charged for unless a person is disabled. Disabled phone users must register with the phone service provider before they are eligible for this service.

I'm always getting phone calls from people I don't know. How can I stop them?

If the phone calls are from people trying to sell you something then you can sign up to the Telephone Preference Service. This service is free. Companies should not make phone calls to people who have signed up to this service. For details of how to register, contact the Telephone Preference Service (0845 070 0707; www.tpsonline.org.uk). If the phone calls are from strangers who do not give their name and are being offensive then contact the police. This sort of nuisance call is against the law and people can be prosecuted if they are discovered doing this.

Repairs, rebates and compensation

Each phone service provider has a different policy on repairs, and you will need to check their code of practice to find out more.

Codes of practice on repairs will usually cover issues such as whether there is a time limit during which repairs should be started once a problem has been reported and whether faults are repaired free of charge. This is often the case unless the phone service provider decides the fault was due to damage caused by the customer.

If your phone is not working properly for more than a certain time after being reported, you may have a right to a rental rebate on the standing charge. The phone service provider may also have to pay compensation for the period when the phone service was not available. Details will be in the code of practice.

Claiming the cost of repairs on insurance policies

You may be able to claim on your house contents insurance policy for the cost of repairing or replacing damaged phone equipment if this is not provided free of charge by the phone service provider. Check your policy to find out whether there is an excess or loss of no-claims bonus since the cost of replacing damaged telephone equipment is usually quite low.

Entering land for installation and repairs

If a phone service provider wishes to install cable, telephone poles or pylons or other equipment, it must first get permission in writing from the occupiers of any land concerned, including land needed for access. Various problems can arise:

- you may not want poles on your land or wires going over your property;
- you may not want your land dug up for cable laying or may not agree to the phone service provider's plan;
- there may be disputes about how near to a building the phone service provider wants to install overhead wires;
- you may be willing to allow entry to the phone service provider but want to know if you are entitled to compensation and, if so, how much.

It is worth getting legal advice on this if you want to withhold permission. A previous owner of the land may have agreed to installation of cables or poles and you may be bound by the agreement. If permission is refused, the phone service provider could apply to court for an order allowing installation.

The right to a phone service

BT has an obligation to provide a phone service to anyone who asks for it, unless a prospective customer has been in debt with BT before. In this case, BT can refuse to provide a new service.

If a prospective customer lives somewhere remote, the price of providing a phone service may be extremely high, and the person may not be able to pay the full connection cost.

None of the phone service providers other than BT have an obligation to provide a phone service.

If you want information or advice about changing to a new phone service provider, you could consider contacting **OFCOM** (0845 456 3000; www.ofcom.gov.uk), which can give general information about what to check when considering whether to change to a new phone service provider and provide a list of the licensed phone service providers in your area. OFCOM cannot recommend individual phone service providers.

Number portability

All phone service providers must allow customers to keep their phone number when changing phone service provider. This is known as number portability. This only applies if you are changing the phone service provider you use without changing your address. Some phone service providers offer an additional service where a customer may change address and phone service provider and still keep the same phone number. However, phone service providers are not obliged to offer this service. Phone service providers may make a reasonable charge for providing number portability.

Carrier pre-selection

Carrier pre-selection (CPS) is a phone service that allows a BT customer to make calls using another phone company. You can do this either by dialling a short code or freephone number on your BT phone (which connects you to the other phone company) and then dialling the number wanted. Alternatively, you can have an adaptor plugged between the socket and the phone that allows calls to be diverted to another phone number without your having to dial a code first. Carrier pre-selection must be made available to BT customers. Other phone companies – for example, mobile phone companies – can choose whether to make it available to their customers.

Certain types of call are not included in CPS – for example, emergency numbers, operator assistance, directory enquiries and flat-rate internet access. You will still have the same access to these.

You do not have to make every call using CPS. For example, you may want to use a CPS provider for international calls but another provider for local calls. In such a case, once you have arranged to have international calls put through via a certain provider, you dial the code for that provider before dialling the international number. You can choose four options for CPS: national calls only, international calls only, national and international calls and 'all calls', which includes local, national, international and mobile phone calls.

BT will still own, run and send you the bills for your phone line. Your phone number will not change. However, you will get a separate bill for call charges from each different phone company that you use. More information about CPS is available from OFCOM (0845 456 3000; www.ofcom.gov.uk).

Phone bills

Disputing the size of the bill

Your phone service provider may offer an itemized billing service, showing the date, time, duration and cost of calls costing more than a certain amount, or it may show all calls made. You will need to check with your phone service provider to see if it offers such a service, and if there is any charge. This will help you to minimize disputes about the size of the bill.

You may consider that a telephone bill is too high. In general, it is rare for phone equipment to give wrong information but it is possible for there to be a fault. Occasionally a handset may be faulty and fail to disconnect at the end of a call.

If you have a high bill as a result of calls made by someone who is not a joint-account holder – for example, a friend or a lodger – you will have to pursue that person for the money. If the calls were made to premium rate services, you could also contact the Independent Committee for Supervision of Standards of Telephone Information Services (0800 500 212; www.icstis. org.uk) for help with claiming compensation.

Payphones installed by landlords

If a landlord has a payphone put into a property, they are responsible for the rental and for paying the phone service provider for calls made. Some payphones can be programmed (by the landlord) with a special scale of charges. This may be considerably higher than public payphone charges. The landlord must display the charges on or near the payphone. If charges aren't displayed you can make a complaint to OFCOM.

Disconnection

Each phone service provider has its own policy on disconnections and it is vital that you refer to their code of practice.

Rebate, discount and low cost schemes

Many phone service providers offer a range of special discount and rebate schemes, including schemes for light and heavy users of their phone services. Information on these schemes is available from individual phone service providers.

Phones for disabled people

Someone who is assessed by social services as having a particular need may get help with telephone charges. Some local authorities will pay for installation, others will pay for the rental costs. Phone companies can provide a range of special equipment and services for elderly or disabled people.

Problems in rural areas

There is usually a standard charge for running a phone line into a property and installing a phone. However, if you live some distance from the nearest cable, the phone service provider may charge for part or all of the cost of laying new cable, poles and so on. Contact the phone service provider for details of, for example, how near you are to other customers or phone cables, and the likely costs of connection.

Nuisance calls

Stopping unsolicited phone calls and faxes

All direct marketing companies are banned from making unsolicited phone calls to people who have registered with the **Telephone Preference Service** (0845 070 0707; www.tpsonline.org.uk). Direct marketing companies in the European Union are not allowed to send unsolicited faxes to anyone who has not given their consent to receive faxes from the company, and this is the case whether or not they have registered with the **Fax Preference Service** (0845 070 0702; www.fpsonline.org.uk).

Harassing, obscene or malicious phone calls

Making an obscene, harassing or malicious phone call may be a criminal offence. If you receive such a call, report it to the police. The police can, for example, authorize the phone service to trace malicious calls. If the person who is making the calls is prosecuted, you may have to give evidence in court. The phone service provider may have procedures that deal with malicious, obscene or harassing phone calls. Check the phone service provider's code of practice. For example, BT has a special phone number to call – 0800 666700 – for a 24-hour recorded message.

Caller display/caller return

Almost all phone service providers supply a service called 'caller display' or 'caller return'. Caller display shows the number of the caller, provided the phone receiving the call has a visual display unit. Caller return enables the person receiving calls to find out the number of the last caller by phoning 1471. To delete the last incoming number, dial 1475.

Caller return may be of limited use in the case of malicious calls, as the person making the call can withhold their number by dialling 141 before making the call. This does not mean that the number cannot be traced once the police have authorized this. In the case of nuisance calls, the phone service provider can trace the caller's number even if the number from which the call was made has been withheld. You can also decide not to answer a call if the caller's number is not displayed.

Helplines and premium rate phone lines

If you get itemized phone bills, any calls to telephone helplines will be listed. This means that other people in the household will be able to see that you have phoned a helpline. Almost all phone service providers supply a last number redial service, which means that other members of the household can check the last telephone number that was called.

Some phone service providers itemize only those calls above a certain limit and so, to protect confidentiality, you could make a very brief call to a helpline and ask them to call you back. Most helplines that do this do not use caller display equipment and they withhold their number when making or returning calls to customers. Calls to freephone numbers beginning 0800 or 0500 are not itemized on the phone bill unless made through a switchboard. If you do not want the helpline to know your telephone number, you should dial 141 before entering the helpline number. This works only if you get through to the helpline immediately; it does not work if you press a 'redial' key. Premium rate services give information and provide entertainment over the phone – for example, weather information, competitions and message exchange services.

Premium rate calls cost more than ordinary phone calls, and rates for calls from mobile phones, telephone boxes and hotels can be higher still. Charges from an ordinary domestic phone must be shown in the advert for the service. Most premium rate service numbers begin with 090 and services of an adult nature begin 0909. If you have problems with premium rate phone services contact ICSTIS on 0800 500212 (www.icstis.org.uk).

Complaints about a phone service

The contract covering the service provided by the phone company is covered by the usual law of contract and you will have your usual consumer rights. If you have a problem with the services provided, check the code of practice for details of the complaints procedure you should follow. If the problem is not being dealt with properly, it may be referred to arbitration if the phone service provider belongs to an arbitration scheme. BT has an arbitration scheme. None of the other phone service providers are required to have one, but some do.

If you are still dissatisfied, OFCOM (0845 456 3000; www.ofcom.gov.uk)

or Otelo (the Office of the Telecommunications Ombudsman: 08450 501614; www.otelo.org.uk) may be able to investigate a complaint. OFCOM is a government organization set up to regulate telecommunications in the UK. It has various roles including monitoring the activity of licensed phone service providers and promoting competition between them. OFCOM can also look into or take up complaints by individuals about any aspect of phone service providers. It cannot help negotiate reduced or deferred payment of a bill.

OTELO may be able to help with a complaint about a telecommunications company if the company is a member of OTELO. You must have first used the company's own complaints procedure.

PHONE SERVICES – MOBILE PHONES

There are a number of points to consider before deciding which mobile phone service to choose, such as:

- the cost of calls. This varies depending on the time of day and it usually costs more to phone a mobile from a fixed line phone than it does to call another ordinary phone.
- the type of contract, and length of the contract;
- reception in the area where you live;
- what facilities are available, like voicemail.

Reception signals for mobile phones may be stronger in some areas, for example cities or towns, and weaker in others, for example rural districts. If you are thinking about buying a mobile phone and live in a rural area, you need to find out how good the reception signal will be.

Pay-as-you-go services

Instead of a contract where you pay monthly rental charges and the cost of the calls, you can choose a pay-as-you-go service, where calls are paid for in advance. With these you enter into a contract to pay a set figure for a phone package that includes a handset, battery and free calls for a certain period of time, for example one month, or you may be given a voucher to pay towards the first calls that you make on the phone. When the voucher has been used up, you can buy more vouchers from the mobile phone company. In this sort of arrangement, you enter into a contract for goods and services when you first buy the package and then into a contract for service each time you buy a voucher, even though this contract may be unwritten.

Contracts

It is important to establish who the contract is with in case you:

- want to end your contract for a mobile phone;
- have a fault on your mobile phone;
- want to make a complaint.

Your contract may be with:

- the network operator which is the company that allows airtime so that you can make and receive calls. Examples of network operators are O2, T-Mobile, Vodafone and Orange.
- the service provider who buys airtime from the network operator and sells it to shops, outlets or the public;
- the outlet that sells mobile phones. Some outlets may also be service providers or they may act as agents for service providers.

Here we use 'mobile phone company' to cover whichever type of company your contract is with.

You may find it difficult to arrange a contract if you are not on the electoral register. This is because all mobile phone companies make a credit check and someone not on the electoral register may automatically fail this.

Ending a contract

If you want to cancel your contract you can only do so if there is a clause in your contract allowing you to cancel. If there is a right to cancel, the mobile phone company may impose a charge. However, if you signed a contract in your own home or bought the mobile with credit or by distance selling methods you may have a right to cancel – see *Consumer Affairs*, p. 310, for more details.

Selling a mobile phone to someone else

If you want to sell your handset to someone else, check whether your contract allows this. Someone who wants to buy a second-hand mobile phone handset should check whether it is possible to use airtime that was originally bought by another person. Sometimes the mobile phone company may agree to a transfer, but make a charge. The mobile phone company will also check whether the phone has been stolen before agreeing to transfer the contract.

Stolen mobile phones

If your mobile phone is stolen, immediately inform the mobile phone company and the police. The mobile phone company will usually disconnect the service so that you do not have to pay for unauthorized phone calls. You may still have to pay for line rental for the minimum term of the contract, but check the terms of your contract. If your mobile phone is stolen, it may be covered by your household insurance: check whether a claim can be made.

Broken mobile phones

If your mobile phone breaks, immediately inform the mobile phone company. You should check your contract to find out if you must continue to pay rental charges for this period.

Driving and mobile phones

It is a criminal offence to use a hand-held mobile phone when driving. The ban also applies when you are waiting at traffic lights or in a traffic jam. Although hands-free phones are not included in the ban and can be used while driving, you can still risk prosecution for failure to have proper control of your car or for careless or dangerous driving. There is a fixed penalty for breaking the law by using your hand-held mobile when driving, or up to a maximum sum if you are convicted in court. Drivers of buses, coaches or goods vehicles face a higher maximum fine.

You can find out more about mobile phones and driving on the Department of Transport website (www.dft.gov.uk).

Mobile phone bills

Disputing the size of a bill

It is possible that a fault may have occurred that is the responsibility of the mobile phone company. However, mobile phone companies usually offer an itemized billing service, showing date, time, duration and cost of calls, so you can check whether or not a high bill is due to the calls made or a fault.

How to complain

If the mobile phone or phone service is unsatisfactory

If you have a problem with the phone (handset), it is the *seller* and not the manufacturer or the service provider who is responsible for dealing with your complaint. Remember, the law says the handset must be of satisfactory quality, fit for purpose and match its description.

If you have a problem with the mobile phone service, you will need to contact the person or company that you have a contract with. This will be the network operator (for example, Vodafone or O2), the service provider or the supplier.

The contract covering the service provided by a mobile phone company is covered by the usual law of contract. To complain, contact the appropriate office of the mobile phone company.

If you feel that a complaint is not being dealt with appropriately, follow the complaints handling practice of the mobile phone company. You can get a copy from the mobile phone company, or it may be printed on the back of a phone bill, or it might be in the code of practice.

Some mobile phone companies, including Orange and T-Mobile, belong to an arbitration scheme run by the Chartered Institute of Arbitrators (020 7421 7444; www.arbitrators.org) called the **Communicators and Internet Services Adjudication Scheme** (CISAS).

If you are still dissatisfied, **OFCOM** (0845 456 3000; www.ofcom.gov.uk) or **Otelo** (the Office of the Telecommunications Ombudsman: 08450 501614; www.otelo.org.uk) may be able to investigate a complaint. OFCOM can investigate a complaint about any aspect of mobile phone services. Otelo will only be able to investigate if the telephone company is a member of Otelo and you have first used the company's own complaints procedure.

POSTAL SERVICES

The Royal Mail operates to a code of practice and service standards that are described in the customer services section of their website (www.royalmail.com). You can also find out about Royal Mail service standards at your local post office. You can contact **Post Office Customer Services** (08457 740740) for help and advice about lost, delayed or damaged mail or to make a complaint. You can also e-mail a complaint via the website.

If you have made a complaint and you are not satisfied with the response you have received from Royal Mail, you can contact **Postwatch** (08456 013 265; www.postwatch.co.uk), the independent watchdog for postal services.

TELEVISION LICENCES

Everyone who uses a television set or video recorder needs a television licence. You will also need a licence if you use a computer that is capable of receiving authorized broadcast programmes (that is, the BBC, ITV, Channel 4, Channel 5, cable or satellite television).

A television licence allows the person named on it and any member of their household to use one or more television sets or video recorders. If you only have a black-and-white television you only require a black-and-white television licence. If you have a colour television or a video recorder you will require a colour television licence. This will apply even if the video recorder is used with a black-and-white television set.

There are set fees for colour and black-and-white television licences. These are increased annually. The increase is effective from midnight on the day of announcement. For details of current fees contact your local post office or **TV Licensing** (0870 576 3763; www.tvlicensing.co.uk).

Rules for particular groups

People who are aged 75
Free television licences are available for anyone who is 75 years old or over. The TV licence reminder includes details of how to apply along with an application form for the free over-75 licence. There is a special helpline to answer queries on 0845 603 6999.

If you are 74 you can apply for a special short-term licence that lasts until you are 75. For details of the cost of this licence contact your local post office or TV Licensing (0870 576 3763; www.tvlicensing.co.uk).

People who are registered blind
If you are registered blind by the local authority you will get a reduction in the cost of your television licence if you produce the local authority certificate or doctor's certification form when you buy the licence. The reduction is 50 per cent of the cost of a colour or black-and-white television licence.

If you are registered as partially sighted you cannot get a reduction. For details of the reduction contact your local post office or TV Licensing (0870 576 3763; www.tvlicensing.co.uk).

A TV licence is not necessary in order to install or use a television sound-only receiver. These are made for blind people and are manufactured on behalf of the Royal National Institute for the Blind. Television sound-only receivers are available on loan from the British Wireless for the Blind (01634 832 501).

People living in care homes

If you live in a care home you may be entitled to a reduction in the cost of a television licence if you are:

● retired and aged 60 or over; *or*
● have a physical or learning disability or mental illness.

This type of licence is called a licence for Accommodation for Residential Care (ARC). It is a group licence and must be applied for by the providers of the accommodation. It can only be obtained from TV Licensing (0870 576 3763; www.tvlicensing.co.uk). The provider of the accommodation is responsible for collecting the licence fee from each person covered by the ARC.

Students

If you are a full-time student living away from home, you will usually need a television licence. If you are living in a hall of residence and use a TV in your room you will need a separate TV licence. You will also need your own licence if you share a house with others but have a TV in your own room for which you have a separate tenancy agreement. If you have a separate tenancy agreement but there is only one TV being used in a communal area, only one licence is needed. If you share a house with others and have a joint tenancy agreement, you will only need one TV licence regardless of where the TV is located in the house.

Students can apply for a refund of an unused portion of their TV licence. If you have bought a licence at the beginning of the autumn term and do not remain in university accommodation or lodgings over the summer, you are entitled to a refund of any unused quarter (three full calendar months).

Buying a television licence

As soon as you get a television set or video recorder for which you need a licence you are responsible for buying the licence. You can do this by completing a form and paying the fee at any post office, or by writing to TV Licensing (0870 576 3763; www.tvlicensing.co.uk) asking for a form to complete. You will not be covered until the licence is issued, even if you have sent a completed application form and payment to TV Licensing. You can get a licence issued immediately if you go to a post office. A licence issued for the first time will last for one year from the first day of the month of issue.

You can renew a current licence at any post office or by post to TV Licensing. You can apply to renew a licence up to a month in advance. The new licence will last for one year from the original date of expiry, not from the date the licence is renewed.

You can only get a refund for a television licence in limited circumstances.

If you do not have a licence

You can be prosecuted for having or using a television set or video recorder and not having a licence for it. You can be prosecuted even if you are not the owner or hirer of the set. If TV Licensing decide to prosecute, the case will be heard in the magistrates' court. If you are found guilty, the maximum fine that can be imposed is £1,000. The court cannot confiscate the television set or order you to pay the television licence fee arrears.

Using a television set or video recorder away from home

If you have a television set or video recorder that you use at another address on a temporary basis – for example, at weekends or during holidays – you will need to have a separate licence for it. This is the case even if you already have a licence for a television in your main home.

Television sets or video recorders in rented accommodation (including guest houses and bed and breakfast)

In rented accommodation, the tenant is responsible for obtaining the licence unless the landlord installed the set, in which case the landlord is expected to obtain the licence. However, the user of the television set or video recorder will always be ultimately responsible for ensuring there is a television licence and could therefore be liable for prosecution. If you are the tenant, make sure there is a licence, either by ensuring the landlord buys the licence or by buying it yourself.

A landlord who lets more than one unit of accommodation with a television set or video recorder in the building for overnight, as opposed to long-term, accommodation, may be eligible for a hotel licence – see below. If a building is divided into bedsitters or flats, each separate unit of accommodation is regarded as one household unit. This means that each household unit with a set needs a separate television licence. Lodgers, paying guests and other residents, including relatives, who occupy separate accommodation at the same address count as separate households and need a separate licence for their own use of a television.

Where people jointly rent a flat or house, only one licence is required as long as they all live together as part of the same household, sharing all the facilities and the bills. People who live under this type of arrangement may have to produce evidence of this, for example the joint tenancy agreement. The licence will need to be in the name of one individual, and if that person leaves the flat they are entitled to take the licence and transfer it to their new address. A television licence is not transferable from one person to another except in the case of a free over-75 licence.

If a tenant installs a television set, their landlord is under no obligation to ensure that the tenant has a licence.

Television sets or video recorders in holiday accommodation (including caravans)

Television sets or video recorders installed by the landlord for the use of temporary guests on holiday must be licensed. A separate full licence must be obtained for each unit of accommodation with a television set or video recorder. For example, in a house divided into self-contained flats, each flat will need a licence. However, on a caravan site, the proprietor who owns the caravans may be eligible for a hotel licence. If you are a holidaymaker and have a set in a touring caravan, this will be covered by a licence for your home address. If the caravan is static, a licence for your home address provides sufficient coverage if television sets are not used at the same time at home and in the static caravan.

Television sets or video recorders in hotels

Hoteliers can obtain special comprehensive licences (hotel licences). Only one licence fee is required for television sets or video recorders provided by the hotelier in up to fifteen rooms. Each additional licence fee will cover up to five more rooms. A room may have more than one television set or video recorder in it without affecting this rule. Guests and staff who are permanently resident in the premises will require separate licences to use their own sets in their rooms. More information about hotel licences can be obtained from TV Licensing.

If you do not use your television set or video recorder to watch or record authorized broadcast programmes

If you do not use your television set or video recorder to watch or record authorized broadcast programmes (that is, BBC, ITV, Channel 4, Channel 5, cable television or satellite television) you will not need a licence. This means that you would not need a licence if, for example, you only:

- use the television set as a computer monitor;
- use the television set to play electronic games;
- watch pre-recorded videos, whether these have been bought or recorded by someone else on a licensed video recorder.

However, the television set or video recorder must be incapable of receiving all authorized broadcast programmes. This could be done, for example, by making sure that neither the television set nor the video recorder is tuned into any channels and ensuring that they are not connected to an aerial.

I am going to university soon and I want to take my television with me. Do I need a separate licence?

Most students will need a television licence. There are a few exceptions – for example if the TV set cannot receive television programmes and you are only using it as a computer monitor. If you are living in a hall of residence and use a TV in your room, you will need your own licence. If you are living in a house with other people you will only need one licence if you all live as one household, i.e. share bills and kitchen and other facilities.

If your house is divided into bedsits or flats with their own facilities, then each unit will need its own TV licence.

3
Consumer Affairs

CONTENTS

INTRODUCTION

There's no doubt about it: we live in a consumer society. Most of us make thousands of buying decisions every year, from choosing a plumber or where to go on holiday to deciding which insurance policy to go for, so understanding our rights as consumers is more important now than it has ever been.

The rights of the consumer really took off in the post-war 'never had it so good' boom of the 1950s, when almost full employment saw more people with more cash to spend. Coupled with that increased spending power was a massive increase in the production of consumer goods, alongside an explosion in the advertising and marketing industries. Add into the mix more recent moves away from state provision of pensions, and the privatization of many previously state-owned suppliers, like water and energy, and, like it or not, we now make more personal choices over every area of our lives than ever before.

Cheaper foreign travel and the growth of the holiday industry have meant that we are also consumers abroad, bringing the added challenge of understanding foreign consumer law. And buying over the internet is now a fact of life for many of us. But do we understand our rights for this and other forms of distance selling?

This chapter looks at what our basic consumer rights are, how we can enforce them and how to decide what choices to make in the first place.

PROBLEMS WITH SOMETHING YOU HAVE BOUGHT

When you buy goods, the law says that they must be:

- of satisfactory quality. This means that the goods must be free from faults, including minor ones.
- accurately described. It is a criminal offence for a trader to put a false description on goods.
- fit for their purpose.

Technically speaking, if one or more of the above conditions is not met, it means that your consumer rights may have been breached.

If there is a problem with something you have bought, deciding what outcome you want is the best place to start. You may want to reject the goods and get a refund, compensation or both, or you may want the goods replaced or repaired. If the trader is not able to replace or repair the goods, you may be able to get some money back, or end the contract you made when you bought the goods.

Even if your statutory rights under consumer law have not been breached – for example, even if the champagne flutes you ordered for your daughter's wedding are of satisfactory quality, have been accurately described and are fit for the purpose, but arrived during the honeymoon – there are still things you can do to resolve your problem. You may be able to take action against the trader for breaking a specific condition of the contract – i.e. the agreed delivery date. Or you may be able to use a trade association code of practice or guarantee to help you resolve the problem with your goods. If things have gone seriously wrong, you may need to claim compensation from a trader for injury or damage, and you may want to consider reporting the trader to your local Trading Standards Department.

You won't have a case against the trader if:

- you examined the goods, or a sample of the goods, when you were buying them, and the fault you want to complain about was so obvious that you should have noticed it; *or*
- the trader pointed out the defect that you now want to complain about; *or*
- you have damaged the goods yourself.

There are other situations where you do not have your usual legal rights. These include private sales, some auctions, business-to-business sales, and where goods have been given to you.

Codes of practice

Some traders follow codes of practice. Although not legally binding, they can give you extra protection. However, if the trader is a member of a trade association and is not following the code of practice, the association may be able to put pressure on them to resolve the problem.

Some codes of practice include an alternative dispute resolution scheme, such as mediation, an ombudsman or an arbitration scheme. If you go to arbitration the outcome is legally binding.

Getting a refund for goods

Goods bought from a shop must be of satisfactory quality, accurately described and fit for their purpose. If any of these conditions is not met, then you may have a legal right to reject the goods and get your money back.

You are allowed a short time to examine goods and try them out, but you must tell the trader about the fault as soon as you discover it. If you know you won't be able to get back to the shop for a few days, you should telephone to let the seller know there's a problem and that you want a refund. If you have kept an item for several weeks without properly checking it out and then discover a problem or fault, you might have difficulty in getting a refund because you would have had what is called 'reasonable' time to use the goods. To make matters more complicated, there is no legal definition of what a 'reasonable' time is.

There are some types of sale to which these legal rights do not apply. For example, if you bought the goods from a private individual, you only have a legal right to get your money back if the seller described them wrongly. Also you will not be able to get a full refund if you have continued to use the goods or tried to repair them in some way, so think twice before you do this.

There are some 'grey area' situations in which you may not get a full refund, even if it looks as though one of your consumer rights has been breached – for example, if the goods are faulty, but you have been using them for some time before they show signs of being faulty. In that case, the trader may offer you some money as compensation, instead of a full refund. They may offer you alternatives, such as a repair or an exchange.

Some traders refer you to the manufacturer or say that you should claim on the guarantee. However, you do not have to accept this and you would still be entitled to ask for financial compensation. Remember: it is the person who sold you the goods who is responsible for sorting your problem out, and not the manufacturer, so don't be pushed into claiming on a maker's guarantee, unless you want to.

If you want a refund but the trader does not offer one, you can go to court or use an alternative dispute resolution scheme to enforce your rights. Both these procedures can be straightforward and do not usually need a solicitor; a Citizens Advice Bureau (CAB) will give you the information and advice you need to enforce your legal rights.

When you buy something, the trader may give you additional rights over and above those that the law allows you. For example, some shops allow you to return items to them during a short period after the sale, even if there is nothing wrong with them. Because the shop offers this in addition to your legal rights, you will often be given a credit note or an exchange rather than cash back.

I bought a DVD player in a sale and it's faulty. Can I ask for my money back?

You have just as much right to expect the item that you are buying to be of good quality as if you had bought the item before the sale. The only difference with sale items is that if they were clearly marked as 'shop soiled' or imperfect you would not be able to ask for a refund because you would have been aware when you bought the item that it was not going to be perfect.

All legal rights still apply to goods bought in a sale. They must be of satisfactory quality, fit for the purpose you are buying them for and as described on packaging or labels. That means that if a saucepan is described as non-stick, the egg you are frying should not stick to it, and the 100 per cent cotton blouse you buy should be exactly that.

Repair or replacement of goods – the six-year rule

If one of your rights under consumer law has been breached, you can ask the trader for a free repair or replacement. You can do this at any time within six years of buying the goods, as long as it is reasonable for them to have lasted that long. Taking back a T-shirt to a market stall after five and a half years and expecting a replacement is probably not reasonable! If you don't discover the problem within six years of buying the goods, you will not be able to claim a repair or a replacement.

If the trader does not agree that there was a problem with the goods at the time of sale, it is the trader's responsibility to prove this if you have complained within six months of receiving the goods. If you make your complaint after six months, it is your responsibility to show that the problem existed at the time of sale.

A trader who agrees to carry out a repair or provide a replacement must do so within a reasonable period of time, and without causing you any significant inconvenience. If you ask the trader for a repair but this turns out to be impractical or too expensive, the trader will not be obliged to repair your goods, but you can choose to have a replacement instead. In the same way, if you have asked the trader to replace your goods and this turns out to be impractical or too expensive, the trader will not be obliged to replace your goods, but you can choose to have a repair instead.

If neither repair nor replacement is practical, you may be able to get the price reduced, or even to get a full refund if:

- it is impossible to replace or repair the goods; *or*
- replacing or repairing the goods would cost more than reducing the price or giving you a full refund; *or*
- the trader did not replace the goods or repair them within a reasonable period of time, or was not able to do so without causing you significant inconvenience.

You are likely to get the price reduced if the goods had performed well up until the point when you stopped being able to use them. If you have been unable to use the goods at all, you may be able to give them back and get a full refund.

Compensation for dangerous goods

If you have bought dangerous or faulty goods that have caused damage to property or personal injury to you or someone else, you can claim additional compensation to cover the costs of the damage, as well as getting some money back because the goods were unsatisfactory. Dangerous goods should be reported to your local Trading Standards Department.

Compensation for delivery delays

Goods must be delivered within a reasonable time, even if you have not been given a specific date for the delivery. 'Reasonable' depends on the circumstances – for example, the type of goods, the conditions in the trade concerned and whether the delay was due to circumstances beyond the trader's control.

Time is of the essence

If your goods don't turn up in a reasonable time, arrange a new date making 'time of the essence'. You should write to the trader, giving a firm date for delivery. If that date comes and goes with no delivery, you can claim compensation from the trader. The trader may offer you a fixed amount, but you can also claim for the real losses of waiting for goods that do not arrive – for example, the costs of a day off work to wait in. You could also cancel the agreement and ask for your money back. However, you may have to go to court or use an alternative dispute resolution procedure to enforce your claim.

I ordered a scooter for my little boy's birthday, which was last week, and it hasn't turned up. Is there anything I can do to make up for his disappointment?

Under consumer law, delivery dates don't form part of your contract with the trader. However, if you agreed a specific delivery date with the trader and the scooter still failed to arrive, you might consider taking legal action to get some sort of compensation.

Goods that are damaged during delivery

The trader is responsible for goods bought until they are delivered to you. If your goods have been damaged during delivery, you should complain to the trader.

Credit notes and goods

You cannot insist on a credit note, and you do not have to accept a credit note if one is offered. However, if you accept a credit note, you cannot change your mind later and get a full refund, or compensation, even if you were entitled to it.

A credit note does not have to take any particular form. It may be offered as a gift voucher and it can also have conditions attached to it. You may have to use it within a given time limit.

Check the conditions on the credit note and make sure that the trader has goods that you want to buy.

I have found a hole in the sleeve of a jumper I bought last weekend and am planning to take it back to the shop. Do I have to accept a credit note?

If you take goods back to the seller because they are of unsatisfactory quality, not fit for their purpose or do not match their description then you do not have to accept a credit note and you are within your legal rights to ask for your money back.

However, if you accept a credit note when you were entitled to your money back, you cannot later change your mind unless you can prove that you were forced to accept the credit note by the seller.

If you have taken goods back to a seller because you simply changed your mind about them – for example you don't like the colour – then you would have no legal right to ask for your money back. If the seller is offering you a credit note in these circumstances they are doing more than is required by the law.

Guarantees, warranties, servicing and spares

You have no automatic right to a guarantee, a warranty or servicing. In general, a guarantee is given to you free when you buy goods. You often pay for a warranty or a service contract. There is no law that says that spare parts for goods must be available for any length of time, or even at all.

If there is a guarantee or warranty, it may give you rights in addition to your normal legal rights. Guarantees and warranties often have terms and conditions attached to them which limit what they offer you.

However, it might be easier for you to claim under a guarantee or warranty where the trader is refusing to give you what you want, or if you have no legal rights against them. If you have bought goods in a distance sale (over the internet or by telephone, for example) it can be more convenient for you to claim on the guarantee or warranty. Guarantees and warranties can be very useful if you have problems with goods and the trader has gone out of business. Guarantees given free with goods must be written in clear English and be available for you to see. The conditions of the guarantee are legally binding. Both free guarantees and guarantees you pay for may offer you protection in addition to your legal rights.

My new washing machine has come with a guarantee. What exactly does this cover?

A guarantee is extra protection over and above your legal rights when you buy an item. The seller does not have to give you a guarantee.

Guarantees given free with goods must be written in clear English and be available for you to see. The conditions of the guarantee are legally binding.

In some cases a guarantee allows you to have faulty goods repaired or replaced. Giving a guarantee does not mean that the seller can ignore your legal rights as a customer – for example, your right to get your money back in certain circumstances if there is a problem with the goods.

If a trader tries to ignore a customer's legal rights they may be committing a criminal offence, in which case you could contact their local Trading Standards Department – the number will be in the telephone directory.

What you can do if you have no rights under consumer law

Even if you have no rights you can enforce under consumer law, perhaps because your goods weren't faulty when you bought them, or because more than six years have gone by since you bought them, there are still a few things you could try to get what you want. For example:

- you can try and negotiate with the trader for what you want – you may be able to get a good result;
- you can choose to accept a credit note from the trader;
- you can use your additional rights under a guarantee, if you have one;
- if the trader is a member of a trade association, you may be able to ask that trade association to put pressure on the trader. Some trade association codes of practice include an alternative dispute resolution scheme. These schemes use a third party, such as a mediator or ombudsman, to help the parties reach a solution.

How to go about getting what you want

Once you have decided what outcome you want – for example, refund, repair, replacement or compensation – you will need to contact the trader to put your case. If you approach the trader in the early stages and prepare your case well, your negotiations are more likely to have a successful outcome. You should put together all the information that you will need to pursue your case. This includes information on whether you have any rights in the situation and, if so, what they are.

You will need:

- a description of the goods. This includes anything that was said to you, anything in an advert or anything given to you in writing.
- some details about the trader. If the person who sells you the goods is a private individual, you have fewer legal rights.
- details of the problem with the goods;
- details of how long you have had the goods, or, if you have not had the goods at all, when you were supposed to have received them;
- details of when you first noticed the problem;
- details of whether the goods have caused any damage to people or property;
- details of what you have done about the problem, if anything;
- if you have already approached the trader, details of what was said;
- copies of any documents – for example, an order form, credit agreement or price quotation;
- copies of instructions, an advertisement or a guarantee;
- if you have paid anything, a note of how much, together with any bills or receipts;

- a note of how you were to pay for the goods, for example by cheque, cash or credit;
- copies of any letters between you and the trader, dealing with the problem;
- details of where you were when you made the agreement – for example, in a shop, at home, or at work.

Write to the person who sold you the goods first of all, at the address of the shop or the catalogue where you bought them, or e-mail the website if you bought them over the internet. Keep a copy of your letter or e-mail. If the trader has a head office address, send a copy of your letter there. If you bought the goods on credit, send a copy of your letter to the credit company.

Your letter or e-mail to the trader should say:

- what you bought and when, with a full description of the goods and reference numbers if possible;
- how much you paid;
- what the problems are, and when you first discovered them;
- what solution you would like – for example, a full refund, a replacement, a repair, or compensation.

You should also give the trader a firm date by which to reply to you. The date that you give should usually be seven to fourteen days after you send the letter.

You may prefer to phone the trader, or go and talk to them. Even if you get nowhere with this approach, it is always a good idea to follow up a visit or a phone call with a letter or an e-mail. The letter or e-mail should follow the format suggested above.

Credit where credit's due

If you bought goods costing more than £100 and less than £30,000 on credit, you may be able to enforce your rights against the company that gave you the credit, instead of the trader. This can be useful in situations where you have a claim against the trader who sold you the goods, but they have gone out of business or have no money to compensate you.

If you've tried negotiating with a trader but are not successful, you may want to consider going to court. Before taking legal action, you should make sure that you have tried all other options for resolving your dispute, like alternative dispute resolution (ADR).

CRIMINAL OFFENCES AND THE SALE OF GOODS

It is a criminal offence for a trader to:

- discriminate on the grounds of sex, race or disability when supplying goods;
- make a written statement that you have no legal rights;
- put a false description on goods;
- ignore the safety laws;
- try to charge for goods sent that you did not order;
- sell short measure or short weight;
- give a misleading price, either in writing or verbally.

These are only some of the criminal offences relating to the sale of goods. If you think that a trader has committed a criminal offence, you should report the matter as soon as possible to your local Trading Standards Department (details can be found at www.tradingstandards.gov.uk).

WHAT YOU CAN DO IF THE SUPPLIER GOES OUT OF BUSINESS

Sole traders, partnerships and limited companies

If the supplier of the goods or services has gone out of business, the action you can take will depend on whether the supplier was a limited company, an individual (sole trader) or a partnership. If you have a guarantee, you may find it easier to claim under the guarantee.

Sole trader/partnership

If you were dealing with a sole trader or a partnership, they remain liable even if they have ceased trading. You should continue to negotiate with the owner or partner and could consider suing for compensation if your negotiations fail. Before you take court action, you will need to find out whether the trader is able to pay. If the trader has gone personally bankrupt, there is not much point pursuing them through the courts. If you have already lost money on faulty goods or services, it is not worth losing more money on suing someone who cannot pay you.

Limited company

If the supplier is a limited company, it may have gone into receivership or liquidation. Receivership is where a receiver is appointed to take control of all the company's assets and sell them for the best possible price. This may mean selling the business as a going concern. However, the company may subsequently have to go into liquidation. A limited company may go into 'voluntary' liquidation following a shareholders' decision that the company is no longer solvent, or go into liquidation because of a court order. Once the company is in liquidation, a liquidator will be appointed to collect and redistribute all the company's assets using the rules set out in the insolvency laws. This is known as winding up. Once the winding up is complete, the liquidator sends the final accounts to the Registrar of Companies and the company is considered to be dissolved (gone out of business) three months later.

Disappeared off the face of the earth?

If you no longer have contact details for the business you have a problem with, contact your local Trading Standards Department. If it has them, it may be able to pass contact details on to you for the purposes of court action.

Is the supplier in receivership or liquidation?

You can find out whether a supplier is in receivership or liquidation and details of the receiver or liquidator from one of the following sources:

- the Trading Standards Department of your local council;
- a local traders' association or chamber of commerce;
- a trade association (if the trader was a member);
- Companies House (www.companieshouse.co.uk or 0870 3333 636) will tell you whether a company is in liquidation, free of charge;
- local firms of accountants or solicitors who deal with receiverships;
- the local Official Receiver's office.

When a company is in receivership or liquidation, you cannot insist that the liquidator sort out your problem but you should make a claim for compensation, which will only be met if there are assets left after the priority creditors have been paid in full. If the company is a member of a trade association, it may have a bonding scheme that covers you for this situation. For example, the Association of British Travel Agents (ABTA) will repatriate stranded travellers if their travel agency goes into liquidation.

You will have to negotiate with the receiver or liquidator to solve problems, such as:

- **return of deposit.** You are entitled to ask for your deposit returned, but this is unlikely to happen unless there is any money left after all the secured or priority creditors, such as the company's landlord and the Inland Revenue, have been paid. You should write to the receiver or liquidator enclosing proof such as a receipt, cheque stub or credit card voucher and keep a copy of your letter.

- **delivery of goods ordered.** If the goods you ordered have been earmarked for you by the supplier (for example, they have placed your name on them), you are entitled to have them and should contact the receiver or liquidator to prevent them from being sold. If not, you may be able to negotiate with the receiver to sell you the goods, but cannot insist that this happens. If the company goes into liquidation, the liquidator may sell the goods to raise sufficient money to pay the priority creditors, but will sell you the goods if they are still available once the priority creditors have been paid. You are unlikely to be given a guarantee, but may wish to accept the goods and pay the balance, if they are covered by a manufacturer's guarantee.

- **work not carried out.** If a company has gone into receivership, you may be able to have any work it was doing for you completed. You should contact the receiver to see if this is possible, but cannot insist that it happens. Should the company go into liquidation, the receiver will not be able to guarantee the work and you will have to decide whether to have the work done without a guarantee or lose your deposit. You may be able to negotiate a reduction in price to compensate you for the inconvenience and loss of a guarantee. You can only claim compensation for breach of contract once the secured creditors have been paid in full. If the company is in liquidation, you can make a claim for compensation, but cannot insist that work be carried out. If the company is a member of a trade association, it may have a deposit protection scheme that allows for the work to be completed by another of its members.

- **unsatisfactory goods or services.** If goods are faulty, the receiver may arrange to have the goods repaired or the work remedied or completed. You should contact the receiver to see if this is possible, but cannot insist. If the receiver refuses, you will find it difficult to enforce your rights, as there are unlikely to be sufficient assets to pay compensation. If the company has been sold as a going concern, you will have to negotiate with the new owner, who will take over the company's assets but not its liabilities. You cannot enforce a guarantee or maintenance agreement, but the new owner may agree to honour the guarantee or agreement if it appears beneficial to do so.

- **goods held by the company.** If your goods are being held by a company, for example awaiting a repair, you have a right to have them returned. You should write to the receiver or liquidator asking for their immediate return and for an undertaking that they will be kept safe until returned.

WHAT TO DO IF THERE ARE PROBLEMS WITH SERVICES YOU HAVE ORDERED

Services are everything from work done by professionals, such as solicitors, estate agents and accountants, to leaving a coat in a cloakroom, or using a parking space, in return for payment.

If the plumber's been but the tap still drips, you are entitled to have matters put right. It is the seller of the services who is responsible for sorting the problem out. Services must be performed with reasonable care and skill; they must be done within a reasonable time and you must be charged a reasonable price.

If you are unhappy with work that has been done for you, decide what it is that you want from the trader – do you want your money back, a repair, the service done again or the job finished? You may want to claim under a guarantee, or just pay less or not pay at all.

If things have gone seriously wrong, you may want to claim compensation from a trader for injury or damage, or even to see the trader prosecuted.

Problems can often be sorted out in the early stages and most negotiations end successfully, especially if you have prepared your case well.

You are entitled to inspect the service and examine the goods that are supplied with it, so check those new taps work before the plumber leaves your house. You must tell the service provider if you see any faults as soon as you discover them. If you want to stop the service, you should do so straight away, and discuss the problem with the trader.

The law does not say that you must allow the trader a chance to put things right. However, it would be reasonable of you to suggest it and you should not let someone else alter things or do repairs unless it is an emergency. If you want someone else to carry on with the work, you should get two or three estimates of the cost, and choose the cheapest one. You may be able to claim for extra expenses from the original trader, but they must always be reasonable.

Write to the trader first of all at their address, or e-mail the website if you contacted the trader over the internet.

Keep a copy of your letter or e-mail. If the trader has a head office address, send a copy of your letter there. If you bought the services on credit, send a copy of your letter to the credit company.

Your letter or e-mail should say:

- what was to be done, and what goods were to be used, if any;
- how much you have paid so far, or were going to pay;
- what the problems are – in detail – and when you first discovered them;
- that you are stopping the service and you want a full refund, together with any compensation for extra expenses.

You should also give a trader a firm date by which to reply. The date that you give is usually seven or fourteen days after you send the letter.

You may prefer to phone the trader, or go and talk to them. Even if you get nowhere with this, it is always a good idea to follow up a visit or a phone call with a letter or an e-mail. The letter or e-mail should follow the format suggested above.

Refunds for services

You are only entitled by law to have a full refund in certain circumstances. If the problem is serious, and the service is a total failure, you can get back any money that you have paid. If you are entitled to a full refund because something has gone seriously wrong with the service, you may also be able to claim additional compensation to cover the extra costs of putting things right. This could include, for example, site clearance before building or landscaping work starts again. If the trader has caused damage to property or personal injury to you or someone else, compensation may be awarded to cover the costs of damage.

You will not be entitled to a full refund if there is nothing seriously wrong with the service. However, you may be able to claim some money as compensation if there are minor faults, if you have been overcharged, or if the trader has taken an exceptionally long time to carry out the service. The trader may offer you a repair, or suggest that you can claim under a guarantee. These may be practical solutions, and you may want to accept them, but you are still entitled to ask for some money back. However, the amount of compensation you can get will probably be less than the value of a repair or replacement.

The trader may refuse to refund you, even if you have the legal right to ask for your money back. They may offer you alternatives such as repairs, or starting the service again. Some traders claim that the problem lies with the manufacturer of the goods they are using.

If you want a refund and the trader does not offer one, you can go to court, or use an alternative dispute resolution procedure to enforce your rights. Both these procedures can be straightforward and do not usually need a solicitor.

Repair or replacement

If you bought goods with services and the trader has not installed them properly, you may have the right to a repair or replacement. If the trader does not repair or replace the goods, you may be entitled to a partial refund, or to end the contract you made for the goods and their installation.

My favourite suede jacket has been comprehensively trashed at the dry-cleaners. What can I do about it?

First, remember that dry-cleaning may not remove all stains and may highlight existing wear, like the weakening of curtains by exposure to sunlight. If your jacket has been poorly cleaned, you can ask for a refund. The law says that a dry-cleaning service should be carried out with reasonable care and skill so you have a right to expect this. If the cleaner offers to re-clean the item, it is reasonable to let them do that. If that doesn't work, you may be entitled to compensation. You may also be entitled to compensation if the cleaner was negligent – for example, advised you that your jacket was safe to be dry-cleaned when it wasn't, and now it is in tatters.

If you cannot agree on what has caused the fault or who is to blame, find out whether the firm is a member of the Textiles Services Association (020 8886 7755). The TSA has an informal conciliation service that will attempt to resolve the matter. If this fails, they may suggest assessment by an independent test house. There will be a charge for this, and the fee will be paid by the losing party. If the dry-cleaner makes an alternative offer, be realistic about what you will accept. You may not get a better offer by going to court. Always keep dry-cleaning tickets, as you may have difficulty claiming your property without them.

Delays in starting and finishing services

Been waiting in all week for the builders to start work on the conservatory? If the trader has not started work in a reasonable time from the date of the order, or finished within a reasonable time from the date of starting, you can make 'time of the essence' of your agreement. Write to the trader, giving a firm but reasonable date by which to start or finish. What is 'reasonable' depends on the circumstances – for example, the conditions in the trade concerned and whether the delay was due to circumstances beyond the trader's control.

Once you have a proper date for the start or completion of the services, and these dates have been missed, you can claim compensation from the trader. They may offer you a fixed amount, but you can also claim for the real losses of waiting for the work to be done – for example, the costs of time off work, or of employing someone else to do the job. If you want to bring in someone else, you should get three estimates of what it will cost to do the work, and send them to the trader.

You could also cancel the agreement, and ask for your money back. However, you may have to go to court or use an alternative dispute resolution scheme to enforce your claim.

GUARANTEES, WARRANTIES AND MAINTENANCE CONTRACTS

You have no automatic legal right to a guarantee, warranty or maintenance agreement. In general, a guarantee is given to you free when you buy goods or services. You often pay for a warranty or a maintenance contract.

If there is a guarantee or warranty, it may give you rights in addition to your usual legal rights. Guarantees and warranties often have terms and conditions attached to them and set limits on what they offer you.

A trader may give you manufacturers' guarantees or warranties on goods that they installed as part of a service. These may be useful if the trader has gone out of business, so that you can no longer claim against them. But if you claim under a guarantee or warranty you may have to pay for someone else to come and do any necessary work – for example, to replace a double glazed window if the seal has blown within the guarantee period.

COOLING-OFF PERIODS AND YOUR RIGHTS TO CANCEL

You may be legally entitled to a 'cooling-off' period. This is the right to cancel within a certain period of time, usually quite short. If you cancel within the agreed time, you will not have to pay anything.

If you are not on the trader's business premises when you agree to buy, you have a right to cancel the agreement.

If you buy goods from a trader without having face-to-face contact with them – for example, by telephone or over the internet (called distance selling) – you have a *seven-day* cooling-off period in which to cancel the agreement.

If you buy goods from someone face to face but away from trade premises (called doorstep selling), you have an automatic right to a *seven-day* cooling-off period in which to cancel the agreement.

If you sign a credit agreement in your own home, after a face-to-face discussion with the seller, for goods costing more than £35, you are entitled to a cooling-off period of *five days*. After signing the agreement, you should be given a copy of the credit agreement clearly setting out your cancellation rights. You should also receive, by post, a second written notification of your cancellation rights. The five-day cooling-off period only begins on the day after you have received the second notification of your cancellation rights. If you wish to cancel your credit agreement, you should write to the credit company immediately. Send your letter by recorded delivery and keep a copy of your letter.

BUYING OVER THE INTERNET, BY TELEPHONE AND MAIL ORDER

Goods that are bought by the following means are all examples of 'distance sales':

- by telephone or fax;
- by mail order;
- electronically through the internet, e-mail or digital television;
- through a shopping channel, or teletext;
- from a catalogue;
- through a newspaper or magazine advert order form.

If you buy goods in any of these ways from a UK-based trader, you have rights *in addition* to those you have when you buy goods in a shop. These include the right:

- to be given the name and address of the trader;
- to be given the price of the goods, including taxes and delivery charges;
- to be given a cooling-off period of seven working days and information about your right to cancel the order;
- to receive the goods within thirty days;
- to keep or dispose of any goods you received but have not ordered. If a seller demands payment for unsolicited goods, you don't have to pay for or return the goods.

If you use a credit card to buy goods in any of these ways, you also get special protection against the fraudulent use of your credit card details.

I've had a personal letter telling me that I've won a prize in a lottery. How can I find out whether it's genuine or not?

If you find that you have unexpectedly won an exciting prize in a prize draw, lottery or other form of promotion you should be suspicious. While some of these approaches are genuine, some are dishonest attempts to trap you into parting with your money. Many common scams take the form of prize draws or lotteries designed to trick the unwary. Scams are usually based outside the UK, although they may use UK Post Office boxes.

You can find out about common scams on the Office of Fair Trading website (www.oft.gov.uk).

Buying over the internet

When you buy goods over the internet from a UK-based company, you have the same rights as if you bought them from a shop.

You also have additional rights when you buy over the internet, including the right to:

- clear information before you decide to buy, including the name of the seller and the price of the goods, including 'extras' like VAT or delivery charges. If you pay any money before the goods are delivered, the seller must also give you their full postal address, either in a letter, fax, e-mail or on the website. *And*

- cancel your order at any time up to seven working days after you received your goods and get your money back, although you might have to pay to return them. You cannot cancel if the goods were made to order, perishable, newspapers, or software, audio or video recordings which have been unsealed. *And*
- have the goods delivered within thirty days of ordering, unless you and the seller agreed otherwise. If the seller realizes later they cannot deliver within the time, they must give you the option of cancelling and getting a full refund. *And*
- protection from fraud if you pay by a credit, debit or store card. If someone uses your card fraudulently you can cancel the payment and the card issuer must refund all the money to your account.

These rights *do not* apply when buying:

- financial services, like insurance or banking;
- timeshare agreements (although there are other laws that protect you when you buy a timeshare);
- services like accommodation, catering or leisure services that you order for a certain date;
- goods at an online auction.

If the goods are damaged when they are delivered or are substantially different from their description on the website, you are entitled to ask for a full refund, including the cost of all postage and packaging. Faulty goods are not subject to the return time limit, but you must contact the seller within a reasonable time.

More about e-commerce

In addition to the rights mentioned above, there are other rules that apply to traders who sell using electronic commerce, or e-commerce, which includes selling by e-mail, on the internet, interactive TV, or by sending and receiving written information on a mobile phone. All traders based in the UK must follow these rules even if the customer is in a different EU member-state when buying the goods or services. There are a few exceptions (for example, betting or lotteries) but generally all electronic promotional material must contain certain information and must be correctly presented. It must, for example, identify the trader who sent the message, and you must be given in a permanent, easily accessible way the name of the trader, a postal address and an e-mail address. The price of goods must state whether it includes tax and delivery costs. The trader usually has to provide a facility that allows you to identify and correct any errors that were made when inputting the order.

There is a voluntary membership scheme called Euro-label for traders throughout the UK who use websites to sell goods and services. Its members must comply with a code of conduct and, if you have a dispute with a trader who is a member, you could use the Euro-label dispute resolution scheme. You can find them at www.euro-label.com.

What happens if mail order goods don't arrive

If the goods aren't delivered by the agreed date or within thirty days you have the right to cancel the order and get your money back.

If you paid for the goods in advance and the seller has gone out of business, you might get your money back if the seller is a member of the Mail Order Protection Scheme (MOPS: 01628 641930; www.mops.org.uk) or the Periodical Publishers Association (PPA: 020 7404 4166; www.ppa.co.uk). Check the advert to see if it has the logo of one of these associations. If it does, write to the advertising manager of the publication in which the advertisement appeared within three months of the date of the publication, giving the seller's name and address, the publication date of the newspaper or magazine, the date you placed the order, how much you paid and a summary of any action you have already taken.

Who can help?

Many large companies that sell through catalogues belong to the **Mail Order Traders' Association** (MOTA: 020 7735 3410) and its members have to comply with a code of practice. MOTA also runs an independent arbitration scheme which you can use if you cannot resolve the problem directly with the trader. There is a small charge for using the scheme, although this would be refunded if the arbitration finds in your favour. Many of the companies that advertise through direct marketing, which includes book and music clubs, charities, motoring associations and companies that advertise through inserts placed in magazines or papers, belong to the **Direct Marketing Association** (DMA: 020 7291 3300; www.dma.org.uk). DMA runs an independent arbitration scheme which you can use if you cannot resolve the problem directly with the trader. There is a small charge for using the scheme, although this would be refunded if the arbitration finds in your favour.

All mail order advertisements that appear in the UK must be legal, decent, honest and truthful. If you think a mail order advertisement describes goods or services in a misleading way in order to sell them, you should contact the **Advertising Standards Authority** (ASA: 020 7492 2222; www.asa.org.uk).

The **Direct Selling Association** (DSA: 020 7497 1234) is concerned with all types of direct sales agreements made in the home. Under the DSA's Consumer Code, member firms must give customers a fourteen-day cooling-off period. This applies whether or not the customer asked the sales person to call and regardless of the value of the sale. You can check whether a firm is a member of the DSA by looking at its website (www.dsa.org.uk). If you have been unable to resolve the problem with the seller, the DSA has an independent complaints procedure. Although the decision is binding on the seller, it does not prevent you taking legal action.

BUYING ON THE DOORSTEP

If you buy goods or services from a trader who visits your home, for example from a door-to-door salesperson or a double-glazing representative, or if you buy from a home party or party plan sale, you have the same rights as if you bought them from a shop. The goods must match their description (if a pair of sheets is described as fitted then they must be fitted) and must be of satisfactory quality. This means the goods meet the standards that any reasonable person would expect, taking into account the description, the price and all other relevant information. The goods must also be fit for their purpose. For example, if you tell a door-to-door salesman you need a cleaning product that is suitable for cleaning your car, he should not sell you one that will scratch the paintwork.

If you make an agreement to have a service carried out – for example, you agree to have a patio laid – the work must be carried out with reasonable care and skill, finished in a 'reasonable' time, unless a specific time has been agreed, and provided at a reasonable cost, unless a specific cost has been agreed. All these elements form part of the contract between you and the seller. This contract exists even if nothing is written down.

Cancelling an agreement made in your own home

If you decide you don't want the goods or services, you have a right in certain circumstances to cancel the agreement as long as you do so within seven days. This is known as the cooling-off period. Some sellers may allow a longer cooling-off period. If you cancel during the cooling-off period, you are entitled to get your money back, although if some work has already been carried out you will have to pay for that part of the work. The trader may have committed an offence if they do not give you written cancellation rights when the contract is formed. Your local Trading Standards Department will be able to advise you further on this.

You **do not** have the right to cancel agreements made at home if:

- the goods or services you bought cost less than £35, *unless* you signed a credit agreement at home, in which case you can cancel the agreement regardless of the amount you paid (see *Cooling-off periods and your right to cancel*, p. 310); *or*
- you contacted the seller and asked them to visit you; *or*
- the service included new building works, such as a conservatory. However, the right to cancel does include agreements for home repairs and improvements, such as fitting double glazing. *Or*
- you bought food or other perishable goods; *or*
- you bought the goods from a home party sale.

BUYING GOODS FROM A TRADER OVERSEAS

If you buy goods from a trader overseas, for example when you are on holiday, your rights usually depend on the laws of the country where you bought the goods.

Buying goods and services within Europe

Generally, when you buy goods or services from a seller in another European Union member-state, your rights will depend upon what the law says in the country where the seller is based. However, your consumer rights will be similar in most EU countries, because consumer law in each EU country comes from EU law. You will have UK rights and the rights of the country where the seller is based if:

- the seller advertised in the UK and you concluded the contract in the UK – for example, you bought shoes from a mail order company in Italy which advertised in a UK magazine and you sent the order from the UK; *or*
- the seller received your order while in the UK; *or*
- you bought the goods or services in another EU member state during an excursion organised by the seller to encourage you to buy – for example, you bought wine in France while on a wine-tasting trip organized by the wine seller.

You will not usually be entitled to UK rights as well as those of the country where the seller is based if the contract involves:

- a service not usually provided in the UK; *or*
- transport (although there are some exceptions to this, including package travel contracts); *or*
- insurance; *or*
- land or property – for example, buying or selling an apartment.

It is not clear whether you would be entitled to UK rights if you bought something from the website of a company in another EU member-state. This is because the question hasn't yet been tested in the courts, but it seems likely that you would be entitled to your UK rights if a website based in an EU member-state were targeted at the UK market – if, for example, prices were given both in euros and sterling.

You will not have to pay additional VAT or other tax when you buy goods in another EU country and bring them back to the UK, although it is a good idea to check before you buy, as special rules apply for some goods, including new and nearly new cars, motorbikes and boats.

If you bought goods and services by credit card and they cost between £100 and £30,000, the credit card company may be equally liable, for example if the goods are faulty. It may be easier to get redress from the credit card company than from a seller based abroad.

There is a network of European Consumer Centres (ECC) in many EU countries that provide information about consumer law and procedures for enforcing your rights. Citizens Advice Bureaux, with the support of the national Citizens Advice organization, operate the UK European Consumer Centre. (If you have a query, contact your local CAB, visit www.euroconsumer.org.uk or e-mail: euroconsumer@citizensadvice.org.uk).

PRIVATE SALES AND CAR BOOT SALES

If you buy goods from a private individual, for example through an advert in a newspaper or shop window, or at a car boot sale, you have very few legal rights that you can enforce as a consumer. However, if the goods are described, the description should be accurate. It is important to check goods before you buy, because generally goods bought from a private seller do not have to be free from faults, so you would be unlikely to get a refund on the basis of a discovered fault. However, if you were told by the seller that the goods were in a good working order and they weren't, you might be able to take action on the grounds that the goods did not match their description. Sometimes people who sell goods as part of their business pose as private sellers because then the customer has fewer rights. This is a criminal offence and, if you think that a private seller is actually in business, you could inform your local Trading Standards department, which can take action against the seller.

It is also an offence for a private seller to sell an unroadworthy car. Again, you should report suspected offences to your local Trading Standards Department.

Remember: if the seller arranged credit to pay for the goods, or you paid by credit card and the goods cost more than £100 and less than £30,000, the credit company may be equally liable for any breach of contract.

It is unlikely that you would be able to claim against a guarantee that came with goods bought from a private seller, as usually guarantees are only valid for the person who first bought the goods.

You may be entitled to compensation if:

- the seller has described the goods wrongly, although this may be difficult to prove unless it was in a written advert or you have a witness; *or*
- someone has been injured by an unroadworthy vehicle; *or*
- the seller knowingly made a false statement about the goods in order to persuade you to buy them.

It is always worth taking legal advice before deciding whether to accept an offer of compensation for personal injury.

Second-hand goods

You have the same rights when buying second-hand goods as you do when buying new, but you must take into account the fact that they are second-hand and so won't necessarily be of the same quality as new. Even though you can still claim your money back for faulty goods, you won't be able to claim that the goods are faulty if the faults are down to reasonable wear and tear or were obvious when you bought them. So be sure to check the goods carefully before you buy.

AUCTIONS

If you buy *new* goods at an auction, you have the same legal rights that you have if you buy goods in a shop.

If you buy *second-hand* goods at an auction, you only have legal rights if you weren't given the opportunity to attend – for example, at an internet auction, such as eBay. You'll also lose your rights if the auction house makes it clear that you don't have normal consumer protection or that the goods are sold 'as seen'.

When you buy goods at an auction, you enter into a contract with the owner of the goods, not the auctioneer, so if there is a dispute you will have to take action against the owner and not the auction house. In addition, the auction house is not obliged to give you the owner's details, so tracing them may be difficult. However, the auction house must not make false statements about the goods. Contact the auction house as soon as possible if you have a problem. If you have paid an indemnity fee, check whether it covers your particular problem. For example, if you discover that the car you have bought at auction is recorded as a 'write-off' you may have a claim under the indemnity policy.

These rules apply to distance auctions in the UK. If you buy something

---

Did you know . . .

that if you buy goods for your business, the legal rights that you normally have as a private consumer may not apply?

via an internet auction from a firm based outside the UK, the law of that country will usually apply. If you have a dispute in these circumstances it's a good idea to seek specialist advice.

KEEPING LOST, FOUND AND UNCOLLECTED GOODS

If you want to find out whether you can keep something you have found, you must first check whether the goods are:

- uncollected or abandoned;
- stolen;
- lost;
- treasure;
- goods found in the sea or on the seashore.

Uncollected or abandoned goods

A person may leave goods that belong to them with someone else and appear to have abandoned them. Examples might include scaffolding or other equipment left by builders on site, uncollected goods left by a tenant in a landlord's property or goods ordered and received but then rejected or not paid for.

If you have uncollected or abandoned goods, you have a duty to look after them. You may be liable for any damage caused to the goods while they are in your care.

If you are in possession of another person's goods you can sell or otherwise get rid of them if they remain uncollected, as long as you make reasonable attempts to get the owner to collect them and provide the opportunity for the owner to take the goods away. If you want to sell the goods you must take reasonable steps to trace the original owner if they or their whereabouts are unknown. Money received from the sale has to be returned to the original owner or, if this is not possible, kept on account for them. The owner only loses their right to the money after six years.

Stolen goods

When goods are stolen, the original owner still retains their legal right of ownership over the goods. When stolen goods are found a court can order the return of the goods or a compensation payment for the value of the article to be made to the original owner.

If you get stolen goods, even if you have paid a fair price and are unaware that the goods were stolen, the general rule is that you do not get a legal right of ownership. You must inform the owner and allow them to take the goods away, if you discover that they were stolen. If you buy something that you later find out was stolen, you could try to claim compensation from the seller.

Lost goods

If you find goods that appear to be lost, then you can keep the goods as long as:

- you did not find the goods dishonestly or while trespassing;
- you did not find the goods on your employer's property;
- the goods are actually lost, and not uncollected or abandoned, stolen or treasure;
- you have taken reasonable steps to find the owner of the goods – for example, left them to be claimed at a police station for a reasonable length of time;
- the goods were found on premises or land where the occupier does not exercise much control – for example, an air terminal lounge, the public part of a shop, or a recreation ground. (Sometimes it can be the owner of the land rather than the finder who has the right to keep the goods.)

Goods handed in to the police

The usual police practice is that the finder can have the goods back and keep them if they are not claimed within six weeks. However, the police may want more time if there are special circumstances and they want to investigate – for example, if they suspect the goods are stolen or think that the owner can be traced. Once the property has been returned to the finder by the police, the original owner cannot usually then claim the goods.

Treasure

Treasure is the property of the Crown. Anyone who finds treasure should report this directly to the coroner for the district where the object was found within fourteen days of the find (or of first having reason to believe the object may be treasure). A finder who fails to report a discovery without a reasonable excuse will be committing a criminal offence. The coroner may hold an inquest to determine whether the object is treasure and, if so, who the finder was. This process can take several months.

An object is normally only treasure if it is at least three hundred years old and made of silver or gold.

When an object has been declared treasure it is dealt with in one of the following ways:

- if it is not required for any museum, it is returned to the finder, who can then sell the object (the finder must have had permission to be on the land where the treasure was found); *or*
- if the find, or any part of it, is kept for a museum, the finder is paid a sum equal to the market value of what is kept.

It is to the finder's advantage to report the find at once. The finder will either get the find back or its market value as an ex gratia reward. A finder should generally receive a reward within twelve months of having delivered the find. If the find is not required by a museum it will be returned to the finder within six months.

Goods found in the sea or on the seashore

Property found in the sea or on the seashore could be from a ship and is known technically as 'wreck'. All wreck must be reported to the Receiver of Wreck. This can be done by downloading a form from the Receiver's website (www.mcga.gov) or by calling 02380 329474.

BUILDERS

Most of us need to employ builders at one time or another, so it's best to know what the deal is from the start.

When you have building work done, the law says the work must be performed with reasonable care and skill, done within a reasonable time and you must be charged a reasonable price. Any goods or materials provided as part of the work must match their description and be of satisfactory quality. This covers the normal use associated with the goods or materials. For example, if you tell the builder that you want a block-paved drive that will withstand the weight of vehicles, it shouldn't crack when you drive on it.

Who is the contract with?

Before you deal with a building problem, you will need to work out who you have the contract with. It could be:

- a **builder**, if you made an agreement with a building firm who agreed to carry out the work, or agreed to subcontract part of the work to other builders;
- an **architect or structural engineer**, who took responsibility for employing the builders;
- an **individual contractor**, if you employed each worker yourself;
- a **subcontractor**, if you have agreed for them to carry out additional work. For example, if you ask a plumber, who was contracted by your builder, to service your central heating system, then you have a contract with that subcontractor.

If you are unsure with whom you have a contract, any action you take should be against all the builders and subcontractors involved.

General tips on dealing with builders

- You cannot usually cancel the work because you have changed your mind or have found another builder who will do the work more cheaply.
- Only pay the final amount when the work has been completed to your reasonable satisfaction.
- Do not sign any document that says you are satisfied with the work until you have had sufficient time to test it.
- If you used your credit card or the trader arranged finance for you, and the cost of the work is over £100 and under £30,000, the credit company may be equally liable for any breach of contract – for example, if there was any damage to your house during fitting.

What to do if the work is shoddy or the goods supplied are unsatisfactory

So, the double-glazing has been installed, but the windows don't open properly. What can you do about it? First you will need to ascertain whether the windows themselves are faulty or the trader has installed them incorrectly.

If you buy goods from a trader who installs them for you, you can ask them to **replace or repair** the goods free of charge if they are faulty, or if they were installed without reasonable care or skill.

If it is impossible to replace or repair the goods, or it would be unreasonably costly for the trader when compared to alternative remedies, or if the trader fails to replace or repair within a reasonable timescale, or causes you significant inconvenience, then you can ask for a partial or full refund, the amount of which would take into account any use you have had out of the goods.

You may be entitled to **compensation**:

- if the work was not carried out with reasonable care, or takes an unreasonable length of time to be completed;

A builder I hired to build us a garden wall is taking a very long time to complete the job. Is there any way that I can make him finish it?

When you hire a builder to work for you, you are buying a service and are entitled to expect that it should be done with the care and skill you would expect from a tradesman. That means that any walls built should not crack or roofs be leaky.

You do not need to have agreed a timescale before the work is started but you can expect it to be carried out within a 'reasonable' time. There is no legal definition of 'reasonable' but it would not be reasonable to expect a builder to build a complete house in two weeks or for it to take three months to build a barbecue.

If you think that the builder is taking an unreasonable time, you could begin by keeping a diary of the times that the builder is doing your work and photographs of the stages of the work as it is going on. This could be used as a form of evidence if you decide to take legal action. If you talk to the builder about your concerns and this makes no difference it would be a good idea to write to the builder (keeping a copy of the letter) setting out what you want. If this still makes no difference then you may be able to take court action.

If you agreed with the builder that the work would start on a certain day, you've paid a deposit and the agreed date has passed, you may be entitled to a refund. This is because a condition of the contract has been breached.

- if the trader has been negligent – for example, if your new windows let in rain and you have to redecorate;
- if the goods or services are unsafe and someone has suffered an injury. Always take legal advice before accepting compensation for personal injury.
- if you have incurred additional expenses, like the cost of employing someone else to rectify any faults.

If you think a **criminal offence** has been committed – for example, the trader has described the glass as safety glass, but you believe it is not – you should contact your local Trading Standards Department before allowing the trader to rectify the work. Strict rules apply to the construction of new buildings/extensions, and so you should discuss your concerns with your local Building Regulations department.

Steps to work through

1. Once you've decided where you stand, collect all the relevant documents together and contact the trader as soon as possible, either by telephone or by visiting their offices. Explain the problem calmly but firmly and ask for a refund, repair, replacement or compensation. Set a time limit. If you can't agree who is responsible for the problem, try to arrange for the trader to visit your home to examine the work.
2. If you are still dissatisfied and cannot reach a satisfactory agreement, try to find out whether the trader is a member of a trade association that might be able to arbitrate.
3. If the matter is still not resolved, or there is not a trade association who can help, write to the trader (and the credit company, if applicable) repeating your complaint and what steps you have taken to resolve the matter. Say you are giving them fourteen days to resolve the problem, or you will ask another trader to carry out the work and that you intend to recover the charges from them. You can add that you will consider legal action. Send the letter by recorded delivery, with a copy to their head office, if applicable, and remember to keep a copy yourself.
4. If the trader then makes you an alternative offer, you can either accept or continue to negotiate. Be realistic in what you will accept – you may not get an improved offer by going to court.

Court – the last resort

If you do not receive a reply to your letters, or the trader refuses to do anything or makes you an unacceptable offer, you will have to consider going to court. Before going to court, you need to consider whether you have sufficient evidence. You will have to prove in court that the trader is responsible for the problem and you may have to provide expert evidence. You will also need to find out whether the trader is solvent, as there is no point suing a person or company who has no money. And if you have lost money on shoddy building work, don't waste any more on a case you can't win!

Who can help?

The **Architects' Registration Board** (020 7580 5861) deals with complaints against architects.
The **Royal Institute of British Architects** (020 7580 5533) has an internal conciliation and arbitration scheme to deal with complaints against its members.
The **Federation of Master Builders** (FMB: 020 7242 7583) has a complaints procedure to deal with disputes.

BUYING SECOND-HAND CARS

Getting a new motor? After buying a house, a new set of wheels is probably one of your biggest one-off purchases, so it's worth spending some time getting to know your rights.

When you buy a second-hand car, your rights will depend on whether you buy the car from a dealer, at an auction or from a private seller.

Buying from a dealer

If you buy a second-hand car from a dealer, it must:

- match the description given by the seller and this includes any written description in an advertisement or catalogue; *and*
- be of satisfactory quality – i.e. be in reasonable condition, considering its age and make, its past history and the price paid.

It must also be fit for its purpose. For example, if you request a vehicle that is capable of towing a large caravan, it must be up to the job.

It must also be roadworthy. In fact, it is a criminal offence to sell an unroadworthy car. A car is not roadworthy if its brakes, tyres, steering, or construction make it unfit for the road.

You will not have these rights if:

- the dealer pointed out the full extent of any fault before you bought the car;
  or
- you examined the car and should have noticed the fault. This mainly applies to cosmetic defects if examined by a lay person. The dealer would not be able to evade responsibility for mechanical defects if they were not apparent on your examination.

Vehicle checks

Before purchase, it is worth carrying out a check to discover whether the car has been the subject of an insurance write-off or stolen, or whether there is outstanding finance from a previous sale. Mileage checks may be available. For peace of mind, you may wish to get the vehicle inspected for mechanical faults by an expert. There is a charge for these services. For further information about organizations that can do vehicle checks go to www.consumer.gov.uk.

Criminal offences

A criminal offence will have been committed if the dealer:

- gives a false description (for example, states there has been one careful owner when the logbook shows four former keepers); *or*
- sells an unroadworthy car; *or*
- alters the mileage reading or sells you a car with an altered mileage reading; *or*
- pretends to be a private seller.

If you think that any of these might apply to your situation, before taking any action against the seller you should report the matter to your local Trading Standards Department and, in the case of personal injury, take legal advice on your claim.

Changing your mind

Do not agree or sign anything unless you are absolutely sure that you wish to go ahead with the purchase, and beware of signing any document that states that you have examined the car and found it satisfactory in all respects.

- If you are paying for the car by cash, there is no cooling-off period. You would normally be legally bound from the moment you both agreed the deal.
- If the deal is subject to finance, but you have not signed a finance agreement, neither party is legally bound until the finance agreement has been signed by both parties.
- If you have signed a finance agreement but the finance company has not yet approved it, you may be able to withdraw if you act **very quickly**. Telephone the finance company immediately and follow it up with a letter confirming withdrawal.

Guarantee or extended warranty

If the car was sold with a guarantee or an extended warranty, you may have additional rights. The guarantee or warranty cannot take away your statutory rights. You should check the small print on your warranty. Many have exclusions such as wear and tear. If you are buying a high-mileage car, you need to ask yourself if the warranty is likely to cover the problems most likely to occur and consider whether the warranty offers value for money.

Special rules if you paid by credit

If you used your credit card or the seller arranged the finance for you to pay for the car, and it cost more than £100 and less than £30,000, the credit company may be equally liable for any breach of contract. This means that if the car is faulty, you may be able to claim a refund or the cost of repairs from the finance company, the dealer, or both jointly. The rules regarding hire purchase and conditional sale are different to other agreements in that it is the finance company that is solely responsible.

Your rights if the car is faulty

Refund

Whether you can return the car and demand your money back depends in part on how long you have had the car and how many miles it has travelled before you report the fault. If the fault is serious and you have not done many miles and return (reject) it very shortly after purchase, you may be entitled to a full refund. If, however, you keep the car for a longer time without returning it, you may lose this right, although you may still be entitled to ask for the fault to be rectified. If you are entitled to a refund, this will include both the money you paid for the faulty car and the return of any part-exchanged car. If the part-exchanged car has since been sold, you are entitled to the cash value as represented on your paperwork.

Replacement or repair

You can ask the seller to replace or repair the car free of charge if it is faulty. If you do this within six months of receiving the car, and it is reasonable to expect it to have lasted for the period of time you have had it, it will be assumed that the problem existed when you bought the car, unless the seller can show otherwise. However, you can still ask for a replacement or a repair for up to six years from the date that you bought the car, if it is reasonable for it to have lasted that long. In this case it will be up to you to show that the car was faulty at the time of sale. The longer you have had the car, the more difficult it is to prove that the fault was there at the time of sale. You can ask for a partial or full refund if:

- it is impossible to replace or repair the car; or
- replacement or repair would be unreasonably costly for the seller when compared with alternative remedies; or
- the seller fails to replace or repair the car within a reasonable time of having agreed to do so, or causes you significant inconvenience.

The amount of money you get back may be reduced to take account of any use that you have had out of the car.

Compensation

You may be entitled to compensation if:

- the contract has been broken (breach of contract) because the vehicle is not as described, of satisfactory quality or fit for its purpose; or

- the dealer has made a false statement about the car to make you buy it (for example, telling you it has had a new engine fitted when the engine is reconditioned); or
- you have had an injury because the car is unroadworthy or unsafe (you should always take legal advice before deciding whether to accept an offer of compensation for personal injury); or
- a fault with the car caused damage to something else; or
- you accept a repair which turns out to be unsatisfactory; or
- you have incurred additional expenses because of the dealer's breach of contract – for example, having to make telephone calls or pay for alternative transport.

How to solve your problem

Once you have decided what your rights are, contact the dealer. It is the dealer and/or the finance company and *not* the manufacturer who is responsible for dealing with your complaint.

Follow the steps below:

- Stop using the car.
- Collect all your documents together, including your sales invoice, guarantee or warranty and/or credit agreement.
- If someone has been injured or if you feel a criminal offence has been committed (for example, the car is unroadworthy), you should contact your local Trading Standards Department before going back to the trader.
- Contact the dealer and the finance company (if applicable) as soon as you discover the fault. Take the car back, and ask to speak to a manager or the owner. Alternatively, write to the manager or owner, enclosing a copy of your sales invoice. Keep a copy of your letter. Explain your problem calmly but firmly and ask for a full refund, a repair, a replacement, or compensation and set a time limit.
- If you are still dissatisfied, write to the dealer and/or the finance company repeating your complaint and the steps that have been taken. Say that you will give them fourteen days to sort out the problem or you will consider legal action. Send your letter by recorded delivery with a copy to the head office. Be sure to keep copies of all letters.
- If the dealer makes an alternative offer (for example a replacement car), you can either accept or continue to negotiate. Be realistic in what you will accept. You may not get a better offer by going to court.
- If the dealer doesn't reply to your letters, refuses to do anything, or makes a

final offer that you are unwilling to accept, your only other choice is to go to court. If you are claiming the cost of repairs make sure you have obtained sufficient evidence to prove your claim – for example, expert reports, photographs, etc. – before you allow another garage to repair the car.

Remember, court is your last resort. You also need to find out if the dealer is solvent. It is not worth suing a person or a firm that has no money, and if you have lost money on a faulty car don't waste more money on a case you cannot win.

Getting an expert opinion

If the cause of the problem is in dispute, it may be necessary to obtain an expert opinion. This could be obtained through a trade association or could be from anyone suitably qualified who is willing to put their findings in writing. Reports must usually be paid for, and you should reach agreement with the seller in advance on the choice of expert and that you will both be bound by the expert's findings. You should then be able to recover the cost if the complaint is upheld. If you go through a trade association, it may offer conciliation or arbitration. Arbitration is often legally binding. If you would like more information before you commit yourself, contact the trade association for further details.

Buying a car at an auction

If you buy a second-hand car at an auction that you have the opportunity to attend in person, your rights may be limited if the car turns out to be faulty. You should check the terms and conditions of business of the auction, for example in the catalogue or on notices on display. If they state that your rights under the Sale of Goods Act 1979 are excluded, then you are buying the car *as seen*, and it is your responsibility to check the car before you bid for it.

Some auctions will offer insurance against the vehicle turning out to be stolen and some may offer you a cooling-off period (although this may often be very small – a matter of a few hours).

Buying a car from a private seller

If you buy a car from a private seller, you will only be able to take action against the seller if the car is not as described. Sellers will be liable for a false description even if they believed the description to be true. Be wary of a seller who wants to meet you away from his private address, whose name is not on the logbook, or who is evasive about answering your questions.

Who can help?

If you have a dispute regarding a warranty from a manufacturer or from a mechanical breakdown insurance company that is a member of the **Society of Motor Manufacturers and Traders** (0870 7518270), you may be able to use the SMMT conciliation service.

The **Retail Motor Industry Federation** and the **Society of Motor Auctions** (01788 538317) are both part of the same organization and members must follow a code of practice. There is an internal conciliation service and an independent arbitration scheme run by the Chartered Institute of Arbitrators to deal with complaints against its members.

INSURANCE

You buy insurance in order to protect, or 'cover', yourself against unexpec-ted financial loss that can result from, for example, personal injury, illness, or damage to your property or personal possessions. Some of the most common types of insurance cover are:

- motor insurance;
- household contents insurance;
- buildings insurance;
- travel insurance;
- private health insurance;
- life insurance (often called life assurance).

You can buy insurance direct from an insurer, through an insurance agent (usually employed by one insurer) or through an insurance broker or independent intermediary. An insurance broker or intermediary is not usually tied to any one particular insurer, but will receive commission for selling you an insurance policy. It is sometimes quicker and easier to go to an intermediary than directly to an insurer, and they are useful if you want insurance for something special. You can also buy insurance through a bank, building society, solicitor, travel agent, mail order agent or accountant.

Companies and individuals who sell, arrange or give advice on the common types of insurance must be registered with the Financial Services Authority (FSA), and must comply with FSA rules.

When you apply to buy insurance, you must answer the insurer's questions, or those of the person selling you insurance, truthfully, as the insurer may refuse to pay out on a future claim if you withhold information. Your insurance policy will contain the terms of your contract with your insurer. This will include what is known as a 'schedule'. The schedule has your personal details on it, and the particulars of your specific policy. You have the right to a full copy of your policy. It is important to make sure that the information in your policy is correct, and you should check it very carefully as soon as you receive it.

The amount you pay for an insurance policy is called a 'premium'. Premiums can either be paid to your insurer in one lump sum or in instalments.

A 'no-claims bonus' increases for every year that you make no claims on your policy, up to a maximum amount. Most insurers will let you transfer the discount, if you want to change your insurer. If you make a claim, you will also need to compare the amount by which your no-claims bonus would be reduced.

Claiming on your insurance policy

If you want to make a claim on your insurance policy, do this without delay, and follow the procedure set out in your policy document.

You do not have to make a claim on your insurance policy, even if you are entitled to do so. However, you should think very carefully about this decision as costs that you have to pay yourself may turn out to be higher than you think. It is always advisable to make an insurance claim if someone has been injured. Personal injuries can be expensive, and they can have unexpected and long-term effects on your health.

Even if you don't wish to make a claim, you must always tell your insurer about an event. If you do not report it, you may find that this leads to problems later on when you do wish to make a claim.

An insurance policy may include an 'excess', which is the fixed amount of any claim, for example the first £50, that you must pay yourself.

If your claim is substantial, you may want to employ loss assessors to help you with your claim. Make sure that they are members of the Institute of Public Loss Assessors (01494 782342). Get details of all fees and services offered, in writing, before any work is carried out. You may be able to claim the fees back.

Cancelling your insurance policy

You may want to cancel an insurance policy if you have just bought it and have changed your mind. You have a right to do this if you bought your policy over the phone, on the internet, or from someone who called at your home or place of work. You may also have a right to cancel your insurance policy if you paid for it by a credit agreement that you signed in your own home or anywhere other than the offices of the credit company, or if the insurance contract itself says that there is a right to cancel.

How to resolve an insurance problem

If you have a problem with your insurance policy, or an insurance claim, write to your insurer, giving details of your complaint and how you would like it resolved. If you are not satisfied with your insurer's response, make a formal complaint, using their official complaints procedure. If you are still not satisfied with the outcome of the formal complaints procedure, consider taking the complaint further.

All insurance companies must be covered by the rules of the financial watchdog, the Financial Services Authority (FSA). This means that if you have a complaint about an insurer you can complain to the Financial Ombudsman Service (FOS). There is a free service to policy-holders who have already followed their insurer's complaints procedure. The FOS will try to resolve the problem through mediation between yourself and the insurer. A decision made by the FOS is binding on your insurer, but if you do not agree with it, you can still take your insurer to court.

To find out whether the FOS can investigate your complaint, you can contact them on 0845 080 1800, or visit their website (www.financial-ombudsman.org.uk).

If your insurer is a member of Lloyd's, contact Lloyd's Complaints Department on 020 7327 5693. If you are not satisfied with the outcome of this complaint, you can then go on to complain to the FOS.

If you have tried all the options for resolving your complaint through the complaints procedures, but have not met with success, or if your insurer is based outside the UK, you may wish to consider taking legal action. However, you should only consider going to court as a last resort. This is because the amount of compensation a court may award you could be reduced if you have not tried other ways of resolving the problem before taking legal action.

If your insurer has disappeared

If you want to trace an insurer, intermediary or broker, contact the
Financial Services Authority (FSA: www.fsa.gov.uk).
If your claim has not been settled because your insurer has gone out of
business, you may be able to get help from the **Financial Services
Compensation Scheme** (www.fscs.org.uk). If your insurer is a member of
Lloyd's, you should contact the complaints department at Lloyd's
(020 7327 5693).

Motor insurance

(see *Travel and Transport*, p. 381)

Household contents insurance

Household contents insurance (sometimes known as home contents
insurance) covers most of your personal belongings and household possessions against loss or damage. This includes furniture, domestic equipment, electrical appliances, furnishing, clothing, food and drink, some
valuables and cash up to a certain limit.

Household contents insurance covers the possessions belonging to you
and to close family members who live with you. Some insurance companies
automatically include people who are cohabiting or same-sex couples in
their definition of 'family members', but you may want to check. A friend
who lives with you or who is staying with you would not normally be
covered, unless their name was included in your policy. There is no legal
requirement for you to take out household contents insurance, but it is
advisable for you to do so.

Your household insurance policy will only cover some forms of accidental
damage. It will normally cover damage due to fire, floods and storms as
well as accidental damage to mirrors and fixed glass in furniture. You can
often extend your policy to cover accidental damage to all of the contents
of your home. You will have to pay extra for this.

If you rent any of your possessions, for example a television set or a video
recorder, it is advisable to take out insurance cover for these items. This is
because you are legally responsible for any loss or damage that occurs to
them.

If you rent your home and it has some contents belonging to your landlord, for example furniture or a television set, you may be responsible for any loss or damage to them and will need to arrange insurance cover. Check your tenancy agreement to see if this is the case.

Making a claim

Contact your insurer as soon as possible and request a claim form. Complete the claim form carefully and keep a copy.

If your claim is substantial, you may want to employ loss assessors to help you with your claim. Make sure that they are members of the Institute of Public Loss Assessors (01494 782342). Get details of all fees and services offered, in writing, before any work is carried out. You may be able to claim these fees back.

Buildings insurance

Buildings insurance covers the cost of damage to the structure of your property. This includes the roof, walls, ceilings, floors, doors and windows. Outdoor structures such as garages and fences are also included.

Buildings insurance covers permanent fixtures and fittings, interior decoration and underground tanks, pipes, cables and drains for which you are responsible from your home to the mains supply. Buildings insurance commonly covers loss or damage that happens as a result of fire, storms, floods, theft or vandalism.

Your buildings insurance should cover the full cost of rebuilding the property. This should include costs such as demolition, clearing the site, and architects' fees. Make sure any special features such as a luxury fitted kitchen or a conservatory are also included. The **Association of British Insurers** (ABI 020 7600 3333; www.abi.org.uk) produces yearly guidelines on rebuilding costs.

You can extend a buildings insurance policy to include cover for accidental damage to the inside of your home. This will cost extra. However, anything that is not clearly listed in the policy is not usually covered.

A buildings insurance policy will usually also cover the cost of alternative accommodation up to a certain limit, if you have to leave your home while repairs are carried out.

If you own the property, you can also be insured against legal responsibility if someone dies or is injured when they visit your property. You can also get cover for damage to someone else's goods or property when they visit you.

Who should have buildings insurance

If you are an owner-occupier with a mortgage, it will be a condition of the mortgage that your home is insured. Your mortgage lender will make sure that the amount of cover is sufficient to meet the outstanding amount of your mortgage. However, you should make sure that this is enough to cover the full rebuilding costs of your home.

Your mortgage lender should give you the choice of at least three insurers, or allow you to propose one you have chosen yourself. Your mortgage lender will usually accept your choice of insurer, as long as the policy provides adequate cover. They may make a small charge for this. Your mortgage lender does have the right to turn your choice of insurer down, but they cannot insist that you take out their own insurance policy unless you have agreed to a special mortgage package that includes insurance.

If you buy or sell a house, responsibility for the buildings insurance passes to the new owner when contracts are exchanged. It is therefore very important that, if you are buying a house, you insure the property from the day that contracts are exchanged. This is because if the house is damaged or destroyed, you will be expected to cover the loss. If you are selling your house, you have a legal responsibility to look after the property until the sale is completed, and you should therefore keep on your buildings insurance until then.

If your mortgage lender repossesses your home, you are still responsible for the insurance until it is sold. Your insurance policy may no longer cover you if you are not living in the property. You should explain the circumstances to your insurer so that they can change the terms of your policy. They may want assurances that someone, for example a neighbour, is watching over the property while it is empty.

If you are a freeholder without a mortgage, you do not have to take out buildings insurance, but it is advisable to do so.

If you are an owner-occupier who is a leaseholder, you may have a condition in your lease that says that you have to take out buildings insurance with a specified insurer. This may be the case even if you don't have a mortgage.

Alternatively, the freeholder of your building may take out the insurance and charge you for the premium.

If you are a tenant, your landlord usually has responsibility for the buildings insurance. Check that your landlord has taken out buildings insurance. You may also have some responsibility for certain loss or damage to fixtures and fittings. Check your tenancy agreement for this. Your household contents insurance may cover some of these losses.

Making a claim

If your claim is substantial, you may want to employ loss assessors to help you with your claim. Make sure that they are members of the **Institute of Public Loss Assessors** (01494 782342). Get details of all fees and services offered, in writing, before any work is carried out, and do not arrange for permanent repairs to be done without your insurer's permission. Your insurer may ask a claims inspector or loss adjuster to visit you, to investigate the circumstances of your claim. If your claim is accepted, your insurer will either arrange for a company to do the repairs, or ask you to get estimates for their approval before going ahead with any work.

Travel insurance

(see *Travel and Transport*, p. 391)

ALTERNATIVE DISPUTE RESOLUTION

If you have a dispute over the supply of goods or services that you have been unable to settle through negotiation, you may wish to consider using an alternative dispute resolution (ADR) scheme rather than taking court action.

These schemes use a third party such as an arbitrator or an ombudsman to help you and the supplier reach a solution. You will usually have to complete the supplier's internal complaints procedure beforehand and you may have to pay a fee for using the scheme. This is usually refunded if you are successful.

Some schemes are legally binding, which means you cannot take court action if you aren't satisfied with the decision, except to enforce an award. If your claim is over £5,000, you should discuss the possibility of ADR with your solicitor. If your claim is less than this amount, you should look at the pros and cons of ADR and small claims actions and decide which would be the best course of action for you.

The main advantages of using an ADR are:

- you may resolve your problem;
- you may be awarded compensation;

- the procedure is less formal than going to court;
- in some schemes, the decision may be binding on the trader but not on you, leaving you free to pursue the action through court if you wish;
- it may cost you less than going to court;
- the procedure is confidential.

You might want to think about these points:

- The costs involved. Compare the arbitrators'/mediators' fee with the costs involved in going to court.
- Would you prefer to have a hearing, where you can put your point across in person, or have the matter dealt with on paper, in a 'documents only' process?
- If the arbitrators' decision is legally binding, it will prevent you taking the matter through the courts.
- You may have to pay further costs to enforce the arbitrators' decision through the courts.
- Most schemes have a time limit within which you must start the complaint. This time limit may be shorter than those for taking court action.

Types of ADR scheme

The main types of ADR scheme that deal with consumer disputes are conciliation, arbitration and mediation and are usually provided by trade associations. If you wish to use one of these schemes, you should ask the suppliers whether they are members of a trade association and, if so, contact the trade association to find out whether it has a conciliation or arbitration service.

Conciliation

In consumer disputes, conciliation is usually the first stage in the arbitration process and the conciliator is usually a member of the trade association. Both you and the supplier will be asked to give written details of the complaint, including any evidence, and the conciliator will give an opinion on the best solution. Any decision is not binding and won't prevent you from taking court action. If you disagree with the opinion offered, you can then proceed to the arbitration stage or consider suing in court. There is usually no charge for conciliation.

Arbitration

Arbitration is a procedure for settling disputes in which both you and the supplier usually agree to accept the decision of the arbitrator as legally binding. This means you cannot take court action, except to enforce the award if the supplier doesn't pay. The arbitrator will usually be a member of the Chartered Institute of Arbitrators (020 7421 7444; www.arbitrators.org) and often acts independently of the trade association. The arbitrator will make a decision based on the written evidence presented by you and the supplier. The decision is confidential and cannot be made public without the supplier's agreement. You will have to pay a registration fee, which may be refunded if you are successful. Some contracts for services and delivery include an arbitration clause stating that you will refer any dispute to arbitration. Although this is binding once you have signed the agreement, if the total cost is below the small claims limit (£5,000) you cannot be forced to arbitrate unless you gave your agreement after the dispute arose.

Mediation

If you use a mediation scheme, the mediator will help you and the supplier to negotiate an acceptable agreement and will act as a go-between if you don't want to meet. If the supplier agrees to mediation, you will both be asked to give details of the dispute, including copies of any evidence, and will be asked to sign a mediation agreement giving a framework for the mediation. The mediator may arrange joint or separate meetings with you and the supplier and will help you to identify the strengths and weaknesses in your case. Any agreement reached will be legally binding unless you state otherwise and will prevent you from taking court action except to enforce any award. Mediation can be expensive but you may be able to apply to the Community Legal Service (CLS) for help under the legal help scheme or the publicly funded legal representation scheme. Contact your local Citizens Advice Bureau for more help.

Ombudsman schemes

Many services have an ombudsman scheme that you can use, but you will only be able to refer the matter to the ombudsman after you have completed the supplier's internal complaints procedure. You will need to give written details of your complaint, together with copies of any of your evidence. The ombudsman will make a recommendation or a ruling, which is usually accepted by the supplier, but isn't legally binding. Hence you can still take court action if you aren't satisfied with the decision. However, the court will take the ombudsman's ruling into account when deciding your claim. All the ombudsman schemes are free.

Who can help?

If you are interested in ADR, you should find out whether the trader is a member of any trade association that offers such a service. If you have any difficulty contacting the trade association or finding out whether there is a relevant ombudsman scheme, or if the trader is falsely claiming membership of an association, you should contact your local Trading Standards Department. You should find their number in your local telephone directory. You should enquire whether there is a charge for their services before you commit yourself. The Law Society has established a Civil and Commercial Mediation Panel (01527 517141, extension 3460) to help members of the public find qualified solicitor mediators.

If you bought the goods or services in another European country, a European Consumer Centre or the European Extra-Judicial Network (EEJ-Net) might be able to help you find a suitable alternative dispute resolution body (go to www.euroconsumer.org.uk).

STARTING COURT ACTION

If you have been negotiating with a trader to resolve a consumer complaint but have not been successful, you may want to consider going to court. Before taking legal action, you should make sure that you have tried all other options for resolving your dispute, like alternative dispute resolution (ADR – see above).

Most consumer cases are heard in the county court. If the case is defended by the trader, the court will allocate the case to one of three tracks: the small claims track, which deals with claims of £5,000 or less; the fast track for most cases between £5,000 and £15,000; or the multi-track for cases above £15,000.

In a small claims case you won't be awarded costs to pay for a solicitor even if you win the case, so only the least complex cases are dealt with in this way.

You may decide to take court action rather than using an ADR if:

- the trader is not a member of a trade association with a conciliation or arbitration scheme; *or*
- the amount you are claiming is under £5,000 and will be dealt with as a small claim; *or*
- you have a reluctant witness – only a court can order a witness to attend; *or*
- there is no limit on the amount of compensation you can claim, for example in a negligence claim. An ADR may have limits on the level of payments it can award.

Can the trader afford to pay?

You are unlikely to get your money if the trader is:

- unemployed or on a low income; *or*
- bankrupt, or the company has been wound up. You can find out whether an individual is bankrupt by telephoning the Insolvency Service (020 7637 1110; www.insolvency.gov.uk) or a company has gone into receivership or liquidation by contacting the Companies Registration Office (0870 333 3636; www.companieshouse.gov.uk). *Or*
- in debt and cannot afford to pay. You can find out whether the trader has other unpaid county court judgments by contacting the Registry Trust on 020 7380 0133. *Or*
- has no money and owns nothing else of value.

You would be wasting your money taking court action against a bankrupt or a company in liquidation. If the trader has a very low income, you may get your money if you are prepared to accept very low payments (sometimes as little as £1 per month).

Do you need a solicitor?

If you are claiming over £5,000, or making a claim such as replacement or repair of faulty goods, or making a claim for negligence or personal injury, you should consult a solicitor before starting court action. These cases are more complex and you could find yourself paying the legal costs of the other side if you lose the case.

Is there a time limit?

There are time limits within which you can start court action. These are usually six years for consumer contract issues. The time starts from the date the problem arose. If you are unsure about whether you have missed the time limit, you should consult a solicitor.

Do you have the trader's details?

You will need the full address of the individual or firm you are suing. If you are suing:

- a limited company, you will need to claim against the company, not the owner(s). You should send the claim form to its registered office or to the address of the shop you have done business with. If you want details of the registered office, you can obtain this by telephoning Companies House (0870 333 3636).
- an individual (sole trader), you must name the individual you are suing and not just sue the trading name. The address for service can be either the trader's home address or business address.
- a partnership, each partner is fully liable for any debts. You should sue all the partners at the same time, as you cannot sue them one after the other. A business that does not trade under the names of the partners should display details of the owner or partners on its headed notepaper or at its premises or be willing to provide them if asked. If it fails to do so, it may have committed a criminal offence and should be reported to the Trading Standards Department of your local council or to the police.

For more information, see *The small claims procedure*, p. 473.

GENERAL ORGANIZATIONS THAT HELP WITH CONSUMER COMPLAINTS

Organizations that help with complaints about communications and the media

The **Advertising Standards Authority** (020 7492 2222; www.asa.org.uk) supervises the British Codes of Advertising, Sales Promotion and Direct Marketing and deals with contraventions. It will take up complaints in writing about all forms of advertising.

The **Press Complaints Commission** (020 7353 1248; www.pcc.org.uk) is concerned with maintaining high professional and commercial standards in the British press. It will investigate any complaints about newspapers or magazines, except those involving advertising, where compensation is sought or where the complaint might result in a court case. Complaints should be sent in writing to the Director.

Organizations that help with complaints about travel and transport

The **Retail Motor Industry Federation** (08457 585350; www.rmif.co.uk) operates an internal conciliation service, and an independently run arbitration scheme.

The **Society of Motor Manufacturers and Traders** (New Car Code Conciliation Service: 0870 7518270; www.smmt.co.uk). If you have a problem with a new car which is still under a manufacturer's guarantee or extended warranty, and have been unable to resolve it, contact the SMMT. The SMMT operate an impartial conciliation service and arbitration scheme.

The **Society of Motor Auctions** (01788 576465) represents car auctioneers and has a code of practice, which members must comply with. The SMA has an internal conciliation and arbitration service.

The **British Vehicle Rental and Leasing Association** (01494 434747; www.bvrla.co.uk) represents firms that rent or lease vehicles. The BVRLA will investigate complaints made against its members.

The **Motor Cycle Industry Association** (024 76250 800; www.mcia.co.uk) has an internal conciliation scheme and an independent arbitration scheme to deal with complaints against member firms.

The **Vehicle Builders and Repairers Association** (0113 253 8333; www.vbra.co.uk) has an internal conciliation scheme and an independent arbitration scheme to deal with complaints against VBRA members.

Organizations that help with complaints about property and building services

The **National Association of Estate Agents** (01926 496800; www.naea.co.uk) investigates complaints against members and helps with complaints against non-members. The Association operates an indemnity scheme to protect the public against loss of money held by the Association's members.

The **British Association of Removers** (020 8861 3331; www.bar.co.uk) gives general advice on removals and produces a range of free leaflets. These include advice on choosing a removal firm, preparing to move and moving abroad. BAR has a conciliation scheme and also an independently run arbitration scheme.

The **National House-Building Council** (01494 434477; www.nhbc.co.uk).
To check if a builder is NHBC registered, call 0845 845 6422. The NHBC
is an independent organization with over 25,000 builders on its register.
Before being accepted on to the NHBC register, builders must be able to
show that they are technically and financially competent, and agree to
abide by the NHBC Rules and Standards. These cover technical
requirements and guidance on practical design, suitable materials and
quality of workmanship. The NHBC runs the Buildmark scheme, which
covers homes built by NHBC-registered builders once the NHBC has
certified them finished.

The **Federation of Master Builders** (020 7242 7583; www.fmb.org.uk) gives
advice on how to choose a builder and details of member firms in the
customer's area. It also has a complaints procedure to deal with disputes
with its members, and an independently run arbitration scheme.

The **Confederation of Roofing Contractors** (01206 306600;
www.corc.co.uk) has about three hundred members. There is a free
internal conciliation and arbitration scheme to deal with complaints
against members and non-members.

The **National Federation of Roofing Contractors** (020 7436 0387;
www.nfrc.co.uk) has an arbitration scheme to deal with disputes, for
which a fee is payable.

The **Painting and Decorating Association** (02476 353776;
www.paintingdecoratingassociation.co.uk) operates an internal complaints
and arbitration scheme to deal with complaints against members.

The **National Inspection Council for Electrical Installation Contracting**
(020 7564 2323; www.niceic.org.uk) is an independent consumer safety
organization that publishes a Roll of Approved Electrical Installation
Contractors of over 10,500 electrical contractors, who work to the
technical standards set by the NICEIC. It operates an internal complaints
procedure to resolve disputes over the technical standard of work carried
out by members. The NICEIC will not investigate if the complaint is just
about the cost of the work.

The **National Heating Consultancy** (020 7936 4004) investigates
complaints about defective domestic heating or insulation work. Members
of the NHC are qualified heating engineers who can act as independent
experts. Telephone advice is given free.

The **Association of Plumbing and Heating Contractors** (024 7687 0626;
www.aphc.co.uk) can provide details of member firms in your area, and
operates internal conciliation and arbitration schemes to deal with

complaints against members. There is a fee to use the arbitration scheme, which may be refunded if you win your case.

The **Institute of Plumbing and Heating Engineering** (01708 472791; www.iphe.org.uk) keeps a register of qualified plumbers and can provide details of its members in your area. The IoP runs a free internal arbitration scheme to deal with complaints against members. The IoP cannot award compensation or order that a member remedy faulty work, but it can remove a member from its register.

The **Glass and Glazing Federation** (0870 042 4255; www.ggf.org.uk) produces free leaflets giving advice on choosing new windows, doors and conservatories, a list of member firms and the Customer Charter. The GGF has an internal conciliation service, and an independently run arbitration scheme, to deal with complaints against its members.

The **Conservatory Association** (020 7207 5873) produces Minimum Technical Specifications and a Recommended Code of Practice for conservatory construction and a list of member firms. The Association has an internal arbitration scheme for disputes between customers and member companies.

The **British Pest Control Association** (01332 294288; www.bpca.org.uk) can give general advice on pest control and has an internal arbitration scheme to deal with complaints. It operates the BPCA Code of Practice.

Organizations that help with complaints about clothing and household goods

The **Independent Footwear Retailers Association** (01295 738 726; www.shoeshop.org.uk) represents shoe shops and wholesalers. Shoe shops that are not members can affiliate to the IFRA if they agree to abide by its code of practice.

The **Multiservice Association** (01536 760374; www.the-msa.org.uk) represents some shoe repairers. Members must follow their Code of Practice for Shoe Repairers. Multiservice has a free internal arbitration scheme to resolve complaints against its members.

The **Textile Services Association** (general inquiries: 020 8863 7755; dry-cleaning information bureau: 020 8863 8658; www.tsa-uk.org) represents most dry-cleaners and launderers and has a conciliation service that can be used to resolve a dispute between a customer and a TSA member. The TSA can also give information on which TSA members specialize in cleaning particular items, for example antique fabrics.

The **National Association of the Launderette Industry** (020 8856 9798) has a code of practice that its members must follow and an internal conciliation scheme to deal with complaints against its members. NALI does not deal with dry-cleaners.

The **National Carpet Cleaners Association** (0116 271 9550; www.ncca.co.uk) represents carpet and upholstery cleaning firms and will give advice to customers on cleaning carpets, curtains and upholstery, including information on dealing with stains. The NCCA has an internal conciliation and arbitration scheme to resolve complaints against its members.

The **Association of Manufacturers of Domestic Appliances** (020 7405 0666; www.amdea.org.uk) represents British manufacturers of domestic appliances, but does not deal with radios, televisions or stereo equipment. Members of the AMDA must comply with the Principles for Domestic Appliance Servicing. If you have a complaint about the way in which an electrical appliance has been serviced by the manufacturer of the appliance, the AMDA has an internal conciliation scheme to resolve the problem. There is also an independent arbitration scheme. The AMDA cannot deal with complaints where someone other than the manufacturer has serviced the appliance, or where the manufacturer is not a member of the AMDA.

The **Domestic Appliance Service Association** (01920 870 173; www.dasa.org.uk) represents firms that service and repair domestic electrical appliances. DASA members should provide service within three working days at reasonable cost and carry adequate stocks of spare parts to meet reasonable demands for repairs and to resolve customer complaints.

The **Radio, Electrical and Television Retailers Association** (01234 269110; www.retra.co.uk) represents shops selling domestic electrical appliances, including televisions, radios and stereo equipment. RETRA has a conciliation procedure for disputes involving its members.

The **Hampers Industry Trade Association Ltd** (01482 647227; www.hitauk.co.uk) represents the retailers of hampers, which are defined as 'collections of foodstuffs'. HITA will investigate, and attempt to resolve, complaints against members.

Organizations that help with complaints about door-to-door and distance selling

The **Direct Selling Association** (020 7497 1234; www.dsa.org.uk) represents traders who sell from door to door and those who sell at parties in the customer's home. The Association has an internal complaints procedure to deal with complaints against its members. A list of members is available through the Direct Selling Association website.

The **Direct Marketing Association** (020 7291 3300; www.dma.org.uk) manages the Mail Preference Service, the Telephone Preference Service and the Fax Preference Service. They will remove your name from lists so that you no longer receive advertising from companies. The Association also runs a conciliation service that deals with complaints against member companies.

The **Mail Order Traders' Association** (0151 227 9456) represents firms that sell through catalogues. It has an internal conciliation scheme, and an independent arbitration scheme, to deal with complaints against its members.

Organizations that help with complaints about financial services

The **British Bankers' Association** (www.bba.org.uk) is the main trade association for banks operating in the UK. It produces free information sheets called Bankfacts that cover most aspects of banking practice. They are available by telephoning the BBA Bankfacts orderline (020 7216 8801).The BBA will not give advice or take up an individual problem about a bank.

The **Banking Code Standards Board** (020 7661 9694; www.bankingcode.org.uk) is the body that makes sure that banks and building societies that subscribe to the Banking Code honour their commitments to it. If the BCSB receives a complaint that a bank or building society has failed to comply with the Banking Code, it will ask the bank or building society for an explanation and insist that it complies.

The BCSB cannot deal with claims for compensation, nor intervene in a dispute between you the customer and your bank or building society. However, the BCSB is interested in hearing about cases where a bank or building society appears to have breached the Banking Code.

The **Association of British Insurers** (020 7600 3333; www.abi.org.uk) is the trade association for most insurance companies and has codes of practice that its members must follow. It will take up complaints about its members. Although it does not operate an arbitration procedure and cannot insist that any of its members follow a particular line of action, it can exert pressure to resolve a dispute. If the problem is not resolved, or if an insurance company is not a member of the ABI, you should complain to the Financial Ombudsman Service.

The **Financial Services Authority** (FSA) (0845 606 1234; www.fsa.gov.uk/consumer) is an independent watchdog that regulates financial organizations and protects consumers in the UK. The FSA can provide basic information and guidance on financial services, including pensions, mortgages, insurance and Individual Savings Accounts (ISAs). The FSA does not deal with specific consumer complaints, recommend firms or give financial advice.

The **Financial Ombudsman Service** (0845 080 1800; www.financial-ombudsman.org.uk) can deal with consumer complaints about most personal financial matters including financial advice, banking services, insurance and personal pensions advice. The FOS can investigate complaints only if the problem has not been resolved after going through the company's formal complaints procedure.

The **Motor Insurers' Bureau** (01908 830001; www.mib.org.uk) can give compensation to someone who is involved in a motor accident caused by an uninsured driver or untraced driver. If the driver was uninsured, the MIB can pay compensation for personal injury or death and/or damage to property. If the driver has not been traced, the MIB can only pay compensation for personal injury or death.

4
Travel and Transport

CONTENTS

INTRODUCTION

Years ago, you were born, lived and died sometimes without leaving your village. From Shanks's pony to space travel, the world has got smaller since then, with some people thinking nothing of jetting to another continent for lunch. With Richard Branson promising to send tourists into space within three years, it'll soon be teatime on Mars. But, for most of us, the trials (and pleasures) of travelling about by bus, train and car are enough to keep us busy. The first public bus service is thought to have been Mr Shillibeer's horse-drawn carriage, which started to charge passengers in 1829 for taking them from Paddington station to the City of London. The private railways were taken into public ownership after the Second World War and then, for the most part, privatized again in the 1990s. The first automobiles began to appear on the roads in the late nineteenth century, quickly followed by laws to regulate their use, like the one stating that self-propelled vehicles on public roads must be preceded by a man on foot waving a red flag and blowing a horn.

This section looks at passengers' rights and responsibilities in the world of modern travel and who to complain to if you run into trouble on the move.

PUBLIC TRANSPORT

Bus and coach travel

Bus services outside London are run by private operators or are services subsidized by a Passenger Transport Executive or a local authority. There are six Passenger Transport Authorities (PTAs) in England.

Local authorities may provide some bus services and they must provide bus services to meet the needs of elderly and disabled people. The local authority will normally have a public transport officer responsible for bus services.

Bus services in London are the responsibility of Transport for London (TFL), which gives contracts and licences to private bus operators.

All coach services in Britain are privately operated.

Penalty fares on buses

In London only, you may be liable to pay a penalty fare if you travel without a ticket or valid pass. A penalty fare is not a fine but is a fare set at a higher rate than the normal fare.

If you do not pay the bus penalty fare when asked, you must give your name and address to the official representative of Transport for London (TFL). Refusal to supply these details is a criminal offence and you could be prosecuted. If you want to appeal against being charged a penalty fare, whether you have paid it or not, you have twenty-one days to do this. TFL then has to show why you should pay and, if you continue to refuse, will have to take proceedings in the county court. If you want to appeal, write to Revenue Protection Services at: London Bus Services, PO Box 3893, London SW1W 9TN.

If you feel you have been unfairly treated by being charged a bus penalty fare you should complain in writing to **Transport for London Buses** (020 7918 4300; www.transportforlondon.gov.uk).

Complaints about bus services

If you have a complaint about any bus service (for example, unsafe driving, overcharging, late running, unacceptable staff behaviour) you should complain directly to the bus operator. The name and address of the operator must be shown on the vehicle and will also usually be displayed inside.

In London, you can complain directly to Transport for London Buses (020 7918 4300).

Many private operators and Passenger Transport Executives (see below for contact details) have charters or codes of practice setting out how complaints are dealt with and what a passenger can expect.

If you have complained about a bus service outside London and are not satisfied with the way the operator has dealt with your complaint, you can take it to:

- the **Bus Appeals Body**, whether the service is operated privately or subsidized (023 9281 4493; www.nfbu.org); *or*
- the Traffic Commissioner for the area, the local authority responsible for the

service or the local Passenger Transport Executive (contact details listed below).

If you have complained about a London bus service and are not satisfied, you should contact the **London Transport Users' Committee** (020 7505 9000; www.ltuc.org.uk).

If you are travelling outside London and have a general complaint about bus services – for example, about the lack of a service in your area or where a bus stop or shelter is situated – you should contact the local authority or, if you are in an area covered by a Passenger Transport Authority, the Passenger Transport Executive (contact details below).

In London, you should contact **Transport for London Buses Customer Service Centre** (020 7918 4300).

Complaints about coach services

Anyone who has a complaint about the quality of a coach service should address the complaint to the operator. If you are not satisfied with the way in which the operator has dealt with the complaint you should complain to the **Bus Appeals Body** (023 9281 4493, www.nfbu.org).

Rail and underground services

Penalty fares (rail services)

Railway operators can only impose a penalty fare on a passenger who travels without the correct ticket in some areas. This will be an on-the-spot penalty above the normal fare and is not a fine. If the fare you should have paid is less than £5.00, the penalty is £10.00. If the fare was over £5.00, the penalty fare is double the fare.

You may want to appeal against a penalty fare if:

- there was insufficient notice that you were travelling in a penalty fare area – because, for example, signs were inadequate;
- English is not your first language, or you were unable to read the notices because you are visually impaired;
- there was inadequate opportunity to buy a ticket to travel because, for example, there was a long queue at the ticket office and the ticket machine was not available, or you were unable to use a machine because of a physical disability.

An appeal should be made to the **Independent Penalty Fares Appeal Service**, PO Box 14697, London SE1 8ZJ.

It is a criminal offence to travel on a train with the intention of avoiding paying the fare.

Penalty fares (underground services)
Penalty fares are only imposed on London underground services and not underground services outside of London. Penalties are imposed for the same reason as on buses, and are dealt with in the same way.

If you want to appeal against a penalty fare, you should write to the **London Underground Penalty Fares Appeals** office – London Underground Ltd, PO Box 4092, London SW1H 9EG. If you feel you have been unfairly treated by being given a penalty fare you should complain in writing to the **Customer Service Centre** (0845 330 9880; www.thetube.com).

Complaints about rail services
If you have a complaint about a train journey or a train delay or cancellation, you should address it to the train operator's customer services officer. You may be entitled to compensation for late or delayed services. You should check this with the train operator's customer services officer. If you are complaining about a station, you should find out whether the station is run by a train operating company or by Network Rail. You can do this by checking the logo displayed at the station. You should then address the complaint to the appropriate customer services officer.

Train operators must have a passengers' charter that has been approved by the Rail Regulator. As well as setting out service standards, the charter gives information on how to complain. If you want to make a complaint you can get a complaint form at a station or you can complain by telephone. Notices at stations and on trains give complaint addresses and telephone details.

If a complaint is likely to involve more than one company, or you are not sure which company you should make your complaint to, complain to whoever seems most likely. This company should then deal with the complaint or forward it to the appropriate company or companies.

If you are travelling outside London and you are not satisfied with the way in which the train company or Network Rail has dealt with your complaint, you should complain to the Rail Passengers' Committee. The **Rail Passengers' Council** (020 7505 9090) can give you the address of your local Rail Passengers' Committee.

In London, you should contact the **London Transport Users' Committee** (020 7505 9000; www.ltuc.org.uk).

If my train is late, what compensation can I get?

You are unlikely to get compensation for the full value of your original ticket. The national conditions of carriage for trains only allow for a voucher of at least 10 per cent of the value of your ticket if your train arrived more than an hour late. If you chose not to make the journey on discovering how late the train was, then you can claim a full refund. If you start your journey and have to finish it by taxi, you should inform the Duty Officer at the destination station when you arrive by taxi. Get a receipt for the fare, which you must provide to the train company in order to get a refund.

Complaints or requests for vouchers or refunds should be made to the customer services officer of your train's operator. You can get details from the ticket collector on your train or from the station where you bought your ticket. You will have to write and enclose your ticket or other proof that you bought it, for example a credit card receipt.

It is always wise to check with the **National Rail Enquiry Service** (08457 484950) shortly before you travel to avoid having your travel plans disrupted. They should have up-to-date information about timetable alterations and engineering works. There is another complaints procedure if the information they give you is wrong, and they can give you details of this.

Complaints about the National Rail Enquiry Service

The **National Rail Enquiry Service** (08457 484950) gives telephone information on timetables, fares and tickets on any route. It also gives information about engineering works and the best or cheapest route to use. If you have been given incorrect information, complain to the Rail Passengers' Committee. The **Rail Passengers' Council** (RPC: 020 7505 9090) can give you the address of the local Rail Passengers' Committee. You will need to give the RPC the date and time you made the call to the National Rail Enquiry Service and your own telephone code for them to identify the call centre that handled your original enquiry.

Complaints about underground services

Outside London, there are underground services in Merseyside, Tyne and Wear, and Glasgow. They are the responsibility of the Passenger Transport Executive for the area (contact details listed below). Underground services in London are the responsibility of Transport for London (0845 330 9880; www.thetube.com).

If you have a complaint, contact the service operator. The operator's name and address must be displayed on the train and will also be displayed in the underground station.

In London, if you are not satisfied with the outcome of your initial complaint to the line manager you can complain to **London Underground Customer Service Centre** (0845 330 9880; www.thetube.com).
If you are still not satisfied, you should complain to the **London Transport Users' Committee** (020 7505 9000; www.ltuc.org.uk).

Taxis and minicabs

In all areas outside London, the local authority regulates taxis and minicabs and their drivers.

In London, taxis, minicabs and their drivers are licensed by the Metropolitan Police at the Public Carriage Office (020 7941 4500).

Complaints about taxis and minicabs

Taxis
If you have a complaint about, for example, a driver's behaviour, unsafe driving, the driver not taking the direct route, or the meter apparently being wrongly set, complain to the taxi operator. If you are not satisfied with the response and you are outside London, then complain to your local authority, quoting, where possible, the licence number. The licence number is usually displayed both inside and outside the taxi.

If you are complaining about a taxi service in London and are not satisfied with the response you have received, take the complaint to the **Public Carriage Office** (020 7941 4500), giving the driver's badge number and as much information as possible about the complaint.

Minicabs

You should first complain to the operator. If you are not satisfied with the result of a complaint to the minicab operator, contact your local authority or the **Public Carriage Office** (020 7941 4500) if you live in the London area.

Personal injury and damage to property

If you are injured or your property is damaged while travelling on public transport other than a train (if, for example, you have fallen downstairs on an escalator), you should report it to the operator. You may also want to consider whether you can get compensation for any injury or damage caused by the accident. You should get specialist legal advice before you consider making a legal claim for compensation.

If you are injured or your property is damaged on a train, complain to the train operator or **Miller Rail Claims**, Room A201, MacMillan House, Paddington, London W2 1YJ. If you suspect there has been a health and safety breach you should report it to the Health and Safety Executive (020 7717 6533; www.hse.gov.uk).

Passenger Transport Executives (PTEs)

Greater Manchester PTE: 0161 242 6000
Merseyside PTE (Merseytravel): 0151 227 5181
South Yorkshire PTE: 0114 276 7575
Tyne and Wear PTE (Nexus): 0191 203 3333
West Midlands PTE (Centro): 0121 200 2787
West Yorkshire PTE: 0113 251 7272

Traffic Commissioners

Northern: 0113 254 3291
Eastern: 01792 454390
West Midlands and South Wales: 0121 609 6801
Western: 0117 900 8577
South Eastern and Metropolitan area: 01323 452400

Who can help?

Office of the Rail Regulator (ORR: 020 7282 2000; www.rail-reg.gov.uk)
The Strategic Rail Authority (020 7654 6000)

TRANSPORT OPTIONS FOR DISABLED PEOPLE

Driving

Buying or hiring a vehicle

If you are disabled and want to buy a vehicle you may be able to get a discount. The **Royal Association for Disability and Rehabilitation** (020 7250 3222; www.radar.org.uk), which gives information and advice on all aspects of living with a disability, including transport and mobility, can give information on dealers who may be willing to give a discount.

Motability (0845 456 4566; www.motability.co.uk) can sell or hire new or second-hand cars to anyone receiving the higher rate mobility component of Disability Living Allowance or war pensioners' mobility supplement.

If you are not entitled to either of the above allowances, contact car dealers and ask if they operate any disabled drivers discount schemes.

Some commercial hire companies offer discounts to disabled people when they hire a car or van. It is worth checking to see if a discount is available.

Adaptations to vehicles

A car may need to be adapted to suit the needs of a disabled person. The Department of Environment, Transport and the Regions' **Mobility Advice and Vehicle Information Service** (MAVIS) offers advice on car adaptations for drivers and passengers (01344 661000; www.dft.gov.uk).

Exemption from road tax

Any vehicle that is used only for a disabled person (whether they are the driver or the passenger) will be exempt from road tax. To get exemption, the disabled person must be either:

- receiving the higher rate mobility component of Disability Living Allowance;
  or
- receiving war pensioners' mobility supplement.

The vehicle must be registered in the name of the disabled person or in the name of someone authorized to act on their behalf.

Parking concessions

The Blue Badge scheme allows certain groups of disabled people to park in parking-restricted areas. For example, the blue badge enables disabled people to park free of charge and without time limit at on-street parking meters. Some London boroughs, and some town centres, do not operate the Blue Badge scheme.

You are eligible to apply for a blue badge if you are a driver or passenger who:

- receives the higher rate mobility component of Disability Living Allowance or war pensioners' mobility supplement, or is registered blind;
- has a permanent and substantial disability that means you are unable to walk or can walk only with considerable difficulty;
- has very severe upper limb disabilities (drivers only).

To apply for a blue badge, contact your local authority social services department. There is a small fee.

If you have a blue badge you may be able to get parking concessions when travelling in another country that also recognizes the badge. However, each country continues to determine its own set of parking concessions for which the badge can be used. There is further information on the Department for Transport website (www.mobility-unit.dft.gov.uk).

Rail services

All station and train operators have a disabled persons protection policy that sets out what provision a station or train operator makes for disabled people using its services. Information on these services and a copy of the protection policy is available from the local train or station operator. Alternatively, most local authorities and Passenger Transport Executives publish guides for disabled travellers that are a useful source of information on the facilities at railway stations.

If you need assistance when travelling by train – for example, if you are a wheelchair user and need help getting on and off the train, or you are visually impaired and need to be guided to the train – contact the train operator and ask them to arrange assistance. Try to give the operator at least forty-eight hours' notice of when you intend to travel and the type of help you require. Most mainline stations have a staff member who deals with requests for assistance. That person will be able to make any arrangements needed with other operating companies.

Concessionary fares

If you are disabled, you can buy a disabled person's railcard that entitles you and an accompanying adult to one third off the price of a rail ticket. Application forms are available from main stations, or from the **Disabled Persons Railcard Office** (0191 218 8103; www.disabledpersons-railcard.co.uk). Existing railcard users can renew their railcard by telephone.

Complaints

If you are not satisfied with any arrangements made or any aspect of accessibility, complain to the train operator. If the operator has not kept to the terms of its disabled persons protection policy, a complaint should be made to the **Office of the Rail Regulator** (020 7282 2000; www.railreg.gov.uk).

Buses

Outside London, most Passenger Transport Authorities and local authorities with responsibility for public transport publish guides for disabled travellers. In London, a person with an enquiry about disability access to buses should contact **Transport for London Access and Mobility** (020 7222 1234).

In some areas there are dial-a-bus schemes providing door-to-door services for disabled people. You can get information from the local authority social services department or a local organization for disabled people.

There are regulations covering coaches and buses so that disabled people can get on and off in safety and reasonable comfort. These depend on when a bus was brought into service, but may include the need for ramps, steps and priority seating. A driver or conductor must help you get on or off the bus if you ask, unless there are health and safety concerns about doing so.

Concessionary fares

Most local authorities offer concessions to disabled people. Details are available from local social services departments.

Disabled people living in Wales are entitled to a free concessionary bus pass and a discount of at least 50 per cent on all bus travel in Wales. Disabled people living in England are entitled to a free bus pass and a discount of at least 50 per cent on all bus travel within their local authority concession area.

Complaints

If you are dissatisfied with access to a bus service, complain to the bus operator. You may also want to draw the problem to the attention of the director of your local authority. The local authority may take up the complaint but will have no formal powers to make the operator respond.

Coaches

There are similar provisions for disability access to coaches as for buses (see above). If you plan to travel by coach you may want to contact the operator when arranging the journey to let the operator know what arrangements you need and to see whether the facilities exist to meet them.

Underground services

There are similar provisions for disability access to underground services as for coaches and buses – see above. To check provisions for disabled people on the underground service in your area, contact the Passenger Transport Executive for travel outside London, or Transport for London's Access and Mobility for travel in London (020 7222 1234).

For more information on how to complain about underground services and addresses of Passenger Transport Executives, see *Public transport*, pp. 355, 356.

Taxis and minicabs

Drivers of licensed taxis and minicabs are required to carry a guide dog and hearing dog, or an assistance dog accompanying a person with epilepsy or a physical disability, free of charge.

Escort services

The **Red Cross** provides an escort service to enable disabled people make short or long journeys that they would otherwise find difficult. Escort services include providing a companion for a journey on public transport, a private car with a driver or a Red Cross ambulance. A charge is made.

Who can help?

The **Disabled Drivers' Motor Club** (01832 734724; www.ddmc.org.uk) gives help and advice on motoring problems, vehicles and conversions. The **Disabled Drivers' Association** (08707 703333; www.dda.org.uk) provides advice and information to members on all aspects of mobility.

CAR TRAVEL

Can I use my mobile phone in the car?

It is now a criminal offence to use a hand-held mobile phone when driving. The ban also applies when you are waiting at traffic lights or in a traffic jam. Although hands-free phones are not included in the ban and can be used while driving, you can still risk prosecution for failure to have proper control of your car or for careless or dangerous driving. There is a fixed penalty of £30 for breaking the law by using your hand-held mobile when driving, or up to £1,000 if you are convicted in court. Drivers of buses, coaches or goods vehicles face a higher maximum fine of £2,500.

Driving tests

A driving test is made up of a theory test and a practical test. You cannot normally take the practical test without first having passed the theory test. You have to pay a fee for each part of the test.

Before you can apply for a test, you must have a valid Great Britain provisional driving licence.

The theory test

The theory test is in two parts. The first is a computerized touch-screen test in which you have to select the correct answer from a number of choices. The second part is called the hazard perception test. You will be shown a set of video clips of driving hazards and asked to click the mouse button as soon as you spot a hazard. You have to pass both parts of the theory test at the same sitting in order to pass.

If you have special needs, the **Driving Standards Agency** (0115 901 2500; www.dsa.gov.uk or see contact list below for area offices) can make special arrangements.

You do not have to take a theory test if you:

- want to upgrade your licence in the same category – for example, upgrade your car licence to be able to drive a car towing a large trailer;
- have a licence to drive automatic cars and/or motorcycles and want to upgrade your licence to a manual gearbox for the same type of vehicle;
- have passed a theory test and a practical moped test, and now want to upgrade to a motorcycle licence;
- have full entitlement to drive certain motor vehicles – for example, motor tricycles, because you have a full motorcycle licence issued before 1 February 2001;
- have a full licence for an invalid carriage.

You can apply for the test:

- in writing, by completing an application form available from theory test centres, driving instructors or the theory test booking line (0870 010 1372 or 0870 010 0372 if you want to apply in Welsh);
- by phone on 0870 010 1372 using a credit or debit card;
- by fax on 0870 010 4372;
- online (www.dsa.gov.uk).

You have to pay a fee for the test.

Candidates with special needs

If you have special needs – for example dyslexia or deafness, or if you need special physical access to the centre or want to take the test in a language other than English – the **Driving Standards Agency** (0115 901 2500; www.dsa-.gov.uk or see contact list below for area offices) can make arrangements. Indicate what your special needs are when you book the test.

If you are ill and have to cancel your theory test, you should normally send the DSA a doctor's certificate within ten days of the test day if you want to be given another date without having to pay the fee again. Otherwise, you must pay another fee. You must give three working days' notice to cancel for any other reason.

The practical test

You cannot take the practical test until you have passed the theory test unless you are exempt. The practical test will test your ability to exercise adequate control of your vehicle and normally lasts forty minutes.

The practical test also includes two questions on vehicle safety, designed to make sure that you know how to check the safety of your vehicle.

You must have completed a course of compulsory basic training (CBT) before applying for a motorcycle test, and must show your CBT certificate when you take your practical test. Information on the CBT is available from the **Driving Standards Agency** (0115 901 2500; www.dsa.gov.uk).

If you fail, or do not take the practical test within two years of having passed the theory test, you will have to take the theory test again and pass it before you can apply for a practical test.

Applying for a practical test

You will have to pay a fee for the test. There is no fee for a test to drive an invalid carriage. You can apply for the test by phone and pay by debit or credit card, or by post and pay by cheque or postal order.

You can choose to take the test at any test centre but often the choice is determined by the driving instructor and the availability of the instructor's car for the test.

Candidates with special needs

The DSA (0115 901 2500; www.dsa.gov.uk or see contact list below for area offices) can make provision for a candidate with special needs if you ask when you book the test. If you are deaf, you can ask for the test to be carried out in stages to enable sufficient time for the examiner to give instructions. A friend or family member can act as an interpreter or signer and the examiner can allow stopping at safe places on the route for the signer (who will sit in a rear seat) to communicate with you.

If you have a physical disability you may be asked to demonstrate any special controls on the vehicle in which you are being tested before the start of the test.

Practical test result

At the end of the practical test, the examiner will tell you whether you have passed or not.

If you fail the practical test, you can only appeal on the grounds that the test was not conducted in accordance with regulations.

When you have passed the practical test, you must apply to the **Driver and Vehicle Licensing Agency** (DVLA: 0870 240 0009) for your full licence within two years of the test date. Otherwise you will have to take the practical test (and the theory test) again.

When you pass the car or motorcycle-only practical test you will be subject to a probationary period.

Probationary period

When you pass your driving test for the first time you will be subject to a two-year probationary period. This applies to anyone driving on a licence issued by the DVLA. The two-year period begins on the day you pass the practical test.

If during the probationary period you are convicted of driving offences for which six or more penalty points are awarded, your driving licence will be revoked.

If your full driving licence is revoked, you will revert to learner status and be treated as if you had never passed a driving test. To continue driving, you will have to get a provisional driving licence and drive with learner's plates until you have passed both the theory and practical parts of the driving test. You cannot appeal the revocation of your licence. However, if you appeal against the conviction or sentence that brought the number of penalty points up to six or more, you can apply to the DVLA to have your licence restored pending the result of the appeal. If the court notifies the DVLA that the sentence is under appeal, the full licence should be restored without a further test.

There is no minimum period for which the licence must be revoked. As soon as you have passed both the theory and practical parts of another driving test, you can apply for a new full licence. However, the penalty points will remain on the driver's licence for four years from the date of your offence. After four years you can ask the DVLA to have them removed from your licence.

Disqualification/extended driving test

For some offences, a court can disqualify you or order that you be re-tested. If the offence is very serious the court can order that you are 'disqualified until test passed' and that you must take a double-practical driving test known as an 'extended driving test'. The fee to be paid for this test is higher than that for a normal test.

A motorcyclist who is disqualified by a court will have to retake compulsory basic training in order to ride as a learner and will have to retake the practical test.

Fees
You can find details of current driving test fees on the Driving Standards Agency website (www.dsa.gov.uk).

Complaints

Step one
If you want to complain about the way in which any part of your test was administered, you should contact either the Theory Test Operations or Practical Test Operations at the Driving Standards Agency (DSA). You can contact the offices by phone but in most cases you will have to put the complaint in writing.

If you want to complain about the *theory test* you should contact the **Driving Standards Agency's Customer Service Unit** (0870 241 0204 or 0870 010 0372 for Welsh).
If you want to complain about the *practical test*, you should complain to the Driving Standards Agency (0870 0101 372).

Step two
If you are not satisfied with the outcome of your complaint about any general administration of the test you can write to the DSA chief executive at the DSA's headquarters. You can also ask one of the following to investigate your complaint:

- an independent complaints assessor. You would need to contact the DSA's chief executive at the DSA headquarters (0115 901 2500; www.dsa.gov.uk) about this. *Or*
- the Parliamentary Ombudsman. You would need to ask your MP about this. See *Civil Rights*, p. 453.

Who else can help?
Driving Standards Agency area offices:

London and the South East: 020 7468 4712

Northern: 0191 201 8161
Midlands and Eastern: 0121 697 6762
Wales and Western: 029 2058 1218

There is more information about the Driving Standards Agency, the Driver Vehicle Licensing Agency and the Vehicle Inspectorate at www.direct.gov.uk.

Driving licences

You need a licence to drive most vehicles on a public road. You do not need a licence to drive any vehicle on a private road. A private road is one to which the public does not have access, for example a road on a private estate.

However, there are some vehicles which do not require a licence, either on a public or a private road. The most common examples of these are bicycles and horse-drawn carts.

Ages at which you can drive

Age	Vehicle
14 years	• electrically assisted pedal cycles
16 years	• mopeds • cars. This applies to people receiving Disability Living Allowance at the higher level • small agricultural tractors • small mowing machines or any other small pedestrian-controlled vehicle
17 years	• motorbikes up to 125 cc power • cars • large agricultural tractors • small road-rollers
18 years	• medium lorries • vans and lorries if you are a member of the young driver scheme
21 years	• large road-rollers • all other vehicles

| 70 years | • A provisional or full licence only lasts until your 70th birthday. Once you are 70, you must apply to renew your licence. The licence will normally be renewed for three years, after which you will need to apply to renew again. |

The young driver scheme

The young driver scheme provides an opportunity for a young person to obtain a full licence for large vehicles at the age of 18 rather than 21. The scheme is run by the **Road Haulage and Distribution Training Council** (01908 313360).

The type of vehicle the licence covers

These are the most common types of vehicle which you require a licence to drive. For full details of all of the categories of vehicles that need a licence contact the DVLA (www.dvla.gov.uk).

Vehicle	Category
Cars (including cars with a trailer weighing up to 750 kg)	B
Motorbikes	A
Mopeds	P
Vans and lorries weighing up to 3,500 kg (including vehicles with a trailer weighing up to 750 kg)	B
Vans and lorries weighing between 3,500 and 7,500 kg (including vehicles with a trailer weighing up to 750 kg)	C1
Buses with fewer than nine seats (including vehicles with a trailer weighing up to 750 kg)	B
Buses with more than eight but fewer than seventeen seats (including vehicles with a trailer weighing up to 750 kg) provided they are not used for hire or reward	D1
Invalid cars	B1

Vans, lorries and passenger-carrying vehicles

These vehicles do not require a special licence but do require you to have additional entitlements, for example to drive vans, lorries or passenger-carrying vehicles. If you are unsure what type of licence you need you should consult the Driver Vehicle Licensing Agency (DVLA 0870 240 0009; www.dvla.gov.uk).

Types of driving licence

A driving licence is either a 'provisional' licence or a 'full' licence.

Provisional driving licence
You must apply for a provisional licence if:

- you have never had a full driving licence; *or*
- you are unable to show you are entitled to a full driving licence.

If you want to drive a motorbike, and are applying for a provisional licence, you should indicate this on the application form. If you already have a full licence to drive a moped, car or certain vans and buses you can use it automatically as a provisional licence for driving a motorbike.

A provisional licence has certain restrictions on its use. If you have a provisional licence to drive a car or other vehicle (except a motorbike):

- you must display 'L' plates on the front and back of the vehicle (or 'D' plates in Wales);
- you must not drive on a motorway;
- if the vehicle has more than one seat, you must have someone with you whenever you are driving. The person supervising you must sit in the front passenger seat and be fit to drive the vehicle – for example, they must not have drunk more than a legal amount of alcohol. They must also be aged 21 or over and have had a full driving licence for at least three years.

However, if you have passed a driving test and are still waiting to receive a full licence you are not subject to the above restrictions.

Full driving licence
You are entitled to apply for a full driving licence if you have passed a driving test in the UK within the previous two years.

If you have a full driving licence issued outside the UK, the Isle of Man and the Channel Islands, see *Driving abroad*, p. 372.

Restrictions on the use of a full licence
A full licence does not have any restrictions on its use other than those relating to:

- the age of the driver;
- supervision of learner drivers;
- the type of vehicle the licence covers;
- the medical condition of the driver – for example, defective eyesight that cannot be corrected by glasses.

How to apply for a driving licence

You apply for a driving licence by filling in Form D1, which is available from the post office. This form is used for applying for either a provisional licence or a full licence. You must send the fee with the completed application form and a recent colour photograph and:

- your valid passport (this is the preferred document and should speed up the application); or
- your birth/adoption certificate or other similar official document.

Unless you send a UK, EU or EEA passport with the application, you will also need to get your photograph verified by a doctor, lawyer, teacher, police officer, MP, magistrate, minister of religion or another similar professionally qualified person. If you are a foreign national and you do not want to send your passport, and you do not know anyone who can verify your photograph, you may be able to take your application form, photograph and passport to your local vehicle registration office (details from DVLA: 0870 240 0009; www.dvla.gov.uk) as some VROs operate an over-the-counter identity checking service. Your application will be checked and your passport handed back to you.

You must tell the DVLA about any health condition that affects or may affect your ability to drive – for example, giddiness, heart attack or mental illness. If you have a disability, you will have to inform the DVLA of its nature. They may require you to undergo a medical examination.

If the DVLA refuses to give you a licence on medical grounds, you can appeal to a magistrates' court.

Licences are issued in two parts. One section is a credit card-sized photocard and contains details of the categories of vehicles that you are entitled to drive. The other section is a paper document setting out your licence entitlement history and any valid endorsements, including penalty points and disqualification periods. These licences are called photocard licences.

Paper licences issued before the introduction of photocard licences remain valid until they run out or the details on them need to be changed.

Photocard licences must be renewed every ten years to ensure the photograph remains up to date.

When you can start driving

If you have applied for a first provisional licence, you must not start driving until you receive the licence. This will usually take at least three weeks. If you have a medical condition, you may have to wait longer because more information may be needed before the licence is issued.

Compulsory basic training for motorcycles and mopeds

All learner moped- and motorcycle-riders (except for those listed below) must complete a compulsory basic training (CBT) course.

These people do not have to complete a CBT course:

- people who are learning to drive a motorbike and who have already obtained full moped entitlement as a result of passing a moped test on or after 1 December 1990;
- people riding a moped with the full entitlement given automatically with a full car licence.

CBT courses are run by motorcycle training bodies approved by the Driving Standards Agency (0115 901 2500). They are listed under 'motorcycle training' in the Yellow Pages or 'motorcycling instruction' in Thompson directories.

Disqualifications and endorsements

Disqualifications

If you have been disqualified from driving, you can have a licence again either:

- at the end of the disqualification period; or
- earlier if the disqualification is lifted.

If you intend to wait until the end of the disqualification period, you will usually receive a reminder from the DVLA to apply for a new licence eight weeks before the end of the disqualification period. If you do not receive a reminder, you should fill in form D1 available from the post office and send it to the DVLA. You can apply to the court that dealt with your case to have the disqualification lifted if you have been disqualified for a total of more than two years.

Endorsements

You may incur penalty point endorsements on your licence for being convicted of committing certain driving offences. After a certain time, you can apply to the DVLA on form D1 to have endorsements removed (for a small charge). The time you will have to wait to have endorsements removed from your licence will vary according to the type of driving offence committed.

Lost, stolen or defaced licences

If your licence is stolen or lost, you should tell the police as soon as possible. You should also apply for a duplicate licence using form D1. You can obtain this form from the post office and send it to the DVLA. There is a charge for obtaining a duplicate licence. Duplicate licences may also be obtained by phoning the DVLA.

If your licence is destroyed or defaced in some way so that the information on it is no longer clear, you have to apply for a duplicate licence. You do not have to tell the police in this situation.

Change of name or address

Paper driving licences

If you hold a paper driving licence and you need to notify a change of name or address, you must complete a D1 application form, available from most post offices.

Photocard driving licences

If you hold a photocard driving licence and you need to notify a change of address, you should complete the 'changes' section on your paper counterpart licence and send it to the DVLA (0870 240 0009; www.dvla.gov.uk) together with your photocard licence. If you need to notify a change of name, you should use form D1.

For both paper and photocard driving licences, documentary evidence of a change of name is required – for example, a birth certificate, passport or deed poll. You can continue to drive whilst you are waiting for the licence to be returned to you. The DVLA does not make a charge for changing the details of your name and address. However, you may be fined for not telling the DVLA about a change in your name or address.

Driving abroad

Driving in the EEA

If you have a full Great Britain (GB) driving licence, you can drive in any EEA country on this licence. An International Driving Permit is not required if you have a licence.

You can exchange your GB licence for one of the country in which you are living if you want to.

Driving outside the EEA

If you wish to drive abroad as a visitor, for example on holiday, you may need to apply for an International Driving Permit (IDP). If you need an IDP you may apply by post to one of the motoring organizations or get one in person from a major post office. You do not have to be a member of the organization. You can only be issued with an IDP if you have a full GB licence.

If you go to live permanently in another country you may be able to exchange your licence for a driving licence in that country. You should check with the driver licensing authority in the country in which you are going to live. The appropriate embassy may be able to provide this information.

Driving licences issued abroad

Licences issued in another EEA country

If you have a full and valid driving licence that has been issued in another EEA country (a 'Community licence'), you may be able to drive in the UK on this licence. You do not have to exchange it immediately for a GB licence. Provided the Community licence remains valid in the issuing country, and it is a licence to drive an ordinary car, you can use it to drive here until you are 70, or for three years after you become resident. If it is a 'vocational licence', for example a licence to drive a minibus or bus, the rules are different.

However, if you want to, you can exchange your driving licence for a full GB licence. You should complete form D1 available from post offices and send your own driving licence with the application form. A photocopy will not be accepted. A fee is payable.

Licences issued outside the EEA

If you have a full and valid driving licence that has been issued in a country other than an EEA country you can drive in the UK on this licence for twelve months.

If you intend to be resident in the UK beyond this period, you can exchange your licence for a full GB licence if it is a British Forces Germany licence or if it was issued in certain countries, including Australia, Barbados, Canada, Hong Kong, Japan, New Zealand and South Africa. For some other countries you must take a UK driving test to obtain a full GB licence if you intend to drive after the initial twelve-month period.

Traffic accidents

An accident is defined as a traffic accident if it occurs on a road or in a place to which the public have access. This can include footpaths and bridleways. A driver involved in a traffic accident should stop whether or not the accident was their fault if:

- anyone, other than themselves, is injured; *or*
- another vehicle, or someone else's property, is damaged; *or*
- an animal in another vehicle or running across the road is injured; *or*
- a bollard, street lamp or other item of street furniture is damaged.

If the driver has to stop, they must remain near the vehicle long enough for anyone who is involved directly or indirectly in the accident to ask for details. This could be, for example, the owner of an injured animal, a relative of someone who is injured, or the police. The driver must then give their name and address, the name and address of the owner of the vehicle (if the driver is not the owner), and the registration number of the vehicle.

The driver may also have to report the accident to a police officer or at a police station, in person, as soon as practicable and in any case within twenty-four hours. This duty arises whenever the driver has not given their name and address at the scene of the accident, whether or not they were asked to do so.

If any personal injury is caused to another person, the driver must also produce a valid insurance certificate if asked to do so by a police officer, an injured person, or anyone else directly or indirectly involved in the accident. If the insurance certificate is asked for, but not produced at the time, the accident must be reported to a police station as soon as practicable, or in any case within twenty-four hours, and the insurance certificate must be taken to a police station within seven days of the accident. However, if the driver is asked at the time of the accident to produce insurance details and does so, there is no further obligation to report the accident to the police, as long as they have complied with the duties described above.

In the case of a damage-only accident, the driver must give insurance details to anyone who may wish to make a claim against them. In all accidents, drivers should inform their own insurance company.

If you are involved in a road accident it's helpful if you can establish the following:

- full details of the accident – where and when it happened and who was involved (sketch plans and/or photographs would be useful);
- whether anyone was responsible for the accident;
- whether there was any injury or damage;
- whether there is any independent evidence about what happened – for example, witnesses or police reports;
- whether any criminal proceedings have been started or threatened;
- whether any civil proceedings have been started or threatened;
- what type of insurance the people involved have;
- whether free legal advice or assistance – for example, from a motoring organization or under an insurance policy – is available.

It is important to establish, as soon as possible after the accident, whether anyone was at fault. It may be obvious that someone caused the accident and there will be no dispute about liability. However, there will be cases where it is not obvious, or where the extent of liability is difficult to work out.

As a general rule, the driver of a vehicle that runs into the back of another vehicle will be held liable for the accident. This is the case even if the car in front has braked sharply or unexpectedly, because drivers are required to drive a safe distance behind other vehicles. However, there may be circumstances when this does not apply, and if liability is disputed legal advice will be necessary unless the insurance company is dealing with it.

Independent evidence about what happened

It is important to establish whether there were any witnesses to the accident – for example, other people involved in the accident, other drivers, pedestrians or police who saw what happened. If there are no witnesses it may be difficult to prove liability, especially if the other party denies responsibility.

I have had an accident in my car but the other driver is refusing to give me his details. What can I do?

A driver involved in an accident is required to give information. The keeper of a vehicle can also be required to provide the police with information on who was driving a vehicle at the time that an offence was committed. There is no legal requirement for anyone else to provide information. Drivers include motorcyclists but not cyclists.

If a driver involved in a traffic accident refuses to give details, such as name and address, at the scene of the accident, this information can be obtained in other ways. If the registration number of the vehicle has been noted and the accident has been reported, the police can trace the owner (not necessarily the driver) of the vehicle and their insurance company. However, the police can refuse to pass on this information.

The **Driver and Vehicle Licensing Agency** (DVLA: 0870 240 0009; www.dvla.gov.uk) can give the name and address of the person registered as the keeper of the vehicle to anyone who has a good reason for needing it. Someone who wants this information should write to the DVLA explaining why it is needed. A fee is payable. The registration number, make and model of the car and the date of the accident must be given. If the DVLA does not consider there are adequate reasons for providing the information, it will return the fee.

If a driver is driving illegally

If an accident happens involving a driver who is driving illegally, they will not be in a strong position to take any action, even if someone else caused the accident. Examples of illegal driving are driving:

- alone on a provisional licence;
- without a driving licence, tax or insurance;
- while disqualified from driving;
- a stolen vehicle;
- an unsafe vehicle;
- without an MOT certificate;
- while drunk or under the influence of drugs.

Accidents caused by sudden illness

If an accident occurs because a driver has become ill – for example, through a stroke or heart attack – they will not be prosecuted for the way they were driving. However, in some circumstances they could be liable to pay compensation. This may be covered by their insurance.

Payment for hospital treatment following an accident

Immediate treatment

The driver of a vehicle involved in a road accident may be charged for any emergency medical treatment provided by a doctor (other than one working in or called from a hospital), for example a hospital doctor who is off duty and happens to be passing by the accident. There is a standard charge plus, in certain circumstances, a mileage allowance. The driver will receive a bill from the doctor some time after the accident. This charge should be included as part of any claim for damages. The driver's insurance company will usually pay this charge without affecting their no-claims bonus.

Further hospital treatment

If anyone involved in the accident receives further hospital treatment in a non-NHS hospital, as an in-patient or an out-patient, the hospital may claim from the driver's insurance company up to a certain amount for the cost of treatment. The hospital will write to the patient, or their parents if a child was injured, asking for the driver's name and address, details of their insurance company, whether or not the patient is making a claim against the driver and if a solicitor is acting for the patient.

If a person has a road accident and receives further hospital treatment at an NHS hospital, the Department of Health can require the insurance company of the other driver to meet some of the costs. Where the driver who caused the accident is not insured or cannot be traced, the costs will be recovered from the Motor Insurers' Bureau (01908 830001).

The Department of Health automatically recovers NHS charges from the insurance company on behalf of the hospital. There is no need for the injured person to be involved in routine cases. In cases where the person takes civil legal action against the other party, there is no need to include a claim for NHS charge recovery.

Failure to respond to claim letters

If someone does not reply to a claim letter holding them liable for damages following a road accident, you should take one of the following courses of action:

- if you have fully comprehensive insurance, let the insurance company pursue the claim. If the insurance company does not manage to recover damages from the other person you will lose your no-claims bonus, unless you can successfully sue the liable person.
- if you have no insurance, or have only third-party insurance, you will have to pursue the claim yourself. If the other person does not respond, you may have to take court action.
- if the police were involved, they can be contacted to ask whether they are following up the accident and whether they have heard from the other person.

Civil court proceedings

If you do not have an insurance company acting for you, because, for example some losses are uninsured, you may have to sue the liable person. Where this is the case, bear the following points in mind:

- if the claim is defended and is allocated to the small claims track at the county court (that is most claims of £5,000 or less), you will not usually be entitled to claim solicitors' costs, and will therefore have to deal with the case yourself, or pay for a solicitor;
- if the claim is defended and allocated to either the fast track or the multi-track at the county court, you will need legal advice and representation. This may be available under the legal help scheme or other publicly-funded legal services.

If a claim form has been issued against you, you need to respond quickly, as time limits for entering a defence are quite short. You may admit you are liable for some or all of the damages claimed but you may have a good counterclaim to make and this must be done quickly.

Traffic accidents related to work

If you are an employee and have a traffic accident while travelling for work (or possibly on the way to work) you should bear in mind the following points:

- if the vehicle is insured by the employer, you will be covered by the employer's vehicle insurance, whether or not they were responsible for the accident;
- if you are an injured pedestrian or cyclist, the employer will normally be

liable in the same way as for any industrial injury, unless you clearly acted
negligently;

- if you are a trade union member and are injured you will usually get free
  legal help from the trade union;
- you may be able to claim benefits under the industrial injuries scheme.

Learner drivers

Learner drivers who are driving legally are in exactly the same position as
any other driver in relation to a traffic accident. The supervisor of a learner
driver must do all that is reasonable to prevent the driver from driving in a
way likely to cause danger to others. It is the duty of the driver to report an
accident and the liability and responsibility of the supervisor depends on
the particular circumstances.

The police have the power to require the supervisor of a learner driver to
produce their licence and certificate of insurance.

Bicycles

If you have been in an accident involving a bicycle, you should be aware
that cyclists do not have to be insured for damage to the bicycle or any
other vehicle or for personal injury. However, the cyclist may be covered
under another insurance policy, for example their home contents policy. If
the accident happened on the way to or from work, or while at work, the
person who had the accident may be covered by their employer's insurance
or may be able to obtain advice and assistance from a trade union.

If the cyclist has inadequate insurance it will probably be easier to claim
on your own insurance and let the insurance company take action against
anyone who is liable.

If none of these is possible, the cyclist could be sued in court for compensation.

Children

If you are involved in an accident caused by a child, you should check
whether the child was accompanied by a responsible adult at the time of
the accident. If it can be shown that the adult acted negligently, the adult
may be liable for any accident caused by the child and could be sued in the
civil court for damages caused by the child.

If the child was unaccompanied and it can be shown that an adult was
negligent by failing to supervise the child adequately at the time of the

accident, then they may be liable for any accident caused by the child and could be sued in the civil court for damages.

Children can be held liable for their own negligence. However, it may be difficult to prove that a young child's behaviour is negligent. Even if negligence by the child can be proved, it may not be worth pursuing any legal action as the child is unlikely to have any money.

Stationary or fixed objects

If someone hits a stationary object, either on the road itself or alongside the road, they should consider the following:

- was the object adequately marked or lit to enable the driver to see it clearly and in time to avoid it, for example an unlit car, skip or roadworks? If not, it will be necessary to find out who was responsible for failing to do so: for example, if the object was a parked car, the responsible person is the owner, or, in the case of roadworks, whoever is carrying out the roadworks is responsible. It will be necessary to find out whether this was the local authority or a gas, water or electricity company or contractors doing the work on their behalf.
- had the object been left on the road either unlawfully or in an unsafe way, for example a car parked on a blind corner? If so, the owner of the object or vehicle may be liable.
- have there been any similar accidents caused by the object? If so, this is evidence that the object had contributed to the accident.

The condition of the road surface

An accident may be caused by the condition of the road surface, for example by pot holes, ice, mud or leaves. Adequate warning may not have been given of a problem with the road surface, for example:

- the local authority may have failed to respond reasonably to a problem with the road surface. If so, they may be liable for any accident caused.
- individuals or firms, for example farmers or contractors. may have left mud or grease on the road surface for an unreasonable period of time without adequate warnings. If so, they may be liable for any accident caused.

Animals

If an accident is caused by or to an animal, the following points should be considered:

- if the animal is a cat or poultry, the incident does not count in law as an accident. This means that the driver is not required to stop. The driver must stop if a horse, cattle, ass, mule, pig, sheep, goat or dog is injured.

- if it can be shown that the owner of an animal has been negligent in allowing the animal on the road, for example failing to maintain a fence they are responsible for maintaining, then the owner will be liable. Owners are not responsible for the actions of their cats or poultry.
- if a driver is responsible for an injury to an animal, other than cats or poultry, then they may be sued for damages.

Emergency vehicles

Emergency vehicles have no special exemption from liability for accidents that they are involved in or cause. The same rules apply as with any other accident.

Drivers from abroad

If an accident happens in the UK and the driver is from abroad their obligations are the same as if they came from the UK.

It may be difficult to get compensation for any damage or injuries. You could:

- contact the Motor Insurers' Bureau (01908 830001), which can obtain details of the driver and their insurance company if the vehicle's registration number can be provided and the driver comes from a country participating in the green card scheme. If the driver was not insured, or the insurance company does not have an agent in the United Kingdom, the Motor Insurers' Bureau will take up the case. If the insurance company does have an agent in the UK you will be advised to contact them.
- seek advice from a motoring organization;
- take action against the driver's insurance company if it has an agency agreement with another insurance company in the UK;
- claim on your own insurance policy if you have comprehensive cover. This will affect any no-claims bonus.

If you cannot pursue the claim in the UK, you should consider carefully before proceeding with a claim against the driver in their own country. Claims heard abroad can be difficult, time-consuming and expensive and a solicitor's help would be needed. A claim pursued through the UK courts could become very involved and expensive if the driver refused to attend court.

MOTOR INSURANCE

If you drive your vehicle on the road, or leave it parked in the street, the law says that you must have motor insurance. It is a criminal offence not to insure your motor vehicle.

Types of motor insurance

There are three main types of motor insurance:

Third-party insurance

This is the minimum amount of insurance cover that you must have by law for your vehicle. Third-party insurance only covers you for damage to someone else's vehicle or property, or injury to someone else in an accident that involves your car. This includes accidents caused by your passenger. If your vehicle is damaged in the accident you will have to pay for the repairs yourself.

Third-party, fire and theft insurance

This includes third-party cover and, additionally, damage to or loss of your car by fire or theft.

Comprehensive insurance

This includes third-party, fire and theft insurance. In addition, it will also pay for repairs to your car. There is a range of extra cover that some policies provide, including cover for your own death or injury, or that of your partner or other member of your family, up to a limited amount, cover for your personal belongings if they are stolen from your vehicle, medical and legal expenses, and hire of a replacement vehicle.

Motor insurance policies normally run for a year. Your insurer does not have to send you a notice reminding you to renew but most companies do send out notices. When you take out or renew motor insurance, you will get a cover note at first. This will be valid for thirty days or until you get a copy of the full insurance certificate. It is a criminal offence to drive without a cover note or full insurance certificate, so do not rely only on a telephone conversation in which someone has told you that you are covered. The police can ask you to show them your insurance certificate or cover note. If you can't produce the right document, they will give you seven days to do so at a police station of your choice. If you are stopped under the 'fixed penalty system' they can specify the station.

How to make a claim

If your car has been stolen

If your car has been stolen, tell your insurer and the police immediately. Your insurer will wait a few weeks before settling your claim to allow time for the car to be found. Check your policy to see whether it covers the cost of hiring another car during this time. If you were paying your premium by instalments, you may have to carry on paying, even though you have no vehicle to insure.

If your car is found after your claim has been settled, it will belong to your insurer. If your car is not found, your insurer will offer to pay you the market value of the car, which is the amount you could have sold it for before it was stolen. This payment will bring your policy to an end, and you will not have the rest of your premium refunded, unless this is included in your policy. If you are not satisfied with the offer, try to get evidence that the car is worth more, by using car price guides or prices of similar vehicles in local papers.

If your car has been in an accident

If you have an accident:

- never admit that it was your fault at the scene of the accident, as this could make your policy invalid;
- exchange names, addresses, and insurance details with the drivers of the other vehicles involved, and get the details of any independent witnesses. If someone refuses to give you details about themselves or their insurance, your insurer may be able to trace them through the registration number of their car.
- tell your insurer about the accident straight away, even if you do not intend to make a claim. If you do not make a claim for the accident, you will not risk losing your no-claims bonus.

Third-party and third-party fire and theft policies

Third-party and third-party fire and theft policies do not cover accidental damage to your car, but they may cover damage or personal injury to the other party, depending on who is to blame for the accident. Always make a claim against the other party first, and allow the insurer to decide who is responsible for the accident. If they decide that you are responsible, you will have to pay for the repairs yourself.

To make a claim from the other driver, write to them saying that you intend to make a claim from them. Say that you hold them responsible for the accident and ask them to tell their insurer. Tell your own insurer that you are claiming from the third party. The other driver must report the accident to their own insurer before the claim can be dealt with. The insurer can only act on the instructions of their own policyholder. If the driver was uninsured, or cannot be identified, the Motor Insurers Bureau (MIB: 01908 830001) may be able to settle your claim. In certain circumstances, an insurer may be able to deal with your claim, even where the driver is technically uninsured.

Comprehensive insurance policies

If you have a comprehensive insurance policy, it is usually best if you claim from your own insurer. Be aware that you may lose your no-claims bonus if your insurer is unable to recover the money from the other driver's insurer. You will still need to claim from the other driver's insurer for any injuries you have suffered or any losses that are not covered by your insurance policy.

To make a claim, get a claim form from your insurer, or write to the other driver or their insurer, giving full details of the accident and the driver's policy number. Tell the insurer about any independent witnesses, and send them any witness statements as soon as possible. If you used a broker or an agent to buy your insurance policy, they may help you to prepare your claim. Be sure to keep copies of all documents, including letters, claim forms and statements.

Don't arrange to have your car repaired without the insurer's permission, as you will be responsible for the cost. The insurer may ask an engineer or a motor claims assessor to inspect your car, and use an approved repair firm to carry out the work. Alternatively, you may be asked to get estimates yourself and send them to your insurer for approval before you can go ahead with the repairs. You may have to pay part of the repair costs yourself if your vehicle ends up in a better condition after it has been repaired than it was before.

Insurance when driving abroad

You will have third-party motor insurance to drive in any European Union (EU) country as long as your policy was bought from any EU-based insurer. This includes those based in the UK. However, third-party cover is often inadequate and it is advisable to contact your insurer to arrange extra cover. Your policy may also give you third-party cover to drive in some non-EU countries. Check with your insurer to see if the country you are travelling to is included in your policy. If it is not, you will need to take out extra cover. Your insurer can issue you with a green card to show that you have increased insurance cover. Some countries abroad require you to have a green card.

Motor cycle insurance

There are two different types of motor cycle insurance:

- Specified cycle policy
  This is the more common type of motor cycle insurance policy. It insures you to drive one specific motor cycle.
- Rider policy
  This type of policy insures you to drive any motor cycle up to a certain cc rating, with the owner's permission.

Motor cycle insurance is usually limited to one person only. If you want someone else to drive your motor cycle then you must either name them on your policy, or make sure that they have their own motor cycle insurance. There is usually a compulsory excess on motor cycle insurance and you do not generally get a no-claims bonus.

TRAVEL AND HOLIDAYS

Package holidays

When you buy a package holiday your general consumer rights apply. The holiday must:

- match its description, so if the brochure says the hotel is within walking distance of the beach, it must be so; *and*
- be of a reasonable standard, bearing in mind the price paid and the location.

For example, you would not expect a budget priced holiday to be of the same standard as a luxury holiday, but whatever the price, you would expect basic standards of hygiene to apply.

Once a holiday booking is confirmed, there is a binding contract between the holiday organizer and the person who booked the holiday. Problems with package holidays are usually a result of one or more terms of the contract having been broken. For example, if the brochure said that the hotel had certain facilities, such as a swimming pool, and there wasn't one, you may be entitled to compensation.

Remember: as with other purchases, if you used your credit card to pay for the holiday and the cost was more than £100 and less than £30,000, the credit card company may be equally liable for any breach of contract. This means that you could claim against the travel operator, the credit card company, or both of them jointly.

Prices

The law says that all holiday brochures must give the price legibly, comprehensibly and accurately. Once confirmed, the price of the holiday can be increased only if the booking conditions state that this is allowable, there are at least thirty days before your departure date and the increase is for one of the following reasons:

- an increase in transport costs, for example fuel; *or*
- to cover fees and taxes for services, such as landing fees; *or*
- variations in the exchange rate.

If the contract allows for an increase in price, the first 2 per cent must be absorbed by the tour operator. If the increase is significant, you should be given the opportunity to cancel the holiday. No price increase should be passed on in the period of thirty days before departure.

Refunds and compensation

Once a holiday booking is confirmed, you have a right to a refund without having to pay a cancellation fee if:

- the organizer cancels the holiday. If an alternative holiday is offered, you can choose whether to accept the alternative or the refund. The alternative holiday should be of at least the same standard as the one you booked or, if it is of a lesser standard, you should be refunded the difference in price between the original holiday and the alternative. *Or*

- the organizer has made significant changes to the package holiday. An example of this kind of change would be that the price of the holiday has been significantly increased or the departure date has been moved.

Also, once your holiday booking is confirmed, you may be entitled to compensation if:

- there is a breach of contract that, for example, results in the holiday being a complete disaster, or the departure date is altered significantly. You would not be able to claim compensation if circumstances were outside the operator's control, for example if it rained continuously. *Or*
- the tour operator has been negligent and as a result someone booked on the holiday suffers injury, illness or loss. Always take legal advice before deciding whether to accept compensation for personal injury. *Or*
- your luggage has been lost. However, in practice it is usually quicker and easier to claim through any holiday insurance. *Or*
- you have incurred additional expenses or suffered inconvenience because of a breach of contract or negligence, for example if your flight was delayed for twenty-four hours and you had to take an extra day off work.

Dealing with the problem

Once you have decided what your rights are, contact the person who put together your package holiday. This is usually the tour operator but sometimes it is the travel agent. Whoever organized the holiday is responsible for dealing with most complaints. Even if the problem has been caused by the actions of a third party, for example staff at your hotel, the organizer may still be responsible if they were aware there was a potential problem but did nothing to rectify this.

Complain as soon as possible after the problem arises, if possible to a representative of the tour operator in the resort, and insist that they complete a report on the problem. Gather as much evidence as you can. Take photographs, and ask for witnesses' names and addresses. Back this up with a letter to the tour operator within twenty-eight days of your return. Refer in your letter to any booking reference number, or send a copy of your invoice. Keep a copy of your letter and send it by recorded delivery.

If someone has been injured or you suspect that a criminal offence has been committed – if, for example, the tour operator claims that the hotel has a swimming pool or air conditioning but it does not – you should report the matter to your local Trading Standards Department.

If you aren't happy with the response, write to the tour operator and the credit card company, if applicable. Repeat the complaint and request any compensation. Give them fourteen days to resolve the matter or tell them you will consider taking legal action. If the operator has sent you a cheque for compensation you can cash the cheque, but write back explaining why you feel the amount is inadequate and say you are accepting the money on account. But *don't* cash the cheque if the letter says 'encashment is deemed acceptance', because, by doing so, you are accepting the amount as a final settlement.

Not good enough . . .

If you are still dissatisfied, find out if the tour operator or travel agent is a member of a trade association such as the Association of British Travel Agents (ABTA), which represents travel agents and has a code of practice which its members must follow. If one of its members breaks the code, ABTA's legal department will investigate the matter internally but it doesn't take up cases on a customer's behalf. However, ABTA does operate an arbitration and conciliation service to resolve disputes, which can deal with claims up to £7,500 per booking, but doesn't deal with claims for compensation for illness or injury. You can contact ABTA on 020 7637 2444. There is a fee, but this will be refunded if the claim is successful. The deadline for applying to use the service is nine months from the end of the holiday.

You should try to use an arbitration and conciliation service, or alternative dispute resolution scheme (ADR), where available, before taking court action. This is because the amount of compensation a court may award you could be reduced if you have not tried other ways of resolving the problem before going to court.

If you choose not to use ABTA, and if the tour operator doesn't respond, simply refuses to do anything, or makes a final offer you are unwilling to accept, your only other choice is to go to court. But remember that court should be your last resort. Before starting court action you need to consider whether you have sufficient evidence. You also need to find out if the tour operator is solvent. It's not worth suing a person or company with no money. And you should consider whether, if you've lost money over a holiday, it is worth losing more on a court case you may not win.

Overbooking

Package holiday accommodation

> *Help! Our hotel room was double-booked and the holiday company sent us to a hotel on the other side of the island. It was perfectly pleasant but not really where we wanted to be. We're home now, but would like to know if we can claim compensation.*
>
> Generally speaking, if your holiday plans were changed as a result of an overbooking, it is likely that the agreement between you and the holiday company was broken. When a contract is broken in this way, you are entitled to claim compensation or a refund from the provider. In law, the contract is made up of things like the booking conditions printed on the back of a ticket, a letter confirming a booking and information given in the brochure or by a travel agent. If an overbooking problem is in connection with a package holiday, you should take action against the organizer, not the provider of the transport or accommodation. If you used your credit card to pay for the accommodation or travel and the cost was over £100, the credit card company may be equally liable for any breach of contract. This means you may be able to claim a refund from the credit card company, if you get no joy from the holiday company. In this case, unless you made it clear at the time you accepted the alternative accommodation that you were doing so 'under protest' and that the alternative accommodation was of a lower standard than the one you booked, it is unlikely that a claim for compensation will be successful.

If your holiday accommodation was overbooked and you could not stay there, the organizer should offer you:

- a full refund; *or*
- alternative accommodation of a similar standard to the one you booked; *or*
- if an alternative cannot be agreed, transport back to a place where you can return home and compensation.

How to solve your problem

Once you have decided what your rights are, contact the company, and the credit card company if applicable, as soon as possible. Keep copies of your letters. Explain your problem calmly but firmly and ask for what you want, a refund or compensation. Send proof of your booking, including the dates of your holiday, confirmation letter or tickets. Send photocopied evidence of any extra costs you incurred, for example hotel receipts, if you are claiming compensation. Send a copy of the letter to the travel agent, if the booking was made through one.

If you are not satisfied with the response and booked through a travel agent, find out if the agent is a member of the **Association of British Travel Agents** (ABTA: 020 7637 2444) or **Association of Independent Tour Operators** (AITO: 020 8744 9280), both of whom operate a conciliation service to help resolve disputes. Conciliation is usually free. Arbitration is chargeable and any decision will be legally binding and likely to prevent you taking court action.

If you decide not to use conciliation or arbitration, write to the owner or manager of the company and the credit card company, if applicable, repeating your complaint and the steps you have taken so far. Say you are giving them fourteen days to resolve the problem or you will consider taking legal action. Send the letter by recorded delivery with a copy to the head office of the company, if applicable. Keep copies of all your letters and a note of any phone conversations you have in connection with the problem.

If the company makes you an offer, be realistic in what you will accept. You may not get an improved offer by going to court. If the company doesn't respond, refuses to do anything, or makes a final offer you are unwilling to accept, your only other choice is to go to court.

Overbooking of flights

There are special rules covering compensation for overbooked flights from airports in the European Union. These rules also apply to flights from airports outside the European Union, but flying into a European Union airport on a European Union airline. The compensation is available if you are overbooked on a scheduled or charter flight.

You can get compensation for overbooking of your flight, as long as you meet certain conditions. You must have a valid ticket, which has been confirmed for the overbooked flight, and you must have checked in by the deadline given to you by the airline. As long as you meet all these conditions you will be able to get:

- a full refund of your ticket and a free return flight to your first point of departure, if you need it; *or*
- another flight as soon as possible or at a later date of your choice.

You will also be entitled to:

- compensation in cash, or by cheque or bank transfer, and expenses – for example, for phone calls, meals and refreshments and hotel accommodation if you are delayed overnight.

If your flight is overbooked the airline should give you a form stating what compensation is available. (These overbooking rules only apply if you were not allowed to board the flight, not if you volunteered to take a different flight.)

If you are overbooked on a flight to which the EU rules do not apply, you may still be able to get compensation for overbooking. You will need to check with your airline whether any compensation is available for your particular circumstances.

For more information about overbooking on all flights, see the Air Travel Advice section on the Air Transport Users Council website (www.caa.co.uk/auc).

Overbooking on other forms of transport

If you were booked on a specific ferry or similar sailing, and you could not travel because of overbooking, you may be able to claim compensation from the provider, on the grounds of breach of contract. You could claim an amount for any loss you suffered as a result of the overbooking, for example the cost of staying in a hotel until the next sailing. Also check your travel insurance to see if it covers you for delays caused by overbooking. If it does, it will probably be easier to claim on your insurance than through the courts. You would not be entitled to compensation if you were travelling by coach or train unless you had tickets for a specified service, for example the 10:51 London to Edinburgh express.

If the transport was booked as part of a package holiday, you would need to claim from the organizer.

Travel insurance

Travel insurance can provide you with cover for:

- cancelling or cutting short your trip for specific reasons outside your control – for example, your unexpected illness or that of a close family member or a member of your travelling party;
- missed transport or delayed departure for reasons outside your control;
- medical and other emergency expenses;
- personal injury and death;
- lost, stolen or damaged personal property, including baggage;
- accidental damage or injury you cause to someone else.

You can buy travel insurance to cover a single trip, or an annual policy covering several trips. If you are taking out a single-trip policy, take it out when you book your trip so that you are covered if you have to cancel. Some package holidays offer to include travel insurance, but you do not have to accept this. You are free to make your own arrangements. A travel agent must not charge you more for a package holiday because you do not buy their insurance. If a travel agent tries to do this, you should contact your local Trading Standards Department.

Ask for quotes from several insurers, to help you get the best deal for your circumstances. Some policies exclude dangerous activities or high-risk sports such as skiing or scuba diving, and if you are going on a holiday involving one of these activities, you may have to pay more for your insurance.

It is worth checking your household contents insurance policy, as this may cover you for loss or damage to your personal belongings while you are abroad. You may decide that you only want to take out insurance for some of the other risks you can be covered for while you are abroad.

Your credit card company may provide you with some free insurance cover when you use it to pay for a holiday. Check carefully what is covered. In general, this should not be used as a substitute for your own insurance as it may not cover you for everything.

Remember to take a copy of your travel insurance policy away with you.

Making a claim

If you need to make a claim on your travel insurance policy, check that you are within the time limits for making a claim and that you are covered for the situation you are claiming for. There is usually a maximum amount that can be claimed under each section of the policy, and a limit on the amount you can claim for any single item. Contact your insurer as soon as possible to request a claim form. This may be once you have returned home. Your insurer may have an international helpline that you can use to get advice on the procedures you must follow.

Lost, stolen or damaged personal property or luggage

You will be expected to take reasonable care of your belongings, and to minimize any losses. Your insurer will want evidence of the loss or damage. This may mean making a report to the local police, which should be done within twenty-four hours, if possible.

If you have to replace any essential items that are lost – for example toiletries or clothing – make sure you ask for receipts as you will probably need to provide your insurer with copies. Ask for receipts for any essential services that you need to pay for as well.

Remember that unless you have a 'new for old' policy, the amount you get for an item may be less than the cost of replacing it. This is to take account of any use you have had out of the item.

Medical emergencies and personal injury

If you need medical treatment while you are away, contact your insurer by phone as soon as possible to get authorization for the treatment. If possible, you should try to contact them before agreeing to the cost of the treatment. Get receipts for treatment and medication.

Some insurance policies will not cover you for the treatment of a health problem that you knew about at the time the policy was taken out. You may also be excluded from claiming for the cost of medication that you usually need and may have to take while travelling.

In some European countries, urgent medical treatment is available free of charge if you have a form E111. Some countries in other parts of the world also have agreements with the UK that allow you to get free emergency treatment. You can get form E111 from post offices and can find out more by visiting **Health Advice for Travellers** (www.dh.gov.uk).

Travel insurance usually covers you if you are pregnant, as long as you are in normal health.

Cancelling or shortening your trip

Your insurer will only meet a claim for a cancelled or a shortened trip if you can show that you had good reason to cancel or shorten it. A list of reasons will be included in your policy.

Buying a timeshare property

When you buy a timeshare, you buy the right to use holiday accommodation for a set amount of time each year. The accommodation is usually a villa in a resort, but you can also get timeshares in caravans, cottages and flats. How you pay will vary, but usually you pay a one-off lump sum, and then annual maintenance charges.

Please note that this section covers your rights if you buy a timeshare from a company, but not if you buy it from a private individual.

When is a timeshare not a timeshare?

Holiday and vacation clubs are not timeshares because they do not give you the right to stay in a specific property. As a general rule, accommodation on boats is not covered by timeshare laws. However, it is not clear whether timeshares for canal boats in the UK are covered or not.

Factors to consider before buying

- Do you want this type of holiday every year?
- Is it value for money? Don't forget that the cost of transport to the resort is not included.
- Shop around.
- Ask for a brochure.
- Insist on full details in writing. Do not rely on verbal promises alone.
- Do not be tempted by free gifts offered as an incentive.

Before signing a timeshare agreement

When you buy a timeshare, you sign a binding agreement with a timeshare company. It can be difficult to cancel the agreement, so it is important to get as much information as possible before you sign, including details of:

- the full costs, including charges for things like legal fees, gas, electricity and water, annual management and maintenance charges;
- the duration of the agreement. If you are asked to sign a contract for less than three years, this is usually a deliberate attempt to avoid giving you legal rights.
- what the resort is like. If it is still being built, check that planning permission has been granted, the extent of the development and the amount of work still to be completed.
- the type of ownership you will have and whether you will own the title to the property and an interest in the land which, for example, you could sell or leave in a will (this is unusual);
- the terms and conditions of the agreement;
- who is responsible for the day-to-day running of the resort and maintenance of the property;
- whether there is an owners' committee or association and what powers it has, for example whether it can dismiss the management company.

Cancelling a timeshare agreement

Once you have signed a timeshare agreement, the law gives you a cooling-off period, during which you can cancel the agreement and have your money back without having to pay a cancellation fee. You are entitled to a cooling-off period only if the timeshare lasts at least three years and is for a property or caravan in the European Economic Area (EEA).

The length of the cooling-off period will be fourteen days if:

- you signed your timeshare agreement in the UK; *or*
- the timeshare accommodation is in the UK; *or*
- you are normally resident in the UK and the timeshare accommodation is in an EEA country.

In some EEA countries, a lawyer has to witness you signing the agreement. The timeshare seller does not have to refund the cost of this if you cancel the agreement.

Timeshare sellers in the UK and EEA must tell you about the cooling-off period when you sign the agreement. If they don't, the cooling-off period will be extended, usually by three months.

After the cooling-off period, you can cancel the agreement if the terms of the agreement allow for this. If you want to sell your timeshare, a timeshare resale company or the original timeshare company may be able to arrange this for you, although they will charge you commission. You may be asked to pay a fee upfront and you should be wary before you get involved with a company offering to sell your timeshare. In the past some owners have handed over money only to find that the company offering to sell on their behalf has disappeared.

Protection if you pay by credit card

If you want to cancel your timeshare agreement, and you paid for the timeshare with your credit card, your credit card company might agree to get the money back. In these circumstances, it is essential that you write to both the timeshare seller and the credit card company, notifying them that you wish to cancel the agreement, within ten days of signing the timeshare agreement. You should check whether your credit card company offers this type of protection.

What to do if there are problems

Your rights depend upon the terms of the agreement and the law that applies to it. That could be the law in the country where the agreement was signed, the law in the country where the timeshare company is based, or the law of a third country that the agreement says applies to it. You may need the help of a specialist solicitor to decide which law applies. The organizations below might be able to recommend a specialist.

Compensation

You may be entitled to compensation if:

- the terms of your agreement have been broken, for example if the agreement says the resort has a well-maintained swimming pool and in fact the swimming pool has been out of action for two years; or
- repairs and maintenance aren't carried out in line with the agreement; or
- the seller invites you to attend a presentation, offering a reward in return and you don't get the reward, or it is not the same as what was offered.

If any of these apply, you could sue for breach of contract.

How to solve your problem

Once you have decided what your rights are, you will need to contact the timeshare seller. Contact the company as soon as possible. Write to the manager and keep a copy of your letter. Explain your problem firmly but calmly, and ask for what you want – to cancel the agreement or compensation.

If you are not satisfied with the response and the timeshare is in Europe, find out if the company is a member of the OTE or VOICE. These organizations operate a conciliation service to help resolve disputes. If you use these services, any decision will be legally binding and is likely to prevent you taking court action.

If you decide not to use conciliation, write to the owner or manager of the company and the credit card company (if applicable) repeating your complaint and the steps you have taken so far. Say you are giving them fourteen days to resolve the problem, otherwise you will consider taking legal action. Send the letter by recorded delivery with a copy to the head office of the company, if there is one. Keep copies of all your letters and a note of any phone conversations you have in connection with the problem.

If the company makes you an offer, you can either accept or continue to negotiate. Be realistic in what you will accept. You may not get an improved offer by going to court.

If the company doesn't respond, refuses to do anything, or makes a final offer you are unwilling to accept, your only other choice is to go to court.

Who can help?

If you have bought a timeshare in a European Economic Area (EEA) country and you ask for a brochure and this is not provided; the seller takes money from you during the cooling-off period; or the seller makes false or misleading claims about the timeshare, a criminal offence may have been committed, and you should contact your local **Trading Standards Department**.

The **Organization for Timeshare in Europe** (Fax +32 2533 3061; www.ote-info.com) will be able to refer you to a specialist. The OTE gives general advice about timeshares to prospective purchasers, explains current legislation in the United Kingdom and Europe, and provides information sheets. It also offers a free conciliation service to those in dispute with its members.

The **Timeshare Consumers Association** (01909 591100; www.timeshare.org.uk) deals with complaints about timeshares and can provide help and specialist advice.

VOICE (0870 240 8993) offers an information and free advisory and conciliation service for people with disputes about timeshares.

If an advertisement describes a timeshare in a misleading way, the advertiser could be committing a criminal offence and you could complain to the **Advertising Standards Authority** (020 7492 2222; www.asa.org.uk).

The Association of British Travel Agents (020 7637 2444; www.abta.com).

The **Association of Independent Tour Operators** (020 8744 9280; www.aito.co.uk), which represents independent tour operators, has a code of practice that all its members should follow. It also runs an independent mediation service that charges a non-refundable fee.

The **Advertising Standards Authority** (020 7492 2222; www.asa.org.uk). If the holiday is not as described in the brochure or advertisement, you can complain to the ASA. It cannot award compensation but can take action to have a brochure or advert withdrawn or changed so that it does not mislead others.

The **Countryside Agency** (01242 5333222; www.countrysideaccess.gov.uk) gives information about rights to access in the countryside.

5
Utilities

CONTENTS

INTRODUCTION

It is a truth universally acknowledged that not much in life comes
for free and even keeping warm will cost you. Since peat started
being used as domestic fuel at least 1,300 years ago, we've been
searching for cheap sources of fuel. Along with supplies of clean
water, fossil fuels like coal, oil and gas are the staples upon which
our comfortable lives depend. With the re-privatization of those

industries in recent years, it has fallen more and more to us, as consumers, to make sure that we are getting what we pay for. This section looks at your choices, what you can expect from the utility companies and what to do if their services don't come up to scratch.

GAS

Until 1996, all domestic gas users had their gas supplied by British Gas. Since then, competition has been introduced and you can now choose your supplier. All gas suppliers are licensed by the Office of Gas and Electricity Markets (Ofgem). Complaints about gas suppliers are dealt with by **energywatch** (0845 906 0708; www.energywatch.org.uk).

You have a right to a gas supply unless:

- your gas pipes are in a dangerous condition;
- there is a debt, or disconnection;
- the gas supplier wants financial security that is unavailable.

If you are refused a supply of gas for reasons other than those listed above, take the matter up with energywatch.

Dangerous pipes

If gas pipes are in a dangerous condition, they must be repaired before gas can be supplied. Pipes located on the house side of the meter are the responsibility of the house owner. Pipes on the mains side of the meter are the responsibility of British Gas Transco, which can be contacted through a customer's gas supplier.

Getting a gas supply or changing supplier

When you move to a new home, tell the gas supplier the date you want to take over the supply. If it has to be reconnected, the supplier may make a charge – energywatch can advise on whether a charge should be made and what is a reasonable amount. If the supply has not been disconnected, read the meter and inform the supplier of the reading. Keep a copy of the reading. If you want to change your gas supplier, notify both the current and the new gas supplier. Both will want a final meter reading taken on the day you change suppliers. Some suppliers will send a meter reader; others will ask you to read the meter and send the reading to them. In either case, keep a note of the meter reading in case there is a dispute later. Energywatch can provide advice on what to check if you want to change suppliers and a list of local gas suppliers. Energywatch can also advise you on free internet price comparison services. If you have a gas debt, you may not be accepted by a new supplier. A protocol exists that ensures that if you have a debt of up to £100 and use a prepayment meter you are allowed to transfer to a new supplier and take your debt with you. For more information about this protocol, contact energywatch.

Providing financial security

In some circumstances the gas supplier will refuse to connect the gas supply until you have provided suitable financial security. You may be asked to:

- join a regular payment plan; *or*
- agree to have a prepayment meter; *or*
- provide a guarantor; *or*
- make a cash deposit.

The gas supplier will normally only require security in certain circumstances, for example if you are a new customer and cannot provide proof of your identity or previous address or have a poor payment record at your present or last address.

Guarantors
If you name a guarantor, the gas supplier will check whether their record of gas payments is satisfactory. The guarantor will be legally responsible for paying your gas bills if you don't pay.

Deposits
The gas supplier must only request a 'reasonable' amount as a deposit and the maximum you can be charged is a sum based on the estimate of the highest six months' use in the year following the request for a deposit. The gas supplier will review the deposit after one year. If the bills have been paid in full, the deposit will be returned within two months of the end of the year.

Meters

A gas supplier must provide an appropriate meter to a customer who asks for one. There are two main types of meter:

● credit or quarterly meters, where you use the gas and pay for it later;
● prepayment meters, where you pay in advance for your gas supply.

The gas supplier will normally supply a credit meter, although you can ask for a prepayment meter.

If you are over pension age or disabled, you can have a prepayment meter if you want, as long as it is the best way to pay and it is safe and practical. For example, it may not be safe and practical if the meter can easily be broken into or cannot be installed in an accessible place.

Credit meters

Most customers will have a credit meter, which records gas consumption. A bill is sent out quarterly and calls to read the meter are made every six months. Estimated bills are sent in alternate quarters. You can pay the bill in a number of ways, for example by cheque or by direct debit.

Prepayment meters

In most areas, coinless prepayment ('smartcard') meters have replaced token, key and coin meters and are the only option for a new installation. The meter will record the amount of gas used.

Meter readings

Gas meters are usually read every six months. If the gas supplier has been unable to gain access to read the meter it will leave a card for you to fill in with your own reading. If you are disabled, chronically sick or of pensionable age, you can ask the gas supplier to read your meter every three months. The gas supplier must inspect and test the meter at least once every two years.

If you are disabled, chronically sick or of pensionable age and find it difficult to read your meter because of its position, you can ask the gas supplier to move the meter, where reasonably practicable, free of charge.

Theft from and tampering with a meter

If you have a coin prepayment meter for your gas or electricity supplies, you are responsible for taking reasonable care of it and the money in it. If the meter is broken into, you are responsible for proving to the gas supplier that the break-in was done by a third party, so report the break-in to the police as soon as possible. If you have taken adequate care to secure the premises, you will not be held liable for any money stolen.

Gas marketing

Most suppliers have agreed a code of practice on the face-to-face marketing of gas. You may be entitled to compensation if a sales agent fails to follow the guidelines in the code. For example, agents must only call at your home between 9 a.m. and 8 p.m., except at your request, and if they are visiting sheltered accommodation must first approach the warden. Sales agents must try to make sure that customers have understood any contract signed and their right to cancel.

If a gas sales agent has broken the code of practice, contact the supplier and claim compensation. If you are unsuccessful in reaching agreement with the supplier, contact energywatch. If energywatch cannot resolve the complaint they may refer it on to Ofgem.

Dual fuel offers

Some gas and electricity suppliers are licensed by Ofgem to supply customers with both gas and electricity. Some gas suppliers supply both fuels under one contract, while others give one contract for gas and another for electricity.

Suppliers who make dual offers will often give a discount off the total bill as they make administrative savings by issuing combined bills and collecting combined payments. However, this does not necessarily mean that gas and electricity under a dual offer will be cheaper than that bought from separate suppliers.

Arrears and disconnections

If you have gas arrears, you risk being disconnected.

A gas supplier cannot issue a disconnection notice until at least twenty-eight days after issuing a bill. A disconnection notice must be in writing and will give you seven days' notice of the gas supplier's intention to disconnect, giving you an opportunity to pay the arrears, provide a security deposit, or have a prepayment meter installed as an alternative to disconnection.

A gas supplier must not disconnect a gas supply for arrears during the winter period (1 October to 31 March) if you:

- are of pensionable age and live alone, or with other pensioners or children; *and*
- have arrears because you could not afford your bills.

Even if you do not meet the above conditions, the gas supplier should always offer a prepayment meter as an alternative to disconnection.

Gas safety

A gas supplier can authorize its officials to enter premises to inspect the gas installation and appliances. If a gas leak is reported, it will be made safe free of charge. Making safe can often mean simply turning the supply off. If an appliance is faulty and has to be disconnected, you or your landlord will be responsible for buying a replacement and getting it installed. **Transco**, the main public gas transporter, runs a 24-hour freephone national gas emergency service (0800 111999).

The gas supplier will provide a free gas safety check of appliances and fittings for some older or disabled people. One free check a year can be requested. The check includes a basic examination and very minor work. Any additional work must be paid for.

Buying and installing gas appliances

Anyone supplying a gas appliance must ensure that it is safe and that it meets European safety standards. Anyone installing or repairing a gas appliance or equipment must be registered with the Council for Registered Gas Installers (CORGI). They must carry an ID card listing the types of gas work that they are competent to carry out.

Complaints

If you have a complaint about your gas supplier, first raise it with the supplier. If you are dissatisfied with the way the gas supplier dealt with a complaint, take it up with **energywatch**.

Energywatch will inform Ofgem that a complaint is being dealt with. If energywatch cannot resolve the problem and the supplier has broken a term in its licence, energywatch will refer the matter to Ofgem.

Your gas supplier may have standards of service together with a scheme to pay compensation if it fails to meet these standards, although this is not a requirement of licence conditions. Ask your gas supplier for details.

Who can help?

Energywatch (08459 060708; www.energywatch.org.uk), the gas and electricity consumer watchdog, is an independent organization that represents and protects the interests of gas consumers. It can help with complaints about the supply of gas.

Ofgem (Office of Gas and Electricity Markets) is an independent regulatory body, set up by the Government to monitor and regulate the activities of gas suppliers. It has the power to make a gas supplier supply gas to a particular customer, or not disconnect a gas supply. Consumer complaints are dealt with by energywatch.

The **Council for Registered Gas Installers** (CORGI: 0870 401 2300; www.corgi-gas-safety.com) is an independent organization that promotes gas safety. You can complain to them about a gas installer, or get details of CORGI-registered gas installers.

ELECTRICITY

All electricity suppliers must have a licence from the Office of Gas and Electricity Markets (Ofgem). One of the licence conditions is that an electricity supplier must produce codes of practice on things like complaints procedures, payment of bills and dealing with arrears, as well as energy efficiency and services for older, disabled and chronically sick people.

Although the codes of practice are not legally enforceable, they will be useful when negotiating with an electricity supplier and any breach should be reported to energywatch.

Ofgem sets Standards of Performance that cover many areas of customer service and compensation is payable if the electricity supplier fails to meet them. However, the Standards only apply to some electricity suppliers.

Choosing an electricity supplier

If you are considering changing your electricity supplier you should be aware that the pricing structures, services offered and policies will differ between the different electricity suppliers. You should carefully check the information and contracts of the competing electricity suppliers, and compare these to your current terms, to make sure that you choose the best deal for your needs. Energywatch can give you details of a number of free internet price comparison services.

Dual fuel offers

Dual fuel is the supply of gas and electricity by the same supplier. Some gas and electricity suppliers are licensed separately by Ofgem to supply customers with both fuels. Some electricity suppliers will supply both fuels under one contract, while others will give one contract for gas and another for electricity.

Suppliers who make dual offers will often give a discount off the total bill as they can make administrative savings by issuing combined bills and collecting combined payments. However, this does not necessarily mean that the cost of gas and electricity under a dual offer will be cheaper than buying gas and electricity from separate suppliers.

Electricity marketing

The licence conditions

Another of the licence conditions, by which all electricity suppliers must abide, covers marketing of electricity. The licence condition states that:

- the electricity company must have procedures covering the selection and training of sales staff calling on people at home;
- customers who sign a contract must be contacted by the electricity supplier within fourteen days to make sure they are aware they have signed a contract, and that they are happy with the sales approach used;
- where a contract is signed two months in advance of the change of electricity supplier, the electricity supplier must keep in touch with the customer;
- sales agents are not allowed to ask for money in advance;
- there must be a compensation scheme, and a record must be kept of complaints about sales representatives or marketing techniques. Electricity suppliers must publish reports about this.

If it appears to you that one of the conditions above has been broken, you should contact energywatch with details of the time and date of alleged incidents. Energywatch can investigate, negotiate with the electricity supplier and recommend that the electricity supplier pay compensation. The amount of compensation is not laid down, but will be decided by the electricity supplier according to the circumstances of the case. If energywatch cannot resolve the complaint it can refer the matter to Ofgem, who will give the electricity supplier formal notice that it has breached its licence conditions.

Marketing code of practice

All the major suppliers have agreed a code of practice on the face-to-face marketing of electricity. You may be entitled to compensation if a sales agent fails to follow the guidelines in the code. For example, agents must only call at your home between 9 a.m. and 8 p.m., except at your request, and if they are visiting sheltered accommodation must first approach the warden. Sales agents must try to make sure that customers have understood any contract signed and their right to cancel. If an electricity sales agent has broken the code of practice, contact the supplier. If you can't reach agreement you should contact energywatch.

How to get an electricity supply or change supplier

You have a legal right to a supply of electricity if it is 'reasonable' to provide a supply. If your home is not connected to an electricity main there will be a charge to connect the supply.

There is no duty to supply electricity where the wiring in your house is in a dangerous condition, where the supply has been disconnected and there is no obligation to reconnect, where security has been requested and not paid or where a prepayment meter has been refused. If you are refused a supply of electricity for reasons other than these, you should take the matter up with energywatch.

When you move to a new home, you should tell the new electricity supplier the date on which you wish to take over the supply. The electricity supplier may be your current electricity supplier, or you may wish to change to a different supplier when you move. You may have to change if your current electricity supplier does not supply electricity in the area to which you have moved.

The amount of notice you have to give your current electricity supplier to cancel the contract, and whether you have to pay a cancellation fee, depends on the type of contract you have and the circumstances. Your current electricity supplier can object to you changing to another electricity supplier in certain circumstances, for example if you are in arrears. If you are simply moving home, the electricity supplier cannot object.

Remember to cancel any standing orders or direct debits once you have paid the final bill to your current electricity supplier.

Your current and new electricity suppliers will want a final meter reading taken on the day you change electricity suppliers. Some electricity suppliers will send a meter reader and may make a charge for this, while others will ask you to read the meter and send the reading to them. The new electricity supplier is responsible for sending the reading to the previous electricity supplier. In either case, you should keep a note of the meter reading yourself in case there is a dispute later.

You must give your new electricity supplier the supply number for the meter at your home. The supply number is an identification number for the meter and is shown on the bill relating to the meter. If you are moving home, you will have to ask the present occupiers for the supply number.

If the supply of electricity has to be reconnected, the electricity supplier may make a charge for reconnection. If you think the reconnection charge is unreasonable, you can refer the matter to energywatch.

Getting advice about changing to a new electricity supplier

For information and advice about changing to a new electricity supplier, contact energywatch (0845 906 0708; www.energywatch.org.uk). Energywatch can provide advice on what to check if you want to change suppliers and a list of local electricity suppliers. They can also provide details of internet and telephone fuel price comparison services. If you have an electricity debt you may not be accepted by a new supplier. A protocol exists that ensures that if you have a debt of up to £100 and use a prepayment meter, you are allowed to transfer to a new supplier and take your debt with you. For more information about this protocol you can contact energywatch, whose details are given above.

Providing security

Most customers will have a credit meter and receive regular bills, but if you are a new customer, cannot provide proof of your identity or have a poor payment record, the electricity supplier may refuse to supply until you have provided suitable security. The electricity supplier should first ask you to agree to a prepayment meter being fitted. Only if you refuse a prepayment meter should the electricity supplier ask for alternative security, but they will normally ask you to do one of the following:

- join a regular payment plan;
- pay by direct debit;
- provide a guarantor – the guarantor will be legally responsible for paying your electricity bills if you do not pay;
- make a cash deposit – the electricity supplier can only request a reasonable amount, usually up to a maximum of one and a half times the average amount of a quarterly bill.

Meters

Most customers will have a credit meter and will receive bills four times a year – quarterly billing. The electricity supplier will call to read the meter at regular intervals or contact the customer and ask them to read the meter and pass on the reading. The meter must be read at least once a year, but it can be read by the customer rather than the electricity supplier.

Prepayment meters are used when the customer wishes or is asked to pay in advance for an electricity supply. In most areas, cashless prepayment meters have replaced coin meters and are the only option for a new installation. They have an electronically coded card, token or key that carries the customer's reference number and the meter's serial number and cannot be used to buy electricity for anyone else. The electricity supplier will give you a list of the places you can get the card, token or key charged, which may include vending machines.

The card, token or key will have an emergency credit facility, so that if you use all the credit you have paid for you will be allowed to continue to use electricity for a short while.

The electricity supplier can set the meter to collect arrears.

Coin meters are no longer being installed, as they are not being made and are increasingly difficult to maintain as some spare parts are unavailable. If you already have a coin meter you can continue to use it until the meter breaks down and cannot be repaired or until you choose a different type of meter.

Meter readings

A customer who is disabled, chronically sick or of pensionable age can ask the electricity supplier to read their meter every three months if neither they nor anyone else in the household can do so. However, the bill will be estimated if the electricity supplier cannot gain access.

A customer who is disabled, chronically sick or of pensionable age can get information and advice about:

- special controls or adaptors for prepayment meters or electricity appliances owned by the electricity supplier;
- resiting of the meter if it is owned by the electricity supplier and it is in a position which makes it difficult for the customer to read it.

Information and advice, and resiting of the meter, must be provided free of charge. However, a charge can be made for any special controls or adaptors for the meter or appliances.

Tampering with a meter

The electricity supplier may disconnect your electricity supply by removing the meter if it has sufficient evidence that you have tampered with your meter. To prevent disconnection, you must convince the electricity supplier you did not tamper with the meter and took proper care of it.

Electricity bills

Electricity bills will be sent to you at regular intervals. If you are blind, or have impaired sight, the electricity supplier may make special provision, for example making regular quarterly telephone calls to keep you up to date with your account or offering a bill reading service. You can ask for your bills to be sent to someone else if you wish.

The standing charge is a fixed daily amount charged to electricity users, regardless of how much electricity is consumed. There are different charges for credit and prepayment meters. Your electricity supplier may offer you the option of not paying a standing charge, but paying a slightly higher rate for the electricity used instead. You would need to work out, from your bills, whether this option would be cheaper for you.

Complaints

If you have a complaint about your electricity supplier, you should first raise it with the electricity supplier, who may have a compensation scheme. If you are dissatisfied with how the electricity company has dealt with your complaint you can take it up with energywatch.

Who can help?

Energywatch (08459 060708; www.energywatch.org.uk), the gas and electricity consumer watchdog, is an independent organization that represents and protects the interests of electricity consumers. It can help with complaints about the supply of electricity.

Ofgem (Office of Gas and Electricity Markets) is an independent regulatory body, set up by the Government to monitor and regulate the activities of electricity suppliers. It has the power to make an electricity supplier supply electricity to a particular customer, or not disconnect a supply. Consumer complaints are dealt with by energywatch.

WATER

Water is supplied by a number of private water companies. As a domestic customer living in a property, you have the right to a water supply and there is no charge for taking over a water supply that is already connected.

The supply of water

A supply of water for domestic purposes must be:

- constant. If a company needs to interrupt a supply of water, it must give reasonable notice.
- safe to drink. Fluoride may be added in some areas.
- supplied at an adequate pressure;
- sufficient for normal domestic use. If there is a serious shortage of water in the area, the company can impose a temporary hosepipe ban to restrict the watering of private gardens or the washing of private cars.

Calculating water charges

There are several different methods of calculating charges for water. The cost will be based on a standing charge and:

- an unmeasured charge based on the rateable value of the property, on a flat rate charge or on a banding system; *or*
- a measured charge (using a water meter) based on the amount of water used,

usually per cubic metre, at a rate approved by the Director General of the Office of Water Services (OFWAT).

You may be able to choose which method is used. The choice will usually be between a water meter and another charging method.

Water meters

You may want to request that a meter is installed if you use very little water, the property has a high rateable value or you want more control of how much water you pay for.

However, disadvantages include the inconvenience of having it read, water lost through leakage after the meter is installed, which must be paid for and the uncertainty of how much the annual bill will be.

All household customers can elect to have a water meter installed in their homes free of charge, unless it is not practical or would be unreasonably expensive to install. You may wish to do this to find out whether this will help to reduce your bills. You will normally be able to switch back to your old charging method, as long as you do so within twelve months of the start of metered charging.

Companies are entitled to install water meters in areas that have been declared areas of water scarcity, or where people use a high volume of water for non-essential purposes, for example:

- using a sprinkler system to water the garden;
- using a system that replenishes a pond or swimming pool with a capacity in excess of 10,000 litres;
- using a 'power shower';
- filling a bath with a capacity of more than 230 litres.

Water bills

Your water bill may include the following:

- a standing charge;
- a charge for water, based on a meter reading or another charging method;
- a charge for sewerage. If your sewerage service is provided by a different company, you may receive a separate sewerage bill.

Bills are usually sent once or twice a year, depending on the company's practice. If the water charge is on an unmeasured basis, the bill will be for the forthcoming billing period. If the water charge is a measured charge the bill will be for the preceding billing period.

Help with water bills

Some people may be able to get help with the costs of their water supply, for example people with water meters who use a high volume of water because of certain medical conditions, or because they have three or more children under 16, and are receiving a qualifying benefit. They may benefit from a bill calculated as an average charge for domestic customers of that company rather than on their actual measured use of water.

All companies have provisions in place to help people who have difficulty paying their bills, for example budget schemes.

Who is liable to pay the bill

The occupier of the property is normally responsible for paying water charges. If someone shares accommodation, the liability is shared even if the bill is only in one name.

Arrears

Water companies cannot disconnect a domestic customer for water arrears. The company would have to take action in the county court for debt to recover money owing for water charges.

Arrangements to pay the arrears

If you are in arrears you will have to negotiate a repayment schedule with the water company. They should take your ability to pay into account and you shouldn't offer more than you can realistically afford to pay. In some cases, the water company may even agree to write off the arrears. If you are receiving Income Support, income-based Jobseeker's Allowance or Pension Credit, you may be able to use the 'third-party deduction' scheme. The Department for Work and Pensions will pay an amount each week from your benefit directly to the water company.

Compensation

All water companies have certain standards of service covered by the statutory Guaranteed Standards Scheme with which they must comply. These standards cover:

- keeping appointments;
- responding to account queries;
- responding to complaints;
- interruptions to supply;
- water pressure;
- installing meters;
- sewer flooding.

If the company fails to meet a standard of service, you can claim £20 compensation. If your water pressure falls below a certain level twice in twenty-eight days you can claim £25. Usually, compensation will be automatically paid or credited by the company. If the complaint is about an interruption of supply, low pressure or sewer flooding, you must claim compensation in writing within three months of the incident.

As well as the standards of service and minimum compensation levels required of all companies, some companies may operate their own higher standards and/or compensation levels.

Who can help?

The **Office of Water Services** (OFWAT: 0121 625 1300; www.ofwat.gov.uk) is the independent regulatory body set up by the Government to monitor and regulate the activities of the water companies. If you have a problem with your water company, you should initially take up the complaint with the company. If you are not satisfied, you can take up the complaint with the local WaterVoice Committee (see below). If the company does not accept the WaterVoice Committee's recommendation for resolving a complaint, the matter will be referred to OFWAT.

WaterVoice Committees can investigate and take up complaints about the water and sewage industries. WaterVoice committees are appointed by OFWAT (the address of your local WaterVoice committee is available from www.watervoice.org.uk).

The **Drinking Water Inspectorate** (020 7082 8024; www.dwi.gov.uk)

monitors the quality of water. If you are unhappy about the quality of your water, you can complain to the local WaterVoice Committee or the Drinking Water Inspectorate.

Basic Rights

1
Civil Rights

CONTENTS

INTRODUCTION

'The nature and limits of the power which can be legitimately exercised by society over the individual.' That's how John Stuart Mill described civil rights in his essay *On Liberty* in 1869. The relationship between the citizen and the state is a subject that has been taxing hearts and minds since Greek and Roman times and long before in the great early civilizations. The rights and duties of the common person – what you can and cannot do in the privacy of your own home or in public, to yourself or to other people, what is expected of you and how you can contribute to the democratic process – is the stuff upon which modern politics is based. Today, ordinary people enjoy social and political rights that many did not have even a hundred years ago. Bodies like the United Nations, Amnesty International and Human Rights Watch have been founded to monitor and fight for the human and civil rights of people across the globe.

This chapter looks at the basic voting system, some of the laws that govern us and how you can enforce your rights within them, including making complaints to the ombudsman responsible.

VOTING

The electoral register

There are two versions of the electoral register. The full version lists everyone in the constituency who is eligible to vote. This is available to political parties, some government agencies and credit reference agencies. It is also available for public inspection all year round at council offices and selected other places. There is also an edited version of the electoral register. This is available for open sale and you have the right to opt out of this version of the register.

To be included on the electoral register you must:

● be aged 18 or over; *and*
● have one of the types of citizenship described below; *and*

- be resident in the constituency in which you wish to vote; *and*
- not be a person who is excluded from voting.

Age

If you are going to be 18 during the twelve-month period after the register is published, you should be entered on the register so that you will be able to vote as soon as you become 18. Your date of birth must be given on the electoral registration form.

Citizenship

The following people can register to vote in European parliamentary elections, British parliamentary elections (this means general and by-elections) and local government elections:

- British citizens;
- Citizens of the Republic of Ireland who live in the UK;
- British nationals overseas (parliamentary elections only);
- British Overseas Territories citizens;
- Commonwealth citizens.

If you are a Commonwealth citizen who wishes to register to vote in local elections, you must either:

- have leave to enter or remain in the UK; *or*
- be a person who does not require such leave.

EU citizens

European Union (EU) citizens have the right to vote in European parliamentary and British local government elections. European nationals who are not EU citizens do not have this right. EU citizens cannot vote in British parliamentary elections.

For European parliamentary elections, an EU citizen may vote in either their 'home' country or the EU country in which they are currently living. They cannot vote in both.

To be eligible to vote in British local government elections, an EU citizen must be included on the electoral register for the constituency they vote in.

Residency

To register to vote you must generally be resident in the constituency on the date on which you make the application to register. If you are temporarily away from home, for example if you are studying away from home, you can still vote or declare a local connection in the constituency where you usually live.

There are some exceptions to the rules about residency – for example, people who live abroad, some homeless people, and people in psychiatric hospitals (see below for a fuller explanation).

Who cannot vote

The following people are not eligible to vote:

- anyone who is not on the electoral register on polling day;
- people from abroad (other than EU citizens, citizens of the Republic of Ireland and qualifying Commonwealth citizens who are resident in the UK – see above);
- people aged under 18;
- certain people convicted of corrupt or illegal electoral practices;
- peers of the realm who remain members of the House of Lords (for British parliamentary elections only);
- people who have a severe mental illness and are unable to understand the voting procedure.

Getting on the electoral register

The electoral register is compiled annually but amended throughout the year. Every local authority has an electoral registration officer who is in charge of the process. Each year, around August or September, all households in a constituency will receive an electoral registration form or, rarely, be visited by a member of the electoral registration officer's staff. If you do not receive a form, for example because you are homeless, you can get one from the electoral registration officer.

The form should be completed according to the instructions, and should include everyone in the household who is eligible to vote and who will be resident in the household on 15 October. If someone is temporarily away from home, they should still be included on the form. Someone who will become 18 during the twelve-month period after the register is published (on 1 December that year) should also be included, to be able to vote on becoming 18. The relevant dates of birth for anyone affected must be given on the form.

From the information you provide, the electoral registration officer compiles a register. This is published by 1 December each year and is open for inspection all year round at local council offices and other public places, for example main post offices and libraries. You can apply to be added to the register or to have your details amended on the register at any time throughout the year, although, when an election is held, registration applications must be received two to four weeks before polling day, depending on the election timetable.

I don't want my ex-husband to know I am back in the area. Can I register anonymously?

You cannot register anonymously even if you feel at risk, for example from an ex-partner. Failure to provide information to the registration staff or to complete the registration form, or giving false information, may result in your being prosecuted and fined. Some electoral registration officers may allow people who feel at risk to register in another name – for example, a maiden name or half of a double-barrelled name. However, this is subject to the officer's discretion and you cannot insist on registering in this way. Alternatively, you could change your name and register under the new name.

If you have not been included in the register
If you consider you are eligible to register, but discover you have not been included in the register, you can obtain a form from the electoral registration officer on which to make an application for registration. Alternatively, the application can be made in the form of a letter containing all relevant information. This application can be made either by you or by someone else on your behalf.

How to object to an inclusion in the register
You may wish to object to the inclusion of your name, or someone else's name, in the register, for example because you believe they are no longer resident in the constituency or are not entitled to vote. Any person on the electoral register (not necessarily in the same constituency) may make such an objection. You can also object to the inclusion of your details in copies of the register that are sold to commercial organizations. If you wish to object you should contact the electoral registration officer and put your

objections in writing. The local authority may have a standard form that you can fill in.

If the registration officer decides to disallow your objection immediately, you will be notified of the decision and the grounds on which it was made. You then have three days from the date of the registration officer's notice to ask for a hearing.

Overseas voters

If you live abroad, have been resident in the UK, and have been registered as a UK resident elector within the previous fifteen years, you can make an annual declaration. This will allow you to be included each year on the electoral register in the constituency where you were last registered before you went abroad. Registration as an overseas voter is voluntary.

If you are now old enough to be included on the register, but you were too young to be included when you left the UK, you can also make such a declaration, provided you have lived in the UK within the last fifteen years and your parent or guardian had been included on the electoral register.

> *My father has been living abroad for ten years and has just asked me if he can still vote in UK elections.*
>
> People who have been on a UK electoral register in the last fifteen years can make an 'annual declaration', which lets them be included on the electoral register they were last on in the UK. British consulates abroad have the forms, which must be sent to the electoral registration office of their last constituency.

Anyone who is eligible, and who wishes to register as an overseas elector, must complete the necessary forms, normally available from British consulates and diplomatic posts. You must return the completed forms to the electoral registration officer for the constituency in which you were last registered. You must do this annually. The first time the declaration is made, you must give details of your British citizenship, which is the only type of citizenship that counts to be an overseas voter. You will get a reminder from the registration officer to renew your overseas elector declaration. Once registered, you can vote at any parliamentary or European parliament election that occurs while you are on the register. You cannot vote in local government elections or in elections to devolved assemblies, for example the Welsh Assembly.

Special arrangements for specific groups when registering to vote

There are special arrangements for some groups of people when registering to vote. These groups are:

- homeless people – see below;
- patients in psychiatric hospitals – see below;
- people resident in more than one constituency – see below.

A *declaration of local connection* may be made by homeless people and patients in psychiatric hospitals. This should be used if you are in one of the above groups and do not fulfil the usual residence requirements but are otherwise entitled to register to vote.

The declaration must:

- give your name; *and*
- provide an address for correspondence to be sent to, or an undertaking to collect such correspondence from the electoral registration office; *and*
- give the date of the declaration; *and*
- state that you fall into one of the categories that is allowed to make a declaration and state the relevant category that applies to you; *and*
- state that you fulfil the nationality requirements; *and*
- state that you are at least 18 years old or, if not, give your date of birth.

A declaration enables you to apply to register to vote. You must submit the declaration to the registration officer within three months of the date on the declaration and you will be treated as being resident at the address you have given. This registration will be valid for twelve months unless cancelled or superseded.

Homeless people

If you are homeless, you should make a declaration, giving the address of a place where you spend a substantial part of your time, or the address of somewhere near to that place. This could include a café or drop-in centre.

Patients in psychiatric hospitals

If you are a short-term patient in a psychiatric hospital you can register to vote by completing the usual electoral registration form. You should give your usual address outside the hospital as your place of residence.

If you are a long-term patient in a psychiatric hospital, when a new electoral register is being drawn up you are entitled to register to vote. You can register at your address outside the hospital. Alternatively, you can register at the address of the hospital if the registration officer considers that you have been, or will be, in the hospital for a long enough period of time for it to be regarded as your place of residence.

If your usual address is the hospital's address, you can make a declaration of local connection. The declaration must give both the name of the psychiatric hospital and the address where you would be living if you were not in the hospital. If you cannot provide your most recent home address, you should provide an address in the UK where you have lived at any time.

If you are detained under the Mental Health Act 1983 you may not vote in person, but must instead vote by post.

People resident in more than one constituency

Your position if you have more than one home is complex. Your rights to be included on the register and vote in a particular constituency depend on your circumstances. It will be necessary to consult the electoral registration officer in this situation. It is illegal to vote twice in an election.

You can be entered on more than one electoral register if you are resident in more than one constituency. For example, if you are a student you may be registered at one address by your parent/guardian and may also register yourself at your college/university town if you are living away from home.

However, in some situations, you may be prevented by the electoral registration officer from registering in two places. For example, if you have a holiday home but spend only a few days there each year, you may not be considered to be 'resident' there. However, if you spend most weekends there, the registration officer may well consider you are eligible to be included in the register.

Although it is not illegal to be registered in more than one place, it is illegal to vote twice in an election. For example, in a general election, you may choose which constituency to vote in on polling day.

If you are not in the constituency where you wish to vote on polling day and wish to apply for a proxy vote, you must satisfy the registration officer that you are eligible. If a proxy vote is refused, there is a right of appeal in the county court. You can vote by post without having to meet any specific criteria.

How to vote

Before polling day, everyone entitled to vote will be sent a polling card, unless a proxy or postal vote has previously been agreed. The card will give details of the polling station and the hours it is open. You do not need to take the polling card to the polling station when you go to vote, but it may be more convenient to do so.

If you do not want to, or cannot, attend the polling station in person, you can apply for a postal vote or a proxy vote if you meet the relevant criteria.

In some areas of the UK, in some elections, voting may be by post only. You can find out whether this applies by contacting your local authority electoral registration officer.

Help for disabled people

If you are disabled, you may be able to vote by post or by proxy.

If you are partially sighted and choose to vote in person, the polling station must display a large-print version of the ballot paper to assist you. If you are blind or partially sighted the polling station must also provide a device to enable you to fill in your ballot papers without any need for assistance from anyone else.

If you are physically disabled or unable to read, you may take a companion to help you complete the ballot form and put it in the ballot box. Your companion must be aged 18 or over and be entitled to vote, and must make a written declaration to this effect.

Your companion cannot help more than one disabled voter to vote at that election. The presiding officer has to be satisfied that you need the help of a companion in order to vote.

Alternatively, you can ask the presiding officer to mark the ballot paper on your behalf.

Postal votes

Once you are registered to vote, you can choose to vote by post at both parliamentary and local government elections for an indefinite period, a particular period or a particular election.

To make an application for a postal vote, you must:

- state your full name; *and*
- provide the address where you are or will be registered; *and*
- provide the address to which the ballot paper must be sent; *and*
- stipulate the period or the particular election for which the application is made; *and*
- state whether the application is made for parliamentary elections, local government elections, or both; *and*
- sign and date the application.

Complete the application form available from your electoral registration office or from the postal voting website (www.postalvotes.co.uk). Only one application form can be used for each person. Alternatively, you can apply in writing, although care must be taken to ensure that the letter contains all the information necessary, as listed above.

An application for a postal vote has to be received by the registration officer at least six working days before the date of the poll. If you have already registered to vote by post and then change your mind – for example, you want instead to vote by proxy or to be removed from the record – the registration officer must receive your application at least eleven working days before the poll. Once a successful application has been made, you should be added to a section of the register known as the absent voters list.

You should receive confirmation that you have been given a postal vote (if there is enough time before the election). You will receive a ballot paper (with a prepaid envelope if you are in the UK) with a declaration of identity which you must sign in the presence of a witness who knows you. The witness must also sign and print their name, along with their address. If you are registered and have applied to vote by post and you do not receive your postal ballot paper by the fourth working day before the day of the poll, you may apply to the registration officer for a replacement ballot paper. The application for a replacement ballot paper must include evidence of your identity. You should then be issued with a replacement ballot paper.

Proxy votes

Voting by proxy means that you appoint someone else to vote on your behalf. The person appointed as a proxy must be eligible to vote.

Once you are registered to vote by proxy, you will be able to do so at both parliamentary and local government elections for an indefinite period, a particular period or a particular election.

Anyone can apply to vote by proxy for a particular election, but only the following people may be eligible to vote by proxy for a particular or indefinite period:

- people registered as service voters, for example members of the armed services;
- people registered as overseas electors – people in this situation cannot vote in local government elections;
- people who cannot go in person to vote without making a journey by sea or air;
- people who cannot reasonably be expected to vote in person because of the general nature of their occupation or that of their spouse (evidence is required);
- people who cannot reasonably be expected to vote in person because they or their spouse are attending a course provided by an educational institution (evidence is required);
- people who are blind or have some other physical incapacity and who, as a result, cannot reasonably be expected to vote in person at the allotted polling station or cannot reasonably be expected to vote unaided.

If you wish to apply to vote by proxy for a particular election and you are not in one of the groups listed above, you must satisfy the registration officer that, on the date of the poll for that election, you cannot reasonably be expected to vote in person at your allotted polling station.

To make an application for a proxy vote, you must:

- state your full name; *and*
- provide the address where you are or will be registered; *and*
- provide the full name and address of the proxy together with their family relationship to you, if relevant; *and*
- state the grounds on which you claim to be entitled to a proxy vote – see above; *and*
- stipulate the period or the particular election for which the application is made; *and*
- state whether the application is made for parliamentary elections, local government elections, or both; *and*

- sign and date the application – see below.

An application for a proxy vote has to be received by the registration officer at least six working days before the date of the poll. If you have already registered to vote by proxy and then change your mind – for example you want instead to vote by post or to be removed from the record – the registration officer must receive notification of this at least eleven working days before the poll. Once a successful application has been made, you should be added to a section of the electoral register known as the absent voters list.

You should receive confirmation that you have been given a proxy vote (if there is enough time before the election) confirming the name and address of the proxy and the length of time they may act as your proxy. The proxy will also receive confirmation and, shortly before polling day, will receive a proxy poll card or a proxy postal ballot paper, depending on the chosen method of voting.

Blind or physically disabled voters

If you are applying for a proxy vote (for a particular or indefinite period) on the grounds of physical incapacity, the application form must be signed by a GP, Christian Science practitioner or registered nurse. If you live in residential care, a local authority care home or sheltered accommodation, you can have your application signed by the person in charge.

The person who signs the application form has to state that:

- they are treating (or providing care to) you for the physical incapacity specified in the application; *and*
- you cannot reasonably be expected to go in person to the allotted polling station or to vote there unaided; *and*
- the physical incapacity is likely to continue either indefinitely or for the particular period specified in the application.

If you are applying for a proxy vote (for a particular or indefinite period) on the grounds of physical incapacity, you will not have to fulfil the requirements listed above if you are:

- registered blind; *or*
- in receipt of the higher rate of the mobility component of Disability Living Allowance; *or*
- registered with the local authority on grounds of physical disability.

Appealing against refusal of a postal or a proxy vote

If the registration officer refuses an application for a postal or proxy vote, you will be notified of this decision and the reasons for it. You can appeal against this decision, but not if you applied to vote by post or proxy in a particular election only.

HUMAN RIGHTS

The United Kingdom first signed and ratified the European Convention on Human Rights (ECHR) in 1950. The Convention enshrines fundamental civil and political rights, but for many years it was not part of our own law. Using the Convention usually meant taking a case to the European Court of Human Rights in Strasbourg. This was often time-consuming and expensive.

Since coming into force on 2 October 2000, the Human Rights Act has made rights from the ECHR (the Convention rights) enforceable in our own courts. This is much quicker and simpler than the old arrangement.

The Human Rights Act means that it is unlawful for public authorites to act in a way that is incompatible with Convention rights. 'Absolute rights' under the Human Rights Act include the right to life and the prohibition of torture and degrading treatment. 'Qualified rights' have to strike a balance between individual rights and the general public interest. Examples include the right to respect for private and family life and freedom of expression. If one of your human rights has been breached, cases can be dealt with in a UK Court or tribunal. You don't have to go to the European Court of Human Rights in Strasbourg.

HUMAN RIGHTS – DISCRIMINATION

Race discrimination

It is generally unlawful to discriminate against someone because of their race, and public authorities have a legal duty to eliminate unlawful discrimination and actively to promote equality. Race discrimination can be 'direct' or 'indirect', or can take the form of harassment or victimization.

If you are taking action over race discrimination, you do not have to demonstrate that there was an intention to discriminate against you. It is only necessary to show that discrimination took place.

You do not have to demonstrate that racial grounds were the only reason for the discrimination you experienced. It is enough to show that racial grounds played a substantial part in the discrimination. For a definition of 'racial grounds', see below.

Direct race discrimination

It is direct race discrimination to treat a person less favourably on racial grounds than another person would be treated in the same circumstances. As well as words or acts of refusal, direct discrimination includes words or acts of discouragement.

A clear example of direct race discrimination would be the refusal to appoint a person from a particular racial group because, according to the employer, 'they wouldn't fit in' or 'the customers would object'. Less obvious examples would be a person being turned down for a job because of a connection with someone of a particular racial group, for example because their partner is Afro-Caribbean, or being dismissed for refusing to carry out instructions that would discriminate against people from that racial group.

Indirect race discrimination

It is indirect race discrimination to set conditions or requirements for a person to meet that may seem to apply to everyone but may place people of a particular racial, ethnic or national group at an unfair disadvantage.

There may have been indirect discrimination involved in such a requirement if:

- people of a particular racial, ethnic or national group are less likely to be able to meet it; *and*
- as a result, people who cannot meet it are placed at a disadvantage; *and*
- it cannot be justified by the person or institution setting it (see below).

There may be indirect discrimination if members of one or more racial, ethnic or national group are less likely to meet a requirement than others. An example would be if an employer insists that candidates for a job should speak faultless English when this is clearly not needed for the type of work. Further examples are banning the wearing of headscarves or insisting on the wearing of skirts at work or school, or an employer insisting that a person has qualifications obtained only in the UK.

Victimization and harassment

You will have suffered victimization if you are treated less favourably because you have complained, brought proceedings or asserted your rights under race discrimination laws. This also includes a person who has assisted or supported you in doing this, for example by giving evidence as a witness in a case of race discrimination. You will have suffered harassment if you have been intimidated or humiliated by another person because of your race.

What are 'racial grounds'?

'Racial grounds' include:

- colour;
- race;
- nationality;
- ethnic or national origins. 'Ethnic origins' is a term that is hard to define. However, discrimination cases have clarified the position of certain groups of people. For example, Jews, Romany gypsies, members of the Irish traveller community and Sikhs were found to be ethnic groups, whereas Rastafarians were not. Welsh and English people are racial groups on the grounds of 'national origins'.

It is not necessary for you to belong to one of these groups for discrimination to take place. Someone may act in a discriminatory way because they believe you belong to a different racial group.

Where race discrimination is unlawful

It is unlawful to discriminate on grounds of race in:

- employment and training;
- education;
- the provision of goods and services, for example financial matters, entertainment and transport;
- housing.

Employment and training

It is unlawful for an employer to discriminate against someone on the grounds of race. This includes all employers, no matter how few workers they employ. Most workers, including employees, trainees and those who are self-employed, have legal protection from race discrimination in all aspects of employment, including recruitment, selection, promotion, training, pay and benefits, redundancy, dismissal and terms and conditions of work.

Trade unions have a duty not to discriminate against their members or those wishing to become members.

I think I'm being treated unfairly because of my religion. Is this legal?

I'm Jewish and need to take Friday afternoons off work in winter to get home before dark and prepare for the Sabbath. At the moment, my boss is happy to let me do this and make up the time during the rest of the week. However, he is thinking of introducing a new shift pattern which means I will not be able to do this any more. Can he do this?

It is unlawful to discriminate against any worker because of their religion or belief. So, if your employer is introducing a new shift pattern that will be difficult for you because of your religion, it may be that you are the victim of indirect discrimination on religious grounds. Your employer would have to show exactly why it is essential for you to work on Friday afternoons. If he is unable to show that there is no other reasonable way to reorganize your work, his behaviour towards you may count as discrimination on religious grounds.

Education

It is unlawful for any school or college to discriminate on grounds of race. This is the case whether or not it is maintained by the local education authority. A school must not discriminate in any of its policies and practices, including its admissions policies, its treatment of pupils, exclusions or decisions about a pupil's special educational needs.

A local education authority must not discriminate in any of the decisions it makes.

Goods, facilities and services

It is unlawful for anyone providing goods, facilities or services in the UK to discriminate on grounds of race, either by refusing to provide goods, services or facilities, or by providing them on less favourable terms or conditions. This is the case regardless of whether the goods, services or facilities are provided for payment or free.

Housing

In most circumstances, it is unlawful for a person or organization responsible for selling or letting a property to discriminate on grounds of race, either by refusing to sell or rent the premises or in the terms on which the premises are offered.

In most circumstances, it is unlawful for local authorities, housing associations or other registered social landlords to discriminate on grounds of race, for example in the allocation of property to people on the local housing lists.

It is unlawful for a landlord to discriminate against a tenant once a property is occupied.

When race discrimination is not unlawful

The law on race discrimination says there are some situations where race discrimination is permitted.

Employment

If certain conditions or requirements in employment can be shown to be a 'genuine occupational qualification' they may not be discriminatory. For example, it may be justified for the owner of a Chinese or a Greek restaurant to ask for a Chinese or a Greek waiter because the restaurant setting requires this. It is justifiable for a hostel for Asian women who have suffered violence to specify that it wants only Asian women workers on the grounds that the women would find it easier to relate to and communicate with people of the same racial group.

Race discrimination is not unlawful if the job involves working for a private household or working abroad for most of the time or when, with regard to certain jobs, the Crown is the employer.

Goods, facilities and services

Clubs, associations and charities set up especially for people of a particular ethnic or national group are allowed to discriminate on the basis of nationality or ethnic or national origin but not on the grounds of colour.

Housing

Owner-occupiers who are selling or letting their property can lawfully discriminate on the grounds of race if they do not advertise or use an estate agent. So can people who are renting out 'small premises', if the landlord or a member of their family has to share facilities with the tenants or prospective tenants.

Courses of action

If you think that you have suffered race discrimination there are a number of courses of action you can take. These include:

- negotiating with the person or body that discriminated against you;
- using an established grievance or complaints procedure;
- publicizing your case through the media;
- taking your own individual case under race discrimination legislation;
- taking legal action not related to race discrimination legislation;
- giving details of the problem to the Commission for Racial Equality (020 7939 0000; www.cre.gov.uk) if you believe the problem is widespread.

The course of action you choose to take will depend partly on the outcome you wish to achieve – for example, financial compensation, justice or publicity, and the speed with which you wish to get a result.

Help with the costs of taking a case

If you are taking a case you will face financial costs. Some help may be available. The Commission for Racial Equality (CRE) may be able to give some help with costs.

If you feel that you have been discriminated against in your job your case will be heard at an employment tribunal (see *Employment*, p. 259).

If you qualify for publicly funded legal services you may be able to get advice and assistance from a solicitor under the legal help scheme. Help is only available to prepare the case. A solicitor will not be able to represent you under the legal help scheme.

For more information and advice on the legal help scheme and other publicly funded legal services, see *Legal System*, p. 488.

Racially and religiously motivated attacks

Racially motivated attacks and religiously motivated attacks are attacks that are carried out because of someone's racial or ethnic origin, or their religion or lack of religion. They include the following:

- a physical attack on a person or family by another person or group of people;
- an attack on a person's or family's home or property, for example breaking a window, throwing an object through a letter box or setting a car alight;
- verbal abuse or threats;

- written abuse, for example a letter, pamphlet, e-mail or telephone text message;
- an abusive slogan painted on a wall or building.

Racial offences

If you have been harassed, distressed, insulted or attacked because of your racial origin, the person who carried out the attack can be prosecuted.

In addition, if someone incites other people to hatred of a particular racial group, for example by publishing or distributing insulting pamphlets, that person may be prosecuted for racial hatred.

Religious offences

If you have been harassed, distressed, insulted or attacked because of your religion, the person who carried out the attack can be prosecuted.

Racially and religiously aggravated criminal offences

If a criminal offence is racially or religiously aggravated, the court can impose a more severe sentence than if it was not racially or religiously aggravated. The offences that can be racially or religiously aggravated are:

- criminal damage;
- actual bodily harm;
- wounding;
- common assault;
- threatening behaviour or intentional harassment, alarm or distress;
- disorderly behaviour;
- harassment.

An offence is racially or religiously aggravated if, at the time it is committed, the offender is insulting about the victim's membership (or presumed membership) of a racial or religious group, or the offence is motivated by hostility towards members of a particular racial or religious group.

There may have been previous attacks in the area that could help to indicate that an attack was racially or religiously aggravated. There may also be a local organization, for example a community group or the Citizens Advice Bureau, that can confirm that there is a history of such attacks in the area. The local Racial Equality Council is also likely to have information. Evidence of a history of attacks in an area may help to prove to the police that an offence is racially or religiously aggravated.

Dealing with a racially or religiously motivated attack

If you have been the victim of an attack, it will help, when reporting it, if you can give the following information:

- how you were attacked;
- if you know it, the identity of the attacker and where they live or, alternatively, what the attacker looked like and/or what they were wearing;
- what, if anything, was said by the attacker, particularly anything insulting about your race or religion;
- why else you regard the attack as having been racially or religiously aggravated;
- if you have been attacked before, when and by whom;
- where the attack was made;
- when the attack was made (date and time of day or night);
- the nature of any injuries sustained (it might be helpful to obtain medical evidence);
- if anyone else was attacked;
- the names and addresses of any witnesses.

Reporting the attack to the police

If you want help or support in contacting the police, you can approach a Citizens Advice Bureau (CAB). If you have been attacked by a member or members of the police, you should always obtain advice.

The Government's own guidance defines a racist incident as 'any incident which is viewed as racist by the victim or any other person'. This means that if either the victim or any other person, for example a witness or a police officer, perceives an attack as racially motivated, the police should record it as such. The definition does not currently take into account religiously motivated attacks.

When you contact the police, you can ask to be interviewed at the police station, your home or a mutually agreed neutral location, for example the CAB (if they allow this). In any case, it is generally advisable for another person to attend with you, for example a solicitor experienced in this type of work, a CAB adviser or a friend.

If you have difficulty speaking or understanding English, you may find it helpful to have an interpreter with you. You can ask the police to provide an interpreter, ask a friend or relative, or approach a local organization, for example the CAB.

Discrimination because of your sexuality or religion

At work, it is unlawful for an employer to discriminate against you because of your sexuality, religion or belief. However, there is no law covering discrimination on these grounds in other situations.

Discrimination at work because of your sexuality

It is against the law for someone you work for to treat you less favourably than other workers because of your sexual orientation. The law calls this direct discrimination. An example of direct discrimination would be refusing to employ you or dismissing you because of your sexuality. It is also against the law for someone you work for to have rules, policies or practices which, though not aimed at you personally, put you at a disadvantage because of your sexual orientation. The law calls this indirect discrimination. An example would be a rule that restricts employment benefits for family members to opposite-sex partners only. Indirect discrimination can be justified if it can be shown to be an unavoidable business need.

Discrimination at work because of your sexuality could include:

- denying you opportunities at work for development, promotion, or other benefits such as pension and insurance schemes and cheap travel (unless the benefits depend on marital status);
- dismissing you because of your sexual orientation;
- bullying at work because of your sexual orientation;
- refusing to give you a reference, or giving you an unfair reference when you leave your job;
- treating you differently, for example if your employer expects workers to bring an opposite-sex partner to business meals but same-sex partners are not welcome.

Discrimination at work because of your religion or belief

It is against the law for someone you work for to treat you less favourably than other workers because you follow a religion or similar belief. The law calls this direct discrimination. An example of direct discrimination would be refusing to employ you or dismissing you because of your religious belief. It is also against the law for someone you work for to have rules, policies or practices which, though not aimed at you personally, put you at a disadvantage because of your belief. The law calls this indirect discrimination. An example would be a rule that requires everyone to dress in a particular way, meaning you can't wear an item of clothing you regard as part of your faith. Indirect discrimination can be justified if it can be shown to be an unavoidable business need.

Having a religion or similar belief may mean:

- belonging to an organized religion such as Judaism or Islam;
- having a profound belief that affects your way of life or world view;
- belonging to a smaller religion or sect, such as Scientology or Rastafarianism;
- taking part in collective worship.

Discrimination at work because of your religion or belief could include:

- making you dress in a certain way or remove sacred items;
- making you work at times that are against your religion;
- bullying at work because of your religion.

Age discrimination

There is no law to protect you from discrimination because of your age. Age discrimination will be illegal from 2006.

Sex discrimination

The Sex Discrimination Act 1975 makes it unlawful to discriminate against a person on grounds of their sex. Sex discrimination can be direct or indirect. It can also take the form of victimization.

Direct sex discrimination

It is direct sex discrimination to treat a person less favourably on grounds of their sex than someone of the other sex would be treated in the same circumstances.

Examples of direct sex discrimination include:

- refusing credit to a married woman without her husband's signature, while a married man is not required to have his wife's signature;
- refusing to accept a woman's salary as the basis for a mortgage because of her sex;
- allowing women (or men) free entry to a club or cheap drinks when this concession is not given at the same time to men (or women);
- advertising a vacancy for a 'waiter', implying that the job is only open to men;

- sexual harassment;
- dismissing an employee because she is pregnant.

Indirect sex discrimination

It is indirect sex discrimination to set conditions or requirements which, while apparently applying to everyone, have a greater effect on one sex.

Examples of indirect sex discrimination include:

- a requirement that an employee should not have young children – the proportion of women having responsibility for young children is much higher than that of men and this is also unlikely to be a justifiable requirement for employment (regardless of sex);
- the dismissal of all part-time workers in a firm where all of the part-time workers are female – this may also be direct sex discrimination;
- a mortgage provider insisting that only people who work full time can be given a mortgage. This is more likely to have an adverse effect on women than men, as women are more likely to work part time.

Victimization

Under the law, victimization occurs where you are treated less favourably as a result of complaining, bringing proceedings or asserting your rights under sex discrimination legislation. It is also victimization if you are treated less favourably because you have supported someone else taking action, for example by acting as a witness in a sex discrimination case.

Where sex discrimination is unlawful

It is unlawful to discriminate on grounds of sex in:

- employment and training;
- education;
- the provision of goods and services, for example financial matters, entertainment and transport;
- housing;
- advertisements.

Employment and training

It is unlawful for an employer to discriminate on the grounds of sex. Employment is defined as employment under a contract, which includes employees and self-employed people contracted to do a job personally.

Discrimination in employment also includes discrimination in recruitment and in vocational training.

The Equal Pay Act 1970 gives you the right to be treated equally in terms of pay in comparison to a member of the opposite sex. The people who are being compared must be working in the same place or working at different establishments for the same employer. A woman who believes she is being discriminated against would have to show that she is employed:

- in 'like work' – that is, work that is the same as or broadly similar to a man's; *or*
- in work that has been rated as equivalent to a man's job under a job evaluation study; *or*
- in work that is of equal value to that of a man in terms of, for example, effort, skill and decision making.

Pregnancy and employment

It is direct sex discrimination to dismiss a woman because she is pregnant. As only a woman can become pregnant, dismissal on the grounds of pregnancy is automatically discrimination on grounds of sex.

A woman who is dismissed because she is pregnant can also claim that she has been unfairly dismissed, regardless of how long she has worked for her employer. However, as there is a maximum limit on the compensation that can be awarded for unfair dismissal, but no limit on compensation for sex discrimination, a woman dismissed for being pregnant should claim sex discrimination as well as unfair dismissal.

Transsexual people

It is unlawful to discriminate in employment and vocational training against someone who intends to undergo, is undergoing, or has already undergone gender reassignment.

Married people

In the case of employment, it is sex discrimination to discriminate against you for being married whether you are a woman or a man. There is no provision covering discrimination against a person for being single, although it may be possible to argue this.

Education

It is unlawful for a state or private educational establishment to discriminate in its admission policies, unless it is a single-sex establishment. For example, a mixed-sex school should not refuse admission to a student on grounds of their sex, or attempt to maintain a gender balance in the school by admitting one sex and not another when places are limited.

A girl and boy must have the same access to the school curriculum – that is, they must be given exactly the same subject options and the same amount of subject teaching.

It is unlawful for any educational establishment to discriminate in the way it provides services to its students. For example, school students should have equal access to course option consultation and careers guidance. Any counselling provided must not be discriminatory.

Goods, facilities and services
It is unlawful for anyone providing goods, facilities or services to discriminate by refusing to provide the goods because of your sex, or to discriminate in the way in which they are provided. This is irrespective of whether the goods, services or facilities are provided for payment or free.

Financial services
It is unlawful for a financial services provider to discriminate by, for example, asking a married woman to provide a guarantor for a loan (unless a man in a similar position would also be asked to do this), insisting that a married woman seeking a loan must apply jointly with her husband (unless all married applicants are asked to apply jointly) or setting more stringent conditions when a woman asks for a business loan than when a man does. It may be lawful, however, to discriminate when providing insurance cover.

Pubs and clubs
It is unlawful for a pub to discriminate by, for example, refusing to serve a woman a drink in a pint glass (unless the same restriction also applies to men) or for a club to discriminate by offering free entrance only to women. However, discrimination may be lawful in the case of a private club.

Concessionary travel passes
It is not unlawful for a local authority to give concessionary travel passes to women at 60 and men at 65 (that is, their respective relevant pension ages).

Housing
It is unlawful for a person or organization responsible for selling or letting a property to discriminate on grounds of sex in the terms on which the

premises are offered. It is unlawful to discriminate in the treatment of people listed as needing accommodation, for example in local authority housing lists. It is also unlawful to discriminate against a tenant once a property is occupied.

Advertisements

It is unlawful for someone to publish an advertisement that indicates an intention to discriminate on grounds of sex. For example, it is unlawful for a club open to the public to advertise free admission for women while making men pay or for an employer to use expressions that have a gender connotation in advertisements, such as 'craftsman', 'manageress' or 'handyman'.

Where sex discrimination is not unlawful

There are a number of situations in which it is not unlawful to discriminate on grounds of sex.

Charities

It is not unlawful for a charity to provide benefits to people of one sex only, provided this is set out in the charity's constitution or rules.

Housing

Communal accommodation

It is not unlawful to discriminate on grounds of a person's sex in the provision of some types of communal accommodation, for example a women's refuge.

'Small dwellings' exception

It is not unlawful to discriminate on grounds of a person's sex in a 'small dwelling' or for sub-letting accommodation where:

- the proprietor or a close relative is also living; *and*
- there is shared accommodation with other people living there; *and*
- there is not normally accommodation for more than two households as well as the proprietor's own, or six people in addition to the proprietor.

Insurance

It is not unlawful for an insurance company to discriminate on the grounds of a person's sex when the company is assessing risk, provided that the company can:

- provide information to justify the discrimination; *and*

- show that the information was obtained from a reliable source; *and*
- show that the discrimination is reasonable in relation to the information available.

Examples of legitimate discrimination would be:

- in the case of life assurance, women and men have different life expectancies and can therefore be charged different rates;
- in the case of travel insurance, a woman who is pregnant may be refused cover on the grounds that she is not considered fit to travel.

Private clubs

It is not unlawful for a genuine private members' club to discriminate on the grounds of someone's sex in the way that it treats its members. Examples are working men's clubs, golf and bowling clubs, and gentlemen's clubs.

It is not unlawful for a club to have different types of membership that are restricted to one sex only. An example would be a club that has 'full' membership for men, with full voting rights and other privileges, and 'associate' membership for women, with more restricted rights.

Sport

It is not unlawful to limit participation in some sporting events to one sex only, provided physical strength, stamina or physique is important in the particular sport to the extent that, for example, a woman would be at a competitive disadvantage to a man.

It is not unlawful to discriminate on sex grounds in situations where a member of one sex might object to physical contact with a person of the opposite sex. For example, it is legitimate for a self-defence class to restrict itself to women participants.

It is not unlawful for a genuinely private members' sporting club to discriminate on grounds of sex.

Positive discrimination

The law against sex discrimination does not allow positive discrimination in favour of one sex. For example, it is unlawful to discriminate in favour of a woman in recruitment or promotion on the grounds that women have previously been adversely affected by discrimination. However, positive action is allowed.

Positive action

The law against sex discrimination does allow positive action in favour of one sex, particularly in training and advertising. Positive action is intended to redress the effects of previous unequal opportunities by providing special encouragement to the minority sex without actively discriminating against the majority sex. Examples of positive action are:

- a training agency may use positive action if it appears that very few or no people of one sex have been engaged in a particular kind of work over the past twelve months;
- an employer who has very few or no employees of one sex engaged in a particular job, or in management positions, may use positive action to provide training for that work to employees of the minority sex only;
- a trade union or political party is allowed to use positive action to ensure that members of both sexes are represented at all levels of the organization. A trade union can, for example, reserve seats on a committee for one sex where it is under-represented.

Taking action about sex discrimination

When taking action about sex discrimination, you do not have to demonstrate that there was an intention to discriminate against you. It is merely necessary to show that discrimination took place.

When taking action under legislation against sex discrimination, a comparison must normally be made between how a woman has been treated and how a man has been treated. However, if a woman cannot identify a man who is being treated, or has been treated, more favourably, she can still take a case if she can show that a man would have been treated more favourably. If you think you have suffered sex discrimination there are a number of actions you can take. These include:

- taking your own individual case under the Sex Discrimination Act;
- negotiating with the person or body that discriminated against you;
- using an established grievance or complaints procedure;
- taking legal action not related to the Sex Discrimination Act;
- giving details to the Equal Opportunities Commission (0845 601 5901; www.eoc.org.uk).

Any course of action is likely to be complicated, could include confrontation and may involve court action. If you are contemplating action you should consult an experienced adviser, for example at a Citizens Advice Bureau.

Disability discrimination

The Disability Discrimination Act 1995 (DDA) deals with the discrimination faced by disabled people in various areas of their lives. Many common examples of discrimination, however, will not be covered by this Act. The DDA will only be fully implemented over a number of years. This information covers the areas in force at the time of writing.

The following areas are currently covered by the DDA:

- discrimination in employment (this includes discrimination in recruitment and selection, terms and conditions, and dismissal and redundancy);
- access to goods, facilities and services (this includes most goods and most services provided direct to the public either commercially or through local/central government, although there are some important exemptions);
- letting or selling land or property (but there are limitations);
- educational services.

The DDA covers discrimination against people who are disabled or who have been disabled in the past. Disability means a physical or mental impairment that has a substantial and long-term adverse effect on a person's ability to carry out normal day-to-day activities.

The definition of 'impairment' includes sensory impairments, such as impaired sight and hearing, or mental impairments, including learning disabilities and clinically recognized mental illnesses.

The disability must have a substantial and long-term effect. Although a minor impairment may not, on its own, count as 'substantial', you may have a number of minor impairments that together may be held to have a substantial effect. 'Long-term' means:

- that the disability has lasted for at least twelve months; *or*
- that the disability is expected to last for at least twelve months; *or*
- that, in the case of a person expected to live for less than twelve months, the disability is likely to last for the rest of their life.

Some special rules have been made about what is or is not to be classed as a disability for the purpose of the Act. Some severe disfigurement is classed as disability. Some conditions that can worsen over time, such as multiple sclerosis and HIV/AIDS, are covered as soon as symptoms start to appear, even before the symptoms start to affect day-to-day activities.

'Day-to-day activities' means normal activities that most people carry out on a regular basis. An impairment will be treated as affecting your ability to carry out normal day-to-day activities if it affects at least one of the following:

- mobility;
- ability to use hands, for example for writing or cooking;
- physical co-ordination;
- going to the toilet;
- the ability to lift, carry or move ordinary objects;
- speech, hearing or eyesight;
- memory, or the ability to concentrate, learn or understand;
- being able to recognize physical danger.

Employment

It is important to remember that the rights disabled people have through the Disability Discrimination Act are in addition to any other statutory or contractual employment rights that they may have.

It is unlawful for an employer to:

- directly discriminate against a disabled person;
- give a disabled person less favourable treatment unless this can be 'justified';
- fail to make 'reasonable' adjustments to the work environment to enable a disabled person to work;
- harass or bully a disabled person, for example by making jokes about their disability;
- victimize a person for taking action under the DDA or helping someone else to take action.

Access to goods, facilities and services

It is important to remember that the rights disabled people have through the Disability Discrimination Act are in addition to any other statutory or contractual rights that they may have. For example, all people, disabled or not, have a statutory right that the goods they buy are of satisfactory quality. It is unlawful for a provider of goods, facilities and services to discriminate against a disabled person.

Examples of the types of goods and services covered by the DDA include services provided by hotels, banks, building societies, solicitors, local authorities, advice agencies, pubs, theatres, shops, telesales, transport termini (such as railway stations), churches, doctors and law courts. It does not matter whether the service is free or has to be paid for.

Education and transport vehicles are not covered by this part of the DDA. Insurance is covered by the Act, but insurers are allowed to treat disabled people less favourably if this treatment is based on reliable information about risk.

Buying or renting land or property

It is important to remember that a disabled person's right to be protected against discrimination is in addition to their other rights, for example as a tenant.

It is unlawful for someone who is selling, managing or renting land or property to discriminate against a disabled person. Discrimination includes:

- refusing to sell or let a property or offering a property for sale or rent on worse terms to a disabled person;
- treating a disabled person less favourably on a housing waiting list or register;
- unreasonably preventing a tenant from using facilities or not allowing them to use these facilities in the same way as a landlord would allow other tenants to do;
- evicting a disabled tenant for a reason connected with their disability or harassing them for that reason.

Landlords who are renting out accommodation in their own homes are not covered by the requirements of the DDA.

The DDA does not require people selling or letting property to disabled people physically to alter existing premises in order to make them more accessible. However, they must make their services accessible. This may mean, for example, that an estate agent has to adapt their office to make it accessible.

Education

It is unlawful for any school or provider of further education, higher education or adult and community education to discriminate against disabled students (both current and prospective students).

Schools

A school might discriminate against a disabled student in three ways:

- less favourable treatment. If a school treats a disabled student or prospective student less favourably than another because of their disability, this will be unlawful discrimination unless the school can justify it. For example, a school might tell a parent who wants their daughter with epilepsy to go to a primary school that the school cannot take her unless she stops having fits. This is likely to count as less favourable treatment for a reason related to the child's disability. If the school cannot justify it, it will amount to discrimination.

- failing to make a reasonable adjustment. This can count as discrimination if it places disabled students or prospective students at a substantial disadvantage compared to non-disabled students. For example, a deaf student who lip-reads is at a disadvantage if teachers continue to speak while facing away to write on a whiteboard. There may be justification for failing to make a reasonable adjustment.
- failing to comply with a statement of special educational needs – for example, failing to recruit a learning support assistant where the student's statement provides for one.

It is unlawful for schools to discriminate in the following ways, unless they can justify the less favourable treatment:

- **admissions**. Schools must not discriminate against a disabled student in the way they decide who can get into the school, including any rules they use when a school is over-subscribed, in their terms for offering a place at the school, or by refusing an application from a disabled student for admission to the school.
- **education and associated services**. This includes all aspects of school life such as education and school trips and extra-curricular activities.
- **exclusions**. It is unlawful to discriminate against a disabled student by excluding them because of their disability. This applies to both permanent and fixed-term exclusions.

Justification for less favourable treatment
In some cases, a school can treat a disabled student 'less favourably' if it can justify this. A school can justify less favourable treatment if it is because of a permitted form of selection. For example, if a child with learning difficulties applies to a school that selects its intake on the basis of academic ability and fails the school's entrance exam, then even though the reason for her performance in the exam was a reason related to her disability, because the school has used objective rules the less favourable treatment (that she is not offered a place at the school) is likely to be justified.

Justification for failing to make a reasonable adjustment
If a school does not make reasonable adjustments to avoid putting disabled pupils at a substantial disadvantage, it can justify this if it has a substantial reason that is relevant to the particular circumstances.

The DDA does not say what 'reasonable' means. It will depend on the circumstances of the particular case and will be decided by the tribunal or appeals panel. However, in deciding what is 'reasonable', a school can take account of:

- its need to maintain academic and other standards;
- money available;
- the practicalities of making the particular adjustment;
- the health and safety of the disabled pupil and others;
- the interests of other pupils.

Provision of aids or services to disabled pupils
Schools do not need to provide aids or adaptations for disabled children under the Disability Discrimination Act. They may, however, be under a duty to provide such aids to children under the special educational needs framework. This might include services such as information available in Braille or audio tape, or personal assistance.

'Reasonable adjustments' to buildings and the physical environment of the school
All local education authorities must have accessibility plans to make their schools more accessible to disabled pupils. Maintained schools, independent schools and non-maintained special schools must produce their own accessibility plans. The plans must be in writing and publicly available.

The Department for Education and Skills has produced guidance for schools on their planning duties under the Act, called *Accessible Schools: Planning to increase access to school for disabled pupils*, available from DfES Publications (0845 60 222 60, available in Braille, large-print and audio tape; www.dfes.gov.uk/sen).

What can you do if you feel that your child has been discriminated against?
Depending on the circumstances of the case, you can take a case to a special educational needs and disability tribunal or, in certain cases, to an admissions appeal panel or an exclusion appeal panel. You are only able to make an appeal to any of these bodies having come to the end of a complaints process with the institution that you feel has discriminated against your child. You can contact a special educational needs and disability tribunal through the Disability Rights Commission (DDA helpline 08457 622633;

textphone 08457 622644; www.drc-gb.org) and can apply to an admissions appeal panel via the LEA or the governing body of the school and the exclusion appeal panel via the LEA. You will be offered conciliation in most situations before you appeal.

Further and higher education

All of the information provided under the heading 'Schools' also applies to further and higher education establishments. The Disability Rights Commission (DRC: www.drc-gb.org.uk) has detailed guidance on how further and higher educational establishments should implement these policies. This guidance is available from the DRC and from the Department for Education and Skills publications unit (0845 60 222 60).

Public transport

The DDA gives the government powers to make regulations about the design of and access to newly built public transport vehicles, taxis and services.

Although public transport vehicles are not yet covered by the Act, public transport termini are and so, for example, a deaf person could complain about the lack of minicom or other accessible information at a train station.

Who can help?

Race discrimination

The **Commission for Racial Equality** (England: 020 7939 0000; Wales: 029 2072 9200; www.cre.gov.uk).

Racial Equality Councils are local organizations that may be able to help with action over race discrimination. They may offer different levels of help. You should check what services or assistance your local Racial Equality Council can offer. For the address of your local Racial Equality Council, contact the Commission for Racial Equality (England: 020 7939 0000; Wales: 029 2072 9200; www.cre.gov.uk).

If you have been the victim of a racially and/or religiously motivated attack, you should always seek advice. You can get this from a CAB. However, you could also get help from the local Racial Equality Council (REC), the local **Victim Support** scheme (Helplines: 0845 3030 900; www.victimsupport.org.uk) or another local organization.

You could also contact the **Monitoring Group** freephone emergency helpline (0800 374 618), which advises victims of racial harassment and abuse. It is available twenty-four hours a day, and is staffed by volunteers recruited from black and ethnic minority communities, to ensure that they can communicate with the caller in the appropriate language. There is also a Home Office support line for Muslims – **'Muslim Line'** (0208 840 4840) – which can give advice if you have been abused because of your religious beliefs.

If you have suffered a personal injury as the result of a racially or religiously motivated attack, you may be eligible for compensation under the **Criminal Injuries Compensation Scheme** (www.cica.gov.uk).

Sex discrimination

The **Equal Opportunities Commission** (England: 0845 601 5901; Wales: 029 2034 3552; www.eoc.org.uk) may be able to help you take a case for sex discrimination. The EOC is willing to advise over the phone or by letter on the best way to argue a case. This is a free service. It can also give details of solicitors experienced in this type of work and may arrange representation.

Disability discrimination

The **Disability Rights Commission** (DDA helpline: 08457 622633; textphone: 08457 622644; www.drc-gb.org) is a national body that may be able to help you take a case under the Disability Discrimination Act. It may also be able to give advice on the Act to disabled people, employers and service providers. For telephone queries about the Act, and advice on how to take a case, contact the DDA helpline, which refers callers to the Disability Rights Commission if it considers this appropriate.

General discrimination

Law Centres can offer free legal advice to people who want to take action about discrimination. If you are represented by a solicitor from a law centre, you may be entitled to publicly funded legal services. Details of the nearest law centres are available from the **Law Centres Federation** (020 7387 8570; www.lawcentres.org.uk).

Members of the **Discrimination Law Association** (01933 228742; www.discrimination-law.org.uk) work in the areas of race, disability and sex discrimination. The Association can provide names of member practitioners. You should remember that most members are likely to be solicitors in private practice and so charges will be made if publicly funded legal services are not available.

INVESTIGATING COMPLAINTS – OMBUDSMAN

An ombudsman is a person who has been appointed to investigate complaints about an organization. The ombudsman is usually a lawyer and investigates from an independent standpoint.

There are a number of ombudsmen:

- the Parliamentary Ombudsman, who investigates complaints about government departments and some other public bodies;
- the Local Government Ombudsman, who investigates complaints about local councils and some other local organizations;
- the Health Service Ombudsman;
- the Financial Ombudsman Service (FOS);
- the European Ombudsman;
- the Legal Services Ombudsman;
- the Ombudsman for Estate Agents;
- the Housing Ombudsman;
- the Prisons and Probation Ombudsman;
- the Funeral Ombudsman;
- The Welsh Administration Ombudsman.

Details about ombudsmen in the UK who are members of the European Extra-Judicial Network project can be found on the Euroconsumer website (www.euroconsumer.org.uk).

There is no charge for the investigations made by an ombudsman. Any money you spend in making the complaint, for example travel expenses, should be reclaimed from the office of the relevant ombudsman.

Even where the ombudsman agrees that the complaint is justified, in most cases an organization cannot be ordered to do anything to compensate you. In addition, the investigation by the ombudsman can take a long time. Complaining to the ombudsman should therefore only be considered as a last resort.

The ombudsman's job is to investigate cases of maladministration. This means the way in which an organization has dealt with a situation, for example whether the procedures used by the organization were fair or reasonable.

The ombudsman will only investigate a case where an individual (or in some cases a group of individuals) has suffered personal injustice, hardship or financial loss because of the action or lack of action of a particular organization. The complaint must be brought by the person who has suffered this injustice, hardship or loss.

The ombudsman cannot investigate a decision made by an organization, only the way in which a decision was reached. More detailed information on which type of complaint each ombudsman can take up is provided below.

You should complain to the ombudsman only if you have given the relevant organization an opportunity to comment on the complaint and resolve any problems. A letter setting out the problem should be sent to the relevant organization. You should always keep copies of any letters sent and any replies received. The ombudsman will not investigate a case if it is about to go to court or if court proceedings are being considered. In some cases the ombudsman will not investigate cases that could be dealt with by a court or tribunal.

How to complain to the ombudsman

The procedure for starting the investigation by the ombudsman differs slightly depending on which ombudsman the complaint is being made to. Most of the offices of the ombudsmen provide an application form for making a complaint. It is not, however, necessary to use an application form. You can send a letter containing the following information:

- name and address of the person making the complaint;
- name and address of the organization the complaint is being made about;
- details of what the complaint is about – that is, what the organization did wrong or failed to do;
- date when you first identified the event you are complaining about;
- what personal injustice, financial loss or hardship was suffered;
- what the organization should do to put the situation right;
- details of how the complaint has been followed up prior to contacting the ombudsman.

Copies of any correspondence relevant to the complaint should also be sent.

Parliamentary Ombudsman

The Parliamentary Ombudsman can take up complaints in England and Wales about the way an individual has been treated by a government department or other public body. The Parliamentary Ombudsman can deal with complaints about maladministration by a public body, for example how procedures are used. Examples of the type of complaint the Parliamentary Ombudsman could deal with are:

- slow and unsatisfactory responses to letters to government departments;
- incorrect or misleading information and advice given by officials of government departments or refusal to give information;
- rudeness, discrimination, unhelpfulness of staff of government departments or refusal to give information;
- failure to follow reasonable rules in procedures and administration.

The Parliamentary Ombudsman cannot investigate the following types of complaint:

- complaints about nationalized industries;
- problems that can usually be taken to court;
- complaints about the way legal proceedings are conducted, for example complaints about the administrative staff of courts, unless the staff acted on the authority of the judge, magistrate, etc.;
- complaints about the police;
- complaints about things that have not caused the complainant hardship or suffering;
- complaints about government policies.

The office of the Parliamentary Ombudsman (England: 0845 015 4033, Wales: 0845 601 0987; www.ombudsman.org.uk) can be approached directly for advice on whether the case is one which they could take up.

Local Government Ombudsman

The Local Government Ombudsman can deal with complaints of maladministration in the following organizations:

- district, borough, city or county councils (but not town or parish councils);
- joint boards of local authorities;
- police and fire authorities (not complaints about individual police officers);
- English Partnerships (some housing and planning matters only);
- the Commission for the New Towns (housing matters only);
- housing action trusts;
- national park authorities;

- the Environment Agency (flood defence and land drainage matters only);
- the Greater London Authority;
- the Norfolk and Suffolk Broads Authority;
- education appeal panels;
- school governing bodies (admission matters only).

The Local Government Ombudsman can only investigate complaints of maladministration that cause injustice, suffering or hardship. This means that they can only take up complaints about the way an organization has done something, or not done something it should have done. Examples of the type of complaint it can investigate are:

- delay or neglect in responding to enquiries or providing a service;
- failure to follow the agreed policies, rules or procedures of the organization;
- rudeness, discrimination or unhelpfulness of staff;
- incorrect or misleading information and advice by officials, or failure to provide advice and information.

The Local Government Ombudsman cannot deal with:

- a complaint that could go, or has already gone, to a court or tribunal or in which a government minister is involved;
- a complaint about something that affects all or most of the inhabitants in a local area, for example a complaint that the council has wasted public money;
- a complaint about court proceedings;
- a complaint about the internal affairs of schools and colleges;
- contracts for the supply of goods and services to the council;
- personnel policies and practices.

Contact details of the Local Government Ombudsmen are listed here. You should contact the Ombudsman for your area.

London boroughs north of the Thames (including Richmond and excluding Harrow and Tower Hamlets), Berkshire, Buckinghamshire, Hertfordshire, Essex, Kent, East and West Sussex, Surrey, Suffolk and Coventry: 020 7217 4620.
London Borough of Tower Hamlets, Birmingham, Cheshire, Derbyshire, Nottinghamshire, Lincolnshire and the North of England (except the cities of York and Lancaster): 01904 380200.
London boroughs south of the Thames (excluding Richmond), Harrow, the cities of York and Lancaster and the rest of England not covered by London: 024 7682 0000.

More information is available from the national helpline on 0845 602 1983 or online (www.lgo.org.uk).

Wales: 01656 661325 (www.ombudsman-wales.org). The Welsh Administration Ombudsman (0845 601 0987; www.ombudsman.org.uk) investigates complaints of maladministration by the National Assembly for Wales and other Welsh bodies.

European Ombudsman

Examples of the problems that can be investigated by the European Ombudsman include administrative delay, refusal of information, discrimination and abuse of power.

Before you can make a complaint to the European Ombudsman, the European institution concerned should be given the opportunity to investigate and try to resolve the problem.

Health Service Ombudsman

The Health Service Ombudsman can investigate complaints about NHS hospitals or community health services.

Some examples of the type of problems the Health Service Ombudsman can investigate are:

- poor service, such as a long wait for treatment or an operation;
- failure to provide a disability aid;
- dirty wards at a hospital;
- unhelpful staff or inadequate staffing;
- the care and treatment provided by a doctor, nurse or other trained professional;
- complaints about GPs, dentists, opticians and pharmacists working for the NHS;
- refusal to give you information to which you are entitled.

The Health Service Ombudsman cannot investigate the following types of problem:

- complaints that have gone or could go to court or a tribunal;
- complaints relating to services in a non-NHS hospital or nursing home (unless paid for by the NHS);
- decisions an NHS authority or individual providing NHS services has a right to make, even if you do not agree with the decision.

The Health Service Ombudsman does not have to investigate a complaint, and the local community health council or the Health Service Ombudsman's office will be able to advise on whether or not the Ombudsman can take up a complaint.

You should complain to the Health Service Ombudsman (England: 0845 015 4033; minicom: 020 7217 4066; Wales: 02920 394621; www.ombudsman.org.uk) in writing, no later than a year from the date when you first became aware of the events that are the subject of the complaint.

Financial Ombudsman Service

The Financial Ombudsman Service (FOS) can deal with consumer complaints about most personal financial matters including financial advice, banking services, building society services, and insurance. The FOS is impartial and is free of charge.

The FOS can mainly deal with consumer complaints about companies that are authorized by the Financial Services Authority (FSA), although they can also deal with a number of unauthorized companies. You should contact the FOS directly (0845 080 1800; www.financial-ombudsman.org.uk) for information on how to make a complaint.

Legal Services Ombudsman

The Legal Services Ombudsman can deal with complaints about solicitors, barristers, legal executives and licensed conveyancers.

The Legal Services Ombudsman will not deal with a complaint if:

- the internal complaints procedure of the lawyer's professional body has not yet been exhausted;
- the complaint is being or has been dealt with by a court of law;
- the complaint is about how a barrister handled a case in court;
- the complaint is made more than three months after the lawyer's professional body has informed you of its decision, unless the Ombudsman decides there are special reasons.

You can contact the office of the Legal Services Ombudsman on 0845 601 0794 (local call rate), online (www.olso.org), or in writing, and get a complaints form to complete and return.

Ombudsman for Estate Agents

The Ombudsman for Estate Agents will investigate complaints about member companies if you have lost money or suffered inconvenience because a company has:

- infringed your legal rights;
- treated you unfairly;
- been guilty of maladministration (including inefficiency and delay).

The Ombudsman for Estate Agents will not deal with complaints if:

- the complaint is not against a member company;
- the complaint is being or has been dealt with by a court;
- the complaint relates to a dispute over a survey;
- the claim is for more than a certain amount;
- the complaint is sent more than six months after the company complained about has made its final offer.

You can write to the Ombudsman for Estate Agents (01722 333 306; www.oea.co.uk) giving full details of the complaint.

Housing Ombudsman (England only)

The Housing Ombudsman Service can deal with complaints about maladministration by any registered social landlord or other private landlord who has joined the scheme voluntarily. Complaints that can be dealt with include:

- failure to make repairs in a reasonable time;
- mistakenly accusing a tenant of rent arrears and not acknowledging the mistake;
- charging you more than other tenants for the same service;
- unreasonably refusing to provide a home or a transfer.

The Ombudsman will not normally deal with complaints which involve:

- the level of rent or service charges;
- matters that have gone to court or which the Ombudsman decides are better dealt with by a court;
- council tenants (complaints can be dealt with by the Local Government Ombudsman instead).

You can write to the Housing Ombudsman Service (020 7836 3630; Lo-call: 0845 712 5973; www.ihos.org.uk) giving full details of your complaint.

Prisons and Probation Ombudsman

The Prisons and Probation Ombudsman can consider complaints about most aspects of a prisoner's treatment in prison, including disciplinary hearings. It also deals with complaints by people on probation. The Prisons and Probation Ombudsman can consider whether a decision taken by the Prison Service was correct and whether the proper procedures were followed in making the decision. This includes action taken by prison staff employed by private companies and by people such as prison probation officers or members of the Independent Monitoring Board.

The Prisons and Probation Ombudsman cannot consider complaints about the actions of outside agencies, for example the police, courts or the Immigration Department.

Complaints can be made to the Prisons and Probation Ombudsman (020 7276 2876 or 08450 0107938; www.ppo.gov.uk). There are strict time limits for dealing with a complaint.

THE NATIONAL ASSEMBLY FOR WALES

The National Assembly for Wales is responsible for certain areas of law and policy in Wales. This means that law or policy can be different in England and Wales – for example, prescription charges differ in Wales and England.

As a broad guide, the Welsh Assembly makes law in areas such as education and training, economic development and industry, health services, housing, social services and local government. It does not have authority in matters of criminal justice, employment law, social security, immigration or taxation.

Contacting an Assembly member

You can contact an Assembly member on any matter that is covered by the Assembly. Names and addresses of Assembly members can be found in *The Wales Yearbook* in libraries, or by contacting the Assembly (029 2089 8200; www.wales.gov.uk).

FREEDOM OF INFORMATION

Your right to information

Under freedom of information laws, anybody can request information from a public authority. This means you have the right:

- to be told whether or not a public authority holds information that you want; and if so,
- to have access to the information.

You do not need to say why you want the information and, generally, there are no restrictions on how you can use the information once you have it.

Any information held by a public authority is eligible for release. However, information does not have to be provided where the authority decides there are good reasons for keeping it confidential, for example where your request relates to someone else's personal details. You may have to pay a fee for the information.

Broadly, freedom of information applies to all public authorities within the following categories:

- central and local government;
- the health sector;
- the police and armed forces;
- the education sector;
- other public bodies in England, Wales and Northern Ireland.

The publication scheme

All public authorities have a publication scheme. This scheme lists the information that the public authority routinely makes available and states whether you have to pay for the information or not. Check the scheme to see if the information you want has already been published as this will save you time and money.

How do I ask for information?

All requests must be in writing, by letter, fax or e-mail. You must clearly state what you want and supply your name and address. You can ask for any recorded information, so the information could be in the form of e-mails, notebooks, videos or tapes as well as paper or electronic documents. In most cases, a public authority must respond to your request within twenty working days. If it cannot, it must explain why and let you know when you will get a reply.

The reply should confirm or deny whether or not the authority holds the information, and either provide the information you requested or explain why it cannot.

What if my request is refused?

If your request is refused, the public authority must give you details of how to apply for an internal review of its decision. If, after an internal review, the public authority still refuses your request, you may ask the Information Commisioner to review that decision. More information is available on the Commissioner's website (www.informationcommissioner.gov.uk).

PRIVACY AND DATA PROTECTION

Personal data is data about an identifiable living individual. Examples of personal data include:

- your health record;
- an entry about you on the police national computer;
- your credit reference file;
- an e-mail about your conduct at work.

There are rules about what personal data can be accessed by others and the way in which data is processed. Data can only be processed for specific and limited purposes: for example, your local authority is not allowed to pass on the names and addresses of Council Tax payers to any commercial organization.

Data must be accurate and, where necessary, kept up to date. It must not be kept longer than necessary and must be secure. There is extra protection relating to 'sensitive' personal data – for example information about your racial or ethnic origin, political opinions or sex life. This sort of data can be processed only if you give your express consent or if it is in connection with legal proceedings.

The **Information Commissioners Office** is the UK independent supervisory authority that oversees and enforces data protection law. Contact the Data Protection helpline (01625 545 745; www.informationcommissioner.gov.uk) for more information.

2

The Legal System

CONTENTS

INTRODUCTION

Access to justice is a basic right in a fair society and we need to trust the laws that support us and those who administer them. The right to a fair trial and to appeal against a decision are cornerstones of the justice system, as high-profile miscarriages of justice that have come to light in recent years have illustrated. Access to publicly funded legal services is also vital so that low income is no barrier to justice. The nature of the justice we demand and the laws that we live by have developed over many centuries and the only similarity between Sir Thomas More, the Lord Chancellor in 1529, and modern-day 'Lord Chancellors' is that both are custodians of the Great Seal, used to show the monarch's approval of important state documents. The face of the legal system has further changed in recent years with changes to the role of the Lord Chancellor itself and the creation of a new Department of Constitutional Affairs with responsibility for providing effective and accessible justice for all, ensuring the rights and responsibilities of the citizen and modernizing the law and constitution.

This chapter looks at the basic structures of our legal system, which courts do what, the prison system, police powers, how to use the small claims court and how to use a solicitor.

JARGON BUSTER

statutory charge	the deduction of solicitors' costs made from any money or property you are awarded as a result of advice or assistance under the legal help scheme
LSC	Legal Services Commission
CLS	Community Legal Services
criminal law	deals with illegal acts committed against individuals or society as a whole
civil law	involves disputes over property, commercial transactions or family matters like divorce and adoption
JPs	justices of the peace
summary offences	criminal offences, dealt with in the magistrates' court, where the defendant is not entitled to trial by jury
VOs	Visiting Orders

THE LEGAL STRUCTURE

The county court

The county court deals with civil (i.e. not criminal) cases, which are dealt with by a judge or district judge. The claimant is the person who makes the claim and the defendant is the person against whom a claim is made. A case can be started in any county court but it may be transferred to the defendant's local court. If the case is defended and the claim is for a fixed amount of money, the case will be transferred automatically by the court to the defendant's local court (if the defendant is an individual not a company). In other cases the defendant can request its transfer.

All claims arising from regulated credit agreements must be started in the county court, whatever their value.

Examples of cases dealt with by the county court

County courts can deal with a wide range of cases, but the most common ones are:

- landlord and tenant disputes – for example, possession (eviction), rent arrears, repairs;
- consumer disputes – for example, faulty goods or services;
- personal injury claims (injuries caused by negligence), like traffic accidents, falling into holes in the pavement and accidents at work;
- undefended divorce cases, but only in some county courts. In inner London, the Divorce Registry in the Strand deals with undefended divorces.
- some domestic violence cases, but these may also be heard in the magistrates' court;
- discrimination cases;
- debt problems – for example, a creditor seeking payment;
- employment problems – for example, wages or salary owing or pay in lieu of notice.

Small claims cases

A case will, if defended, be dealt with in one of three ways. The court will decide which procedure will apply and then allocate the case to the corresponding 'track'. The three tracks are:

- the small claims track;
- the fast track;
- the multi-track.

The small claims track is the usual track for claims with a value of £5,000 or less. The procedure in the small claims track is simpler than in the other tracks and in most cases the losing party will not have to pay the other party's costs.

For more information on using the small claims track, see *Using the small claims procedure*, p. 476.

Magistrates' courts

Magistrates' courts deal with mainly criminal cases but some civil ones too. Cases are dealt with either by justices of the peace (JPs) or by District Judges (Magistrates' Courts) who together are known as magistrates. (JPs are unqualified and are paid only expenses, while District Judges are salaried.) Magistrates' courts usually deal only with cases that arise in their own area.

Criminal cases in the magistrates' court

Magistrates' courts deal with criminal offences where the defendant is not entitled to trial by jury. These are known as summary offences. Summary offences involve a maximum penalty of six months' imprisonment and/or a fine of up to £5,000.

Magistrates also deal with offences where the defendant could choose trial by jury or trial in the magistrates' court, and has chosen the magistrates' court. If the defendant chooses trial by jury, the case will be passed on to the Crown Court.

The youth court

The youth court deals with young people aged between 10 and 17 who have committed criminal offences. The youth court is part of the magistrates' court and up to three specially trained magistrates hear the case. If a young person is charged with a very serious offence, which in the case of an adult is punishable with fourteen years' imprisonment or more, the youth court can commit them for trial at the Crown Court.

Civil cases in the magistrates' court

Magistrates can deal with a limited number of civil cases as follows:

- some civil debts – for example, arrears of income tax, National Insurance contributions, council tax and VAT;
- licences – for example, granting, renewing or taking away licences for pubs and clubs;
- some matrimonial problems, such as maintenance and removing a spouse from the matrimonial home;
- welfare of children, including local authority care or supervision orders, adoption proceedings and residence orders.

Crown Courts

The Crown Court deals with the following types of cases:

- serious criminal offences that will be tried by judge and jury;
- appeals from the magistrates' court, which are dealt with by a judge and at least two magistrates;
- convictions in the magistrates' court that are referred to the Crown Court for sentencing.

Imprisonment and fines in the Crown Court are more severe than in the magistrates' court.

The High Court

The High Court deals with civil cases, hears appeals in criminal cases, and also has the power to review the actions of individuals or organizations to make sure they have acted legally and justly. The High Court has three divisions, as follows:

The Family Division

The Family Division deals with complex defended divorce cases, wardship, adoption, domestic violence, and so on. It also deals with appeals from magistrates' and county courts in matrimonial cases.

The Queen's Bench Division

The Queen's Bench Division deals with large or complex claims for compensation. It also deals with a limited number of appeals from magistrates' courts or Crown Courts, and with libel and slander actions, as well as reviewing the actions of organizations to see whether they have acted legally.

The Chancery Division

The Chancery Division deals with trusts, contested wills, bankruptcy and mortgage foreclosures.

The Court of Appeal

The Court of Appeal deals with civil and criminal appeals. Civil appeals from the High Court and the county court, as well as from the Employment Appeal Tribunal and the Lands Tribunal, are dealt with. Criminal appeals include appeals against convictions in the Crown Court, and points of law referred by the Attorney General following acquittal in the Crown Court or where the sentence imposed was unduly lenient.

The House of Lords

The House of Lords deals mainly with appeals from the Court of Appeal, or where the Attorney General wants an opinion on a particular point of law. Appeals are mostly about civil cases although the Lords do deal with some criminal appeals.

JURY SERVICE

I'm very busy at work. Do I have to do jury service?

Work commitments can be important and hard to break. Being busy at work isn't enough to excuse you from jury service altogether, but you can ask for your service to be postponed until a later date. Postponing for this kind of personal reason is known as deferral of jury service.

Your work commitments may prevent you from serving on a jury at the time that you are summoned but won't prevent you from serving at another date. If your service is deferred, you will be asked to confirm any other dates in the year when you won't be able to attend, so that you are given a new date that is convenient. Jury service can only be deferred once.

You apply to have your jury service deferred by completing the section in the summons form called 'Deferral and Excusal'. When this has been accepted you will get a letter confirming the deferral and giving you a new date for your jury service. You cannot defer twice and must attend on this second occasion.

You can find out more about jury service online (www.juror.cjsonline.org).

Jury service is an important civic duty. You do not need any knowledge of the legal system to be a juror and the experience and knowledge of each person on the jury will differ. Each individual juror will be asked to consider the evidence presented and then decide whether the defendant is guilty or not.

Jurors usually try the more serious criminal cases, such as assault, burglary, fraud or murder, that take place in the Crown Court. Jurors might also be needed to serve in a civil case such as libel, though this does not happen often. When it does, the trial will take place in the High Court or a county court. You might also be needed to serve in a coroner's court.

Jurors are chosen at random from the electoral roll to serve on a jury. If summoned, you are legally required to serve on a jury unless you are disqualified from jury service – for example, if you have been convicted of certain criminal offences.

The jury summons tells you which court you have been summoned to attend and the date and time on which your service will begin. You must reply to a jury summons within seven days of receipt.

If you have confirmed that you are able to serve at the time you have been summoned, you will receive details of how to get to the court and what to expect once you're there.

If you apply to have your jury service deferred or to be excused from jury service you will receive confirmation of whether your application has been granted. You should receive a reply within ten days of sending your letter.

If you are a juror, you are able to get travelling expenses, a subsistence allowance and an allowance for certain other financial losses that you may suffer while on jury service. The cost of childcare can also be reimbursed. If you have any queries about being summoned for jury service, you can contact the Jury Central Summoning Bureau (0845 3555567; www.juror.cjsonline.org).

LAW-MAKING INSTITUTIONS OF THE EUROPEAN UNION (EU)

The European Union has four decision-making institutions:

- the Council of Ministers;
- the European Commission;
- the European Parliament;
- the European Court of Justice.

The Council of Ministers

The Council of Ministers is made up of ministers who represent each of the EU member states. The Council of Ministers makes the final legal decisions on important issues based, mainly, on proposals from the European Commission.

The presidency of the EU rotates every six months, in alphabetical order of country. The country that holds the EU presidency also presides over the Council of Ministers for that period.

The European Commission

The European Commission is the institution that initiates new EU policies and laws. Members of the European Commission (commissioners) are nominated for a five-year term of office by each member-state. The European Commission is based in Brussels. The duties of the European Commission include administering EU funds and investigating complaints of breaches of EU laws by member states.

The European Parliament

The European Parliament is composed of publicly elected members (MEPs) from each member state. Elections are held every five years.

The European Parliament can, in some circumstances, both recommend and decide on legislation in certain areas. The European Parliament is based in Strasbourg.

The European Court of Justice

The European Court of Justice (ECJ) is composed of judges and Advocates-General, who are appointed by member states' governments. Broadly, the ECJ oversees and enforces EU law. It is based in Luxembourg.

Individuals who want, for example, to challenge EU legislation or to force a member state to implement EU legislation cannot take a case directly to the ECJ. These types of cases must be taken through the domestic legal system of the member state concerned and the relevant domestic court will, if necessary, refer the case to the ECJ.

The European Ombudsman

The European Ombudsman can investigate maladministration in the activities of the European community institutions and bodies.

Examples of the problems that can be investigated by the European Ombudsman include administrative delay, refusal of information, discrimination and abuse of power.

How EU law relates to UK law

Under UK law, Acts of Parliament are not challengeable unless they conflict with European law.

The European Convention on Human Rights is one aspect of European law that relates to UK law. As well as treaties there are several ways in which European law is made:

- regulations;
- directives;
- European Court of Justice case law.

A *regulation* takes precedence over any member state's domestic law that is inconsistent with it.

A *directive* sets a goal that must be reached by a certain date.

Who can help?

The **Office of the European Commission:**
in Brussels: 0032 2 235 1111
in the UK: 020 7973 1992
in Wales: 029 2089 5020
The **European Parliament Information Office** (020 7227 4300).
Europe Direct (freephone hotline: 00800 6789 1011;
www.europa.eu.int/europedirect) provides information and advice about citizens' rights in the European Union, for example to work, live or study in another country of the EU. People can order guides and detailed fact sheets covering particular topics by ringing the freephone hotline number or sending an e-mail through the website (see above).
There are twenty-six **Euro Info Centres** in the UK. They are sometimes called European Business Information Centres. They are usually based in existing organizations that have links with the business community. Their function is to provide EU information likely to be of value to small and medium-sized businesses. For the address of the nearest Euro Info Centre, people should contact their local Chamber of Commerce, or check the website of the National Euro Info Centre Network (www.euro-info.org.uk).
The **European Documentation Centres** hold a substantial collection of the publicly available documentation of the EU. There are forty-four

European Documentation Centres in the UK, based mainly in university libraries. Some of them provide an information service and some will provide photocopies of, for example, relevant directives and regulations. They cannot offer legal advice. Contact details of the European Documentation Centres in the UK can be found on the website of the European Union (www.europa.eu.int/comm/libraries/edc/indexen.htm).

There are **European Consumer Centres** throughout most of the EU member states. They can provide information and advice on EU consumer issues and help if you have purchased goods or services from another EU member state. To contact the UK ECC visit their website (www.euroconsumer.org.uk).

The **European Extra-Judicial Network** (EEJ-Net) is a European Union project that helps resolve complaints about goods and services bought from traders in other EU countries. EEJ-Net does this through alternative dispute resolution (ADR). ADR means trying a different way of resolving a dispute without going to court.

If you cannot resolve a dispute with a trader, you can get advice and help from the network of European Consumer centres. If negotiation fails, you may be able to refer the complaint to a suitable ADR organization in the trader's own country.

You can find information about EU-approved ADR organizations in the UK on the ECC and EEJ-Net website for the UK (www.euroconsumer.org.uk).

Citizens Advice Bureaux can advise on a wide range of issues and hold information about situations where European law has an effect on UK law. You can find the address and telephone number of your local CAB in the telephone directory, or on the Citizens Advice website (www.citizensadvice.org.uk).

THE SMALL CLAIMS PROCEDURE

You can start a civil legal action in the county court or in the High Court depending on the circumstances of the case. If the claim is for £15,000 or less, it must be started in the county court. If the case is a simple one, the county court will decide to use the small claims procedure and will allocate the case to the 'small claims track'.

You can use the small claims procedure for claims of £5,000 or less (£1,000 or less for personal injury) against a person or company. It is an informal way of settling a dispute without using a solicitor and the level of costs that you will have to pay is limited.

The most common types of claim in the small claims track are:

- compensation for faulty services provided by, for example, builders, dry-cleaners or garages;
- compensation for faulty goods, like televisions or washing machines that go wrong;
- disputes between landlords and tenants – for example rent arrears or compensation for not doing repairs;
- wages owed or money in lieu of notice.

Can I claim money I am owed by taking a case to court?

If your case is a simple one and the amount owed to you is less than £5,000, then the court will probably allocate the claim to the small claims track if it is defended. The most common claims are for compensation for faulty services, compensation for faulty goods and disputes with employers for wages due or for money in lieu of notice. These are just examples and the small claims track can be used for other claims too.

Although you may be able to get help to prepare your case through the legal help scheme you will not be able to get legal help for representation. If the case is considered to be complex, the judge may decide to use a different procedure that means there can be a full hearing. You must have tried to settle your claim before taking court action, for example by writing to the person who owes you money. You must have also given them time to respond. You need to keep a copy of all correspondence.

You can start a claim by filling in a claim form and taking two copies to the court. You keep a third copy for yourself. You also pay the court fee at this time. You can make applications online in some cases.

The hearing will usually be informal and you and the other party will have a chance to give your reasons for starting the claim and why it is disputed. At the end of the hearing the judge will give the judgment. If you win, you get your court fees back. You can appeal against the judgment but you have only fourteen days to do so.

If a case is complex, the judge may refer it to another track, even if it is below the financial limit of that track.

Costs

If you are using the small claims procedure, the costs you may have to pay include:

- **court fees.** You have to pay a fee when starting your claim (the amount will depend on how much you are claiming), and further fees if the other person (the defendant) defends the case. If you win, these fees will be added to the amount the defendant has to pay. If you are in receipt of Income Support and some other benefits, you will be exempt from payment of the fee. If you are on a low income you can ask the court to consider whether the fees can be waived.
- **witness costs.** If your case is defended and you use witnesses, you may have to pay their travelling expenses and a fixed amount towards the cost of any lost earnings.
- **expert's fees and expenses** – if you need an expert's report to support your case; *and*
- **additional travel costs** – if the case is for a fixed amount of money, the defendant is an individual who defends your claim and the case is transferred to their local court.

If you win, the court may order the defendant to pay all or part of these costs. You may also be able to claim some other costs, such as a limited amount of compensation to cover you for such things as time lost at work and the cost of telephone calls, but you are unlikely to recover all you have paid out.

You should try and take proof of any losses to the court with you. If you lose, you will have to pay the defendant's costs, including travelling expenses and an amount towards any lost earnings.

In most cases, the court will not order solicitors' costs to be paid by the losing party in a small claims case, and if you instruct a solicitor you will have to pay the costs yourself. For this reason most claimants deal with a small claim without the help of a solicitor. It is possible to have the help of a friend or 'lay representative', for example, some Citizens Advice Bureaux can offer trained advisers to help people with small claims. It may be possible to get legal advice (not representation) from a solicitor under the legal help scheme. If your claim is for £5,000 or less (£1,000 or less for personal injury), you will be unable to claim any of your own solicitor's costs from the other side, except a fixed amount to cover the cost of issuing your claim, if you are successful. If you lose, you will not have to pay the defendant's solicitor's costs. If you are unsure about speaking in court and your case is defended, you can ask a relative, a friend or an advice worker to speak on your behalf as your lay representative.

Using the small claims procedure

How to start a small claim

Before you make a claim, you must write to the individual or company with whom you are in dispute, giving them a specific time, such as fourteen days, to put the situation right and stating that, failing this, you will take court action. This is called a '*letter before action*' and should be sent by recorded delivery. If you do not try to settle the case first, the court may penalize you later.

Completing the claim form

You start a claim by filling in a claim form (N1 form). Claim forms are available from local courts, legal stationers, and online (from www.courtservice.gov.uk). Claims for a fixed amount of money can also be issued online (at www.courtservice.gov.uk/mcol). Usually claims will be issued, printed and sent to the defendant on the day the claim is submitted. Court fees for online claims must be paid by credit or debit card.

You will need to give the following information:

- your name and address;
- the name(s) and address(es) of the other party you are suing. If you are suing a limited company, you will have to say whether you are giving its registered office address. If you are suing the owners or partners of a business you will need to add 'trading as' and give their business name after their names. If you are suing a firm you should add 'sued as a firm' after the name of the firm.
- brief details of the claim such as 'return of money for faulty goods' or 'compensation for breach of contract'.
- value, which is the amount you are claiming. The court fee you pay will be based on this amount. You can either put the exact figure you are claiming – for example, if you are claiming back the cost of a faulty item (a 'specified amount') – or you can leave it to the court to assess damages – for example, if you are claiming compensation for a disappointing holiday (an 'unspecified amount'). If you are leaving the court to decide the exact amount, you should

state on the court form 'I expect to recover not more than £. . .'. This amount should not exceed £5,000 if you wish the matter to be allocated to the small claims track.

- particulars of claim. This section explains what the problem is and the steps you have taken to try to solve the problem. You can either complete this section of the form or send your particulars of claim separately within 14 days of sending the form; *and*

- interest. Unless your contract imposes the percentage of interest to be paid by parties in dispute, you should claim interest at the statutory rate of interest. Check with the court for the most up-to-date figure.

- the interest up to the date of issue of the claim form if you are claiming a specified amount. You should use this formula to calculate the interest:
  Step 1 0.00022 x the amount you are claiming = (this is the daily rate of interest).
  Step 2 Multiply the result of step one by the number of days since the contract was breached.

  You must put the following wording on the claim form at the end of your particulars of claim *'The claimant claims interest under section 69 of the County Courts Act 1984 at the rate of x% per year from* [date when the money became owed to you] *to* [the date you are issuing the claim] *of £. . .* [amount from step 2] *and also interest at the same rate up to the date of judgment or earlier payment at a daily rate of £. . .* [amount from step 1].

- if you are claiming an unspecified amount, you do not need to calculate the interest, but should include this wording after your particulars of claim *'The claimant claims interest under section 69 of the County Courts Act 1984 at the rate of x% per annum and continuing at the same rate up the date of judgment or earlier payment.*

- statement of truth. You will have to sign a statement of truth confirming that the facts in your claim are true.

If you need help in completing the form, your local CAB or Trading Standards Department may be able to help. Although court officers can help you to complete your claim form, they cannot give you legal advice, such as whether you have a good claim or who you should be claiming from.

Serving the claim

You may find it easier to return your completed forms (including photocopies) to the court in person, as a court officer will go through the form and may point out any irregularities. You will be asked to pay a fee for starting proceedings. This will be based on the amount you are claiming.

When you issue proceedings you will be given a notice of issue (N205), giving your case number, which you should use whenever you contact the court. The court will post the claim form to the defendant(s) – called 'serving the claim form' – and will inform you when it is served. If it is returned undelivered, you will be informed and must take responsibility for serving it.

What happens next?

The defendant will have a limited time in which to reply to your claim. This is usually fourteen days after the date the claim form was served (sixteen days after it was posted), but can be extended by a further fourteen days if the defendant serves an acknowledgement of service stating that he intends to defend the case.

If the defendant doesn't reply

You can either:

- complete form N225 asking the court for judgment by default (if you started your claim online, you can use an online request form for this at www.court-service.gov.uk/mcol). Obtaining judgment by default means the court will order the defendant to pay you the full amount you have claimed because no reply has been received. You should do this as soon as the court will allow you to do so, as the court will accept the filing of a late defence if this is received before you file your request for judgment in default. You will have to complete a section stating how you want the defendant(s) to pay and will need to take their circumstances into account. You may have a better chance of being repaid if you accept payment by instalments rather than asking for the full amount immediately. *Or*

- complete the bottom of form N205B (which you were given when returning your claim form), asking the court to make an order that the defendant is liable (responsible) for your claim. This is called entering judgment for an amount to be decided by the court. Your claim will be referred to a judge, who will decide whether a court hearing is necessary and if any further evidence is required (giving directions). Both you and the defendant will be sent a copy of the judge's decision (order) and any other directions the judge has given. Your claim will either be allocated to the small claims track or given a disposal hearing. A disposal hearing is a court hearing where the judge gives more detailed instructions about the case or decides how much the defendant must pay.

If the defendant is not defending the case

If you are the defendant and you are not defending the case, you may accept that you owe the money claimed. If so, and you can pay the money immediately, you should send it to the claimant directly.

If you accept that you owe the money but you need time to pay, you can propose, for example, that you pay the money in instalments or all the money in one lump sum at a specified future date. If the claimant accepts this offer, they will have to return a form to court requesting 'judgment on admission'. As the defendant, if you do not keep to the arrangement, the claimant can take enforcement action.

As the claimant, if you do not accept the offer, you must give your reasons and a court official will decide what a reasonable arrangement should be. The court will send both parties an order for payment ('judgment for claimant after determination'). As the claimant, if you are not happy with the order, you should write to the court giving your reasons and you must send a copy of the letter to the defendant. A judge will then decide what is reasonable for the defendant to pay. If the defendant does not keep to the arrangement, the claimant can take enforcement action.

If the defendant is defending the case

If you are the defendant and you are defending the case, you have to respond to the claim form and the particulars of claim within fourteen days of the date of service (this is the second day after posting). If the particulars of claim were served after the claim form, you must respond within fourteen days of the date of service of the particulars of claim. You must respond by filling in the defence form that was sent to you with the claim form.

You can send your defence to the court. However, if you need more time to prepare a defence, you can send back an acknowledgement of service and then the defence within fourteen days (the acknowledgement of service would be sent to you initially with the claim form).

When the defence is returned to the court, the court will send an allocation questionnaire to both the claimant and the defendant. This must be returned no later than the date specified on it. As the claimant, when you return the allocation questionnaire you have to pay a fee, although this may be waived on financial grounds. The court will use the information given on the allocation questionnaire to decide which track the case will be allocated to.

The notice of allocation

When the court has decided to allocate the case to the small claims track, the parties will be sent a notice of allocation. This form will tell the parties what they have to do to prepare for the final hearing. These instructions are called 'directions'. For example, the parties may be told to send copies of all the documents they intend to use to the court and to the other party at least fourteen days before the hearing is due to take place.

There are standard directions for a number of common cases; for example, if the claim is to do with a holiday, there are standard directions about the documents that have to be sent to the other party. If the claimant wants to show a video as evidence in a holiday claim, they have to contact the court to make the arrangements for the video to be shown at the hearing.

The hearing date

The notice of allocation will usually specify the time, date and place where the hearing will take place and how much time has been allowed for it.

If you are the claimant and want to attend the hearing but cannot, you can write to the court and apply for a later date to be set. A fee is payable for this application and the court will agree only if there are good reasons.

If you are the claimant and do not wish to attend the court hearing, for example because the travel costs of getting to the hearing are higher than your claim merits, you can write to the court to ask it to deal with the claim in your absence. The letter must arrive at court no later than seven days before the hearing date, and a copy must be sent to the defendant. The letter will ensure that the judge takes into account any written evidence that you have sent to the court and the defendant.

Sometimes the court will not set a final hearing date at the allocation stage. It could instead:

- propose that the claim is dealt with without a hearing. If the parties do not object, the case will be decided on the papers only. If the parties do not reply by the date given, the judge may treat the lack of reply as consent.
- hold a preliminary hearing. This could happen if the claim requires special directions that the judge wants to explain to the parties personally, or where the judge feels that the claimant (or the defendant) has no real prospect of succeeding and wants to sort out the claim as soon as possible to save everyone time and expense, or if the papers do not show any reasonable grounds for bringing the claim. A preliminary hearing, therefore, could become a final hearing where the matter is decided once and for all.

Preparing the case

It is important to prepare the case carefully – the court has to be convinced. The following points are a general guide to what preparation should be made. But if you are not confident about how to present your case, you should consider taking someone else along to help, or getting specialist advice first. The main points are:

- if you have a low income you can use the legal help scheme to cover the cost of legal advice (but not representation) from a solicitor. This advice can include getting expert reports, for example on faulty goods (but a report may be used in court only with the permission of the court);
- notes about the case should be set out in date order. It is very useful to note down what your case is, for example the points to make, the documents that are relevant, and what they prove. A list of all documents and other evidence is useful to make sure nothing is forgotten.
- damaged or faulty goods should be taken as evidence, if possible – for instance, clothes ruined by a washing machine, shoes, etc. If this is not possible, photographs could be used instead.
- evidence of expenses should be prepared and any receipts taken along;
- all letters (and any other relevant documents, including photographs) about the case should be ready for the hearing;
- in most cases the claimant and the defendant will be the only witnesses. If the court has agreed that other witnesses can attend, they must attend. If a witness has difficulty getting time off work, it may be helpful to serve a witness summons. The court can explain how to do this.

The final hearing

The final hearing is usually held in public but it could be held in private if the parties agree, or if the court believes it necessary in the interests of justice. Hearings in the small claims track are relatively informal and strict rules of evidence do not apply. The judge can adopt any method of dealing with the hearing that they consider to be fair, and they may ask questions of the witnesses before allowing anyone else to do so. The judge may limit the time that parties or witnesses have to give evidence.

A lay representative has the right to speak on behalf of a party at the final hearing, but only if that party attends the hearing.

If you do not speak English as your first language, you might find it helpful to have an interpreter help you to put your case. The court will not be able to assist in finding an interpreter. Your local Citizens Advice Bureau will often hold a list of interpreters, if you need help with finding one.

After the hearing, the judge will give the judgment. The judge has to give reasons for their judgment. The reasons must be given as simply and briefly as possible, and usually will be given orally to the parties present at the hearing. However, the judge may give them later either in writing or at a later hearing.

If you are the claimant and you win your case, you will get the court fees back as well as the amount of the claim, and you can ask for certain expenses also. If you lose, you will not get the court fees back. But it is unlikely that you will have to pay any other costs.

Appeals

You may appeal against a judgment in the small claims track only if the court made a mistake in law or there was a serious irregularity in the proceedings. If you want to appeal, you must file a notice of appeal within 14 days. A fee is payable although this could be waived in cases of financial hardship.

If you want to appeal against a decision in the small claims track, you should consult a solicitor or an experienced adviser.

Enforcement of court orders

As the defendant, if you lose the case and you do not pay the claimant will have to go back to the same court to apply for an order to get the money. This is called enforcing the judgment. As the claimant, you will have to pay a fee to start enforcement proceedings.

SOLICITORS

It is worth remembering that solicitors are not the only people who can provide legal advice. Legal help may be available from:

- other professionals – for example, an accountant who can give advice on tax and company law;
- advice centres, such as the Citizens Advice Bureaux, housing advice centres, money advice centres and law centres;
- other organizations, such as trade unions and motoring organizations.

You may also act for yourself in court proceedings or, if you are acting for yourself, you may have a friend or lay representative to assist you in court. So before paying out for a solicitor – sometimes fees can be hefty – it is worth considering whether there is anyone else who can help.

Choosing a solicitor

If you decide that you do need a solicitor, you should choose one who has experience in the appropriate area of law.

A local advice agency, such as a law centre or Citizens Advice Bureau, should be able to recommend local solicitors who are experienced in the appropriate area of law or will be able to provide information on how to find a suitable solicitor. In some cases, a CAB can refer you to an organization that can offer free legal help. You can also get details of solicitors from the Community Legal Service Directory (www.clsdirect.org.uk). If you are at a police station, or have been charged with a serious offence, you can obtain free legal advice under the duty solicitors' scheme. If you are at the police station, the police will contact the duty solicitor. If you are at the magistrates' or youth court, the arrangements for providing the solicitor will vary.

When you have chosen your solicitor, you will need to make an appointment. This will usually be within five working days. If the matter is urgent, the solicitor should try and arrange an earlier appointment.

You should take all relevant documents to the appointment and it may be helpful to prepare a list of questions for the solicitor in advance.

A solicitor must comply with certain rules and standards laid down by the Law Society. The solicitor must, for example, give you certain information at the first interview. The information should include:

- how the solicitor intends to deal with the problem;
- what the solicitor's next step will be;
- information about costs, which must be confirmed in writing as soon as possible after the interview;
- whether you will be eligible for publicly funded legal services or criminal legal aid;
- the expected timescale of the case;
- whether the solicitor has a relationship with another company that could affect the steps taken in relation to your case.

The Law Society has also produced a document called 'The Client's Charter', which tells you what you can expect from your solicitor and what to do if you want to make a complaint.

You should make sure you understand what the solicitor has told you, and don't be afraid to ask questions.

During the case, the solicitor should keep you regularly informed of progress and costs, even if there are no significant developments. Remember that each contact you have with the solicitor will increase your costs.

Solicitors' costs and bills

At the beginning of the case, the solicitor must give you information about the likely cost of the case and how the charge is calculated – for example, a fixed fee, an hourly rate or a percentage fee.

In some cases, for example personal injury cases, you may enter into a conditional fee agreement with the solicitor. This means that if you lose the case, you will have to pay the costs of the other side and, depending on the agreement, the solicitor's expenses and any barristers' fees. If you win the case, you will have to pay the solicitor's fee at a higher rate. If you are considering entering into a conditional fee agreement, you must be clear what the terms of the agreement will entail and should consider consulting an experienced adviser to discuss the implications.

In all cases, the solicitor must discuss how the costs are to be met and whether you are eligible for publicly funded legal services. If the solicitor does not do publicly funded legal services work, they must still explain the advantages of publicly funded legal services to you if you are eligible, and give you the opportunity of going to a solicitor who does publicly funded legal services work.

The solicitor must keep you informed about the costs throughout the case.

If the solicitor is holding your money, it must be kept in a separate deposit account and you may be entitled to interest.

You should get your bill within a reasonable time after your solicitor has finished the work they have done for you, and it will be made up of three elements: disbursements, fees and VAT. Disbursements are the expenses the solicitor has had to pay out on your behalf – for example, fees paid to court and barristers' fees.

Fees cover the professional services carried out by the solicitor on your behalf. If the work was court work, the fees that the solicitor can charge are subject to court rules. There are no scales that regulate non-court work, but the charges must be fair and reasonable. VAT will be charged on the fees and some disbursements.

If you think the bill is too high

You can:

- ask the solicitor for a detailed account;
- in some cases, ask the Law Society to look at the bill;
- ask a court to look at the bill.

Getting a detailed bill from the solicitor

You can write to the solicitor asking for full details of how some or all of the charges on the bill were worked out. This letter should also include a request for a written reply. Items such as stamp duty for buying a house are fixed amounts and cannot be questioned.

Asking the Law Society to look at the bill

This procedure only applies to work that does not include court work. You can, within one month of receiving the bill, ask the solicitor to obtain a remuneration certificate that approves it or reduces it. There is no charge. You must pay half the bill and VAT and disbursements before applying for a remuneration certificate. Disbursements cannot be questioned. There is a time limit for applying for the remuneration certificate. It is usually one month but may be longer in some circumstances. The solicitor may also agree to waive the time limit. You should check the relevant time limits with the Consumer Complaints Service (0845 6086565), part of the Remuneration Certificate Department of the Law Society that deals with applications and queries.

Asking a court to examine the bill

This procedure can be used for any work done by a solicitor, including court work, and is known as assessment.

The court can examine the whole bill, and can either approve it or reduce it. If the reduction is more than one-fifth, you will not pay the costs of assessment. Some publicly funded legal services may be available.

For non-court work, the court that assesses the bill is the High Court in London. Where court work is involved, the bill will be assessed by the court that dealt with the case. In publicly funded legal services cases, bills may be assessed by the Legal Services Commission.

If you ask for assessment within one month of getting the bill, the court must assess it. Between one month and a year, the court decides whether to agree to assessment of the bill; after a year it is very unusual for the court to agree.

The court cannot agree to assess the bill if it has been paid and more than one year has gone by.

You can ask the court to examine the bill even if you have signed a conditional fee agreement.

If you have problems paying a solicitor's bill, the solicitor might insist on immediate payment. They could also charge interest on bills for non-court work after a month. However, they may agree to let you pay your bill in instalments.

An experienced adviser's help will usually be needed to assess whether you should challenge a solicitor's bill.

Complaints about solicitors

You may be dissatisfied with your solicitor for a number of reasons, for example you may have problems with publicly funded legal services or you may be dissatisfied with the outcome of the case. You cannot complain about these things to your solicitor. However, if you are dissatisfied with the way the case was handled by the solicitor – for example, delays, or losing documents or money – you can complain.

You should first try to resolve the complaint by discussing it with the solicitor. All solicitors' firms must have a written complaints procedure and the firm will tell you who to contact if you have a problem with the solicitor handling the case. The solicitor must give you a copy of the complaints procedure if you ask for it.

If this does not resolve the matter, you should contact the **Consumer Complaints Service** (CCS helpline: 0845 608 6565), which can advise you about whether there are grounds for a complaint and, if so, how to proceed. You will need to contact the CCS within six months of the end of the work that your solicitor did for you, or within six months of your solicitor's final response to your complaint.

If you wish to proceed with the complaint, you should fill in a special form available from the CCS (01926 820082; www.lawsociety.org.uk). The CCS will consider the complaint and, if appropriate, pass it on to a different section of the Law Society that could discipline the solicitor and/or order the solicitor to:

• refund money that has been paid;

- correct any mistakes or take any other necessary action at their own expense;
- pay compensation to you up to £5,000.

I need a solicitor but I don't have much money. What can I do?

Solicitors are not the only people who can provide legal advice. Legal help may be available from other professionals, for example an accountant who can give advice on tax and company law. Legal help can be obtained from advice centres, such as Citizens Advice Bureaux, housing advice centres, money advice centres or law centres and from other organizations such as trade unions and motoring organizations. You can also represent yourself in court proceedings and you may have a friend or a representative who is not a solicitor to assist you in court. If you think that you need a solicitor, you should choose one who has experience in the appropriate area of law. For example, if you are seeking custody of children you should go to a family law specialist. If you need help with legal costs you may be able to get some through the legal help scheme. This scheme helps people on a low income to get free legal advice on any legal problems, writing letters, negotiation, getting a barrister's opinion and preparing a written case for tribunal. The scheme will not pay for you to be represented by a solicitor in court although there are other schemes that may help in limited circumstances.

If you think you qualify for the legal help scheme, you will need to see a solicitor, or an organization with a contract to provide legal help under the legal help scheme, for example a Citizens Advice Bureau or law centre. You will be asked to fill in an application form at the start of the interview to check whether you qualify.

There are other ways of obtaining legal help at a lower cost. These include fixed-fee interviews with solicitors. Trade unions can help with employment problems and motoring organizations can help with many issues from buying a car to insurance.

If you are at a police station, or have been charged with an imprisonable offence, you can get free legal advice under the duty solicitors' scheme.

More details about the CCS are contained in a leaflet called *What to do if you are dissatisfied with your solicitor* available from the CCS (01926 820082; www.lawsociety.org.uk).

If the solicitor has made a mistake that has caused you financial loss of more than £5,000, the CCS cannot deal with the case and you may need to take legal action against the solicitor. You will certainly need to obtain legal advice, and remember that publicly funded legal services may be available.

If you are not satisfied with the way that the CCS has handled your complaint, you may also be able to complain to the Legal Services Ombudsman (see *Civil Rights*, p. 457).

HELP WITH LEGAL COSTS

If you need help with legal costs you may be able to receive some help through publicly funded legal services organized through the Legal Services Commission (LSC). Publicly funded legal services are provided in a number of different ways:

- the legal help scheme;
- the help at court scheme;
- the controlled legal representation scheme;
- publicly funded legal representation.

The legal help scheme

The legal help scheme allows people with a low income to get free legal advice and assistance from a solicitor or other organization. The solicitor or organization has to have a contract with the Legal Services Commission (LSC) to be able to provide legal help under this scheme.

What sort of help does the scheme cover?

The legal help scheme covers help from a solicitor including general advice on any legal problems, writing letters, negotiating, getting a barrister's opinion and preparing a written case for a tribunal.

The scheme will not pay for representation by a solicitor in court or at a tribunal (although the help at court scheme, the controlled legal representation scheme or publicly funded legal representation might). The scheme may cover the costs of mediation. Mediation is a process of negotiation where the parties are helped by a neutral mediator who assists them to find a mutually acceptable resolution.

Legal problems covered by the scheme

The legal help scheme covers advice on general legal problems, including the following:

- maintenance or disputes over children and undefended divorce;
- conveyancing necessary to carry out a court order or following a divorce settlement or legal separation;
- contested adoptions;
- preparing for tribunals, for example employment tribunals (for unfair dismissal) or unified appeal tribunals (for benefits appeals), but not representation at the tribunal itself;
- making a will if you are 70 or over or disabled, or a parent making provision for a disabled child, or you are a single parent appointing a guardian;
- medical negligence cases or cases where personal injury arises from an assault or deliberate abuse.

For the case to qualify for the legal help scheme, there are two criteria that must always be met:

- help will be provided only where it can be shown there is a benefit to you;
- help will be provided only if it is reasonable for the matter to be funded.

In addition to these criteria, there may be other criteria applied, depending on the nature of the case. For example, if the case is about possession of your home, legal help will be refused if the prospects of avoiding possession are poor.

How much work is covered by the scheme?

The amount of help available under the legal help scheme is limited. There is a maximum amount of help available in all areas of law, except for immigration cases where the maximum varies. The maximum amount includes expenses. The solicitor can apply for extra time to finish the work under the legal help scheme. This is known as an extension.

What are the financial conditions for the scheme?

If your gross monthly income (excluding some social security benefits) is over a certain amount you will not be eligible for the legal help scheme.

There is also a limit on the amount of capital that you can have and still be eligible for help under the legal help scheme.

If you are claiming Income Support, income-based Jobseeker's Allowance or the guarantee credit of Pension Credit, you will be considered to have an income within the limits to qualify for the legal help scheme.

If you are not receiving Income Support, income-based Jobseeker's Allowance or the guarantee credit of Pension Credit, eligibility will depend on disposable income. So, if you are receiving any other benefits, whether or not you are eligible for legal help will depend on your income.

Disposable income is the amount of income you have after deductions have been made for National Insurance, tax and dependants' allowances. A deduction will be made from your weekly income for any dependent partner or children living in the household.

If you have a partner, your partner's income and capital may also be taken into account, except where this is inappropriate – for example, where there is a conflict of interest between you and your partner.

More information

If you want more information on financial eligibility, there is an online interactive calculator (www.clsdirect.org.uk).

Extra costs you may have to pay

If you are awarded money or property as a result of advice or assistance under the legal help scheme in a family case, the solicitor's costs may be taken from the award and you will receive what is left. This deduction is called the statutory charge. If the solicitor or organization providing legal help believes it would cause grave hardship or distress to you if they deducted the charge, they need not deduct it. The statutory charge will also not be deducted if the solicitor or organization believes it would be too difficult to enforce the deduction.

If the statutory charge has to be paid, payment can be postponed if the charge relates to your home or the home of your dependants. The statutory charge can also be postponed where it is to be paid out of money that is to be used to buy a home for yourself or your dependants. Your solicitor will give you more information about the statutory charge before you go ahead with a case.

How to apply

If you qualify for the legal help scheme, you will need to see a solicitor, or organization with a contract to provide legal help under the legal help scheme. The solicitor will ask you to fill in an application form at the start of the interview. The solicitor will then be able to decide whether you qualify.

The help at court scheme

In some cases, a solicitor or representative at court will be paid for by the LSC. These cases are those where there is no real defence but where you need help to present issues to the court. Examples of cases where help at court could be given include:

- a debt case where the only issue is when and how the debt is to be paid;
- where there is a dispute about the amount of rent or mortgage and the lender or landlord has taken legal action to repossess the property.

As well as meeting the financial eligibility criteria (which are the same as for the legal help scheme), you must meet the other criteria of the legal help scheme and, in addition, the solicitor or adviser must think it is appropriate and of benefit to you to attend the hearing rather than simply writing a letter on your behalf.

Controlled legal representation scheme

The controlled legal representation scheme means that free representation can be given if you are appearing before certain tribunals. The same financial limits apply as for the legal help scheme and the same criteria for the type of legal help covered.

Publicly funded legal representation

Publicly funded legal representation provides publicly funded legal services for all the work leading up to and including representation by a solicitor or barrister in civil court proceedings.

The granting of publicly funded legal representation is subject to your having income and capital within specified limits.

Being granted publicly funded legal representation also depends on whether your case meets the criteria applicable to the type of case and the form of publicly funded legal representation you are applying for. This includes the LSC considering it reasonable to fund the case.

There are different forms of publicly funded legal representation and the type of help required will depend on the type of case and the work required to help resolve the case.

If you want more information about the different types of publicly funded legal representation you should contact your local CAB.

Which courts are covered by publicly funded legal representation?

The most common courts that are covered are:

- county courts (except cases allocated to the small claims track);
- magistrates' courts – for civil proceedings such as matrimonial cases;
- the High Court and Court of Appeal;
- appeals to the House of Lords.

Publicly funded legal representation does not cover representation at a coroner's court or at most tribunals except for:

- the Employment Appeal Tribunal;
- Lands Tribunals.

Which cases are covered by publicly funded legal representation?

Examples of cases covered by publicly funded legal representation:

- housing – including eviction, repairs and rent arrears;
- debts – to recover debts by going to court;
- consumer problems – compensation for faulty goods or services;
- dismissal – the preparation of a case before the Employment Tribunal, but not representation at the Employment Tribunal itself;
- appeals to the High Court from tribunals such as the Social Security Commissioners;
- personal injury cases are not generally covered by publicly funded legal representation because if you wish to take such a case you are expected to enter into a conditional fee agreement with a solicitor. However, if the overall costs are expected to be unusually high, some publicly funded legal representation may be available.

Publicly funded legal representation may cover the costs of mediation as well as those of court proceedings. Mediation is a process of negotiation where the parties are helped by a neutral mediator who assists them in finding a mutually acceptable resolution on major disputes. For the purpose of publicly funded legal representation, the term 'mediation' covers both commercial mediation and community mediation or conciliation. Work in relation to mediation will be paid for only if it is considered to be reasonable. Some family cases will be considered more suitable for family mediation through publicly funded legal representation rather than publicly funded legal representation being made available for court proceedings.

How to qualify for publicly funded legal representation

The LSC must agree that you have a reasonable case and that the case meets the criteria applicable to it, and the form of publicly funded legal representation applied for. In addition, your income and capital must be below certain limits.

What are the financial conditions?

If you are getting benefits

If you are on Income Support, the guarantee credit of Pension Credit or income-based Jobseeker's Allowance, you will qualify for free publicly funded legal representation. If you are not getting one of these benefits, you have to meet capital and income conditions.

Capital

You will qualify for free publicly funded legal representation if you have capital of under a certain limit and also meet income conditions. If you have capital over the limit, you will not be able to get publicly funded legal representation. If you have a partner, your partner's capital will also be taken into account unless there is a conflict of interest between the two of you.

Income

If your gross monthly income is over a certain amount , you will not qualify for publicly funded legal representation. Disposable income is the amount that you have after deductions have been made for National Insurance, tax, rent, certain other necessary expenses and allowances for dependants. If you have a partner, your partner's income will also be taken into account except where this is inappropriate, for example where there is a conflict of interest between the two of you.

If you want more information on financial eligibility, there is an online interactive calculator (www.clsdirect.org.uk).

Extra costs you may have to pay

If you are awarded money or property as a result of work carried out through publicly funded legal representation, your solicitor's costs – the statutory charge – may be taken from the award and you will receive what is left. In some cases, for example if the money is for maintenance, the statutory charge will not be taken from the award.

Payment of the statutory charge can be postponed if it relates to your home or the home of your dependants. The statutory charge can also be postponed where it is to be paid out of money that is to be used to buy a home for yourself or your dependants. Your solicitor must give you more information about the statutory charge before you go ahead with your case.

If you receive publicly funded legal representation and you lose the case, you may be ordered to pay the legal costs of the other side if the court considers this would be reasonable.

How to apply

You should apply through a solicitor who does publicly funded legal representation work. The solicitor will ask you to fill out an application form, which includes details of your income and capital. The solicitor will then send the form to the LSC, which will assess your financial eligibility for publicly funded legal representation.

If publicly funded legal representation is granted but you are also required to pay a contribution, the contributions must be paid monthly, for as long as the case lasts.

Legal aid for criminal proceedings

For cases involving criminal proceedings you may be eligible for help through legal aid. This could cover the cost of representation by solicitors or barristers, and of bail applications. Getting criminal legal aid depends mainly on whether it is 'in the interests of justice' that you are legally represented.

Criminal legal aid does not cover you if you bring a criminal prosecution yourself.

Criminal legal aid is usually granted in the following cases:

- if you are likely to go to prison if convicted;
- if you are likely to lose your job if convicted;
- if you cannot follow what is happening in the trial because of mental or physical disability or language problems;
- where children are involved in care proceedings, an application for a contact order (if they are the subject of a care order), or adoption proceedings in the magistrates' courts;
- to children or their parents, if a child is charged with or convicted of a criminal offence;
- for appeals against criminal court decisions;
- for contempt-of-court proceedings.

Minor offences such as motoring offences are not usually eligible for criminal legal aid.

How to apply

You can obtain forms from the court dealing with the case. These should be returned to the court, which will decide whether to grant criminal legal aid. For more information, there is a leaflet called 'A practical guide to Criminal Defence Services' (available at www.legalservices.gov.uk/leaflets/lsc/index.htm).

Other sources of legal help

Depending on the nature of the matter, you may be able to get legal help from other sources. Some of these are listed below.

Fixed-fee interview

Some solicitors may give up to half an hour's legal advice for a fixed fee. Some schemes may offer free advice. This can be useful if you want to get an idea of whether you have a case that is worth defending or pursuing.

The fixed-fee interview scheme does not depend on your income or savings: the charge will be the same for everyone.

Your local CAB will refer you to solicitors who can offer this service.

Trade unions

Trade unions may provide free legal representation for work-related problems, including travel to or from work. Free union representation may be better for you than publicly funded legal services. This is because you will not have to make a financial contribution and the union will also be used to dealing with your sort of case.

Motoring organizations
Motoring organizations may offer a cheap or free legal advisory service if you are a member.

Legal expenses insurance
Some insurance companies offer policies that cover the expenses of certain legal matters – for example, consumer disputes, personal injuries, employment problems and motoring offences. It is important for you to consider carefully what the policy offers. Many policies will exclude certain kinds of legal expenses – of, for example, matrimonial disputes – or may not meet the total cost of claims that are covered.

Other organizations, like Which (08453 074000; www.which.net), offer a legal advisory service if you pay a subscription.

Law centres
In some areas, there are law centres that give free legal advice. The cases that they tend to specialize in are housing, employment, immigration, juvenile crime and welfare benefits. A law centre may take up a case where publicly funded legal services are not available, although some may also provide publicly funded legal services.

You can get the address of your local law centre from the Law Centres Federation (020 7387 8570; www.lawcentres.org.uk).

Solicitors' Pro Bono Group
The Solicitors' Pro Bono Group (www.probonouk.net) might be able to guide you in getting legal help.

Conditional fee agreements
In all civil non-family cases, you may enter into a conditional fee agreement with your solicitor. This means that if you lose the case, you will only have to pay the costs of the other side and, depending on the agreement, the solicitor's expenses, including any barristers' fees. If you win the case, you will pay your solicitor a higher fee. In certain cases, you can take out a special insurance policy that can cover your costs if you lose the case.

If you are considering entering into a conditional fee agreement, you must be clear what the terms of the agreement will entail and should consider consulting an experienced adviser to discuss the implications.

PERSONAL INJURY

A personal injury can include, for example, an injury at work or in a traffic accident, an injury received as a result of faulty goods or services, an injury sustained by tripping over paving stones, an injury caused by errors in hospital treatment or one sustained by a victim in the course of a crime. An injury can be physical, psychological or both.

If you have sustained a personal injury, you may want to make a complaint to the person or organization you believe was responsible for the injuries or claim for compensation to cover losses you have suffered as a result of the injury. You should consider whether there are any immediate financial problems arising because of the injury – for example if you are unable to work. You may want to contact an organization that could offer support or counselling.

Whatever you are intending to do about your personal injury, you may want to:

- inform the police if, for example, the injury resulted from a road accident (if the injury was caused by the police, you will need to consult an experienced adviser);
- report it to your insurance company, if the injury resulted from a road accident (remember that the policy may be invalid if the accident is not reported);
- notify your employer if the injury resulted from an accident at work. The accident must be recorded in the accident book. Your employer has a legal responsibility to report the accident to the Health and Safety Executive or the local authority environmental department and can be prosecuted if they fail to do so.
- report the injury to your doctor because it could become more serious. You should do this even if the injury seems minor. If you subsequently go to court to get compensation for the injury, the doctor will be asked to provide a medical report.
- gather evidence about the accident and injuries. It may be useful to take photographs of the scene of an accident and of what caused the injury. You should also, if possible, write an account of the incident while details are still fresh in your mind. If there are witnesses, you should make a note of their names and addresses.

Making a complaint

If you have had an accident or suffered an injury, you might be able to get an explanation of what went wrong and receive an apology. In some cases, there may be an official complaints procedure you can use.

Complaints procedures are often time-consuming and the final result will be no more than an apology. If you have suffered a personal injury and you also want compensation, you should be aware that there are time limits for taking legal action and going through a complaints procedure may delay matters.

If you decide that making a complaint will provide a sufficient remedy, you can complain to whoever caused the injury, for example:

- a government department;
- a local authority;
- your employer;
- the police;
- your school or other educational institution;
- your hospital or other National Health Service institution.

If you want more information about how to complain to these types of bodies you should seek specialist advice from an experienced adviser, like a CAB.

Compensation

There are four main ways of getting compensation for a personal injury:

- using a claims assessor;
- taking legal action in a civil court;
- making a claim to the Criminal Injuries Compensation Authority;
- through a criminal compensation order.

Amount of compensation

If you have sustained a personal injury you may be able to claim two types of compensation: general damages and special damages.

General damages are paid as compensation for an injury, for example a payment for pain and suffering or loss of future earnings. The court will decide on the amount to be paid.

Special damages are paid as compensation for actual financial loss caused by the accident up to the date of the hearing. These can include damage to clothing or other belongings, the costs of care, travel costs to hospital, medical expenses (including the cost of private treatment) and the cost of hiring or repairing a car if it has been damaged in the accident. If a court decides that you were partly to blame for the accident, it may reduce the amount of damages you receive. An example of this would be if you were not wearing a seat belt when you were involved in a traffic accident.

Deduction of social security benefits from compensation

If you have been receiving certain social security benefits because of an accident in which you sustained a personal injury, you may have to pay these back out of any compensation you get. The rules on this are complex and if you think you may be affected you might want to seek specialist advice.

Claims assessors

If you have sustained a personal injury you may be considering using the services of a claims assessor, sometimes known as a claims manager.

Claims assessors offer to take up cases on a 'no win, no fee' basis but there may be some disadvantages, including:

- a claims assessor will not usually be a solicitor and may not have a solicitor taking responsibility for the case. If this is so, the assessor will not be able to claim compensation through the courts and you may receive less compensation.
- the claims assessor may ask you to pay a percentage of whatever compensation you receive to the assessor. You should be aware that while paying 50 per cent of £1,000 damages may be acceptable to you, paying 50 per cent of £10,000 may not.

If you are considering using a claims assessor, you should first seek advice from an experienced adviser.

Taking legal action in a civil court

If you want to take legal action to claim compensation for a personal injury, you will need to get advice from a solicitor specializing in these types of case. This must be done as soon as possible as there are strict time limits on taking legal action.

The most common claim in a personal injury case is negligence and the time limit for this is three years. This means that court proceedings must be issued within three years of your first being aware that you have suffered an injury.

Paying for legal action

Legal action for compensation for a personal injury can be expensive. You may be able to get help with legal costs – see *Help with legal costs*, p. 488.

Conditional fee agreement

A conditional fee agreement means that if you win a case you must pay your solicitor's fees and expenses from the damages you receive. If you lose, you will not have to pay fees to your own solicitor but you may have to pay the other side's costs. Your solicitor will normally ask you to take out insurance to cover this.

Choosing a solicitor

If you want to take legal action over a personal injury you should consult a solicitor who is a member of the Law Society's personal injury panel or clinical negligence panel, depending on the nature of the injury. The Law Society (020 7242 1222; www.lawsociety.org.uk) can give details of solicitors on these panels.

Who can help?

The **Association of Personal Injury Lawyers** (0115 958 0585; www.apil.com) is an association of solicitors who are experienced in personal injuries work.

The **Motor Accident Solicitors Society** (0117 929 2560; www.mass.org.uk) is an association of solicitors experienced in dealing with personal injuries resulting from motor accidents. Participating solicitors provide a free initial consultation.

If you have sustained an injury as a result of a traffic accident and you are a member of a **motoring organization**, you may be able to get specialist legal advice through that organization.

If your injury resulted from an accident at work you should contact your **trade union** if you are a member. The union may instruct solicitors to pursue a claim on your behalf and you will not have to pay for this.

Criminal Injuries Compensation Authority

If you have been injured as a result of a criminal act, you may be able to claim compensation through the Criminal Injuries Compensation Authority (0141 331 2726/0800 358 3601; www.cica.gov.uk). You may have been the direct victim of, for example, an assault or your injury may have been sustained when you were attempting to help the police after a crime had been committed. A close relative of a person who died because of injuries can also make a claim.

You must report the incident to the police at the earliest opportunity and an application must normally be made within two years of the incident. However, in exceptional circumstances, the authority may be willing to extend this limit. An example would be if you are making a claim for abuse you suffered as a child. The details of the crime and injuries that must be entered on the claim form are important and if you are completing the form you may want to consult an experienced adviser.

Criminal compensation orders

A person convicted of a criminal offence may be ordered by the court to pay compensation for injury, loss or damage they have caused to someone else by committing the offence. If you are the person who has sustained the injury or loss you cannot apply for this yourself, so it is important that you give the prosecution full and accurate information about the injuries and losses to put before the court.

The amount of compensation will depend on what the offender can afford to pay, but the maximum is £5,000. If a criminal compensation order is made, the court will be responsible for making sure the offender pays.

Financial problems

If you are having financial problems as a result of a personal injury you sustained in, for example, an accident or an incident of violent crime, you may need to consult a specialist money adviser for help with debt and benefits. You may need financial advice because a member of your family has been injured or killed in an accident or as the result of a crime. You may be able to claim compensation for the loss of financial support.

Support and counselling

There are a number of voluntary organizations and schemes that may be able to give support if you have been injured, or your partner, friend or relative has been injured or killed.

Action against Medical Accidents (08451 232 352; www.avma.org.uk) can provide information, support and referral to solicitors if you are the victim of a medical accident. AvMA has a panel of medical experts prepared to give independent opinions.

The **Disabled Living Foundation** (0845 603 9177; www.dlf.org.uk) gives advice and information about equipment available for people with disabilities.

Disaster Action (01483 799066; www.disasteraction.org.uk) was set up by a group of people affected by major disasters. The group campaigns for changes in the law and for improved counselling and compensation, as well as giving support to people involved in disasters and their relatives and friends. It can also make referrals to specialists.

A number of **self-help groups** have been set up for people who have been injured by, for example, unsafe medicines. A list of groups of this kind can be found in the 'Voluntary Agencies Directory', a copy of which will be available in the local public reference library or a CAB.

Headway, the brain injury association (0115 924 0800; www.headway.org.uk), supports people with brain injuries and their carers. It also campaigns for improvements in health and social care services. It runs a helpline, and can provide a list of solicitors who specialize in brain injury cases.

The **Medical Foundation for the Care of Victims of Torture** (020 7697 7777; www.torturecare.org.uk) provides medical care, counselling and therapy to people who have suffered an injury as a result of torture. It sets up self-help groups and can examine patients, for example to provide forensic evidence of torture injuries. The organization can be of use to people who are applying for asylum.

MIND (020 8519 2122; www.mind.org.uk) promotes the interests of people suffering from mental illness or distress and provides advice and advocacy services.

There are a number of **rape organizations** offering help and advice to people who have been raped. A list of groups of this kind can be found in the 'Voluntary Agencies Directory', a copy of which will be available in the local public reference library or a CAB.

Roadpeace (020 8964 1021) provides support and advocacy for bereaved and injured victims of road accidents. It also promotes public awareness of road dangers, and campaigns for justice for victims.

Victim Support (0845 3030 900; www.victimsupport.org.uk) offers information and support to all victims of crime, except theft of, or from, cars and child abuse in the family. There are local schemes.

Women's Aid (0845 702 3468) provides advice, information and sometimes temporary refuge for women and their children who are threatened by mental, emotional or physical violence, harassment or sexual abuse.

POLICE POWERS

Most of the rules that cover police behaviour are set down in codes of practice. There are also other laws that give the police particular powers. If the police fail to act in accordance with police codes of practice or law, it may mean that they can be sued or convicted in a criminal court. Officers could also be disciplined, or a court might be unable to accept police evidence that had been obtained by the police acting beyond their powers. This information does not cover every situation and if you have problems with the police you should always take further advice. If you are cautioned or taken to a police station you should always contact a solicitor.

Stop and search

The police can stop and search any person or vehicle for certain items. However, before they stop and search they must have reasonable grounds for suspecting that they will find any of the following:

- stolen goods;
- an offensive weapon;
- any article made or adapted for use in a burglary;
- an article with a blade or point;
- items that could damage or destroy property.

The police can also search a football coach going to or from a football match if they have reasonable grounds for suspecting there is alcohol on board or that someone is drunk on the coach.

   In all of these situations where the police have a right to stop and search, they should not require you to take off any clothing other than an outer coat, jacket or gloves.

If you are arrested, the police can search you for anything you might use to help you escape or for evidence relating to the offence that has led to your arrest. Again you should not be required to take off any clothing in public except for an outer coat, jacket or gloves, but the police can search your mouth.

In some circumstances, a police officer of the rank of inspector or above can give the police permission to make stops and searches in an area for a certain amount of time. When this permission is in force, the police can search for offensive weapons or dangerous instruments whether or not they have grounds for suspecting that people are carrying these items. When this permission is in force, a police officer in uniform can also order you to remove any item if you are wearing it to hide your identity.

An officer with the rank of assistant chief constable or above can also give permission for searches in an area in order to prevent acts of terrorism. London is one of these areas and authorizations have been given on a rolling basis since 2001. During one of these searches, you can be required to remove headgear, footwear, an outer coat, jacket or gloves in public.

Where can the police search you?

The police can search you in any place that is generally open to the public. This means they can search you anywhere other than your home and your garden, or the home or garden of someone who has given you permission to be there. If the police have reasonable grounds for believing that you are not, in fact, in your own home or that you are somewhere without the permission of the homeowner, they can search you.

The police can use reasonable force when they stop and search, but must make every effort to persuade you to co-operate. They should only use force as a last resort, and the force used must be reasonable.

Before searching, the police officer should tell you that you are being detained so you can be searched. They should also give you their name, the name of their police station, the purpose of the search and their grounds or authorization for making the search. If the search is connected to terrorism, or if the officers believe that giving their name would put them in danger, they can give their police number instead of their name. You should also be told that you have a right to a copy of the record of the search. If it is impractical to make a record of the search there and then, the police officer should tell you that you have the right to apply for a copy, as long as you apply within twelve months.

When can the police question you?

The police should not question you with a view to getting evidence until they have cautioned you. If you have been arrested, you must not be interviewed before being taken to the police station unless:

- delay could lead to interference with or harm to evidence connected with the offence;
- delay could lead to physical harm to others;
- delay would alert someone suspected of committing an offence who has not yet been arrested;
- delay would hinder the recovery of property that is the subject of the offence.

If you are cautioned without having been arrested, you must be told you are free to leave whenever you want.

Powers of entry

Police can enter premises without a warrant in a number of different situations. These include entry to:

- deal with a breach of the peace or prevent it;
- enforce an arrest warrant;
- arrest a person in connection with certain offences;
- recapture someone who has escaped from custody;
- save life or prevent serious damage to property.

Apart from a situation where the police are preventing serious injury to life or property, they must have reasonable grounds for believing that the person they are looking for is on the premises.

If the police do arrest you, they can also enter and search any premises where you were during or immediately before the arrest. The police must have reasonable grounds for believing there is relevant evidence there relating to your suspected offence. They can also search any premises occupied by someone who is under arrest for certain serious offences. Again, the police officer who carries out the search must have reasonable grounds for suspecting that there is evidence on the premises relating to the offence or a similar offence.

If the police have a search warrant they can enter the premises. The codes of practice state that in most cases they should enter property at a reasonable hour unless this would frustrate their search. When the occupier is present, the police must ask for permission to search the property – again, unless it would frustrate the search to do this.

When they are carrying out a search, police officers must:

- identify themselves and – if they are not in uniform – show their warrant card; *and*
- explain why they want to search, the rights of the occupier and whether the search is made with a search warrant or not.

If the police have a warrant they can use reasonable force to enter if:

- the occupier has refused entry; *or*
- it is impossible to communicate with the occupier; *or*
- the occupier is absent; *or*
- the premises are unoccupied; *or*
- they have reasonable grounds for believing that if they do not force entry it would hinder the search, or someone would be placed in danger.

Seizure of property

The police have wide powers to seize property. They are able to seize goods if they have reasonable grounds for believing that:

- they have been obtained illegally; *or*
- they are evidence in relation to an offence.

In either of these cases they must also have reasonable grounds for believing that it is necessary to seize the goods to prevent them being lost, stolen or destroyed.

Powers of arrest

Arresting someone means that the police deprive you of your freedom to go where you want. Police can arrest you if they have a valid arrest warrant. There are also some situations where they can arrest you without a warrant. Examples are where:

- you are in the act of committing certain offences;
- they have reasonable grounds for suspecting you are committing certain offences;
- they have reasonable grounds for suspecting you have committed certain offences;

- you are about to commit certain offences;
- they have reasonable grounds for suspecting you are about to commit certain offences.

The police can also arrest you if they have reasonable grounds for suspecting you have committed or attempted to commit any offence, or if you are committing or attempting to commit any offence, but it is impractical or inappropriate to serve a summons. However, they can only do this if one of the following conditions applies:

- they do not know, and cannot get, your name;
- they think you have given a false name;
- you have not given a satisfactory address – this means an address where the police can contact you;
- they think you have given a false address;
- the arrest is necessary to prevent you causing physical injury to yourself or others, suffering physical injury, causing loss or damage to property, committing an offence against public decency, or causing an unlawful obstruction of the highway;
- they have reasonable grounds for believing that arrest is necessary to protect a child or other vulnerable person.

If they are arresting you because you have failed to give them a satisfactory address, they must explain that you may be arrested and give you the opportunity to provide the address.

What should happen on arrest

The police should only use reasonable force to make an arrest and they should inform you that you are under arrest as soon as possible. After the arrest they should explain why they have arrested you. The police must caution you unless it is impractical to do so or unless they cautioned you immediately before they arrested you.

If the police arrest you somewhere other than at a police station, they should take you to a police station as soon as possible. If they arrest you for theft, and you were seen taking property but did not have it after a chase, the police officer can retrace your tracks. This may allow them to recover the property. They should take you to the station once they have recovered the property.

At the police station

If you are under 17 years of age and are detained by the police, 'an appropriate adult' – usually your parent or guardian – should be informed as soon as possible. The police should not interview you until your parent is present, unless a delay would mean an immediate risk of harm to someone or serious loss of or damage to property.

People with learning difficulties

If the person arrested has learning difficulties, the police should only interview them when a responsible person is present, unless delay would result in a risk of injury or harm to property or people. The person with learning difficulties should be accompanied at interview by:

- a relative or other person responsible for their care; *or*
- a person who is not employed by the police, and who is experienced in dealing with people with learning difficulties; *or*
- some other responsible adult who is not employed by the police.

People from abroad

If the person arrested is not usually resident here the police may have the right to request help from their High Commission, embassy or consulate in tracing them. Certain countries have special agreements with the UK so that the High Commission, embassy or consulate is automatically informed if one of their nationals is arrested (unless the arrested individual is a political refugee).

If your first language is not English

If you have difficulty understanding English and the interviewing officer cannot speak your language, you should be provided with an interpreter. The police must not interview you until the interpreter is present unless a delay would mean an immediate risk of harm to someone or serious loss of or damage to property.

Deaf people and people with hearing or speech difficulties

If you have hearing or speech difficulties the police should offer you an interpreter. They should not question you until the interpreter is present, unless a delay would mean an immediate risk of harm to someone or serious loss of or damage to property, or unless you agree in writing to be interviewed without one.

What should happen if you are detained

At the police station the police should inform you of:

- your right to let someone know of your arrest; *and*
- your right to talk to a solicitor in private and the fact that this is free of charge; *and*
- your right to look at the police codes of practice.

The police should also inform you that you do not need to use these rights immediately. You can exercise them at any time while you are detained. You should be given a written notice of these rights while you are at the police station, and of your right to a written copy of your custody record when you are released. The police will ask you to indicate on the custody record whether you wish to have legal advice and will also ask you to sign the record.

If you do ask for another person to be informed of your arrest, this should happen as soon as possible, unless you have been arrested for certain offences and an officer of the rank of superintendent (or above) allows a delay. In order to allow a delay, the officer should be satisfied that there are reasonable grounds for believing that informing someone of your arrest would:

- lead to interference with evidence;
- affect the police's ability to recover property;
- lead to other suspects being alerted;
- prevent recovery of the proceeds resulting from drug offences.

If a delay is authorized, the police should tell you and write the reason on your custody record. The maximum delay is thirty-six hours unless you are detained in relation to a terrorist offence, in which case it is forty-eight hours. If someone asks about your whereabouts then, as long as you agree, they should be informed, unless an officer of the rank of superintendent (or above) decides that they should not.

How long can the police hold you?

The police should not detain you for more than twenty-four hours without charging you, unless an officer with the rank of superintendent (or above) or a magistrate gives permission.

A police officer with the rank of superintendent (or above) can authorize detention for a further twelve hours. Magistrates can authorize further detentions up to a maximum of ninety-six hours. Once charged, you should be brought before the magistrates the next day (but not on Christmas Day, Good Friday or any Sunday). Arrests in suspected terrorism cases have different detention rules.

Right to silence

Although you have a right to silence, courts can take your silence into account when deciding whether you are guilty or innocent.

Duty solicitor

If you are arrested, charged or questioned by the police, you should ask for a solicitor. There should be a duty solicitor, available by telephone, who will not charge you for help. You have the right to free, confidential legal advice but in exceptional circumstances a delay of up to thirty-six hours can be authorized, more in cases of suspected terrorism.

Complaints

If you feel the police have treated you unfairly and you want to complain, there are different courses of action you can take. The appropriate course of action will depend on the nature of your complaint. For example, if the police have obtained evidence by breaking code of practice rules, a court can refuse to accept police evidence in any case against you. Alternatively, you may wish to use the police complaints procedure to complain about an individual officer's behaviour or take civil court action.

Making a complaint

You can make a written complaint to the chief constable of the force or, in London, to the Commissioner of the Metropolitan Police. You should send the letter by recorded delivery and keep a copy. If you think you might also take court action, you should ask a solicitor to write the letter. The police station will record the complaint and you will be invited to an interview at the police station. You should take a friend or solicitor with you. If you have been injured you may also be asked to attend a medical examination, which can only be carried out with your consent. The police may ask you whether you want the complaint to be dealt with informally under a procedure called 'local resolution'. If you do not agree, then the matter will be investigated formally.

If after formal investigation the complaint is upheld:

- the police officer may be given an informal warning or words of advice; *or*
- the police officer may be formally disciplined; they may be dismissed or required to resign, suffer a reduction in rank or pay, be fined, given a warning or reprimanded; *or*
- the matter will be referred to the Crown Prosecution Service if there is an allegation of criminal offences by the police officer. (If the complaint is upheld, you may want to consider suing the police.)

The Independent Police Complaints Commission (08453 002 002; www.ipcc.gov.uk) oversees and investigates complaints against the police.

Suing the police

If your complaint is serious you may wish to sue the police. You can sue the police in the same way that you can sue members of the public. If you want to sue the police you should talk to a specialist solicitor.

Who can help?

Liberty (08451 232307; www.liberty-human-rights.org.uk) campaigns on civil liberties issues, including police policies and powers, and can advise people who have problems with the police. However, they can only take on a few cases each year. They can also recommend solicitors with experience in police complaints.

Inquest (020 8802 7430; www.gn.apc.org/inquest) offers legal advice on any problems relating to a coroner's inquest.

Police monitoring groups are campaigning organizations that aim to increase public awareness of police work and improve police policies. Most police monitoring groups are in London. The groups offer free advice, may take up a complaint and will make referrals to a solicitor. To find out whether you have a local group, contact your local authority.

Law centres offer free advice and representation. The Law Centres Federation (020 7387 8570; www.lawcentres.org.uk) can provide details of your local law centre.

PRISONERS

Prisoners' rights

All prisoners have certain rights and privileges. These are set out in standing orders, available in prison libraries.

The **Prison Service** (www.hmprisonservice.gov.uk) and the **Prison Reform Trust** (0207 251 5070; www.prisonreformtrust.org.uk) have co-produced a guide to prisoners' rights, and a copy of this should be given to each prisoner on arrival in prison. You can also buy a copy of the guide from the Prison Reform Trust.

Types of prisoner

A remand prisoner is someone who is awaiting trial or who is in the middle of a trial. A civil prisoner is someone who has been sentenced for a civil offence, such as non-payment of a fine. A convicted prisoner is someone who has been tried for a criminal offence and has been found guilty. They may or may not have already been sentenced.

Prison visits

The basic rules about which family or friends can visit a prisoner apply to all prisoners, whether they are remand, sentenced or civil prisoners. Up to three people, not including children under ten, are allowed on each visit to a prisoner as long as they all visit at the same time. The adults can be relatives, friends or anyone caring for the prisoner's children. However, whether or not you need to give notice to visit or must undergo extra security procedures before your visit will depend on the type of prisoner you are going to see. The governor has discretion to disallow any visit to or from a person under 18, if it is not in the interests of the visitor or the prisoner. If you are planning to visit a prisoner you should telephone the prison first to check that the visit will be allowed.

Professional visitors

If a prisoner wants to see their lawyer, the lawyer can visit as often as necessary. A prisoner may also be visited by other people, for example the prisoner's home social worker or probation officer, or a hostel worker if the

3
Nationality and Immigration

CONTENTS

INTRODUCTION

Britain is a nation of immigrants. From the Roman, Saxon and
Viking invasions, the Protestant refugees from France and the
Low Countries, the Africans brought to Britain via the slave trade
and the waves of Jewish arrivals over the centuries to the Irish
fleeing rural poverty and famine, incoming populations have
always made a huge contribution to life in Britain. More recently,
British citizens from the Commonwealth invited to come to
Britain after the Second World War and the recent migrants from
Eastern Europe and Africa escaping wars and persecution in their
home countries have continued this history of immigration.
Twenty-three per cent of Britain's doctors were born overseas,
two-thirds of independently owned shops are owned by people
from ethnic minorities and Britain's cultural and sporting life has
been hugely enriched by a diverse range of cultural influences.
Political life too has been informed by the experiences of new
Britons from Olaudah Equiano, who as a free man in Britain

fought the slave trade that brought him here from West Africa, to Diane Abbot, who became the first black female MP in 1987. Newcomers have often had a hostile reception, whatever their reasons for coming and, in recent years, have faced increasingly strict immigration controls.

Immigration law is about how and why people from countries outside the UK are allowed to come to the UK and how long they can stay. It is also about what they are allowed to do when they are here – whether they can work, whether relatives can join them afterwards, and whether they can use the National Health Service or claim benefits.

Immigration law is made more complicated because it overlaps with nationality law – that is, the law about who is or is not a British citizen, and the rights of the different types of British citizen. Because these laws are so complicated, it would be misleading to give any general guidelines on them. Instead, this chapter gives some examples of the sorts of problems that may arise, and a list of organizations which may be able to help.

IMMIGRATION CONTROL AND NATIONALITY

The system of immigration control in the UK broadly establishes two distinct groups of people:

- those who have 'right of abode' in the UK and who can live, work and move in and out of the country as they wish;
- those who require permission in order to enter and remain here. The technical term for this permission is 'leave' and people who do not have an automatic right to be in the UK are often described as people who 'need leave' to come and stay in the UK.

There are certain groups of people who do not fit easily into these two groups and who do not have to get leave to 'enter and remain', even though they do not have 'right of abode'. Included in this group are people who can benefit from European rights of free movement.

Where people do need leave to enter the UK, immigration rules (which are law) set out various ways in which it can be granted.

'Visitor', 'spouse', 'au pair' and 'student' are all examples of different immigration categories. In each category, the rules indicate different requirements that must be satisfied before a person will be granted leave to come and stay – for example, students must show that they will follow a full-time course of study. Most of the categories under the rules require that people coming to the UK will be able to support themselves without relying on public funds.

The immigration rules also spell out how long leave to remain in the UK should be granted. Leave can be either 'limited' or 'indefinite'. Limited leave is granted to those people who are coming here for 'temporary' purposes, for example as students. Other categories of applicant may be eligible for 'indefinite' leave with the possibility that the person may be able to apply for citizenship.

People in most 'temporary' categories, such as visitors, will also need to show that they intend to leave the country when the purpose of their stay is over.

Nationality law is a branch of law in its own right in the UK, but questions of nationality or citizenship are closely associated with immigration law because a person's nationality is central in determining what immigration rights they have. It is also important to remember that there are different 'kinds' of citizenship in UK law and not all British nationals have the 'right of abode' that allows them freely to enter and live in the UK.

People who require leave to enter the UK will usually need to get 'entry clearance' to show that they are entitled to enter the UK under the immigration rules. There are detailed rules about how to qualify for entry clearance within each category of applicant coming to the UK. Some groups, such as refugees and asylum seekers, do not require entry clearance, but most do.

Immigration laws are strictly enforced in the UK and the consequences of misunderstanding your right to be here can be very serious. They can include the risk of deportation. It is essential to consult a specialist adviser if you are unsure about your position or the position of family and friends.

For this reason you should seek specialist advice in the following situations:

- you want permission to stay in the UK longer than you originally intended;
- you want permission to do something that you are not at present allowed to do, such as work;

- you want to bring relatives into the country, such as your wife or children;
- you are being threatened with deportation from the UK;
- you are being held by the immigration authorities in a detention centre;
- you want a passport and don't know whether you are entitled to a British passport or some other one;
- you want to apply to become a British Citizen;
- you are already living in the UK but want to travel abroad and are unsure whether you will be allowed back into the UK;
- you are not sure whether you are entitled to use state services or claim benefits;
- you are not sure whether you have the right to vote;
- a relative or friend has been refused entry to the UK at an airport or port.

Who can help?

Registration of Immigration Advisers

All immigration advisers must be registered with the **Office of Immigration Services Commissioner** (OISC: 0845 000 0046; www.oisc.org.uk), or be an adviser with an organization, such as the Citizens Advice Bureaux, that is exempt from registration. Anyone who gives immigration advice and is neither registered nor exempt will be committing a criminal offence. Every registered or exempt advice agency should display a certificate issued by the OISC to show it meets the OISC standards.

A list of all registered and exempt advisers and advice organizations can be seen on the OISC website, which also includes details of how to make a complaint about an immigration adviser. The OISC does not deal with enquiries about immigration problems.

The **Immigration Advisory Service** (IAS: 020 7967 1200; 020 7378 9191 – emergency line; www.iasuk.org) operates a number of regional offices – details are on their website.

The **Refugee Legal Centre** (020 7780 3220 – advice line; 0800 592 398 – detention advice line; www.refugee-legal-centre.org.uk) can give advice and assistance to asylum seekers and refugees. This includes helping with applications, advising on temporary admissions, refusal of asylum, family reunion, and representing appeals in court. Appointments can be made by phoning the main advice line.

I want to marry my Jamaican girlfriend. She is in the UK on a three-year student visa. Do we need to do anything special about her status in this country?

If you marry, your new wife should ask for permission to stay in the UK as your spouse. There are strict requirements that she will have to meet to satisfy the immigration authorities that your marriage is genuine and that she should be allowed to stay. She will also have to show that she didn't intend to deceive the authorities when she entered the country as a student and that, as a couple, you can support yourselves without help from the state. If she does get permission to stay as your wife, she will be given leave to stay for two years. Towards the end of the two-year period she can apply to stay permanently.

Don't forget that UK immigration law is complex and getting it wrong has serious consequences, so it always advisable to consult a specialist adviser.

The **Refugee Council** (020 7346 6777 – advice line; Wales: 029 2048 9800; www.refugeecouncil.org.uk) in England and Wales offers advice and support to all refugees and asylum seekers. As part of this it operates a one-stop service, providing advice and support to newly arrived refugees and asylum seekers on social security benefits, housing, immigration and education. No appointment is necessary, but people are seen on a first come, first served basis. The Refugee Council also offers training and work experience.

The **UK Lesbian and Gay Immigration Group** (UKLGIG: 020 7734 3705 – helpline; www.uklgig.org.uk) is a national lobbying and campaigning organization working for legal equality for lesbians and gay men. UKLGIG is a support and campaign group for lesbians and gay couples with immigration problems that they would not face if they were heterosexual. The group works to change the immigration rules to ensure this discrimination is removed. It also arranges for exchanges of information, provides a support network and advises on and supports applications to the Home Office.

UKCOSA (020 7288 4330 – administration only; www.ukcosa.org.uk) campaigns on behalf of foreign students and produces a number of very useful booklets on students' problems. Individual foreign students looking for advice should consult their local NUS office (contactable through NUS headquarters). In an emergency, you may ring UKCOSA on the public casework line (020 7109 9922).

I'm a Nigerian visitor and would like to stay in the UK to do a degree. Will I be allowed to do this?

When you came to the UK as a visitor from Nigeria you were allowed to enter on the basis that you returned to Nigeria when your visitor's visa ran out. So, under immigration rules, you will not be allowed to stay here to study. If you want to become a student, you will have to leave the UK and re-apply to return as a student at a future date from Nigeria. If you stay on in the UK beyond the date of your visa, you will be in breach of your conditions of entry. This is a serious offence and you can be prosecuted and deported.

The **Joint Council for the Welfare of Immigrants** (JCWI: 020 7251 8708; www.jcwi.org.uk) is an independent voluntary organization financed by trusts and charity. It campaigns for changes in immigration law, both on its own and together with other organizations. It also provides advice and training to other advice agencies. It does not do casework.

The few **solicitors in private practice** who specialize in immigration work are generally based in larger urban areas. To find out whether there are any solicitors in private practice in your area who specialize in immigration work, you can contact the **Immigration Law Practitioners' Association** (020 7251 8383).

The **Community Legal Service** (CLS: www.Clsdirect.org.uk) website contains a directory with contact details of solicitors, advice agencies and sources of specialist advice locally. Information is available in English, Welsh, Urdu, Bengali, Cantonese, Punjabi and Gujarati. You can consult a copy of the CLS Directory for English and Welsh regions in your local library or call the CLS Directory line (0845 608 1122).

Many **local organizations** provide immigration and nationality advice, for example, law centres or race equality councils, but remember that the quality of advice that local organizations give can vary.

Law centres nearly always have a worker who specializes in immigration.

Law centres generally have fairly strict catchment areas, so it is important to check whether a law centre in the area will be able to take on a case. Sometimes, the catchment area will include people who either live or work in the area. If the law centre can offer advice and representation in immigration cases, it will be free. For more information, contact the **Law Centres' Federation** (020 7387 8570; www.lawcentres.org.uk).

My aunt writes to me and says that things are getting very frightening for members of the Movement for Democratic Change political party in Zimbabwe. She's getting afraid to leave the house. She wonders if she could come to the UK for a while until things calm down a bit.

The UK is a signatory of a United Nations Convention on refugees, which means that it is committed to offering asylum to people who are at risk of persecution in their own country. The process of applying for asylum in the UK is extremely complex and you should seek specialist advice to find out whether your aunt might qualify for asylum at the present time. Only a small proportion of asylum applications are successful, so you should also consider whether your aunt could come to this country in another capacity. She may, for example, have family links with the UK that could give her rights to be here while things are unsettled in Zimbabwe.

Money

1

Tax

CONTENTS

INTRODUCTION

We've all been complaining about taxes since Robin Hood started
redistributing wealth and Lady Godiva rode naked through the
streets of Coventry to get her husband to reduce them. Income
tax was introduced in 1799 as a way of funding the war against
Napoleon – 10 per cent on all income over £60. It is still a
'temporary' tax, which expires each year on 5 April, and
Parliament has to reapply it by an annual Finance Act.

Taxes can win and lose elections and have always been centre
stage for politicians fighting for our votes. Whether the politicians
are promising to cut taxes and put more money in our pockets or
planning to 'tax and spend' to pay for public services, taxes are at
the heart of the political agenda.

Like it or not, most of us have to pay them so the best you can
do is make sure you know your way around the tax jungle. This
chapter looks at income tax, tax relief, tax rebates, Self
Assessment, PAYE and 'fringe benefits', like that company car.
There is also a tax 'jargon buster' to help you understand the
lingo.

JARGON BUSTER

deeds of covenant   a way of giving money regularly to charity that allows the charity to reclaim the income tax that was paid on the gift

filing date   the date by which completed tax returns must be received by the Inland Revenue. If a return is not received by this date, you may have to pay penalties. The filing date is the 31 January after the tax year to which the tax return relates.

fringe benefits   non-cash benefits, such as company cars, given to employees. Most fringe benefits are taxable. The Inland Revenue now uses the term employment benefits.

Gift Aid   a way of giving a one-off amount from taxed income to a charity. The charity may then claim the tax back.

inheritance tax   tax paid on a person's estate after death. It was formerly known as estate duty or capital transfer tax. Inheritance tax may also be payable on some gifts made during a person's lifetime.

Inland Revenue   the government department responsible for assessing and collecting most types of tax, but not VAT, which is dealt with by Customs and Excise

ISA   stands for Individual Savings Account. ISAs allow money to be saved in several ways without tax having to be paid on any interest earned.

PAYE   stands for Pay As You Earn and is the way that all employees, and some other people, pay income tax

payments on account   payments of income tax and Class 4 National Insurance contributions that must be paid by self-employed people, or by certain employees. The payments are made in advance of the taxpayer sending in a tax return for a particular tax year, and mean that tax will be paid in two instalments during the tax year.

remission of tax arrears   a taxpayer with tax arrears may have some or all of them 'remitted', that is, the taxpayer will not have to pay all of the arrears if certain conditions are met

Self Assessment Self Assessment taxpayers are responsible for assessing which parts of their income are taxable and filling in a tax return accordingly

stamp duty land tax a tax that is paid on documents that convey a sale of property or shares. The document is sent to the Stamp Office for stamping, and the tax is paid then.

tax arrears a debt to the Inland Revenue for tax owed

tax assessment the amount of tax which someone must pay

tax-exempt income income on which income tax is never payable, for example, some income from National Savings certificates and winnings from gambling

tax-free income not the same as tax-exempt income. Tax-free income is the personal allowances and tax relief that reduce income on which tax would be payable. Once these have been deducted, what remains is called the taxable income.

taxable income the part of total income on which income tax is payable, that is after tax-exempt income and tax-free income have been deducted

tax rebates payments from the Inland Revenue to an individual who has paid too much tax in any particular year. The payment will often not be made until the end of the tax year.

tax return Form SA 100 on which taxpayers must list all income and certain expenses so that the amount of tax due can be calculated. You can do the calculation yourself, or can ask the Inland Revenue to calculate how much tax you should pay.

tax years 6 April one year to 5 April the following year

TESSA stands for Tax Exempt Special Savings Account and, as the name suggests, is a special savings account that allows interest to be paid tax-free. No new ones can be started, but any already in existence can continue until the end of their term.

VAT stands for Value Added Tax, which is a tax on goods and services, and is payable at a certain percentage. It is administered and collected by Customs and Excise, not the Inland Revenue.

INCOME TAX

Income tax is a tax paid on income. It is paid by employees and people who are self-employed and may also be payable if you are not working but have an income, such as a retirement pension or an occupational pension. Not all types of income are taxable and it will seldom be the case that all of your income is taxed. There is no minimum age at which a person becomes liable to pay income tax. What matters is your income. If this is below a certain level, no tax is payable.

There is no single definition in tax law of income. Income tax law divides various types of income into schedules. If an item comes within a schedule it counts as income and income tax must be paid on it. The way the tax must be paid will depend on which schedule it falls into. The most common schedules are Schedule E for employees and Schedule D for the self-employed.

How it is calculated

There are five main steps in calculating income tax:

1. Add together all your yearly income, including social security benefits, income from renting out accommodation, wages, occupational pension and interest from bank and building society accounts.

2. Take off any income that is exempt from tax. Calculate whether you can claim tax relief on any of the money you have spent over the year (tax relief usually applies to people who are self-employed and have to buy items for the business). Deduct this tax relief. This leaves income on which tax may be payable (taxable income).

3. Work out which tax allowances you are entitled to. You will be entitled to a personal allowance (plus age-related additions if appropriate). These allowances are deducted at this stage in the calculation.

4. Multiply the taxable income by the correct tax rate. This gives the tax due to be paid that year (unless you are entitled to married couple's allowance for over 65-year-olds).

5. If applicable, deduct the appropriate percentage rate of married couple's allowance for over 65-year-olds.

Income that is taxable

Income that is taxable includes:

- some social security benefits and pensions, for example, Retirement Pension, Jobseeker's Allowance and Statutory Maternity and Paternity Pay;
- employment-related allowances and benefits;
- earned income, for example wages and salaries and profits from self-employment;
- other types of income, for example profits from the sale of most goods and property;
- some fringe benefits, for example company cars;
- some occupational pensions;
- interest on some types of savings, for example building society and bank accounts.

The percentage rate of tax payable varies according to the amount of the taxable income. Further advice is available from the Inland Revenue helpline (0845 307 3555).

Tax-exempt income

Some income is exempt from income tax, which means that tax is never paid on this income. You should check whether any income is exempt from tax before doing a tax calculation. Examples of such income are:

- interest from some types of savings;
- some benefits and tax credits, for example Child Benefit, Disability Living Allowance;
- other types of income, for example damages and interest awarded for personal injury, and certain pensions.

Tax allowances

Everyone resident in the UK is entitled to receive a certain amount of income each year before they have to start paying tax. This amount is called the personal allowance. There are also other additional allowances that can reduce the tax you have to pay. This means that some of your income, which would otherwise be taxable, will be tax-free.

Tax allowances are announced in the Budget each year. If you are an employee and so are taxed under Pay As You Earn (PAYE), your personal allowance(s) will be spread throughout the year, so that each week or month you will be left with a certain amount of tax-free income after the tax has been deducted. If you are self-employed or have an income but are not working, your personal allowance(s) will be taken into account when the Inland Revenue assesses your tax liability each year.

All taxpayers can claim at least one tax allowance and some taxpayers can claim more than one. The allowances are given to all taxpayers whether they are employees, self-employed or do not work. If you are entitled to an allowance and are not getting it, you should claim it from your tax office. If you have not received allowances to which you are entitled, you can make a backdated claim for them for up to six years.

In practice, if you receive earnings or an occupational pension, this income is taxed through the Pay As You Earn (PAYE) system. This means your allowances are spread over the year and you pay your tax throughout the year, not just when your income reaches the amounts of your allowances. The following tax allowances can be given:

- personal allowances;
- blind person's allowance;
- married couple's allowance for couples where at least one member was aged 65 or over on 6 April 2000.

Personal allowances

Everyone automatically gets a personal tax allowance, whether they are male or female, married or single, and regardless of how young they are. This can be set against all types of income. There are three amounts of personal allowance:

- a standard amount for people aged under 65;
- a higher amount for people aged 65 to 74;
- the highest amount for people aged 75 or over.

Blind person's allowance

You can claim a blind person's allowance for the whole tax year if you are a registered blind person or become a registered blind person during the tax year. You can claim this in addition to your allowance.

If you are married and cannot use all your blind person's allowance because you do not have enough income, you can ask your tax office to transfer the unused part of the allowance to your married partner, whether or not the partner is blind. If both you and your spouse are blind, you can each receive the allowance.

Married couple's allowance for couples aged over 65

See *Income tax and the over 65s*, p. 553.

Tax relief (excluding self-employed people)

As a taxpayer, if you spend money on certain outgoings, the amount you spend can be deducted from your total taxable income and you will therefore pay less tax. Tax relief can be claimed in addition to any personal tax allowances that you are entitled to and can be backdated for up to six years. Some reliefs have to be claimed by writing to your tax inspector, although most are automatic. No action need be taken by you to claim automatic relief. Tax reliefs for employees are spread throughout the year in the same way as personal tax allowances. Tax relief for self-employed people and people who have an income but are not working is taken into account by the Inland Revenue when assessing tax each year, once it has received the taxpayer's tax return.

Types of tax relief

There are six main types of tax relief:

- tax relief available to self-employed people;
- tax relief available to employees;
- tax relief on training and education;
- tax relief on property;
- tax relief on some insurance premiums;
- tax relief on payments to other people, such as maintenance payments and payments to charities.

Income tax rates

Tax is paid at different rates on your total taxable income. Income tax rates are reviewed annually and usually change in April. Contact the Inland Revenue (www.inlandrevenue.gov.uk) for details of current tax rates.

Income on which tax has already been paid

When calculating the tax due, it is necessary to work out whether or not you have received any income on which tax has already been paid – for example, interest on savings in a building society or bank account, where the interest is paid to you after the bank/building society has taken the tax off it. Payments from an occupational pension will also have had tax taken off before the payment is made to you.

When working out the total tax due for the year, it is necessary to take into account the fact that tax has already been paid on this income. This income (which needs to have the tax deducted added back in) will also count towards taxable income on which personal tax allowances are allowed.

National Insurance contributions

When checking whether your tax has been correctly calculated, it may also be useful to calculate the National Insurance contributions that you have to pay, as this will give the figure for your take-home pay. National Insurance contributions are calculated on gross income. National Insurance contributions for employees are deducted at different rates depending on your pension arrangements and on your level of income.

Record-keeping

If you are a taxpayer, you must keep records of your income to enable you to complete a tax return. Personal or non-business records must be kept until twenty-two months after the end of the tax year that they relate to, and business records must be kept for five years after the fixed filing date.

How income tax is collected

Deduction of tax at source

Only a minority of taxpayers pay tax directly to the Inland Revenue every year. The majority of taxpayers pay their tax through deductions that are made from their income before they receive it. This is called deduction at source.

Some of the most common examples of deduction at source are PAYE and deductions from bank and building society interest.

Pay As You Earn (PAYE)

By law, anyone making payments to employees or members of occupational pension schemes has to operate the PAYE system. This means they must deduct income tax and Class 1 National Insurance contributions from the payments that they make, and must send these sums to the Inland Revenue. You are entitled to receive written confirmation of deductions that have been made by:

- payslips, showing gross pay, deductions made and net pay if you are an employee; *and*
- a P60 certificate at the end of each tax year, confirming the amount of gross earnings, and the income tax and Class 1 National Insurance contributions deducted; *and*
- a P45 certificate whenever you change jobs, which shows the tax code operating on your earnings at the time you left and, in some cases, the earnings and income tax deducted in the tax year to date.

Bank and building society interest

Banks and building societies deduct income tax from the interest paid on most deposits made with them by individuals, and pay this over to the Inland Revenue. This is done before the interest is paid to the account holder.

Confirmation of the interest earned in each tax year and the income tax deducted must be provided by the bank or building society free of charge to you, the saver, if you ask for it. A number of banks and building societies send these details to all their investors each year, as a matter of course.

If you do not need to pay any tax on this interest – for example, because your total income from all sources falls below your tax-free income for the tax year – you can arrange to receive your interest gross – that is, without deduction of any tax. This is called taxback. You should ask your branch of the bank or building society for a taxback form. This avoids the need to claim a tax refund.

Collection of tax by Self Assessment

See *Self Assessment*, p. 550.

Tax rebates

A tax rebate is a refund of tax that has been overpaid. There are a number of reasons why tax may have been overpaid, including when:

- you start a new job and are taxed under an emergency code for a while;
- your circumstances change – for example, you marry, reach retirement age or become a single parent;
- the Inland Revenue sends the wrong tax code to your employer;
- the Inland Revenue made an assessment – for example, for a self-employed person – that was too high;
- you are not a taxpayer, but have had tax deducted from your building society or bank interest.

Rebates under PAYE

If you pay tax through PAYE you have your tax adjusted throughout the tax year by your employer. If too much tax has been deducted, the tax office will send your employer a new tax code, which will enable your employer to pay the rebate through your wages or salary.

Rebates for unemployed people

If you become unemployed and claim Jobseeker's Allowance, you will not immediately receive a tax rebate. A rebate will be paid either under PAYE if you go back to work, or at the end of the financial year, whichever is sooner. If you are on Income Support you will be treated in the same way.

Rebates following a death

An overpayment of income tax may arise following a death. The Inland Revenue should be informed of the death in writing as soon as possible and a copy of the death certificate should also be sent to the tax office. Special rules apply to the tax allowances if the person who has died was married. If a refund of tax is made, it is counted as part of the estate of the person who has died.

Rebates for strikers

If you are on strike, you will only be paid a rebate when you either leave the job or go back to work. The rebate will not be paid at the end of the financial year.

Leaving a job

If you leave work and do not claim social security benefits, you may be able to claim a rebate after four weeks of leaving work.

Time limits on claiming a tax rebate

A claim for a tax rebate can usually be made in the six years after the end of the tax year in which tax was overpaid. However, this time limit can be extended in cases where overpayment of tax occurred because of an error by the Inland Revenue or another government department, and where there is no dispute or doubt as to the facts.

Interest on rebates

The Inland Revenue must pay interest on some tax rebates that have been delayed. For interest to be paid, the rebate must:

● have been delayed for more than twelve months after the end of the year of assessment (or the end of the year in which tax was paid, if it was paid late);
● be for a certain minimum amount;
● be for a tax year when the tax payer was resident in the United Kingdom.

PAYE

The Pay As You Earn (PAYE) system is a method of paying income tax. Your employer deducts tax from your wages or occupational pension before paying you your wages. Wages include sick pay and maternity pay. This means that you pay tax over the whole year, each time you are paid. Your employer is responsible for sending the tax on to the Inland Revenue.

If you pay tax on your wages or occupational pension under PAYE, the PAYE system can also be used to collect the income tax of any other taxable income you have. For example, if you pay tax under PAYE on an occupational pension, the tax due on your state retirement pension is collected through PAYE by deducting tax from your occupational pension.

Tax codes

The tax office will tell your employer how much tax to deduct from your wages/occupational pension, but will not give details about how your code has been decided. If the tax office does not have enough information to issue a full tax code, it will use an emergency tax code until more information is received and the tax can be adjusted.

Most PAYE codes are made up of a number followed by a letter:

● the letter relates to the type of allowance(s) you are getting;

- the number shows the amount of income you have as allowances that may be set against tax.

The letter in the tax code

The letter in the tax code, which shows which tax allowances you are receiving, will be one of the following:

L. if you are aged under 65 and getting the personal allowance. You will be given this code if you are a single person or a person who is being taxed on the emergency code.

P. if you are a single person, or a married woman, aged 65–74 who is entitled to the full age-related allowance;

V. if you are a married man aged 65–74; *and*
- your wife is aged 74 or less; *and*
- you are entitled to the full age related allowance; *and*
- the Inland Revenue estimates that tax will be paid at the basic rate.

T. may be allocated for a number of reasons. These include:
- where you request it, because you do not want to reveal your actual code; *or*
- you or your partner is aged 75 or over; *or*
- there is a reduced age-related personal allowance in the code.

K. if you are someone whose untaxed income adds up to more than your personal tax allowances. If your untaxed income is from fringe benefits and/or pensions, interest or social security benefits you may be given a K code.

Y. if you are aged 75 or over and have the full personal allowance;

NT. if you do not have to pay tax. This code does not include a number.

BR. if you have not been given any allowances and tax will be deducted at the basic rate. This code may be given where you have more than one job.

DO. if you have tax deducted at the higher rate;

OT. no allowances have been given or remain after other adjustments have been made. Tax will be paid at the lower, basic or higher rate, depending on the level of income.

The number in the tax code

The number in the tax code represents the total of all available allowances, less any amount to be deducted to cover other income or benefits.

If you are given a PAYE tax code it will be shown on:

- a notice of coding sent by the tax office; *or*
- your payslip; *or*
- your pension statement if you are getting an occupational pension.

Emergency tax codes

The tax office may not be able to give your employer a tax code to allow deduction of the right amount of tax over the whole year. In this case, the tax office gives your employer an emergency code with which to tax you. An emergency code assumes that you are only entitled to the basic personal allowance and your PAYE tax code will include the letter L, which shows that you are only receiving this personal allowance. It does not take into account any other allowances and reliefs you may be entitled to.

You will stop being taxed on an emergency code:

- when the tax office sends your employer (and you) a PAYE tax code, and details of previous earnings and tax paid for that tax year. This enables your employer to deduct the correct tax in future and refund any tax overpaid as a result of the emergency code. *Or*
- at the end of the tax year. Your employer will usually start deducting tax cumulatively, that is, when deducting tax your employer will take into account the amount of tax you have already paid. If, at the end of the tax year, you think you have paid too much tax because you have been taxed on an emergency code, you should claim a rebate by writing to the tax office.

Notice of coding

A notice of coding shows your tax code if you are going to pay through the PAYE system. The notice is usually sent out in January or February for the tax year beginning on the following 6 April. The code shown in the notice is given for that tax year only. The notes that come with the notice of coding explain how the code is worked out.

Not everyone gets a notice of coding each year. It depends on what allowances and relief you are claiming and whether these tend to change from year to year. It is important to check that the notice of coding gives the correct allowances and relief, because if it is wrong you will be paying the wrong amount of tax.

You should check carefully that you have been given all the allowances and relief that you are entitled to claim and that all your income has been taken into account. If help is needed consult a local tax office or an experienced adviser.

There is also a leaflet called 'Inland Revenue PAYE: Understanding your tax code'.

PAYE and Self Assessment

Under the system of Self Assessment, you have to assess how much tax you have to pay on any income which you receive that is not taxed through PAYE, for example:

- income from renting out a room; *or*
- income from freelance work.

You must tell the local tax office if you receive taxable income in addition to that which you pay through PAYE. You will then have to complete a tax return form and either ask the Inland Revenue to calculate how much tax is due (Revenue calculation) or do the calculation yourself (taxpayer calculation). If you owe less than a certain amount in tax on sources of income that are not taxed through PAYE, and you send your completed tax return form back by the 30 September following the end of the tax year, you can pay all your tax through PAYE. If you owe more than this amount, or if you prefer, you can pay the tax due on the other sources of income directly to the Inland Revenue. If you want to check that you are paying the right amount of tax, or, for example, if you think you may have over- or underpaid tax, you should contact your local tax office and ask if you can complete a tax return form. Once you have completed the form you can either ask the Inland Revenue to calculate the amount of tax due, or do the calculation yourself.

Change in circumstances

If your circumstances change during the tax year, for example if you become entitled to a new allowance or incur a new outgoing, you must inform the Inland Revenue as soon as possible.

You cannot rely only on telling an employer of a change in circumstances. In fact, as an employer can do nothing until instructed by the Inland Revenue, you do not have to inform your employer at all. You should write to your tax office with the details of the change.

PAYE: Common problems

Starting a new job

When you start a new job your employer needs to know your tax code. If you have a form called a P45 from a previous job in the same tax year, your employer will use the information on this to deduct the right amount of tax. If you were unemployed and receiving Jobseeker's Allowance, you should give your new employer the P45U you were given by the Employment Service Jobcentre.

No P45 or P45U

You may not have a P45 or P45U. This may be because you:

- are starting your first job; or
- were unemployed but not receiving Jobseeker's Allowance and therefore do not have a P45U ; or
- have lost the P45 or P45U; or
- were not given a P45 by your last employer.

If you cannot give the employer a P45 or a P45U, your employer will give you a P46 form, which, when completed, allows your employer to deduct tax on an emergency code until the right amount of tax to be deducted is worked out. If you have lost your P45 or P45U, you will not be able to obtain a duplicate, as these are never issued. Your new employer, or the Jobcentre if you are claiming benefit, will ask you to complete a P46.

Fringe benefits (benefits in kind)

Fringe benefits are any benefits which you receive from your employment that are not actually included in your salary cheque or wages. On the tax return form they are called benefits in kind. They include such things as company cars, private medical insurance and cheap or free loans. Not all fringe benefits are taxable and some are only taxable if you are earning over a certain limit. See *Fringe (employment benefits)*, p. 544.

More than one job

If you have more than one job, you will get a separate PAYE code for each job in which your earnings are taxed under PAYE, and normally a separate notice of coding for each job. All the reliefs and allowances you are entitled to will normally be included in the tax code for your main job. This means that all your earnings from the second job may be taxed. If so, the tax code you are given for the second job will be:

BR. if you are being taxed at the basic rate of tax; *or*
DO. if you are being taxed at a higher rate of tax.

If the income earned from the second job takes you into the higher rate of tax, all the earnings from the second job will be taxed at the higher rate. If you are in this situation you may find that your tax bill will need adjusting at the end of the tax year.

Other taxable income

If you have other taxable income in addition to wages or an occupational pension, the tax due on this can be deducted from these payments by your employer. This is done by altering the amounts of the allowances given to you, in effect reducing the amount of income you can receive before you have to pay tax. The most common forms of other income that are taxed in this way are state retirement and widow's pensions.

Wage rises

When you get a wage rise you are liable to pay more tax and the adjustments for this will be done automatically by your employer.

Changes to income tax in the Budget

Changes to income tax are usually made by the government in the annual Budget – for example, the amount of the allowances is usually increased. The changes are announced during November and take effect from the following 6 April.

If the allowances go up in the Budget, this increases the amount of tax-free pay you can receive before you start paying tax. If your tax code includes the letters L, P or V, your employer can make the adjustments automatically. This will usually be done in January so that the new allowances can be implemented on 6 April.

If your PAYE tax code includes the letters T or K the tax office has to send a new code to you and your employer before the adjustments can be made. The adjustments should be in place by 6 April, but if there is any delay you will receive a tax refund.

Change in circumstances

Your tax code will be affected if:

- your personal circumstances change, and you are entitled to different allowances; *or*
- your outgoings change and you can claim extra relief; *or*
- your taxable income changes – for example, you start receiving a taxable pension. This other income can also be deducted from your wages through PAYE.

If your tax position changes, your tax code may need amending. You should write to the tax office with full details of the changes and ask for the code to be amended. You should give your full name and National Insurance number and details of your employer's name, address and tax reference number. You can obtain these details from your P60 or by asking your employer. You should enclose your last notice of coding if you have one.

It is important to write as soon as possible because you may be paying the wrong amount of tax because your tax code is incorrect. This could result in either an overpayment or an underpayment of tax. If an underpayment arises the tax office will collect this and has the power to charge interest or impose a fine.

If the tax office needs further details before they can change the code they will sometimes send a tax return for completion. This should be returned within thirty days. If there is any delay in its return, this will result in a change to the tax code being delayed.

Sick or on maternity leave

If you are sick or on maternity, paternity or adoption leave you will have the tax on your pay collected under PAYE.

If you do not receive any pay you will be entitled to a rebate. This is because you did not use your tax allowance during the period when you were unpaid.

The rebate can either be paid when you return to work or while you are off work. If you are not getting any pay, you might prefer to have the rebate as soon as possible rather than wait until you are next paid. You should ask your employer to arrange this or confirm when the rebate will be paid.

Unemployment, short-time working or on strike

If you are unemployed, on short-time working or on strike you may be entitled to a rebate of tax at the end of the tax year. This is because the amount of tax you have paid may be too high for the amount of earnings you are now likely to receive over the tax year. However, if you get Jobseeker's Allowance, which may be taxed, the rebate may be cancelled out.

If you are temporarily on short-time working, your employer should make whatever tax rebate you are entitled to on your normal paydays.

If you are on strike or involved in a trade dispute you will not be able to claim a tax rebate while on strike. Instead, you will have to wait for a rebate under PAYE – in other words when you either leave the job or return to work. If you are still on strike at the end of the tax year, you will not get a rebate until you leave the job or return to work. However, your employer will give you your P60, which will show the rebate that is due as if it had been paid. Your employer must also give you an additional note saying how much tax rebate under PAYE is being withheld until you leave or return to work.

The employer or tax office makes a mistake

Your employer or tax office may make a mistake, for example if the tax office gives your employer the wrong PAYE code or your employer wrongly calculates your tax and deducts too much or too little tax. In these circumstances the amount of tax that you have over- or underpaid will be rebated or reclaimed by adjusting your PAYE tax code for the following tax year. In a limited number of circumstances you may not have to pay all the tax arrears that you owe.

If you think that a mistake has been made in the amount of income tax you have been paying, you should inform the tax office as soon as possible.

Leaving a job

If you leave your job – whether voluntarily, through dismissal, redundancy or because you retire – your employer should give you a Form P45. The P45 gives details of your employer's tax office, your employer's tax reference number, your tax code and the total amount of pay and tax deducted during the current tax year. If tax has been deducted on the emergency code, the P45 will have an X in the box marked week 1 or month 1 and there will not be any details of pay or tax. You should keep the P45 in case you start work again.

If your employer fails to give you a P45 after being asked to do so, you should contact your tax office as they may encourage your employer to issue a P45. If your employer cannot be persuaded, a new employer will ask you to complete a P46 form, which allows your new employer to deduct tax on an emergency code until the right amount of tax to be deducted is worked out.

If you claim Jobseeker's Allowance, you will have to give the P45 to the Employment Service Jobcentre. If you start work again before the end of the tax year, the Jobcentre will give you a P45U, which includes details of the taxable benefit you have received as well as the normal P45 details.

If you leave at the very end of the tax year you should be given a P60 and a P45.

Students

If you are a student who is working during vacations, you will usually pay tax in the same way as other employees. However, you and your employer can fill in a form P38S, which your employer can obtain from the tax office or local tax enquiry centre, which means tax will not be deducted under PAYE. The form must show that all the student's earnings, plus any other income for the tax year, will not exceed the total allowances and reliefs that can be claimed.

Dealing with a PAYE problem

If you have a problem about your income tax, you may be able to resolve it by talking to your employer. Your employer will have guidance from the tax office on how to operate the PAYE tax system and deal with problems.

If the problem cannot be resolved by talking to your employer, you can contact:

- a tax enquiry centre;
- the tax office that holds your records.

FRINGE (EMPLOYMENT BENEFITS)

Fringe benefits are benefits that employees or directors receive from their employment but which are not included in their salary cheque or wages. On the tax return form they are called 'benefits in kind'. They include such things as company cars, private medical insurance paid for by the employer and cheap or free loans. Some fringe benefits will not be taxed, some will, and some will be taxed only for employees who are directors or higher paid.

Tax-free fringe benefits

Some fringe benefits are tax-free and do not need to be entered on your tax return. These include:

- contributions paid by your employer into an approved occupational or personal pension scheme for the employee;
- cheap or free canteen meals, if these are provided for all employees;
- in-house sports facilities;
- counselling services to redundant employees;
- childcare for children aged under 18;
- works buses, or subsidies to public bus services, to get employees to and from work;
- bicycles and cycling safety equipment provided for employees to get to and from work, and workplace parking for bicycles and motorcycles;
- the loan by the employer of computer equipment up to a certain value;
- reasonable removal expenses if you have to move to take up a new job;
- genuine personal gifts given for reasons unconnected with the job, for example retirement gifts or wedding gifts;
- gifts, other than cash, that you receive from someone other than your employer, for example seats at sporting or cultural events, providing they are not worth more than a certain amount;
- if you are disabled, equipment and facilities provided for you to carry out your job.

For fringe benefits that are taxable, tax is paid on the taxable value of the benefit. The way the taxable value is worked out depends on whether or not you are a higher-paid employee or a director.

Common fringe benefits

If you get taxable fringe benefits, you must enter the value on your tax return for the relevant year, even if you have already paid tax on the benefit under PAYE and whether or not you count as higher-paid.

The following paragraphs list some of the more common fringe benefits.

Accommodation

Generally, where any employee, whether higher-paid or not, is provided with accommodation, either rent-free or for a very low rent, the difference between the rent paid, if any, and the annual value of the property is taxable.

There are three exceptions to this rule. No tax will have to be paid on the accommodation if:

- it is necessary for you to live in the accommodation to perform your duties properly; *or*
- it is provided so that you can perform your duties better than you could without it; *or*
- the job involves a special security risk and special accommodation is provided for your safety.

Hotels and temporary accommodation

The cost of hotels and temporary accommodation while travelling for business purposes is not taxed. However, if you are given an overall cash allowance to cover these costs, this will be taxed, but anything you spend on accommodation for the purpose of your job can be deducted from your taxable income as a tax relief.

Company cars and vans

Free private use of a car provided by your employer mainly for business use is normally only taxable for higher-paid employees and directors. Cars that are used only for business, and are not available for private use, are not taxable. In nearly all cases, travel between home and work by higher-paid employees and directors is considered by the Inland Revenue to be private use of a vehicle, not business use, and therefore is a taxable benefit.

Childcare expenses

If you pay childcare costs yourself, you cannot claim these costs as relief against tax. Neither can you claim travel expenses to and from work for childcare reasons.

Clothing

Work and safety clothes provided by your employer, for example overalls and protective helmets or shoes, are not liable to tax. However, any normal clothing provided by your employer is taxable.

Council tax

Where your employer pays your council tax, you will have to pay tax on it. But you will not have to pay tax if it is necessary for you to live in the accommodation to do your job. You may be entitled to Council Tax Benefit.

Credit cards and charge cards
If you use your employer's credit card to buy goods or services for yourself, you will have to pay tax on the cost to the employer of allowing you access to the employer's credit facility. You will not have to pay tax if you buy goods or services for yourself that are necessary for your job.

Fuel
Fuel given by an employer to a higher-paid employee or director for private use is taxable.

Holidays
If you are a higher-paid employee or director and receive a free holiday, you will have to pay tax on its value. Other employees do not have to pay tax on a free holiday as long as the holiday has no resale value, for example if payment is made direct to a hotel. A payment to a travel agent for a holiday abroad would be taxable.

Job-related benefits
Job-related benefits are benefits to employees provided from within the employer's business. They include cheap airline seats for airline staff, cheap rail travel for railway employees and goods or services provided by a business that are offered free or at a discounted price to employees. They are taxable only for higher-paid employees and directors. They do not include company cars and fuel, loans, accommodation or mobile phones, as there are special rules for these items.

Cash allowances given in lieu of job-related benefits are taxable for all employees.

Loans
Interest-free and cheap loans are taxable for higher-paid employees and directors.

Meals
Meals provided in a staff canteen that is available to all staff are not taxable and you do not need to list them on your tax return. In addition, if you get free or subsidized meals at work, and the meals are available to all employees, they will also not be taxable and do not need to be listed on your tax return. This extends to tickets or vouchers given by employers for free and subsidized meals where the meals are not provided by the employer.

Medical insurance

If your employer provides private medical insurance this is taxable for higher-paid employees and directors.

Mileage allowances

If you get a mileage allowance for using your own car for business purposes, you will be taxed on any profit you make from the allowance. This is the amount by which the total mileage allowance paid exceeds the costs incurred in running the car for business. These costs include running costs such as petrol, oil, servicing and tyres, as well as fixed costs such as road tax, insurance and depreciation.

The Inland Revenue operates a 'Fixed Profit Car Scheme', which sets out tax-free rates of mileage allowances. If you are paid less than the tax-free rates, you will not be liable for tax. If your employer pays more than the tax-free rates, you will be taxed on the difference between what the employer pays and the tax-free rate.

Employers do not have to use the 'Fixed Profit Car Scheme', and if you believe your costs are more than the tax-free rate you can still make an individual claim for tax relief.

Relocation expenses

If your employer pays your removal expenses up to a certain amount, this amount is tax-free. This limit applies to each move.

Shares

In most cases, the value of shares transferred to an employee or director at a discount is liable to tax.

Training

If you are on a full-time or sandwich course at university or college that lasts one year or more with an average of at least twenty weeks' full-time attendance, you can get up to £7,000 pay tax-free whilst you are still on the course.

If your employer pays for your training course in order to retrain you for another job, the value of the payment made by the employer is not taxable.

If your employer pays for an external training course that is not intended to train you for another job with the same employer, you will not be liable to pay tax on this payment if:

- the course is for general education and you are aged under 21 when the course starts; *or*
- the course is related to your job and you are going to be away from work on the course for less than twelve months.

If you pay for an external course that you attend whilst still being paid your usual wages, you may be able to claim tax relief.

Travelling expenses

If your employer reimburses you for the costs of travelling to and from work or pays these direct – for example, by buying a season ticket for you – the value of this benefit is generally taxable. However, you can claim tax relief on any travelling expenses paid by your employer to cover the cost of journeys made by you as a necessary part of your job, excluding journeys to and from work.

Vouchers

If you get vouchers, including luncheon vouchers, of more than 15p a day and cheque vouchers that are exchangeable for goods and services, you will be taxed on the cost to your employer of providing the voucher and these goods and services. Cash vouchers, such as Holiday Stamp schemes used in the building industry, are subject to tax in all cases. If the voucher can be exchanged for cash, the tax will generally be paid through PAYE as if it were a payment of cash.

Overnight expenses

If you stay away from home overnight on business and incur personal expenses, for example for newspapers, telephone calls home, or laundry, you can have these expenses reimbursed by your employer without the payment being taxable. The limit for non-taxable reimbursement is £5/night for stays in the United Kingdom or £10/night for stays elsewhere.

How tax is declared and paid on fringe benefits

If you get any taxable fringe benefits, you must enter their value on your tax return for the relevant year, even if tax has already been paid on them under PAYE. Your employer also has to make a return to the tax office with details of any fringe benefits given to you. Your employer makes the return on the form P11D, which lists the benefits and expenses for the relevant tax year. You should get a copy of this form by 6 July following the end of the tax year.

Fringe benefits may be taxed under PAYE by being offset against personal tax allowances in your PAYE code. Otherwise, tax will be collected after the end of the tax year by the issue of an assessment on the fringe benefits.

SELF ASSESSMENT

Tax may have to be paid to the Inland Revenue direct by Self Assessment where the full liability was not, or cannot be, met by deduction at source. This may occur with, for example:

- earnings from self-employment;
- rental income from property;
- interest received gross – for example, on National Savings investments accounts;
- income from overseas;
- fringe benefits received by employees and earnings of employees where an insufficient amount has been paid under PAYE.

Where tax needs to be collected by Self Assessment – for example, because you are self-employed – a tax return form must be completed. You can then either ask the Inland Revenue to calculate the tax due based on the figures in the tax return (Revenue calculation), or calculate the amount of tax due yourself (taxpayer calculation).

If you have completed a tax return, you will usually be sent a statement of account, which is like a tax bill, when the tax is due. If you asked the Inland Revenue to do the tax calculation, the statement of account will show the result of the calculation and how much tax is due. If you did the tax calculation yourself, you will need to enter the amount that you are due to pay on the statement of account. There are set dates in each tax year for tax due to be paid.

Tax return form

A tax return is a form on which you must give details of your income and expenses, if asked to do so by the Inland Revenue. The tax return is then used to calculate the amount of tax that you are due to pay.

You can choose to do the tax calculation yourself by answering the appropriate questions on the tax return, or you can ask the Inland Revenue to do the tax calculation.

Who should complete a tax return

Not all taxpayers are required to fill in tax returns and they are not usually issued to people who have salaries and pensions taxed under Pay As You Earn (PAYE), since it is usually assumed that the correct amount of tax is being deducted at source.

Returns are routinely issued to taxpayers whom the Inland Revenue believes have:

- income from self-employment;
- rental income from property;
- other income that is received gross – that is, where tax has not already been deducted, for example interest on National Savings investment accounts;
- complex tax affairs – for example, higher rate taxpayers or company directors.

Even though returns are not normally issued if you pay tax under PAYE, the Inland Revenue may send one to you as a way of checking that your tax affairs are in order. This is quite common where you have changed jobs, or moved from a salary to an occupational pension.

If you know that you have not paid the correct amount of tax on your income for a particular tax year, you should not wait for the Inland Revenue to send a tax return but should contact your local tax office. Otherwise, you may incur penalties or pay more tax than is necessary.

Where you have received income on which tax is payable, and no tax return has been issued, it is your obligation to notify your tax office of the income received. This should be done in writing, and by no later than 6 October following the end of the tax year in which the income was received. If you fail to notify the Inland Revenue of your income, this can lead to penalties and interest on the outstanding tax. If you write to notify the Inland Revenue of untaxed income, you will be sent a tax return form, so it is often simpler to telephone the Inland Revenue for a tax return form and use this to report the income concerned.

If you believe that you have paid too much tax, you should not rely on the Inland Revenue to find out about this automatically. You should contact your tax office for an appropriate form to claim a refund.

The Inland Revenue has a legal right to demand completion of a tax return from anyone, and where a return form has been issued the tax office will normally insist upon its completion.

Completing a tax return form

The tax return consists of a main form, which everyone who receives a tax return has to complete, and nine supplementary pages, which people with certain types of income have to fill in. There is also an accompanying booklet that gives further guidance on how to fill it in.

If you do not provide all the information required on the form, this will be regarded by the Inland Revenue as the tax return not being completed. This would leave you liable to pay interest and possibly penalties.

You have a duty to keep records of your income and, each year, you should receive documents from your employer or pension administrator that give details of the income you have received, including any fringe benefits. You will need these records and documents to be able to complete a tax return.

Self-employed or rental income

If you have been self-employed, or are receiving rental income from property that is not within the rent a room provisions, details of this income will need to be reported in the appropriate supplementary pages of the tax return.

You will normally have to give details of expenses incurred in the course of running a business, or renting out property that is not within the rent a room provisions.

Deadline for sending back a tax return

You must send your tax return back to the local tax office by the 31 January following the end of the tax year. The tax year ends on 6 April. If you do not do so, you will automatically incur penalties. However, if you want the Inland Revenue to do the tax calculation, you must send the completed return back to the local tax office by the 30 September following the end of the tax year.

Errors on tax returns

If you or the tax office finds a minor error on a tax return, this can often be remedied quite simply by correspondence.

If your income was overstated, resulting in you paying more tax than is actually due, the Inland Revenue will repay the amount of the overpayment with the appropriate amount of interest.

If, however, there is a significant error – for example, if income was under-declared – the tax office may consider this to be grounds for opening an enquiry into the tax return.

Who can help?

The Inland Revenue produces a useful leaflet called 'Self Assessment – Your guide' available from www.ir.gov.uk or from the Self Assessment Orderline (0845 9 000 404).

For general enquiries on Self Assessment, telephone your local tax office or call the Self Assessment Helpline (0845 9 000 444).

INCOME TAX AND THE OVER 65s

If you are 65 or over, you are liable to pay tax in the same way as any other taxpayer but you may be able to claim higher tax allowances than a younger person.

You may have income from a number of sources that may be either taxable or tax-free:

- earnings – taxable;
- an occupational pension – taxable;
- a personal pension – taxable;
- social security benefits (for example, Retirement Pension), Pension Credit – some benefits are taxable and some are tax-free;
- savings or investments. The income from savings and investments is usually taxable. Only a few types of investment income are tax-free.

How much tax must you pay?

You have to pay income tax only on your taxable income. This is worked out for the tax year, which runs from 6 April one year to 5 April the following year. To work out your taxable income, add together your total income from all sources for the tax year concerned. Taxable income is this total less:

- any tax allowances you are entitled to;
- any tax reliefs you are entitled to;
- any income you have that is tax-free.

The amount left is known as taxable income and is taxed at the appropriate percentage rate.

When the tax office has assessed your tax, it will tell you how much tax you have to pay. It will do this by giving you either:

- a PAYE tax code, if you pay tax under the PAYE tax system; *or*
- a notice of assessment, if you pay tax by direct collection assessment.

Types of income and how they are taxed

The following outlines the types of income that people aged 65 or over are most likely to have and how they are taxed.

People whose only taxable income is state retirement pension

State Retirement Pension is taxable (although increases for dependent children are not) but tax on this is never deducted directly from pension payments. If your only taxable income is the basic rate State Retirement Pension (excluding graduated or additional pension), you will not pay any tax, because your allowance(s) will be more than the basic pension.

If you get basic State Retirement Pension plus graduated and/or additional pension (SERPS), but do not get any income from earnings or an occupational pension, you will pay tax directly to the Inland Revenue by Self Assessment, and must complete a tax return form.

People with income from Pension Credit

Pension Credit is not a taxable benefit and no tax is therefore payable on your income from Pension Credit.

People with income from an occupational or personal pension

Occupational pensions are taxable. Any tax will be deducted by your former employer under the PAYE scheme before the pension is paid. If you have other taxable income, the tax on this is also collected through the PAYE system. For example, the tax due on your state pension is collected by deducting extra tax from your occupational pension.

Personal pensions are taxable. Any tax due is deducted by the company providing the pension before the pension payment is made. If you have other taxable income, the tax due on this other income is paid directly to the Inland Revenue by Self Assessment. However, if you have an occupational pension or earnings from employment, the tax due on your income (other than on your personal pension) will be collected through the PAYE system.

People with earnings from employment
If you work for an employer, your earnings are taxed under the PAYE system. The tax due on your other taxable income, for example state retirement pension, is also deducted from your earnings under the PAYE system.

If you are working and getting an occupational pension, your total allowances and reliefs will be set against your occupational pension and, unless the occupational pension is too low to use up all the allowances and reliefs, no allowances will be given against your earnings. The tax code given on your notice of coding will relate to your occupational pension only. Your payslip will show a special PAYE code that is a standard second job code. This code means that you pay tax on all your earnings without any tax allowances or reliefs.

If you are working and getting an occupational pension, and also have another source of taxable income, for example rent from a tenant or lodger, the tax due on this source of income is usually deducted from your occupational pension unless the pension is too small, in which case the tax is collected by reducing your PAYE code.

How income from savings and investments is taxed
The way that income from savings and investments is taxed and paid depends on the type of investment. You can find information on how your savings and investments are taxed earlier in this chapter.

Getting a tax rebate on retirement
When you retire, you may be entitled to a tax rebate if your income drops. If you get an occupational pension or have income from employment, there is no need to apply to the tax office for a tax rebate, as any overpaid tax will be automatically rebated through the PAYE system. If not, you can apply for a rebate. To do this:

- contact your local PAYE Enquiry Office and ask for a form on which to apply for a rebate;
- write to your tax office claiming a rebate. Your former employer will be able to give you the address.

Tax allowances and relief you can claim

Tax allowances

Tax allowances are a type of tax-free income – fixed amounts of income that you can receive before you have to pay tax. Everyone is automatically given a personal allowance but, at 65, you may be entitled to a higher allowance depending on your income.

You may also be able to claim a married couple's allowance if you or your spouse is 65 or more. A blind person can also claim a blind person's allowance.

Married couple's allowance for people aged 65 and over

To claim married couple's allowance, you must be married and living together and at least one of you must have been born before 5 April 1935. You will be treated as living together unless you are separated by a court order or separation deed, or have separated in such circumstances that the separation is likely to be permanent.

From 6 April 2000, the married couple's allowance was abolished for couples aged under 65. If you are part of a couple where either you or your spouse were aged 65 or over on or before 6 April 2000, you will be able to keep the married couple's allowance even though it was abolished on 6 April 2000.

When a personal or married couple's allowance is reduced, if aged 65 or over

The higher tax allowance given to you if you are aged 65 or over is reduced if your total income is more than a certain limit. When calculating your total income for the personal allowance, the income of each partner in a married couple is calculated separately – each partner has an income limit, and the income of the other partner does not count towards it.

When working out the income limit for the married couple's allowance, only the income of the husband counts, irrespective of who claims the allowance. The income of the wife does not count, even if she receives all or part of the married couple's allowance.

If income is over the income limit, the allowance is reduced by £1 for every £2 that the income is over the limit. If the amount of income is so large that the allowance would be reduced to the same amount as, or below, the amount of the basic personal or married couple's allowance, you will only get the basic personal or married couple's allowance.

When calculating whether your income is more than the income limit, any income that is exempt from tax should not be included. Special rules apply to income from which tax has already been deducted. The most common example of this is where tax has been deducted from building society interest before the payments are made to you.

Tax relief

Tax relief is given on certain outgoings – for example, on property that is let out. In practice this means that you will not pay tax on the amount of income you spend on these items.

WHO CAN HELP?

If you have a tax problem and are an employee, you may be able to resolve it by talking to your employer. Your employer will have guidance on how to operate the PAYE tax system and deal with problems.

If the problem cannot be resolved by talking to your employer, or you are not working, you should first contact:

- a tax enquiry centre;
- the tax office that holds your records.

If the problem remains unresolved, you may wish to:

- challenge or negotiate with the Inland Revenue;
- complain to the Revenue Adjudicator;
- complain to the Parliamentary Ombudsman;
- contact TaxAid for help.

Tax enquiry centres

Tax enquiry centres are local tax offices that can help with income tax problems. The centres can help with general enquiries – for example, whether you can claim certain allowances or reliefs – and with specific problems relating to your tax records. Most tax enquiry centres are open to the public and deal with written or telephone enquiries.

Tax enquiry centres are either listed in the local telephone directory under

'Inland Revenue', or details of them will be available from local Inspectors of Taxes' offices.

Tax offices

Each employer has a tax office that holds the tax records for everyone who works for that employer. The tax office may be some distance from where you work.

The employer must give you the following information if you ask for it, as well as providing it on your P45 and P60:

- the name and address of the tax office; *and*
- your tax reference number.

When you contact the tax office you must quote your National Insurance number and your employer's tax reference number. The National Insurance number and the tax reference number are given on forms P45 and P60, or you can ask the employer for them.

Most tax offices only deal with written or telephone enquiries and are not open to the public.

CHALLENGING AND NEGOTIATING WITH THE INLAND REVENUE

You may wish to challenge a decision or negotiate with the Inland Revenue. The procedure to follow, and the office concerned, will differ according to the type of challenge or dispute.

Some of the main procedures are:

- appealing – for example, against a calculation of tax liability or a PAYE code;
- seeking a waiver, because of Inland Revenue delays;
- negotiating tax debts;
- complaining about Inland Revenue conduct.

The Revenue Adjudicator

The Revenue Adjudicator considers complaints of Inland Revenue maladministration, for example:

- excessive delay;

- errors;
- discourtesy.

The Revenue Adjudicator will not consider:

- legal disputes;
- complaints that have already been investigated by the Parliamentary Ombudsman – see below;
- appeals against property valuations, including appeals against Council Tax bandings – these should be referred to valuation tribunals;
- matters relating to a criminal prosecution during the course of legal proceedings.

A complaint should not usually be referred to the Revenue Adjudicator until you have given the Inland Revenue a chance to remedy matters. However, in urgent cases the Revenue Adjudicator may offer immediate help without you approaching the Inland Revenue first, for example if there is a risk that any delay might cause irreparable damage. If you do contact the Revenue Adjudicator's Office directly (020 7930 2292; www.adjudicatorsoffice.gov.uk), you will be guided through the necessary procedures.

The Parliamentary Ombudsman

The Parliamentary Ombudsman may be able to help with complaints against the Inland Revenue if, for example, there has been avoidable delay, failure to give appropriate advice or failure to follow proper procedures. The Ombudsman cannot investigate complaints about government policy or about tax legislation.

If you want to complain to the Parliamentary Ombudsman, you must first contact your MP and ask for the matter to be referred.

TaxAid

TaxAid (020 7803 4959; www.taxaid.org.uk) provides a free and independent tax service offering advice, assistance and advocacy to people needing help with tax. It covers subjects such as tax allowances, PAYE codes, tax arrears, self-employment, tax returns and Revenue administration and complaints. The service is intended for people who cannot afford to employ an accountant. Advice can be given over the telephone and interviews may be arranged.

COUNCIL TAX

Council Tax is a system of local taxation collected by local authorities. It is a tax on domestic property. Generally, the bigger the property is, the more tax will be charged. Some property will be exempt from Council Tax.

Valuation bands

Each local authority keeps a list of all the domestic property in its area. This is called the valuation list. Each property is valued and put into a valuation band. A different amount of Council Tax is then charged on each band. The valuation bands are:

In England

Valuation band	Range of values
A	Up to £40,000
B	Over £40,000 and up to £52,000
C	Over £52,000 and up to £68,000
D	Over £68,000 and up to £88,000
E	Over £88,000 and up to £120,000
F	Over £129,000 and up to £160,000
G	Over £160,000 and up to £320,000
H	Over £320,000

In Wales

Valuation band	Range of values
A	Up to £44,000
B	Over £44,000 and up to £65,000
C	Over £65,000 and up to £91,000
D	Over £91,000 and up to £123000
E	Over £123,000 and up to £162,000
F	Over £162,000 and up to £223,000
G	Over £223,000 and up to £324,000
H	Over £324,000 and up to £424,000
I	Over £424,000

To find out what band a dwelling is in you can:

- inspect a copy of the valuation list;
- look at the council tax banding lists published on the internet by the Valuation Office Agency (www.voa.gov.uk);
- check with your local authority in advance of receiving a Council Tax bill;
- if you are the liable person, you can also find the valuation band from the council tax bill or from an alteration to the valuation list by the listing officer.

A copy of the valuation list is kept at the local authority's main offices and is available for public inspection. Local authorities may also make the list available in other offices, including libraries. You can look at and make copies of the valuation list at the local authority's office or at the local valuation office. There may be a small charge.

If an alteration is made to the valuation list, including adding a new dwelling to the list, the listing officer will inform the liable person.

Properties exempt from council tax

Some property is exempt from Council Tax altogether. It may be exempt for only a short period, for example six months, or for a longer time.

Properties that may be exempt are:

- empty property;
- property that is undergoing major repairs or alterations;
- condemned property;
- property that has been repossessed by a mortgage lender;
- property unoccupied because the person who lived there now lives elsewhere because they need to be cared for, for example in hospital (or with relatives);
- property that is unoccupied because the person who lived there has gone to care for someone else;
- any property that only students live in – this may be a hall of residence or a house;
- a caravan or boat on a property where council tax is paid;
- a property where all the people who live in it are aged under 18;
- a property where all the people who live in it are either severely mentally impaired or are students or where there is a mixture of both;
- a self-contained 'granny flat' where the person who lives in it is a dependent relative of the owner of the main property.

Who has to pay?

Usually one person, called the liable person, is liable to pay Council Tax. Nobody under the age of 18 can be a liable person. A man and woman living together will both be liable, even if there is only one name on the bill.

Usually, the person living in a property will be the liable person, but sometimes it will be the owner of the property who will be liable to pay.

The owner will always be liable if:

- the property is in multiple occupation, for example if it is a house lived in by a number of people who all pay rent, but no one is responsible for paying the whole of the rent; or
- the people who live in the property are all under the age of 18; or
- the people who live in the property are all asylum seekers who are not entitled to claim benefits including Council Tax Benefit; or
- the people who are staying in the property have their main homes somewhere else; or
- the property is a care home.

If only one person lives in a property, they will be the liable person. If more than one person lives there, a system called the hierarchy of liability is used to work out who is the liable person. The person at the top, or nearest to the top, of the hierarchy is the liable person. Two people at the same point of the hierarchy will both be liable.

The hierarchy of liability in England and Wales is:

1. a resident who lives in the property and who owns the freehold (an owner occupier);
2. a resident who lives in the property and who has a lease or who is an assured or an assured shorthold tenant;
3. a resident who lives in the property and who is a protected, statutory or secure tenant;
4. a resident who lives in the property and who is a licensee (this means that they are not a tenant, but have permission to stay there);
5. any resident living in the property, for example a squatter;
6. an owner of the property who does not live there.

How much is it?

Each year, every local authority will set a rate of Council Tax for each valuation band. Not everyone will have to pay the full amount of Council Tax. There are three ways in which your Council Tax bill may be reduced. These are:

- the reduction scheme for disabled people;
- discounts;
- Council Tax Benefit (CTB) and second adult rebate.

Reduction scheme for people with disabilities

If there is someone (adult or child) living in a household who has a disability, the Council Tax bill for the property may be reduced. The reduction is made by charging Council Tax on a lower valuation band than the one the property is in. For example, if the property is in band D, the Council Tax bill will be worked out as if it were in band C. There is also a reduction if the property is in band A. To claim a reduction you must show that a disabled person lives in the property, and also that the property meets that person's needs.

An application for this reduction must be made in writing to the local authority. Many local authorities will have a special application form. Some will ask for supporting evidence, for example a doctor's letter.

Discounts

If only one person lives in a property they will get a 25 per cent discount on the Council Tax bill. When working out how many people live in a property, some people are not counted. These are called disregarded people. If everyone who lives in the property is disregarded, there will still be a Council Tax bill, but there will be a 50 per cent discount. Examples of people who are disregarded are:

- people aged 17 or under;
- people living in the property temporarily and who have their home somewhere else;
- someone defined as a severely mentally impaired person;
- full-time students on a qualifying course of education;

- young people on government training schemes, apprentices, or foreign language assistants;
- hospital patients who live in hospital;
- people living in a residential care home, nursing home, or mental nursing home where they receive care or treatment;
- carers;
- care workers;
- school or college leavers still aged under 20 who have left school or college after 30 April. They will be disregarded until 1 November of the same year whether or not they take up employment.
- a person aged 18 if someone is entitled to Child Benefit for them. This includes a school or college leaver in remunerative work, or a person in local authority care.

A local authority may automatically send a Council Tax bill that includes a discount. The discount will be shown on the bill.

If you believe that you are entitled to a discount and your bill does not show that you have had one, you should apply to the local authority for a discount as soon as possible.

If the bill shows that the local authority has applied a discount and you do not think that you should have one, you must tell the local authority within twenty-one days. If you do not do this, the local authority may later impose a penalty.

Holiday homes

Second or holiday homes in England will be liable for Council Tax but will have a 10–50 per cent discount because no one lives there. In Wales, local authorities can reduce or end the discount in a second home.

Council Tax Benefit and second adult rebate

A person who is liable to pay Council Tax may be able to claim Council Tax Benefit. The amount of benefit they may get will depend on their income and capital.

If you have someone living with you who is not liable to pay Council Tax on your property, you may be able to claim a benefit called a 'second adult rebate'. You will not be able to claim a second adult rebate as well as Council Tax Benefit. If you are entitled to both, you will receive whichever is the higher.

How to pay

Council Tax bills should be sent out in April. You have the right to pay by ten instalments. Local authorities may accept weekly or fortnightly payments. Some may also offer a reduction in the total bill if it is paid all at once, at the beginning of the year.

Arrears

If you do not pay an instalment of Council Tax within twenty-eight days of the date it is due, and have been late with two instalments previously, you lose the right to pay by instalments and become liable to pay the full amount immediately. In practice, most local authorities will still accept payments by instalments.

When you have not paid an instalment of Council Tax within twenty-eight days of the date it is due, the local authority may ask a magistrates' court to issue a court summons for the arrears. If these are not paid by the date of the court summons, the local authority can ask the magistrates to issue a liability order.

A liability order allows a local authority to make arrangements for the arrears to be paid by deductions from a person's Income Support, Jobseeker's Allowance or wages, or for bailiffs to seize a person's goods to the value of the amount owed.

Appeals

Appeals can be made about a range of issues concerning the Council Tax. An appeal must be made to either the valuation office or the local authority depending on what it is about.

Appeals can be made to the valuation office about:

- whether or not the property should be on the valuation list;
- which valuation band the property is in;
- in a property which is partly domestic and partly business, what proportion of the property is domestic.

Appeals can be made to the local authority about:

- whether or not someone is a liable person – this includes someone who is jointly liable because there are two or more people on the same level of the hierarchy or because they are one of a couple;

- whether or not the property is exempt;
- whether or not a discount applies and how much it is;
- whether or not the reduction scheme for people with disabilities applies.

Appeals cannot be made about the level of Council Tax set or the valuation bands for the area.

You can appeal against a decision of the valuation office if you are:

- the owner of the property;
- the liable person, including a person who is jointly liable – there are special rules about when a liable person can appeal about the valuation band of a dwelling;
- the person who would be liable if the property was not exempt;
- the local authority.

The following people can appeal against a decision of the local authority:

- a liable person, including a person who is jointly liable;
- an aggrieved person. This is a person who is directly affected by the decision, for example the administrator of the estate of a liable person who has died.

People who wish to appeal must have moved into the property less than six months before the date of their appeal, or be in a new property that has recently been added to the valuation list.

Appeals to alter the valuation band of a dwelling

The valuation list may be altered to place a dwelling in a different valuation band if:

- there was an error when the list was compiled; *or*
- the dwelling was valued incorrectly – for example, because the valuation officer did not know about internal features of the dwelling that reduced its value; *or*
- in a dwelling that is partly domestic and partly business, the domestic proportion has increased or decreased, or the dwelling has become wholly domestic or wholly business; *or*
- there have been changes to the dwelling that have reduced its value; *or*
- there have been changes to the dwelling that have increased its value and the dwelling has subsequently been sold.

There are special rules about when a liable person can appeal regarding the valuation band a dwelling has been put in – see below.

If the person liable for a dwelling changes, the new liable person(s) will have six months from the date they become liable to make a proposal to change the valuation band. So, for example, if you became the liable person on 13 July 2005 you would have six months from 13 July 2005 to make a proposal to change the list. This is provided that your grounds for the proposal have not already been considered and rejected by a valuation tribunal or the High Court.

If a dwelling has recently been added to the valuation list, the liable person has six months from the date they become the liable person to make a proposal to change the list. In practice this means six months from the date the dwelling goes on to the valuation list.

Appealing to the valuation office

In order to appeal you must first make a proposal to the valuation office saying what you think should be changed and why. If the valuation office does not agree to the changes, the proposal automatically becomes an appeal and is heard by a valuation tribunal.

Properties can only be put in a different band under certain circumstances, for example if something has happened to reduce the value of the property significantly.

Appealing to the local authority

The first stage of an appeal to the local authority involves making a written complaint about the problem to the local authority. If the local authority does not resolve the problem, an appeal can then be made to the valuation tribunal.

The valuation tribunal

In all cases the valuation tribunal will consider all the information about the particular case and will decide what should happen. They may decide on the basis of written representations or may call everyone involved to a meeting to hear their evidence.

Particular circumstances

There are particular points to remember in the following circumstances:

- if you live permanently in a hotel – you will not be liable for Council Tax on the property although the hotel charges would probably include an amount towards any Council Tax payable;
- if you have more than one home – you will probably pay a reduced Council Tax on your second home (if no one lives there) and a full Council Tax on your main home;
- if you own caravans or mobile homes – if you live permanently in a caravan or mobile home you will pay the Council Tax. People who have a fixed caravan as a holiday home will pay business rate. Towing caravans kept at your home will not be subject to either Council Tax or business rate.
- if you are a full-time student in advanced education – you will have to pay Council Tax if you are the liable person for a property. However, if all the people living in the property are students no Council Tax will be payable and if some of the residents are students the Council Tax may be reduced.

2
Credit and Debt

CONTENTS

INTRODUCTION

Years ago, the motto was 'never a borrower or a lender be' and
debt was shrouded in shame. Debtors' prisons, like the
Marshalsea in South London where Charles Dickens's father was
imprisoned in 1824, may no longer exist, but unmanageable debt
is still an invisible prison for those unable to escape from it. Low

rates of unemployment, low interest rates and soaring house prices in recent years have resulted in a substantial increase in mortgage and consumer credit lending, now standing at over £1 trillion.

The credit landscape has undergone dramatic changes in the last thirty years and we now have over 1,400 credit and store cards as opposed to the handful available in 1979. Credit is available at every turn. Offers of loans and credit cards drop unsolicited on to our doormats and opportunities to buy more stuff 'on tick' are offered to us in most high street stores. But, according to the Financial Services Authority, two in three people feel that financial matters are too complicated for them and the underside of the credit boom is the rise in the number of people sliding from handling credit into tackling debt. Citizens Advice Bureaux have seen a 47 per cent rise in the number of people coming to them for advice about debt in the five years to 2002. All in all, it has never been a better time to get your head around your money matters and a grip on your finances.

In this chapter, we cover what to look out for when taking out credit, what to do if you are getting into debt and who can help.

JARGON BUSTER

AER stands for Annual Equivalent Rate. This shows what the interest rate would be if the interest on savings were paid and added to savings at the end of each year. The higher the AER the better the return is on your savings.

APR the Annual Percentage Rate of the total charge for credit. This tells you the cost of a loan, taking into account the interest you pay, any other charges, and when the payments fall due. A loan with an APR of 15 per cent is more expensive that one with an APR of 11 per cent.

basic bank account a type of bank or building society account for people who may have difficulty in opening a standard current account, or who have a current account that is overdrawn. There is no risk of going overdrawn and running up overdraft charges.

CCJ stands for County Court Judgment. This is an order made by a county court judge to deal with debt. CCJs are usually registered and credit reference agencies will note them on someone's credit file.

compound interest this is the type of interest usually paid on a savings account. It is calculated by adding together the amount you have paid into your account (the capital) with the interest paid on it. This is also the type of interest you pay on money you borrow – so the amount you owe can increase quite dramatically over quite a short period of time.

consolidation loan a loan that combines (consolidates) all your outstanding credit cards, housing arrears, loan repayments and household bills into one monthly payment

credit report the information stored about you with a credit reference agency. It will include electoral roll information for your address, how you have handled credit in the last six years and a record of credit checks made about you with that agency.

credit reference agency (CRA) allows creditors to share credit-related information, for example electoral roll entries, to help them lend responsibly

credit repair companies companies offering, for a charge, to advise on how, for example, to erase bad credit from your credit record. Credit repair companies have no special powers to do anything that you couldn't do yourself.

debt management plan (DMP) a debt management plan is a way of deciding how to repay all your non-priority creditors after giving consideration to your priority payments such as mortgage and fuel bills

financial adviser an individual or firm that can assess your financial needs, recommend suitable products, and arrange for you to buy or invest in these products

hire purchase agreement a form of credit agreement which allows you to pay for goods in instalments

interest rate the percentage that is paid on savings or loans. A savings account that was offering 8 per cent would give you a better return than one which was offering 5 per cent. Similarly, borrowing money at 22.5 per cent is going to cost more than borrowing at 18 per cent.

investment financial products that typically involve some risk of losing your original money but give you the opportunity of better returns than you can get from savings – for example, stock market-based investments, such as bonds, shares, trusts and so on.

ISA means Individual Savings Account. You do not have to pay tax on the gains or income from an ISA.

non-priority debts non-priority debts are those where non-payment will not result in the loss of the debtor's home, liberty, essential goods or services

priority debts these are debts that carry the strongest penalties if payment is not made, for example eviction from your home, disconnection of gas or electricity, or imprisonment for non-payment of court fines or council tax

re-financing negotiating a new loan to pay off an existing loan or loans

risk refers to the risk of losing money through savings or investments. Generally, the higher the potential rate of return on your investment or savings, the greater the risk.

secured loan money borrowed from a lender, using your property as an extra guarantee of repayment. If the amount is not paid in full, the lender may repossess and sell the property.

stakeholder a type of pension scheme designed to be good value for money by having low charges and flexible payments

sub-prime lenders (non-status or impaired credit lending) lenders willing to make loans to people who are unable to obtain credit from mainstream lenders, such as high street banks or building societies, because of a poor credit record. Interest rates may be higher than if you get a loan from a mainstream lender.

tax credits means-tested allowances administered by the Inland Revenue

unsecured loan money borrowed from, for example a bank, that is not secured against your home. The lender may only sue for payment if you default on the loan.

CREDIT

'Annual income twenty pounds, annual expenditure nineteen nineteen six, result happiness. Annual income twenty pounds, annual expenditure twenty pounds nought and six, result misery.' Mr Micawber, *David Copperfield*.

If your account is in credit, you have money available to spend. If you obtain goods or services 'on credit' it means that someone, for example a bank or credit institution, has given you the money to make a purchase. The money has been credited to you on a temporary basis, and you must pay it back.

What the law says

Anyone who offers credit must be licensed by the Office of Fair Trading. Most credit agreements for amounts of £25,000 or less are covered by the Consumer Credit Act 1974.

These are called **regulated agreements**. If you have a regulated agreement, you are entitled to:

● have specific information included in your agreement, such as the amount you are borrowing, the length of the agreement, interest rates, any charges, the amount and frequency of payments and your cancellation rights. It must also include the total charge for credit and the Annual Percentage Rate (APR), which is the annual cost of credit after interest and all other charges have been added together. If this information is not included, the agreement may be unenforceable.

- be given a copy of the agreement, which is not binding until signed by both you and the creditor;
- be sent a statement or copy of other documents on request. You may have to pay a small amount.
- be informed of the procedures to be followed, such as sending you a default notice, before court action is taken.

Your agreement will state under its heading whether it is regulated by the Consumer Credit Act. There are some exceptions, such as low cost credit from a credit union. If you want to check whether your loan is regulated, contact your local Trading Standards Department.

Buying on credit

Before applying for credit, you should work out your regular outgoings to be sure you can afford the extra payments each month.

The following steps will help you find the best deal:

- shop around, to see whether you can buy the goods or service cheaper elsewhere, as this will reduce the amount you have to borrow;
- compare the cost of different types of credit by looking at both the APR and the length of the agreement. A fixed interest loan that you arrange yourself may be cheaper than arranging a loan through the supplier. If you are using your credit card, try to estimate how long it will take you to repay the money, taking the monthly interest charges into account.
- you may be tempted by interest-free or other special deals. Look at the total cost of the deal – you may be able to buy the goods cheaper elsewhere. If interest-free credit is offered for a limited period, make sure you check what happens if you don't finish paying during this period. Often there is a high rate of interest payable from the beginning of the agreement.
- ask for a written quotation before you sign anything and read it thoroughly at home;
- if you are offered insurance to cover your payments in certain circumstances, check the cover is right for you and that you do not fall into one of the excluded groups. Some policies exclude, for example, self-employed people or pregnant women. Ask yourself whether you can find cheaper or more inclusive cover elsewhere.
- don't take out a loan secured on your home without considering the consequences. If your circumstances change and you are unable to keep up your monthly instalments, you could lose your home.

Equal liability

If you use your credit card, or if the seller arranged finance for you, the finance company in a regulated agreement is equally liable for the supplier's breach of contract, providing the purchase price was over £100 and under £30,000. This means that you may claim against the credit company, the supplier, or both jointly. If you arrange your own credit, such as a bank loan, the bank will not be liable for problems with the goods or services. The principle of equal liability is especially useful if the supplier has gone out of business. If you buy goods abroad using your credit card, the credit card company may have equal liability provided the credit card was issued in the UK. If your credit card company denies liability, your local Trading Standards Department or CAB may be able to help.

Cancellation of a regulated credit agreement

Cancellation by you

In certain circumstances, you have the right to cancel a credit agreement if:

- you have signed the credit agreement recently; *and*
- you have talked to the seller about the deal face to face (rather than only on the telephone); *and*
- you did not sign the agreement on the seller's business premises; *and*
- the goods have been delivered and it is still possible to return them to the seller in their original state. You will not be able to cancel if the goods are perishable. If you have allowed the seller to install goods (for example, double glazing), you would be able to cancel the credit, but would still be liable to pay the cash price.

In such circumstances, it is essential that you act quickly and notify the creditor immediately in writing that you wish to cancel. When you sign an agreement, you must be given a copy containing cancellation rights and details of how you would exercise these rights. These rights will only last a short length of time.

The *cooling-off period* runs from the date you signed the agreement and ends five days after you received the notice of your cancellation rights. If you have not been given notice of your cancellation rights, the agreement is unenforceable. Keep copies of any correspondence you send and proof of postage.

Even if the above rules do not apply, you may still have the right to withdraw from the deal if the creditor has not yet signed their part of the agreement. In these circumstances, you should telephone the creditor immediately to establish whether they have signed their agreement and, if not, inform them you wish to cancel. Make a note of what is said and the name of the person you speak to. You should then confirm this in a letter. Make a copy of your letter and send it by recorded delivery.

Once you have signed a credit agreement and any cooling-off period has ended, any rights you may have to cancel your agreement will be included in your contract and will depend on the type of credit you took out:

- **credit card agreements** can be cancelled by writing to the creditor, enclosing the card(s) cut in pieces and making arrangements to repay any money you owe. If there is a second card on your account held by someone else, this should also be returned.
- **hire purchase or conditional sale agreements** can be terminated at any time by giving notice that you wish to return the goods and cancel the agreement. This may be an expensive option, as you will be liable for half the total amount payable under the agreement as well as any arrears outstanding and compensation if any damage has been caused to the item. Once you have paid a third of the total amount payable under the agreement, the credit company cannot repossess the goods without a court order. Repossession without a court order in these circumstances cancels the agreement so you can recover all the payments you have made.

Cancellation by the credit company

If you are in breach of your credit agreement (for example, if you are behind in your payments), the creditor must send you a **default notice** before they can take certain types of action against you. This notice must specify the breach, tell you how to remedy it, what action will be taken if you don't and give you a time limit to put the matter right. If you fail to act on this notice, the creditor may be entitled to terminate the agreement, demand early payment of the sum owing, or repossess goods.

Being refused credit

You cannot insist on being given credit. Most creditors use credit reference agencies and credit scoring to decide whether to give credit. Creditors do not have to give reasons for refusing to give you credit, although the codes of practice they follow suggest you should be given the main reason for any refusal.

Credit reference agencies

There are three credit reference agencies, Callcredit (0870 060 1414; www.callcredit.co.uk.), Equifax (0870 010 0583; www.equifax.co.uk) and Experian (0870 241 6212; www.experian.co.uk), who collect and store information on everyone's financial situation. Agency records are not a 'blacklist'. Credit reference agencies provide factual information to lenders, for example banks, building societies, finance houses and major retailers. The lender uses the information provided by the credit reference agency, together with the information given by you on an application for credit, to decide whether or not to grant credit. Information held includes details of county court judgments, bankruptcy, any property repossessed, any other credit accounts you have and a record of everyone who has requested a credit check on your file. The agencies do not hold detailed information about your bank and building society accounts. No details are held about magistrates' court or High Court actions including liability orders for community charge and council tax arrears. Credit information is usually held for six years.

You can check the information held by the credit reference companies by writing to them asking for a copy. Alternatively, you may be able to apply online via the website. A small fee is payable. You can ask that incorrect information be corrected, but cannot ask that correct information be removed.

Credit repair agencies

Beware of companies that promise to repair your credit record for a fee. They have no special powers to do anything you could not do yourself.

Credit scoring

Credit scoring is a system used by most lenders to decide whether credit should be offered. Points are awarded for such things as your age, occupation, marital status and whether you own your own home. If you have been refused credit you can ask the lender to review the decision and you could provide any additional information you think would be relevant.

BASIC DO-IT-YOURSELF DEBT ADVICE

Many people fall into debt at some point in their lives, often through no fault of their own. The information and suggestions given in this section will help you to deal with your debts and remove the pressures of being in debt. The following steps will help you regain control of your finances.

Make a complete list of your debts

Divide them into priority and non-priority debts.

Priority debts
These include mortgage or rent arrears, fuel arrears, council tax arrears, court fines and maintenance (including child support) arrears. They are accepted as a priority because the consequences of not paying them are serious and could lead to your being homeless, or without heating, or in some cases imprisoned.

Non-priority debts
These include benefits overpayments and credit debts such as overdrafts, loans, hire purchase, credit card accounts and catalogues (but not gambling debts, which cannot be enforced), whether or not you are in arrears with your payments. *You cannot be imprisoned for non-payment of credit debts.*

Contact your creditors

Don't ignore the problem. It will only get worse. Contact the people you owe money to (your creditors) as soon as you realize you cannot keep up your payments and explain your problems. Ask them to freeze the interest on your debt. Be sure to keep copies of each letter you write.

Increase your income

You may be able to increase your income by:

- claiming additional benefits and tax credits, including Housing Benefit, Council Tax Benefit, Working Tax Credit, Child Tax Credit, Pension Credit, Jobseeker's Allowance if you are unemployed or Income Support if you are on a low income, and/or Disability Living Allowance, Attendance Allowance and Carer's Allowance if you or your partner/children are sick or have a disability. You can obtain further advice from your local CAB.
- you or your partner finding additional part-time work, but check how this would affect any benefits you are receiving before doing so;
- taking a lodger, but check whether this would affect any benefits you are

receiving. You may also need the permission of your mortgage lender and home contents insurer.

- checking your tax code and whether you are entitled to any tax allowances or tax reliefs that you are not claiming. Your local tax office will be able to advise you.
- borrowing money on better terms to pay off outstanding debts.

Drawing up a personal budget

Work out a weekly or monthly budget so that you know where your money goes and how much you can afford to offer your creditors. Make a rough copy first, as you may need to alter the amounts. Try to ensure that you aren't spending more than you have coming in, but make sure the amounts are realistic. You will find it very difficult to keep up with your payments if you haven't allowed yourself sufficient money to cover all your expenses. Your budget should include the following items:

1. All your household income including:
   - wages or salaries for your partner and yourself – after deductions if you are employed (this should be the amount you regularly receive and if the amounts vary, average them over three or six months);
   - any benefits you are paid – including Child Benefit, Child Support or maintenance;
   - contributions from other members of your family and lodgers.
2. All your expenses including:
   - housekeeping. Include what you spend on food, toiletries, school dinners and meals at work, cleaning materials, cigarettes, sweets, children's pocket money and pet food. Be realistic.
   - housing costs, including mortgage or rent, second mortgage/secured loan, buildings and contents insurance, ground rent, service charges and life/endowment insurance cover attached to your mortgage;
   - council tax;
   - fuel (electricity, gas, coal or paraffin) and water charges;
   - telephone (mobiles and landlines);
   - travel expenses (include both public transport and the costs of running a car such as road tax, insurance, and maintenance);
   - insurance that is not part of your housing costs (see above);
   - child minding;
   - TV rental/licence;
   - clothes and contingencies;

- any other essential expenses, such as medical/dental expenses or support for an elderly relative.

Making offers

Tackle your priority debts first. When you have worked out how much you have left over after paying your expenses, contact each of your priority creditors and make an arrangement to repay your arrears. If they are threatening or have started to take action against you and you need a little time to sort out your finances, send them a holding letter explaining your problems and say that you will contact them again within two or three weeks, whichever is realistic. Ask them not to take any further action during this time. Some priority creditors will want the arrears cleared within a specific time. If you are unable to agree a repayment schedule with them, you should contact your local CAB for further advice.

Make sure you have claimed any benefit you are entitled to, such as Housing Benefit (for tenants on a low income) and Council Tax Benefit. If you are being paid certain benefits, you can repay arrears of rent, fuel, water charges, council tax or your court fines by having a small amount deducted from your benefit each week (direct payments). Contact your local benefits office for more information.

Any money you have left over after paying your expenses and your priority creditors (available income) should be distributed to all your remaining creditors (non-priority creditors) and you will need to ensure that each creditor is treated fairly. This means each creditor should be offered a percentage of the available income, based on the amount they are owed. This will be the balance outstanding on the account. If you don't have recent balances, contact your creditors and ask for them. These offers are called *pro rata* offers.

Add up all your non-priority debts (total debt) and use the following formula to work out each pro rata offer:

For each debt divide the individual debt by the total debt and then multiply by your available income

Ms X owes money to three different people. She owes £100 to A, £150 to B and £400 to C. Her total debt is £650 and her available income is £20 each month.
  Creditor A should get £100/£650 x £20 = £3.50
  Creditor B should get £150/£650 x £20 = £4.00
  Creditor C should get £400/ £650 x £20 = £12.50

This system for working out what you can reasonably afford to pay is accepted by most creditors.

It is essential that you include all your non-priority creditors, *whether you are in arrears or not*, otherwise your remaining creditors will not accept your offers as you will not be treating all your creditors equally. This is because some of your payments would include interest, whilst those you were in arrears with would need to have interest frozen if you were to reduce your indebtedness. You may also find that your repayment arrangements may break down because you cannot afford all your payments.

Once you have worked out your budget and the offers you can make, draw up a financial statement listing your income, expenses (using the main headings such as housing costs, housekeeping, fuel, travel, etc.) and including the amounts you are paying towards your arrears. You should also list your non-priority creditors, the amounts you owe and your offers (if any).

Contacting your creditors

Once you have calculated how much you can afford to pay, write to each non-priority creditor explaining why you have fallen behind with your payments and send a copy of your financial statement. You might, if you have little money available, make them a token offer of £1.00 a month. If you are unable to make any offers to your non-priority creditors, ask them to accept no payments for three to six months and let them know if your circumstances are likely to change during this period. Say you will contact them as soon as your situation changes and you are able to resume making payments. If you are making offers, explain that they have been calculated on a pro rata basis. Always request that interest be frozen to prevent your debt from increasing. If you have credit, debit or store cards, return the cards cut into pieces at the same time and inform your creditor that you have done so.

Start making payments as soon as your offer is accepted and be sure to let your creditors know if your circumstances change and you are able to increase or need to decrease your payments. If your offer is refused, ask the creditor to reconsider and let them know if your other creditors have accepted your offers.

Don't be persuaded by any of your creditors to increase the amount you have offered to them as, by doing so, you will be giving that creditor priority over your other creditors. If you are having difficulty in having your offers accepted, you should contact your local CAB.

Reviews

Most non-priority creditors will only accept an offer for a limited amount of time, usually three or six months. Provided you have made regular payments, they will contact you again at the end of the period to find out whether your circumstances have changed. You should always reply to review letters and may have to send an updated financial statement. Check the balance outstanding on any statements or letters you are sent, to ensure interest has not been added, and when you reply be sure to ask that interest continues to be frozen.

Sample personal financial statement

Use this to illustrate your current financial situation.

Personal Statement of:

Address ....

....

....

Name ....

Number of people in my household ....

1. Income weekly/monthly

Wages/salary _____

Wages/salary – partner _____

Income Support _____

Working/Child Tax Credit _____

Child Benefit _____

Other state benefits _____

Other _____

TOTAL INCOME _____

2. Expenses weekly/monthly:

Housing costs

Mortgage/rent _____

Second mortgage/secured loan _____

Ground rent/service charges _____

Building/contents insurance _____
Life insurance/endowment _____
Council tax _____
Fuel
Gas _____
Electricity _____
Water charges _____
Housekeeping _____
Travelling expenses _____
Telephone _____
Magistrates' court fines _____
Maintenance payments _____
TV rental/licence _____
Clothing/contingencies _____
Prescriptions/health expenses _____
Children's expenses _____
Other (*but not credit/debt payments*)
.... _____
.... _____
.... _____
.... _____

TOTAL EXPENSES _____

3.
TOTAL INCOME   £_____ take away
TOTAL EXPENSES £_____
MONEY FOR CREDITORS £_____

4. Priority debts   **Amount owed**

Rent arrears _____
Mortgage arrears _____
2nd mortgage arrears _____
Council Tax arrears _____
Fuel debts: Gas _____
Electricity _____
Other _____

Magistrates' fines arrears   _____
Maintenance arrears   _____

TOTAL PRIORITY DEBTS   £ _____

5.

MONEY FOR CREDITORS
(see 3.)   £_____ take away
PRIORITY DEBT PAYMENTS
(see 4.)   £_____
REMAINING MONEY FOR CREDITORS
£_____

6. Credit Debt

Creditor	Balance owed	Monthly offer of repayment
1.	....	....
2.	....	....
3.	....	....
4.	....	....
5.	....	....
6.	....	....
7.	....	....
8.	....	....
9.	....	....

TOTAL OWED   _____

TOTAL MONTHLY PAYMENT _____

This is an accurate record of my financial position at ....

Signed ....

Sample debt letters

You should amend these letters to suit your individual circumstances.

Holding letter

Send this letter to creditors if you aren't able to make an offer immediately.

[Name of creditor
Address/postcode
Date]

Dear Sir/Madam
Re: Account No.   ....

I regret that I am unable to maintain my current monthly payments
because .... [*explain your reasons*].

I am writing to all my creditors requesting details of the balance
outstanding on my accounts and would be grateful if you would let
me know how much I owe you. Once I have obtained this
information, I will contact you again with a pro rata offer for
repaying the above debt. [*or*]

I have applied for .... benefit and will contact you again
as soon as I start to receive it. [*or*]

I have been sick/unemployed since .... and am due to
start/return to work on [*date*] and will contact you again once I have
started/returned to work. Meanwhile I request that you hold action
on my account for two months and suspend interest and other
charges to prevent my indebtedness from increasing.

Yours faithfully,
....

Offer letter to non-priority creditors

Send this letter to non-priority creditors when you have drawn up a financial statement and are able to make an offer.

[Name of creditor
Address/postcode
Date]

Dear Sir/Madam
Re: Account No.   ....

Further to my letter dated [*date*], I am now able to make an offer to repay the above debt. [*or*]

I regret that I am unable to maintain my monthly payments at their current level because   .... [*explain your reasons*].

I am enclosing a copy of my financial statement, which gives details of my income and expenses and makes pro rata offers to all my creditors. You will see from this information that I am able to offer you £_____ per month. I propose to make my first payment on   .... I trust you will accept my offer as realistic given my circumstances and agree to suspend interest and other charges on my account provided regular payments are made. I shall of course keep you informed of any changes in my circumstances.

I thank you for your co-operation and look forward to hearing from you.

Yours faithfully,
  ....

No offer letter

[Name of creditor
Address/postcode
Date]

Dear Sir/Madam
Re: Account No. . . . .

I regret that I am unable to pay my current monthly payments
because .... [*explain your reasons*].

I am enclosing a copy of my financial statement, which gives details
of my income and expenses. You will see from this information that I
am unable to make you an offer of payment at this time as I am on a
low income/dependent on Income Support/Jobseeker's Allowance/
Working Tax Credit/Pension Credit, which is a subsistence benefit
only intended to cover my/my family's basic needs.

I request that you hold action on my account for six months and
suspend interest to prevent my debt from increasing.

I am making every effort to increase my income/find work, and will
contact you again as soon as my financial circumstances improve.

I thank you for your co-operation and look forward to hearing from
you.

Yours faithfully,
....

GETTING MONEY ADVICE

If you are having difficulties in dealing with debt problems, you should seek specialist advice. Before seeing an adviser about debt, gather together all your financial papers. These should include any court papers and letters, bills and credit agreements, and details of your income and expenditure and that of your spouse or partner.

If you have to wait for an appointment with an adviser, it may be useful to tell creditors that you have contacted an adviser for help. Most creditors welcome the involvement of a specialist adviser. They may be willing to hold off action to enable an agreement to be reached.

Free advice agencies

Many **Citizens Advice Bureaux** are able to deal with money advice and debt problems. If it is a very complicated case they will usually be able to refer you to a money advice specialist. This may be a solicitor or insolvency practitioner. You can find your local Citizens Advice Bureau in the telephone directory or by going online (www.citizensadvice.org.uk). Help is also available through **Money Advice Centres** or **Law Centres**. The addresses and telephone numbers of Money Advice Centres and Law Centres can be found in the telephone directory.

The **National Debt Line** (0808 808 4000; www.nationaldebtline.co.uk) can give free information to people living in England and Wales. It also provides an information pack on dealing with debt.

Business Debtline (0800 197 6026; www.businessadviceonline.org) is a dedicated advice service for small businesses.

Advice UK (020 7407 4070; www.adviceuk.org.uk) is a large network of advice-providing organizations.

Debt management companies (DMCs)

Debt management companies or agencies (DMCs) offer to help people in debt. They will usually only help with non-priority debts. If this is the case, you will have to negotiate your priority debts yourself.

Most DMCs charge a fee. They offer either to consolidate your debt payments so that you make only one payment directly to the debt management company, or to negotiate with your creditors for you. If you are paying fees to a DMC, this leaves a lot less money from your available income to pay the creditors. Some DMCs do not charge a fee to the customer, but are paid commission by the creditors on the assumption that the DMC will recover some of the debt for them.

Neither advice agencies nor Debt Management Companies can guarantee a favourable outcome for you. Just because a DMC is involved, this does not prevent creditors taking court action against you. Also, if a DMC is involved, creditors are still not obliged to accept reduced payments or to freeze interest and unless they do, the debt will grow.

Not all DMCs produce realistic financial statements, because not all DMCs conduct in-depth interviews with their customers about income and expenditure. You may then be committed to keeping up unrealistic levels of payment. In this case it is more likely that you will default on the payments because they are not affordable.

Some creditors refuse to deal with DMCs. If a creditor will not deal with a DMC, you will have to deal separately with that creditor. However, DMCs often inform customers that they should have no further dealings with the creditors, and that if the creditor does contact the customer, the customer should pass any correspondence on to the DMC. This may result in creditors taking action – including court action – against you which you do not know about.

Advantages of using a DMC

The advantages of using a DMC are:

- some people like the idea that they have a contract with the DMC, and believe that they therefore have more control over how their debts are treated;
- you will have almost instant access by phone to the DMC and will not have to wait to see someone;
- some people like the anonymity of a telephone service run by a DMC;
- you do not have to do any work in relation to your debts, for example drafting letters to creditors;
- there is only one payment to make – to the DMC – and the company distributes the money to the creditors.

Disadvantages of using a DMC

If you are thinking of using a DMC, you should be aware of the following:

- DMCs are usually only interested in customers who have some available income and own their own home, so that the home can be used as surety against the debts;
- many DMCs deal only with non-priority debts and you will have to deal with the more important priority debts yourself;
- if the DMC does deal with priority debts, it may not pay off priority debts before non-priority debts;
- most DMCs charge a fee, which can be quite high. This leaves you with less money to pay off your debts.
- many DMCs will expect a one-off deposit at the start of the agreement with them, in addition to the fee you have to pay. This leaves you with less money to pay off your debts.
- most DMCs also charge an administration fee to the customer each month, to pay for the distribution of payments to creditors, in addition to fees and deposits. You need to check if the DMC does this and if so, how much it is. It may be up to £30 per month. This leaves you with less money to pay off your debts.
- if the debts are rescheduled by the DMC, creditors may consider the account to be in default. Some DMCs take all of the first month's payments as a fee. This puts the account into arrears by a month or more. These arrears will be recorded on your credit file.
- most DMCs do not give financial advice, and cannot advise on, for example, entitlement to benefit;
- most DMCs do not give financial advice and so do not give customers details of all the options open to them with the advantages and disadvantages of each.

BAILIFFS AND DEBT

Bailiffs recover money that people owe the bailiff's clients. In most cases the person who is owed money has to get a court order before being able to instruct a bailiff to recover a debt from you. Bailiffs will ask for a secure method of payment – cash, debit or credit card. If a bailiff visits your home, you will also have to pay a fee, which is set at different rates depending on the type of debt owed and the court that has authorized the bailiff to recover the debt from you. Bailiffs do not generally have the right to force entry into your home. However, they can gain 'peaceful entry' if you let them in, or if they enter through a closed but unlocked door or open window. Also, once bailiffs have gained peaceful entry to your home they can return another time and use force to get in on that occasion. If you cannot repay the debt they may be able to take your belongings and sell them at auction to pay off your debt.

The law on bailiffs is very complicated and the rules depend on the type of debt you owe and who it is owed to. If you are having problems paying a fine or other debt it is always important to try to negotiate and to get specialist advice. At most stages of the debt recovery process there are opportunities to sort the problem out before a court or bailiff gets involved.

BANKS AND BUILDING SOCIETIES

When you open an account, the law says that, like other service providers, the bank or building society must carry out its business:

- with reasonable care and skill. This means, for example, that the bank or building society must act responsibly and keep accurate records of your finances. *And*
- in a reasonable time, unless a specific time has been agreed – what is reasonable would depend on the service the bank was carrying out (for example, it should give a decision on a loan within a couple of days); *and*
- at a reasonable cost, unless a definite price has been agreed.

Some of the bank's or building society's services, such as loans and overdrafts, are covered by the Consumer Credit Act 1974. When you use any of the bank's or building society's services, you will be entering into a contract.

General tips

- You don't have to be given an account or a loan. The bank or building society will want proof of your identity including your full name, date of birth and address before giving you one. However, you cannot be refused a loan on account of your race, sex or disability.
- Your bank or building society can transfer money without your permission from your personal account into your joint account to cover a debt in the joint account but cannot transfer money from your joint account to your individual account without the permission of all the joint account holders.
- Even if your account is overdrawn, you can choose how any further money you pay into the account is used (for example to pay your mortgage or rent). This is called *first right of appropriation*. You will need to write to the bank or building society to tell them this before the money is paid in. You'll have to write to them with new instructions each time you make a deposit.

Your rights if the service is unsatisfactory

You may be entitled to compensation if:

- the contract has been broken (breach of contract), for example if the bank or building society fails to honour a cheque or pay a standing order or direct debit when you have sufficient money in your account to cover it; *or*
- the bank or building society has been negligent in the way it has handled your account. As it is very difficult to prove negligence, you may find it easier to claim breach of contract, for example that it has not handled your affairs with reasonable care and skill.

You will have to show that you have suffered a loss before you can claim compensation and the amount you can claim will usually be limited to the amount you have actually lost.

How to solve your problem

Once you have decided what your rights are, you will need to contact the bank or building society as quickly as possible. The following steps should solve your problem:

- check that the problem has been caused by the bank or building society – for example, the bank or building society will not be responsible if you give someone else your bank card and pin number and they use these to withdraw money without your consent;
- collect all your documents together, including your contract, bank statements and cheque stubs;
- contact the bank or building society as soon as you discover the problem. If you visit, take a copy of all your documents and ask to speak to the person responsible for dealing with your account or the branch manager. Alternatively, write to the branch manager, enclosing copies of your documents, and keep a copy of your letter. Explain your problem calmly but firmly and request the action or compensation that you require.
- if you are dissatisfied with the branch manager's response, you should ask for details of the bank's or building society's complaints procedure. Find out whether the bank or building society subscribes to the Banking Code of Practice. You can obtain a copy from your bank or building society or from the British Bankers' Association (BBA: 020 7216 8801). You should follow each stage of the complaints procedure by writing to the relevant manager, giving full details of your case, including any breaches of the Banking Code

of Practice and stating what action you require. When you have completed the internal complaints procedure, you will be sent a letter of deadlock if your complaint has not been settled.

- if you cannot reach an agreement with the bank or building society, find out if it is a member of the **Financial Ombudsman Service** (FOS: 0845 080 1800; www.financialombudsman.org.uk). The Ombudsman can investigate the majority of banking complaints, but there are some exceptions such as where you are questioning the bank's commercial judgment. You must have followed your bank's or building society's complaints procedure, and have made your complaint to the Ombudsman within six months of receiving its final decision. You cannot use an ombudsman scheme after taking court action.
- if the Ombudsman cannot resolve your complaint, your only other option is to consider going to court. It is extremely rare for a bank or building society to be sued. If you are thinking about doing this, you should see a solicitor.

The Financial Ombudsman Service (FOS)

Your complaint must be brought to the Ombudsman within six months of the deadlock letter. The Ombudsman will try to deal with your complaint informally but if this fails the Ombudsman will make a preliminary decision. You and the bank or building society can make comments on the decision, which the Ombudsman will consider and then make a recommendation or a ruling. The bank or building society must comply with the ruling, but if you are not satisfied, you can take court action. However, if you do so, the court would take the Ombudsman's ruling into account when deciding your case.

Changing to another bank or building society

If your bank or building society subscribes to the Banking Code, it must co-operate with your new bank or building society to help the transfer of your account to take place as smoothly as possible. It must give information about regular payments from your account within three working days. You should not have to pay bank charges incurred as a result of mistakes or delays in the transfer process.

3
Benefits

CONTENTS

INTRODUCTION

It's over sixty years since the British Government asked Sir William Beveridge to write a report on the best ways of helping people on low incomes. His report suggested weekly contributions paid by all people of working age that would help fund the payment of benefits to people who were sick, unemployed, retired or widowed. The system would provide a minimum standard of living 'below which no one should be allowed to fall'. 'Social provision against rainy days' is how the 1945 Labour manifesto put it and, soon after the election victory, that government began the process of implementing the proposals that provided the basis of our modern welfare state.

The benefits and tax credits system that we know today is larger, more all-encompassing and far more complex than Beveridge could ever have envisaged, but one fact remains the same. The number of people entitled to benefits but not claiming them is very high and this is particularly true of people over 75. It may be the stigma of claiming for a generation brought up to 'make do or mend', or long, complicated forms and a confusing claims process, but not claiming can mean scraping by on an unnecessarily low income, struggling to afford the basics.

This chapter looks at the basic benefits and tax credits, what you may be entitled to, how to claim and how to appeal if you think the powers that be have got it wrong.

BENEFITS AND TAX CREDITS

Benefits and tax credits are payments you can get if you:

- are on a low income for the number and ages of people in your family. Your income can be compared to figures set by the Department for Work and Pensions (DWP) to see if you are entitled to any financial help. This is called means-testing. *Or*

- have certain costs to meet because of your situation. Your income may not affect your right to get some payments.

The DWP pays most benefits. However, the local authority where you live helps with Council Tax and rent (Council Tax Benefit and Housing Benefit). The Inland Revenue administers Working Tax Credit and Child Tax Credit. You have to meet a set of conditions for each benefit or tax credit that you want to claim. In order to get the payment, you must meet these conditions and usually have to make an application and provide all the necessary information.

You may be entitled to more than one benefit or tax credit, for example a combination of means-tested payments and payments for extra costs because of your situation. However, some benefits cannot be paid together.

Benefits and tax credits are usually paid directly into your bank or building society account. However, some benefits can be paid by cheque payable at a post office if you do not have, or would find it difficult to manage, an account.

If you have dependent children

If you have a child under 16 (or under 19 and in full-time education), you are entitled to **Child Benefit**. Child Benefit does not depend on having paid any National Insurance contributions or on your income. However, Child Benefit may be restricted if you come from outside the UK and you or the child sometimes live abroad. If you get Child Benefit for a child born after September 2002, they will also qualify for a Child Trust Fund account. This is a savings account to which the state makes a contribution (you can find out more at www.childtrustfund.gov.uk). You may also be entitled to **Guardian's Allowance** if you get Child Benefit for a child whose parents are dead or where one parent is dead and the other is unable to take care of the child.

If you are responsible for a child under 16 (or under 19 and in full-time education) you may also be entitled to **Child Tax Credit**. Child Tax Credit depends on your income but not on National Insurance contributions. You can get extra amounts for a child with a disability.

If you are on a low income

If you are on a low income, your savings are below a set limit, and you are working fewer than sixteen hours a week or not working, you may be able to get either **Income Support** or **income-based Jobseeker's Allowance**. If you can look for work, you should usually claim Jobseeker's Allowance. You will only be able to claim Income Support if you are a person who does not have to be available for work according to rules for getting benefit – if you are a lone parent with dependent children, you are sick or disabled or you are caring for a disabled person. If you are in this situation you may be entitled to Income Support.

If you are on a low income, are not working (or working fewer than sixteen hours a week), and are not entitled to Income Support, you may be able to get **income-based Jobseeker's Allowance** (if you are looking for work) or **Pension Credit** if you are 60 and over.

If your income is not low enough, or your savings are too high, but you have been paying National Insurance contributions in the last two years and are now looking for work, you may be entitled to **contribution-based Jobseeker's Allowance** for a limited period instead.

You may be able to choose between claiming Income Support and income-based Jobseeker's Allowance if you are under 60 and are able to look for work, but do not have to be available for work under the rules for getting benefit.

If you are working sixteen hours a week or more

If you or your partner works sixteen hours or more a week, you may be entitled to **Working Tax Credit,** or **Pension Credit** if you are 60 or over.

Help with rent

If you are on a low income and have savings below a set limit (whether or not you are working) and are paying rent on your home, you may be entitled to **Housing Benefit**. Housing Benefit may help pay all or part of your rent.

Help with Council Tax

If you are on a low income and have savings below a set limit (whether or not you are working) and are liable for Council Tax on your home, you may be entitled to **Council Tax Benefit,** which may help pay all or part of your Council Tax. If you live with someone else who does not pay Council Tax and are on a low income you may be entitled to second adult rebate as well. You may also be able to reduce your Council Tax bill if you are eligible for reductions or discounts.

If you are sick or disabled

If you are unable to work or look for work because of sickness or disability

If you are unable to work because you are sick or disabled, you may be entitled to **Statutory Sick Pay** (paid by your employer) if you usually work as an employee, earn more than a certain amount and have not been sick for more than twenty-eight weeks. If you do not meet these conditions you may get **Incapacity Benefit** instead. Depending on your circumstances, you may have to meet National Insurance contribution conditions to get Incapacity Benefit. If you are not working, and you are not entitled to Incapacity Benefit, but you are on a low income, you may be entitled to **Income Support** or **Pension Credit**. You can also get Income Support to top up Statutory Sick Pay or Incapacity Benefit. You should claim it at the same time. Whether or not you can claim any of these benefits, you may also be entitled to benefits for your care needs or mobility problems.

If you are disabled and work 16 hours or more a week
If you are disabled and work sixteen hours or more a week, you may be entitled to **Working Tax Credit** with an extra amount for your disability. This may apply to anyone who is or has been getting a benefit for sickness and disability.

Other help for sick or disabled people

If you are disabled you may also be able to get **Income Support** or **Pension Credit**. You may be able to get **Housing Benefit** or **Council Tax Benefit** as well. The means-testing for these benefits is more generous for disabled people. This means that you are entitled to a higher combined income of benefits and other money.

If you have care needs or mobility problems

If you have care needs or mobility problems and you are under 65, you may be entitled to **Disability Living Allowance** (DLA). You do not have to be getting help with your care to get DLA. You may get DLA because you cannot prepare a cooked main meal by yourself, or because you need attention for some or all of the time in connection with your bodily functions, or you need supervision to avoid danger to yourself or others. You may get DLA for mobility problems if you have difficulty walking, you cannot walk, or you need guidance and supervision to walk out of doors. You can get DLA whether or not you work.

If you have care needs and you are 65 or over, you may be entitled to **Attendance Allowance**. You cannot get Attendance Allowance for difficulties with mobility, but you can get it if you need attention in connection with your bodily functions, or supervision to avoid danger, throughout the day or for significant periods during the night. You can get Attendance Allowance whether or not you work.

If you are caring for a disabled person

If you care for someone for at least 35 hours a week who has care or mobility problems and is entitled to Disability Living Allowance or Attendance Allowance, you may be entitled to **Carer's Allowance**. To get this you must not be earning more than a set amount. You should be aware that if you get Carer's Allowance, it can affect the amount of any Income Support, Pension Credit, Housing Benefit or Council Tax Benefit the person you care for gets.

If you are 60 or over

If you are a woman aged 60 or over, or a man aged 65 or over, you may be entitled to a **State Retirement Pension**, depending on your or your married partner's National Insurance contribution record. (From December 2005 also the record of someone with whom you have registered a civil partnership.) If you are getting State Retirement Pension, **Income Support** or **Pension Credit** you are also entitled to a one-off payment just before Christmas (the **Christmas bonus**). If you are aged 60 or over you are also entitled to a **Winter Fuel Payment**, which is a one-off annual payment intended to help with fuel costs.

If you are 60 or over you may also be able to get Pension Credit and **Housing Benefit** or **Council Tax Benefit**. The means-testing for Housing Benefit and Council Tax Benefit is more generous for people of pension age. You are entitled to a higher combined income of benefits and other money, and your savings can be higher before they affect these benefits.

> *My neighbour has just come out of hospital and seems to be finding it difficult to cope. Is there any help available for him?*
>
> Depending on how long your neighbour has been ill and the type of help he needs, he may be able to claim Disability Living Allowance if he is under 65, or Attendance Allowance if he is aged 65 or over. Neither of these benefits is means-tested so any capital he has will not be taken into account if he makes a claim. Your neighbour may also be eligible to claim Pension Credit. Pension Credit is a means-tested benefit, so capital such as savings is taken into account in the assessment. If he pays rent for his accommodation he can claim Housing Benefit and Council Tax Benefit. Your local social services department can make an assessment of your neighbour's needs. It may be able to arrange help in a number of ways, for example having rails or lifting equipment fitted to the bathroom, or having someone come to visit on a regular basis.
>
> Your neighbour may also be entitled to help with health costs and visits to hospital.

If you were injured at work or have an industrial disease

If you were injured at work or contracted a disease due to your working conditions, you may be entitled to **Industrial Injuries' Benefit**. You must have been working as an employed earner (not have been self-employed). Only certain diseases in certain types of work qualify as industrial diseases, and you must show that you are disabled as a result of the accident or disease.

If you are pregnant or have recently had a baby

If you are pregnant or have recently had a baby, are off work and usually work as an employee earning more than a certain amount, you may be entitled to **Statutory Maternity Pay**, paid by your employer. If you are not entitled to Statutory Maternity Pay – because, for example, you are self-employed or gave up work before you became pregnant – but you were earning more than a certain amount, you may be entitled to **Maternity Allowance**. If you get Statutory Maternity Pay or Maternity Allowance you may also be entitled to Income Support. If you usually work 16 hours or more each week, you may be entitled to **Working Tax Credit**.

If you are not earning enough to qualify for Statutory Maternity Pay or Maternity Allowance you may be entitled to **Incapacity Benefit** and/or **Income Support.** (This is because you are treated as incapable of work for the period around the birth, and any other day when working would mean a serious risk to your or your baby's health.) You may also be entitled to a one-off **Maternity Grant** if you or your partner are receiving certain means-tested benefits or tax credits at the time of the claim. If you are responsible for a child, you may be entitled to **Child Tax Credit** and you can get an extra amount if you have a child under the age of one.

I've recently had a baby and have heard that the Government is setting up trust funds for children. What are they, and how do I claim?

The Child Trust Fund is a savings and investment account for children. The Government will make payments to children through this account and your family and friends will also be able to contribute. When your child is 18, they will have access to the account and will be able to spend the money however they like. If your child was born on or after 1 September 2002, and you are currently getting Child Benefit, then your child will be eligible for a Child Trust Fund account (CTF).

The Government will make an initial payment of at least £250, followed by another payment on your child's seventh birthday. You and your family and friends can also contribute a sum of money each year to the fund. You do not have to claim or register for the scheme as payments will be made automatically from April 2005.

For more information on Child Trust Funds, call the CTF helpline (0845 302 1470) or visit the Inland Revenue website (www.ir.gov.uk/ctf/parents.htm).

If you are widowed

If you are widowed, you may be able to claim a **Bereavement Payment**, **Widowed Parent's Allowance** or **Bereavement Allowance**, depending on your spouse's National Insurance contributions, their age, and whether you have dependent children. From December 2005, you can also depend on the National Insurance contributions of someone with whom you have registered a civil partnership. If your partner died of an industrial injury or disease, the National Insurance contributions may be waived.

If you have one-off expenses that you cannot afford

If you have one-off essential expenses that you cannot afford, you may be entitled to help from the **Social Fund**. You can get **Budgeting Loans**, **Crisis Loans, Community Care Grants, funeral payments, Cold Weather Payments** and **Maternity Grants** from the Social Fund. If you get a loan, you have to pay it back. You can usually only get help if you are on certain means-tested benefits or tax credits. However, Crisis Loans, which can help with expenses in an emergency or disaster, do not depend on you being on any benefit, as long as you do not have enough resources from anywhere else. You may be able to get a Budgeting Loan for help with essential items such as furniture if you are on income-based Jobseeker's Allowance, Income Support or Pension Credit.

You may be able to get a Community Care Grant if you are on Income Support, income-based Jobseeker's Allowance or Pension Credit and are leaving institutional or residential care, and need help to establish yourself in the community. You may also be able to get a grant if it will help you avoid being taken into care. Community Care Grants can also be paid to help families under exceptional pressure, to help care for prisoners or young offenders who are temporarily released, and to help people who have been homeless and are setting up home. You can get a funeral payment to help with the cost of a funeral if you get Income Support, income-based Jobseeker's Allowance, Housing Benefit, Council Tax Benefit or Pension Credit. You may get a payment if you are on Working Tax Credit or Child Tax Credit. You will only get a funeral payment if it is reasonable for you to take responsibility for the funeral and there is no one else who can pay.

In cold weather, if you are on Income Support, income-based Jobseeker's

Allowance or Pension Credit you may be entitled to automatic Cold Weather Payments if the temperature drops below a certain level.

If you have expenses or costs for school-age children

If you are on Income Support, income-based Jobseeker's Allowance or Pension Credit, or you are otherwise on a low income, you may be entitled to help with health expenses such as prescriptions, dental treatment and travel costs to hospital. You may also be entitled to help with legal costs. If you are getting Income Support, income-based Jobseeker's Allowance or Pension Credit, you are entitled to free school meals for your children if they are under 19. You may also get help with the costs of school clothing, or payments to help children who are 16 and over to continue their education.

How to claim

To claim most benefits, you will need to visit your local Jobcentre Plus office or Jobcentre, which will be listed in the local telephone directory, and speak to a New Claims adviser.

If you want more information about how to make a claim, including help with filling in the claim form, you may want to speak to an experienced adviser, for example at a Citizens Advice Bureau.

Appealing against a benefits decision

Appealing against a benefit decision that you think is wrong can be complicated. If you wish to ask for a decision to be reconsidered or if you wish to appeal you should consult an experienced adviser, for example at a CAB.

There is also a DWP publication – *If you think our decision is wrong* – which is available from your local benefits office or online (www.dwp.gov.uk/publications).

WORKING TAX CREDIT AND CHILD TAX CREDIT

Working Tax Credit (WTC) and Child Tax Credit (CTC) are benefits that are administered by the Inland Revenue.

CTC is available to people responsible for a child or young person and who have income below a certain amount. All households with an annual income of £50,000 or less will qualify for some CTC. The amount you get will depend on how many children you have, and whether they have any disabilities. CTC is available whether or not you are in work and is paid to the main carer in a household, usually straight into a nominated bank account.

WTC is a payment to top up earnings of people working on low incomes, including those who do not have children. Extra amounts are payable if you have a disability, if you work thirty hours or more a week, and where you have childcare costs. If you, or your partner, are employees, you will usually receive WTC through your wages. However, any payments made for child-care costs will be paid direct to the main carer. If you are self-employed, WTC will be paid directly into a nominated bank account.

Tax credits are usually paid for a year, from April to April, but the amount you get may change if your circumstances change during that year, for example if you have another child. If you are a member of a couple who live together, you must make a joint claim. You claim both tax credits on the same form. Claims can only be backdated three months, so you should claim as soon as you can.

I am on Income Support and would like to go back to work. The job I am considering is not that well paid and I am worried I will be worse off if I give up my benefits. Is there any help for me?

If you work for sixteen or more hours a week, you may be able to claim Working Tax Credit (WTC) to top up your earnings. If you have children you may be able to get Child Tax Credit (CTC).

Depending on how much you earn, you might still be able to claim Housing Benefit and Council Tax Benefit with your WTC or CTC, although the tax credits will be taken into account as income when the amount of your Housing Benefit and Council Tax Benefit are worked out. If you stop working during that period, or work fewer than sixteen hours each week, you may be able to get Jobseeker's Allowance or Income Support to top up your income.

Appealing against a tax credit decision

If you think you have been wrongly refused Working Tax Credit or Child Tax Credit, or you think the amount you have been awarded is wrong, you can ask the Inland Revenue to explain its decision. If you are not satisfied with their reply, you can ask for the decision to be looked at again. You must do this within thirty days of receiving a decision from the Inland Revenue.

If your claim is reconsidered and you are still not satisfied, you can appeal to an independent unified appeal tribunal. Appealing against a decision can be complicated and time limits apply. If you want to appeal, you should consult an experienced adviser immediately.

Who can help?

Inland Revenue Tax Credits Helpline (0845 300 3900; textphone 0845 300 3909; www.inlandrevenue.gov.uk/taxcredits).

PENSION CREDIT

Pension Credit is a means-tested benefit for people aged 60 or over. It has two parts – a guarantee credit and a savings credit. Guarantee credit tops up your weekly income to a guaranteed level and savings credit is for people who have a small amount of income or savings. You may be able to claim either part of the Pension Credit separately or both together, depending on your circumstances.

You can claim Pension Credit whether or not you are working and do not need to have paid National Insurance contributions to get the benefit. Arrangements for claiming and paying pension credit are made by the Pension Service. The Pension Service does not have its own offices for people to visit, but you can contact them by telephone, through their locally based services, or through other organizations such as your local benefits office.

Who can help?

Pension Service (national telephone helpline: 0800 99 1234; textphone 0800 169 0133; www.thepensionservice.gov.uk).

BENEFIT FRAUD

To find out whether you are entitled to a benefit, the DWP can carry out certain checks to make sure that the information you have given on the claim form or during an interview is correct. One of the ways in which the DWP can make these checks is to compare what you have said or written on the claim form with records about you held by another government agency. This means that the DWP could ask the Inland Revenue if its records show that you are paying tax, in order to check whether you are working.

Local authorities, who administer Housing Benefit and Council Tax Benefit, can also carry out checks on benefit claims.

Checks on a benefit claim can be made at any time, not just when you first make the claim. Sometimes checks will be made on everyone receiving a certain benefit or on certain groups, such as lone parents.

Authorized fraud officers can request information about you and members of your family from a range of private and public organizations including:

- banks, building societies and credit providers, including credit card companies, money transmission companies;
- insurance companies;
- credit reference agencies;
- education providers;
- water, gas and electricity providers;
- telecoms companies, including mobile phone companies;
- the Student Loans Company;
- overseas authorities.

If you are dishonest in some way with the DWP or local authority, you may be committing benefit fraud, for example if you did not tell them about a change in your circumstances that affected your entitlement to benefit. Even if you are not committing fraud, failure to report a fact or change of circumstances could result in an overpayment of benefit, which you may have to repay.

If the DWP or local authority suspects you of claiming benefit fraudulently, it will carry out an investigation into your circumstances. Benefit fraud is a criminal offence. If the DWP or local authority has evidence that you are committing benefit fraud, you can be prosecuted or be asked to pay a penalty as an alternative to prosecution.

MAKING A COMPLAINT

Everybody has the right to expect a reasonable standard of service from a public sector agency. This includes people who claim benefit, tax credits and Pension Credit or who make National Insurance enquiries or have a child support maintenance assessment. If you have received poor service or have been disadvantaged because of errors or a slow response, you should consider complaining.

You can complain whether or not you have claimed a benefit or tax credit. However, a complaint is not a way of challenging a decision. If you think that a decision is wrong, you should ask for it to be reconsidered or appeal. You can make a complaint as well as asking for a decision to be reconsidered or appealing.

Types of complaint

Poor service

You should consider complaining about poor service if you have experienced any of the following:

- rudeness;
- unwillingness to treat you as somebody with rights;
- refusal to answer reasonable requests;
- not being informed on request of your rights or entitlements;
- advice that is misleading or inadequate;
- bias or partiality, for example because of race, sex or disability. You should make a complaint if you think there has been discrimination.
- not being told about your right to dispute a decision and/or to appeal.

Delay

You should consider complaining if you have had to wait too long for a claim to be decided, or for an explanation to be given. Offices that administer benefits or tax credits usually have target times for deciding a claim. These may be on display in the local office, or you can ask to see them.

Inefficiency

You should consider complaining if there has been inefficiency, for example if the office administering benefit or tax credit loses case papers or stops payment by mistake.

Inadequate information

If you are not satisfied with advice or information you have been given by a government office, you should consider complaining. For example, you may not have been told about a benefit you could have applied for, or you may have been given incorrect information about your National Insurance record.

Difficulty in contacting the office

You should consider complaining if it has been very difficult to contact the office concerned, or they have not responded to letters or telephone calls.

Over- and underpayments

If there has been an over- or underpayment of benefit, you should consider complaining. Even if you are repaid the correct balance of an underpayment, you may have been disadvantaged by not receiving the correct money for a period of time. Overpayments that have to be repaid can also cause unexpected distress.

Interpretation facilities

If your first language is not English, and the office does not provide adequate interpretation facilities, you should consider complaining. You have a right to help with claim forms, letters and understanding your entitlement if you do not speak English as a first language.

Outcomes of making a complaint

Following a complaint, you may achieve, for example:

- an apology for what has happened;
- an explanation of how the problem occurred;
- an assurance that the problem will be put right, if this is possible;
- a change in procedure;
- financial compensation, in certain circumstances.

Compensation

In certain circumstances, for example excessive delay, wrong advice or financial loss, you may be able to obtain compensation. However, these payments are discretionary, so there is no enforceable right to compensation.

Where to make a complaint

You should complain to the office that administered your benefit or tax credit or dealt with your Pension Credit, National Insurance record or child support assessment. Most organizations have their own internal complaints procedure, which should be available on request. There will usually be a customer service manager or equivalent who acts as a point of contact for complaints. There will then be further formal stages for dealing with the complaint.

You should make your complaint about:

Housing Benefit and Council Tax Benefit	to your local authority
benefits and Social Fund payments	to the DWP
Pension Credit	to the Pension Service
child support issues	to the Child Support Agency
treatment at the Jobcentre	to the Jobcentre or Jobcentre Plus
National Insurance contributions	to the Inland Revenue National Insurance Contributions Office
tax credits	to the Inland Revenue Tax Credit Office

You may be able to complain informally by talking to a manager at the relevant local office. If this does not resolve the problem, it may be necessary to put the complaint in writing. The complaints procedure may be explained in a leaflet that will list the different stages of making a complaint and may contain a complaints form which you can fill in.

Taking the complaint further

You may find that an internal complaints procedure takes a long time and does not produce a satisfactory result. There are external, independent procedures for complaining about public services. You are usually expected to have tried any internal complaints procedure first.

Complaints about Housing Benefit and Council Tax Benefit can be investigated by the Local Government Ombudsman.

Complaints about other benefits and child support can be investigated by the Parliamentary Ombudsman. Alternatively, if you have a concern about child support you can complain to the Independent Case Examiner. You can find out more about the Independent Case Examiner and Child Support complaints online (www.ind-case-exam.org.uk).

Complaints about National Insurance and tax credits can be investigated by the Adjudicator for the Inland Revenue.

For more information about using an ombudsman, see *Civil rights*, p. 452.

Using an MP

You can contact your Member of Parliament for help at any stage in an external or internal complaints procedure. For complaints about Housing Benefit or Council Tax Benefit, a local councillor may also be able to help. The MP or councillor may be able to get the complaint resolved more quickly and/or ensure that practices are changed so that the problem does not occur again.

NATIONAL INSURANCE

People in work have to pay National Insurance contributions if they have earnings over a certain amount of money. This amount is called the lower earnings limit. It changes every year, usually in April.

Anyone who pays National Insurance contributions builds up a contribution record. Whether or not you can claim certain benefits will depend on this contribution record.

There are four types of contributions. These are called 'classes'. Credits are contributions that are added to your contribution record either when you are unemployed or unable to work because of illness, or when you have a gap in contributions and apply for credits to fill the gap. The person who gets the credits does not have to pay for them.

Credits are also given to men aged 60–65 who are either getting benefits or who are not paying contributions out of earnings.

Credits don't cover all benefits, and problems with credits are usually quite complex and should be dealt with by an experienced adviser, for example a CAB.

How to get a National Insurance number

A National Insurance number (NINO) is used to identify your contribution and benefit record. The same NINO is used throughout your working life. The number consists of two letters, six numbers and one letter, for example AB 123456 C.

Most young people whose parents receive child benefit for them are automatically sent a plastic card showing a NINO just before they reach the age of 16.

If you have lost your number, for example because you haven't worked for some time or have forgotten it, you should ask the local benefits office for a record of your number. You will be issued with a new card.

If you don't have a number, you can apply to the local benefits office. You must apply for a number if you start work or if you or your partner claims benefit. The local benefits office will interview you and will require evidence of your identity before a National Insurance number can be allocated to you.

If you are an asylum seeker, you can apply for a NINO in the usual way. If you have applied for asylum and your claim has been successful, a NINO will usually be allocated automatically.

I have two jobs. Should I be paying National Insurance contributions on both?

If you have more than one job with different employers you must pay Class 1 contributions on each employment where the earnings from that job are above the lower earnings limit.

If you are an employee with more than one low-paid job, you may not be paying National Insurance contributions at all. This is because the earnings from each employment are treated separately and if they are each below the lower earnings limit no National Insurance contributions are paid.

Paying late contributions

If you are an employee who has not paid contributions when you have had earnings above the lower earnings limit, you can be required to pay and may face a penalty or prosecution.

If you have an incomplete contribution record, for example because you have been studying, you may wish to pay late voluntary contributions. There are a number of issues you will need to consider – for example, whether the late contributions would enable you to qualify for additional benefits.

Married women and widows

Until April 1977 some married women and widows could choose to pay reduced Class 1 contributions. Some women may still be paying the reduced rate contribution and may wish to consider paying the full rate. Reduced rate contributions do not count towards entitlement to contributory benefits. A person has to have paid full contributions to be entitled to these benefits.

Employees aged 60 and 65

As an employee, once you reach 60 (women) or 65 (men), you will not have to pay contributions. You should automatically receive a certificate of age exemption. This form must be given to your employer so that contributions are not paid. If you do not receive your certificate, you should contact your local benefits office.

Index